Public Accountability and Constitutional Law

This book analyses the public accountability of political actors in contemporary democratic states. Accountability as understood here is a necessary condition of democracy: delegation of power with transparency and supervision over those who are chosen to exercise the power of the state. The authors identify paths of executing accountability in the electoral process, as well as in traditional instruments of parliamentary scrutiny and other relationships between the legislative, executive and judicial branches. They track how well-known mechanisms of democracy fulfil the need to report on the exercising of an entrusted power. They also explore how new developments in the constitutional framework, that is, the post-evaluation of legislation, and beyond it in mass social movements, Big Tech companies and social media, are changing the classic and established concepts of accountable power. The book will be a valuable resource for academics, researchers and policymakers working it the areas of Constitutional Law and Politics and Accountability Studies.

Anna Młynarska-Sobaczewska is a lawyer and a professor in the Department of Constitutional Law and European Research at the Institute of Law Studies of the Polish Academy of Sciences. She has been a visiting scholar in law schools in the United States, Italy, Germany, Vietnam (Hanoi) and Spain.

Jacek Zaleśny is a lawyer, political scientist and associate professor in the Department of Political Systems of the Faculty of Political Science and International Studies, University of Warsaw, Poland. His research interests include the political systems of contemporary states, the law-making process and institutions of legal protection.

Public Accountability and Constitutional Law

Anna Młynarska-Sobaczewska and
Jacek Zaleśny

Routledge
Taylor & Francis Group
LONDON AND NEW YORK

First published 2025
by Routledge
4 Park Square, Milton Park, Abingdon, Oxon OX14 4RN

and by Routledge
605 Third Avenue, New York, NY 10158

Routledge is an imprint of the Taylor & Francis Group, an informa business

British Library Cataloguing-in-Publication Data
A catalogue record for this book is available from the British Library

ISBN: 978-1-032-79247-7 (hbk)
ISBN: 978-1-032-79702-1 (pbk)
ISBN: 978-1-003-49341-9 (ebk)

DOI: 10.4324/9781003493419

Typeset in Galliard
by Deanta Global Publishing Services, Chennai, India

The book is an effect of the scientific project "Accountability as a category of constitutional law" no. 2018/29/B/HS5/01771 which has been funded by the National Science Centre, Poland. This project was held in the Institute of Law Studies of the Polish Academy of Sciences.

Contents

Preface *vi*

1 Accountability in constitutional law – assumptions and meaning 1

2 On the illusory nature of political representation and the illusion of its accountability 32

3 Regulatory impact assessment *ex post* as an accountability instrument: Why does it fail to work? 74

4 Parliamentary scrutiny: Toolbox of institutional accountability of government 113

5 Judicial accountability – where to look for it and why is it not there? 149

6 Non-state actors in the constitutional framework: Political impact without public accountability 200

Conclusions 245

Index *259*

Preface

The doctrine of constitutional law attempts to add meaning to what we know about the state and the power exercised therein, and above all: what we know about the relationship between the rulers and the ruled. This relationship has never been easy – neither in practice nor in analysis. Although an incalculable number of philosophical, political and legal texts have been devoted to it, it continues to fascinate and perplex both the public and academics and, hopefully, occasionally those in power.

We are constantly searching for keys to the complex machinery of governance, especially for the methods and concepts to justify its existence in this – and not some other – form. We continue to look for the right words that will properly define the relationships that exist between people and those who exercise power over them in the state – or outside it, for that matter.

Democracy. Checks and balances. The collective sovereign. Parliamentary mandate. Openness. Responsiveness. Democratic legitimacy. Transparency. These are the concepts we have been using for thousands, hundreds or tens of years respectively. However, political relations have constantly brought about distressing falsifications of the model of the world of governance thus constructed.

Therefore, we invent new concepts and categories that enjoy widespread acceptance in order to describe these falsifications and to better label our everyday situation, pointing out its shortcomings and postulating directions for change. And one such concept is accountability, a word that can simply be considered a buzzword, one that has seen a remarkable rise in social sciences in recent years: a bottomless bag, a concept too ambiguous to be of use,[1] or – a keyword that will create a new quality in describing and operating democracy, the Holy Grail, the discovery of which significantly transforms our reality and our perception of it. Also in the sense that it explains this governors-governed

1 Luc Verhey, Hansko Broeksteeg and Ilse Van den Driessche, eds., *Political Accountability in Europe: Which Way Forward? A Traditional Concept of Parliamentary Democracy in an EU Context* (Amsterdam: Europa Law Publishing, 2008), 9.

relationship.[2] Either way, the concept of accountability is enigmatic and highly promising, but it is still being analysed fragmentarily and usually without proper reference to legal institutions actually in place. Often, accountability is proclaimed as part of postulates – rather than analysis. Accountability is most frequently discussed when its absence is addressed, or its deficit, or the new quality it could yield[3] – if only it could be implemented in a manner similar to management or accounting.

Our book aims to demystify this concept. We approach accountability in a holistic way. We relate it to different dimensions of political and legal relations (parliamentary elections, parliamentary control, judicial power, transnational governance, social movements). We seek its manifestations in these different levels of the realisation of political or legal power relations. It is the result of research aimed at identifying and verifying the accountability of public authorities within the framework of constitutional theory. The objective of this publication is to extract and describe both well-established and newly appearing constitutional tools in order to consider the consequences for the legal and political reality. The book is a socio-legal study of the paths and instruments of public accountability, its meaning and its use; it will reveal its actual functions in modern societies. We study the relationship between the dogma of accountability recognised by the legal doctrine and the understanding of accountability in constitutional practice – not just in books.

There are numerous relevant literature items, commentaries and discussions about accountability. Let us list some of them: A. Przeworski, S.C. Stokes, B. Manin, eds., *Democracy, Accountability and Representation* (Cambridge University Press, 1999); C.T. Borowiak, *Accountability & Democracy: The Pitfalls and Promise of Popular Control* (Oxford University Press, 2011); R. Bellamy, A. Palumbo, eds., *Political Accountability* (Routledge, 2010); M.W. Dowdle, ed., *Public Accountability: Designs, Dilemmas and Experiences* (Cambridge University Press, 2006); L. Verhey, H. Broeksteeg. I. Van den Driessche, eds., *Political Accountability in Europe: Which Way Forward? A Traditional Concept of Parliamentary Democracy in an EU Context* (Europa Law Publishing, 2008); S. Rose-Ackerman, *Democracy and Executive Power: Policymaking Accountability in the US, the UK, Germany and France* (Yale University Press, 2021); M. Bovens, R.E. Goodin, T. Schillemans, eds., *The Oxford Handbook of Public Accountability* (Oxford University Press, 2014). It is commonly treated and understood as being closely related to responsibility, transparency, answerability and responsiveness, and these terms tend to be

2 Carol Harlow, *Accountability in the European Union* (Oxford: Oxford University Press, 2002), 15.

3 Michael Dowdle, "Public Accountability: Conceptual, Historical, and Epistemic Mappings", in *Public Accountability: Designs, Dilemmas and Experiences*, ed. M.W. Dowdle (Cambridge: Cambridge University Press, 2006), 1–29, 4.

used interchangeably.[4] Our book differs from previous publications in that we examine whether public accountability actually works and we try to explore what it means for the known instruments and understanding of the separation of powers and democratic governance.

We assume that accountability, regarded as a part of the political and constitutional system, is a relationship consisting of three basic elements:

1. The obligation of agents to report on the entrusted elements of public authority;
2. A forum for interrogating the accountable agents and considering their reports; and
3. An assessment of the reports by those who entrusted power: the principals.

It is – consciously or not – a pivotal category for both democracy and constitutionalism. Democracy is based on civic participation, inclusiveness and equal influence of all members of the political community on public life. Constitutionalism refers to methods and instruments that avoid arbitrary rule – the principles of exercising power limited by the law and controlled by those who entrusted the power to an entity. However, *arbitrary* does not only mean not based on any principle or system. It is also a situation that does not appear to be based on accepted principles and rationales, particularly when the decision-making process does not explain them clearly and fairly. These are the reasons why the relatively new, yet useful concept of accountability may, in our opinion, be used in constitutional law as a tool for analysing and verifying these principles in the current system of entrusting power in the state.

At its core, accountability is associated with the process of being called to report on (give an account of) one's actions by certain authority. It involves social interaction and exchange, and can be treated as a method for keeping the public informed and keeping the authorities in check.[5] From this perspective, accountability is closely related to the principles of the political system, in particular representative democracy, separation of powers and the rule of law – all established as fundamental conditions for a democratic state. If it is true that an exercise of entrusted power in a state should be accountable, every entity performing public power (except for those covered by state secrets) must be prepared to present a report on the actions taken and to demonstrate their legality and purposefulness.

4 Dawn Oliver, *Government in the United Kingdom: The Search for Accountability, Effectiveness and Citizenship* (Maidenhead: Open University Press, 1991), 22; Jerry L. Mashaw, "Accountability and Institutional Design: Some Thoughts on the Grammar of Governance", in *Public Accountability: Designs, Dilemmas and Experiences* (see note 3), 115–56, at 128.

5 Richard Mulgan, *Holding Power to Account: Accountability in Modern Democracies* (Basingstoke: Palgrave Macmillan, 2003).

There are many channels of public accountability in constitutional systems. Most are associated with sanctions to provide consequences for actions. Democratic states employ a wide variety of well-established mechanisms of governmental accountability; there is also a strong presumption of electoral accountability, meant as the capacity of people to reward or punish representatives during elections. It is also a source of many doubts in constitutional practice – for example much of the controversy surrounding judicial accountability stems from the great difficulty in separating judicial independence from the many forms of accountability of judges for their actions and behaviour, as in the case of disciplinary accountability.

However, some of the ways in which public accountability is exercised are not in line with previously established standards and are not followed directly by sanctions. These forms can be categorised as "narrative accountability". This type of accountability can be exercised by simply answering what, why and how something was done by the agent; it is "a verbal bridge between action and expectations".[6]

Our book deals specifically with the forms and instruments of constitutional accountability understood in such a manner, involving reasoning, answering and even "story-telling" in relation to the exercise of power and the presentation of grounds, causes, processes and outcomes. It is much less recognised and undervalued, but in our view this kind of accountability could become a newly established toolbox for the exercise of democratic power. Therefore, its effectiveness and theoretical assumptions need to be reviewed.

We do not intend to present a complete and coherent theory of accountability within constitutional law (especially since we claim that there is no such theory); rather, we want to examine two issues using the concept of accountability. Firstly, we investigate the extent to which the concept of accountability is present in the regulatory system of contemporary states, based on the assumption of giving an account of entrusted power. We examine the principal (forum)–agent relationship in the context of political systems. Secondly, we examine how accountability is achieved (or not) given established regulation and practice. In this way, we analyse the extent to which the category borrowed from the social sciences verifies the relevance of basic assumptions of democracy and separation of powers. First of all, this requires outlining the unique function of accountability within the entrustment of power, identifying selected forms of accountability within the constitutional framework and analysing its constitutional position and practice in a broad comparative review.

We address three main issues. The first concerns electoral accountability, which is often considered a central instrument for the control and legitimacy of power in a democratic state. Our analysis provides conceptual insights to

6 Martin Messner, "The Limits of Accountability", *Accounting, Organizations and Society* [online], 34, no. 8 (2009): 918–38, at 923, available at: https://ideas.repec.org/a/eee/aosoci/v34y2009i8.

demonstrate the illusory nature of accountability for the exercise of power within the electoral process.

The second theme we are addressing is the attempt to present the specific toolbox used to receive an account of the exercise of democratic power. To achieve this, we study the mechanisms of accountability within a classic system of separation of powers, using the traditional tools of constitutional law and conceptual apparatus. This research starts from contemporary principles of power relationships, where the principal is seen as a political community and there are forms of holding those in power accountable for the power entrusted to them. Using this research perspective, we analyse the accountability of public authorities. It compares constitutionally provided structures and mechanisms for exercising power – such as parliamentary oversight and judicial independence intertwined with judicial accountability – with the political and institutional reality in numerous countries, pointing out various traps and deficits in the concept of accountability. In the chapters that follow (3, 4, 5), we attempt to analyse the extent to which the system of governance in these three branches is designed in a way that makes it possible to receive an account of entrusted power and to give feedback on how such a report is made and received in practice by those who entrust the power.

The third thread tries to put newly recognised actors of political power in two categories: Big Tech corporations and mass social movements. We argue that some of their characteristics render them powerful and underestimated political agents who take on the role of principals. We outline the ways in which public authorities deal with them, as well as the weaknesses of the constitutional and political system attempting to deal with such phenomena.

As we understand it, accountability is first and foremost about communication of the exercise of entrusted power. We attempt to find the channels of this communication on governance: to identify the originator, the recipient and the setting in which such reporting takes place. In doing so, we try to define a broader background to these relationships and the phenomena that accompany them – without complaining about a particular system of governance; we look for regularities and sometimes deficits or inconsistencies that hinder these processes. Consequently, our study looks at public accountability from a new angle, with a selection of instruments that shape its scope and content. On the other hand, it allows us to expose some false or outdated assumptions about the functioning of public authority in democratic societies. In a sense, the use of the public accountability paradigm within the framework of constitutional law means introducing a new concept into the old framework of a democratic state, which can lead to an assessment of whether well-established constitutional assumptions are still correct and valid.

Are the existing channels that were designed under the democratic system anachronistic and becoming obsolete? Is the lack of accountability giving rise to a burgeoning populism, the rise of new self-styled candidates for principals? Can an honest account of the extent to which modern power is constrained by law and expert knowledge strengthen the legitimacy of those in power – or does it weaken it? These are the questions we pose as we strive to find if only partial answers in practice and in the thicket of constitutional instruments.

We would like to thank all those who believed in our project, the reviewers and contributors during the first stage of our work, who were available for four years to talk and read about our ideas and sent their comments, questions and feedback. The knowledge, inquisitiveness and kindness of those who believed in our idea and decided to make this project feasible were a huge support to us. We would especially like to thank Dawid Bunikowski, Adam Czarnota, Jan Filip, Anssi Keinänen and Jan Zielonka. Finally, we take responsibility for any potential mistakes and shortcomings.

1 Accountability in constitutional law – assumptions and meaning

The concept of accountability has gained quite a prominence among social scientists, journalists and politicians in recent years.[1] It is such a broad term and has such a positive connotation that it is hardly possible to find opponents to the idea, and invoking it often entails a demand for greater transparency or credibility. At the same time the suggestive potential of the very notion of accountability makes it an extremely fluid and ephemeral concept.[2] However, it is used more as a slogan, a noble yet vague idea,[3] which can be presented with the conviction that it does not oblige one to do anything, and the purposes for which reference to accountability is made determine both its use and its reception.

As underlined by all, accountability is an ambiguous concept,[4] used in various ways, researched and used for various purposes – often with little connection to the original meaning. It is often used in a very broad sense, overlapping with the content of responsiveness, accountability, efficiency[5] or transparency of operations.[6] Typically, it is also used in a normative rather than an analytical context; as a postulate, a desired goal or an environment in which public authorities should operate.

1 Staffan I. Lindberg, "Mapping Accountability: Core Concept and Subtypes", *International Review of Administrative Sciences* 79, no. 2 (2013): 202–26, 204.

2 Mark Bovens, "Analysing and Assessing Public Accountability. A Conceptual Framework", *European Governance Papers (EUROGOV)* No. C-06-01 (2006), http://www.connex-network.org/eurogov/pdf/egp-connex-C-06-01.pdf, 5.

3 Joe McIntyre, *The Judicial Function. Fundamental Principles of Contemporary Judging* (Springer: Singapore, 2019), 234; Andrew Le Sueur, "Developing Mechanisms for Judicial Accountability in the UK", *Legal Studies* 24, no. 1 (2004): 73–98, 73; Charles G. Geyh, "Rescuing Judicial Accountability from the Realm of Political Rhetoric", *Articles by Maurer Faculty* 303 (2006): 911–35, 914. https://www.repository.law.indiana.edu/facpub/303.

4 As noted by Lindberg, it is already possible to find about a hundred meanings of the concept of accountability (Lindberg, 204).

5 Bovens, 5.

6 Probably the broadest spectrum: Jerry L. Mashaw, "Accountability and Institutional Design. Some Thoughts on the Grammar of Governance", in *Public Accountability: Designs, Dilemmas and Experiences*, ed. M. W. Dowdle (Cambridge University Press, 2006), 115–56, 128.

DOI: 10.4324/9781003493419-1

The notion of accountability has been around in constitutionalism[7] in this sense almost since its inception. It is worth recalling that Article 15 of the Declaration of the Rights of Man approved by the National Assembly of France in August 1789 states: "Society has the right to require of every public agent an account of his administration". As Founding Father James Madison warned, "A popular government without popular information, or the means of acquiring it, is but prologue to a farce or a tragedy, or perhaps both".[8] The possibility of demanding information about how power is exercised is closely linked to the planning and functioning of the democratic order.

It is therefore understandable to turn to accountability when reflecting upon political order and democracy, treating it as a necessary relation between the rulers and the ruled,[9] at the same time proclaiming the need for openness, confidence and all the other attributes so readily used postulatively that we would like to associate with what we consider to be good governance. In a sense, this is a golden idea, fitting anytime and anywhere, provided, however, that it relies on the rule of law and democracy. For democracy, in its Enlightenment sense (other than in the classical sense, i.e. Platonic and Aristotelian), envisages opposition to power exercised in an arbitrary manner, even if by a majority. At the same time, democracy affirms freedom identified with the rule of rational law resulting from a full-scale assessment of the consequences of the enacted regulation.

Given these reasons, it is easy to apply this category, especially in the context of deficit of accountability, in the diagnosis of political relations, as well as the needs for reform of political and legal institutions. Therefore, it is a term that is easily shrugged off and relatively difficult to define, particularly in relation to the realities and regulations of the political system. Accountability is therefore frequently proclaimed (usually as a postulate or, in diagnosis, as a deficit), but rarely given serious consideration,[10] and even less frequently applied. Nevertheless, if it is to be used in science, and the science of law at that, as well as in the analysis and diagnosis of constitutional relations, it is

7 Understood here most straightforwardly as the idea according to which the creation, structure and exercise of power in the state are constrained by law, and that the mandate to exercise power exists as long as it is exercised within these constraints. Cf. Wil Waluchow and Dimitrios Kyritsis, "Constitutionalism", in *The Stanford Encyclopedia of Philosophy* (Summer, 2023 Edition), ed. Edward N. Zalta and Uri Nodelman. https://plato.stanford.edu/archives/sum2023/entries/constitutionalism/.

8 These words were recalled in the ruling on the Watergate scandal in 1977, after "High Court to Rule on Right of Public to Nixon's Tapes", *New York Times*, March 29, 1977. https://www.nytimes.com/1977/03/29/archives/high-court-to-rule-on-right-of-public-to-nixons-tapes.html. (accessed 24.05.2022).

9 Johan P. Olsen, "Democratic Accountability and the Terms of Political Order", *European Political Science Review*, 9, no. 4 (November 2017): 519–37, 519. Similarly (governed and governors) Carol Harlow, *Accountability in the European Union* (Oxford University Press, 2002), 15.

10 McIntyre, 231.

necessary to define much more precisely what it means, what it requires and what are its instruments and methods of obtaining accounts of the exercise of power.

Accountability – a postulate or a description of an actual relation

Accountability is a concept well known to the social sciences, including management and economics, but also political science, administration[11] and social psychology.[12] The term is normally used to denote a demand to provide reports, to give an account of one's functions, performance of one's duties and competencies through actions under a requirement, and acceptance of liability for failure, lack of competence or ddishonesty.[13] The notion of accountability, derived from Anglo-Saxon[14] tradition, began to function in the description and optimisation concepts of administrative structures and corporations, in management science and later also in European Union law. It has become remarkably popular over the last decade or so. Bovens points out that the emancipation of this concept has not been accompanied by a uniform understanding of it and often, in the absence of an adequate equivalent in many languages, it gets confused with the concept of responsibility.[15] This confusion comes up particularly often when reflecting on the nature of systemic relations and democracy,[16] where accountability appears almost as a fundamental feature of systems of political power.[17] In political science, the concept of accountability is typically used to describe particular relations: firstly, between

11 Ferris et al. defined the accountability as "the extent to which a person's behaviours are observed and evaluated by others, with important rewards and punishments contingent upon those evaluations". Gerald R. Ferris, Harry Triandis, Peter Carnevale, D. D. Frink, and H. Hopper, "Accountability in Human Resources Systems", in *Handbook of Human Resource Management*, ed. Gerald. R. Ferris, Sherman. D. Rosen, and Darold. T. Barnum Oxford: Blackwell, (1995) 175–96, 187.

12 Lerner and Tetlock defined the individual accountability as "implicit or explicit expectation that one may be called on to justify one's beliefs, feelings, and actions to others". Jennifer Lerner and Philip Tetlock, "Accounting for the Effects of Accountability", *Psychological Bulletin*, 125, no. 2 (1999): 255–75. https://doi.org/10.1037/0033-2909.125.2.255 at 255.

13 Jonathan Bradbury, "Accountability", in *The Concise Oxford Dictionary of Politics* (3rd ed.), ed. Iain McLean and Alistair McMillan (Oxford University Press, 2009).

14 Although Bovens draws attention to the Anglo-Norman origin of the phrase according to Melvin Dubnick, ""Seeking Salvation for Accountability", American Political Science Association 2002, 6, 7–9,

15 Bovens gives examples from French, Portuguese, Spanish, German, Dutch and Japanese ("Accountability: An Ever-Expanding Concept?" *Public Administration* [online], 78, no. 3 (2000): 555–73; also: Harlow, 14–15; Dubnick, 2002, 6.

16 Philippe C. Schmitter and Terry Lynn Karl, "What Democracy Is … and Is Not", *Journal of Democracy* 2, no. 3 (1991): 75–88; Larry Diamond, *Developing Democracy: Toward Consolidation* (Baltimore: Johns Hopkins Press, 1999), 10–12. See Tom Ginsburg and Aziz Z. Huq, *How to Save a Constitutional Democracy* (University of Chicago Press, 2018), 8.

17 For example: the Global Accountability Report 2008, the European Court of Auditors' Report 2014 – "Gaps, Overlapping Legislation and Challenges: An Overview of EU Account-

members of parliament and their constituents; secondly, within the apparatus of government: ministers are held accountable for their decisions by the parliament that scrutinises them, either jointly or individually, and they are also required to provide information (answers) to members of parliament (committees and individual MPs) and are thus held accountable through parliament by their constituents.

The principle of accountability also finds application when describing relations within the bureaucracy – public administration, structured hierarchically, i.e. within the framework of official relations, ultimately held accountable for its competences and the scope of the duties entrusted to it by the relevant political authorities.

Accountability is related to a fundamental and fairly obvious idea concerning power in the state, which is exercised as a consequence of being entrusted by the people subject to it – that there is a certain bond between entrustors and trustees, and that the latter are obliged to give an account of what they do while exercising their functions of power. Meanwhile, accountability mitigates the asymmetry noted by Max Weber on both sides of the hierarchical relationship in which accountability is supposed to occur; one of the parties (the rincipal) has formal authority to impose sanctions or/and give rewards – but the Agent has an informational advantage over the Principal.[18] This reporting may produce temptation to abuse power, as well as to conceal information or to dose it so as to elicit different reactions.[19] This informational asymmetry exists not only in bureaucratic but also in political reporting.

If regulated and applied, accountability is a mechanism that allows the Principal to gain knowledge and the Agent to explain their actions in a fair and objective manner. In this sense, accountability – at least in theory – seems to be a question of proper reporting, truth-finding and securing compliance with the established regime.[20] It makes it possible to have a closer look at those who perform their functions from the perspective of what is expected of them, but also from the point of view of legal compliance, competences and assumed commitments.[21]

The call for accountability of public authorities is becoming increasingly popular – not to say trendy – in both constitutional law and international law,

ability and Public Control Systems". https://www.eca.europa.eu/lists/ecadocuments/lr14_01/qj0214776enc.pdf (accessed 02.09.2024.2022).

18 Gary J. Miller, "The Political Evolution of Principal-Agent Models", *Annual Review of Political Science* 8 (2005): 203–25, 204.

19 Jan-Erik Lane, "The Principal-Agent Approach to Politics: Policy Implementation and Public Policy-Making", *Open Journal of Political Science* 3, no. 2 (2013): 85–9, 85–6.

20 On the shortcomings in achieving this effect: Joseph Benveniste and Mizrahi Shlomo, "Accountability, Governance, and Institutional Change in Intergovernmental Relations: A Theoretical Framework", *Politics & Policy* 51 (2023): 242–55, 245. https://doi.org/10.1111/polp.12520.

21 Olsen, 520.

including European law, especially following the rise of the doctrine of New Public Management. This concept is based on reorientation of the management of public organisations and consists of the abandonment of a procedure-oriented approach and rules of conduct related to expenditure, and instead the implementation of rules based on the analysis of the results achieved in relation to the incurred expenses, adopting a strategic orientation and incorporating a market mechanism into the process of public service delivery.[22]

It appeared among the seven principles of public life in Lord Nolan's Report (1995).[23] Also in the United States, the notion of accountability was given new potential through *Reinventing Government*: the campaign for reform launched during the Clinton administration.[24] In either situation, the reforms were based on the involvement of management methods and techniques known from the private sector and used to manage public affairs, in particular the use of efficiency indicators for administration and public agendas. As such, it assumes the role of an instrument to improve efficiency and openness in economic terms.

However, in recent years, accountability has also been seen as a demand, and an instrument in the hands of populist movements[25] that is easy to use. Widespread frustration with the way in which power is exercised and with the effects of that power, and with the failure to hold public authorities to account for the exercise of their functions, has led to a need for calls for greater accountability and a change not only of elites, but also of political systems.

This steers the consideration of accountability in a somewhat different direction: how the public nature of accountability can – and should be – understood. More precisely: how and where the reception and consideration of accounts of governance are realised, and where is this public that can accomplish this. This inevitably brings to mind the notion of the public sphere, which, according to the already classical definition by Jurgen Habermas, means a realm of our social life in which something approaching public opinion can be formed; access is guaranteed for all citizens. It can appear in every conversation in which people freely assemble and behave as a public body to talk about matters of general interest.[26] As Habermas wrote, it is a certain environment, a network of communication in which public opinion is formed, primarily informed and shaped by the media. But as one can easily notice, this public sphere has changed a lot in the last decades and it is already a reality that, as Habermas

22 Jody Freeman, "Extending Public Accountability through Privatization: From Public Law to Publicization", in *Public Accountability: Designs, Dilemmas and Experiences* (see note 6), 83.

23 Nolan Report, Standards in Public Life, HMSO, London 1995 (1.4. Acountability. "Holders of public office are accountable to the public for their decisions and actions and must submit themselves to the scrutiny necessary to ensure this").

24 Bovens, 6.

25 Ginsburg and Huq, 83, 108.

26 Jurgen Habermas, ""The Public Sphere: An Encyclopaedia Article", *New German Critique* no. 3 (Autumn, 1974): 49–55, 49.

already predicted and further reminded by Steffek, a public sphere, whether national or transnational, may come in the plural; there is a network of various public spheres as overlapping discursive arenas that taken together constitute the public sphere of modern societies.[27] Much has already been written about the phenomenon of disintegration of the public sphere into multiple separate spheres, often competing and completely parallel as to agenda and understanding of general interest. We also address this issue in the last chapter on technopolitics, but at the moment it is only necessary to highlight two circumstances that arise from the recent reshaping of civic society and the public sphere. Firstly, there are now many of these public spheres, they are worldview-oriented and their discourses and the information they use are distinct and produce competing visions of the world, authority, intentions and ways of exercising it. Secondly – when it comes to the areas of reporting by power actors that we have discussed, the public spheres are not always equally interested in them. For example, communication about court judgments is different than interest in government activities and subsequent debate, and the public sphere is shaped very differently under conditions of electoral campaign and with accountability in mind. In essence, this reservation concerns the fact that we are adopting a certain construct to facilitate the imagining and conceptualisation of accountability – but it is somewhat of an abstract figure, necessary for the analysis of accountability, except that it cannot be oversimplified, or standardised, as lawyers, who usually adopt a single designator for a single concept, would like to have it.

Perhaps these reasons underlie the fact that legal science has not been too keen to use this concept for analytical purposes up to now;[28] specifically, the

27 Jurgen Habermas, *Between Facts and Norms, Contributions to a Discourse Theory of Law and Democracy* (MIT Press, 1998), 373; Erik Eriksen, "An Emerging European Public Sphere", *European Journal of Social Theory* 8, no. 3 (2005): 344; Jens Steffek, "Public Accountability and the Public Sphere of International Governance", *Ethics & International Affairs*, 8, no. 1 (2010): 45–68, 56.

28 On the other hand, it is worth noting that accountability appears in positive law and in contexts far removed from those described. So far, in the European legal order, accountability as a category of public law is making an outstanding career in the area of personal data protection. The General Data Protection Regulation in Article 5(2) introduces the principle of accountability, according to which the controller is responsible for compliance with the other principles of personal data processing and, moreover, must be able to demonstrate compliance with these principles. This requires the implementation of procedures and the maintenance of appropriate documentation. Therefore, accountability means that the controller must be able to report on its compliance with the obligations to comply with the personal data processing principles enshrined in Article 5(1) GDPR. It is therefore no longer sufficient to protect personal data in accordance with the Principles – it is still necessary to be able to demonstrate that one protects these data in accordance with the Principles, i.e. that one fulfils the principle of accountability – the ability to give an account of the processing according to the applicable principles and rules for their protection.

concept of accountability has not been consistently and unequivocally recycled so far in the science of constitutional law.[29]

However, if we assume that accountability is likely to become a distinct and recognised category under the legal science, it should be considered in the framework of constitutional law, independently of the concepts used to date in the description and analysis of constitutional systems. There is still no coherent theoretical approach to this issue, as well as no serious comparative analyses that would make it possible to extract the essence, or at least the features, of this category within the framework of classical institutions and the achievements of the science of constitutional law and legal sciences in general. At the same time, if applied in constitutional law without a precise meaning to describe various well-known phenomena and processes, the concept of accountability may lead to certain misunderstandings and even misleading tracks and conclusions, unnecessarily becoming confused with the well-known and classical concepts of liability, responsibility, as well as control, supervision and – particularly within the framework of electoral process – the concept of responsiveness.

However, if accountability raises so many ambiguities and perplexities at the outset, why should it become a useful tool in the analysis of constitutional law?

In our view, this is the case for at least three reasons. The first is that accountability – purposefully or not – is the central, axial category for a democracy based on active participation of citizens, inclusiveness and equal influence over participation in public life. It is also fundamental from the perspective of constitutionalism, the core of which is the principle of the exercise of mandated power and the control of public affairs by those who grant the mandate.

The next reason is power in a democratic state is classically based on the separation of powers and therefore on the subtle system of interactions between the legislature, the executive and the judiciary, a system based largely on a complex web of interdependence, mutual accountability and entrustment. In this environment, giving and receiving accounts of the exercise of entrusted power is prerequisite to function.

And thirdly, public authority operates by means of administration, and this, according to the still partly valid Weberian paradigm, is structured within a hierarchical framework of entrustment of competences and responsibilities – and therefore of accountability for the tasks to be performed – and the top of this hierarchy usually answers to elected political authorities (government vs. central and local government administrative bodies and other entities performing tasks entrusted to them by the government).

29 C. Harlow, "Accountability and Constitutional Law", in *The Oxford Handbook of Public Accountability*, ed. M. Bovens, R. E. Goodin, and T. Schillemans (Oxford: Oxford University Press, 2014), 195–210, 196.

There are also at least three serious values of public life that are well established in constitutional law theory, which argue for the distinction of accountability in constitutional theory and practice. The first is openness – transparency of public life, immanently linked to the democratic form of governance and scrutiny. The second value is the rationality behind the exercise of power – it also does not need to be elaborated further that the necessity to give an account of the function exercised or the actions taken promotes, firstly, the consideration of the rationale behind these actions and, secondly, their presentation in such a way that this rationality is evident. Finally, an important value offered by accountability is the legitimacy of power actions and power structures. Indeed, the legitimacy of the power exercised in a state depends not only on the title by which it was obtained, but above all on the manner in which it is exercised – efficiency, compliance with community goals and the aforementioned rationality, all of which are assessed by the collective entity that entrusts the exercise of power in a continuous and – as we still hope – attentive manner.

Constitutional principles, in particular the principle of separation of powers and the rule of law, are inextricably linked to accountability.[30] These principles determine fundamental conditions for a democratic state – firstly by indicating the boundaries within which the wielder of power is to act, as well as the need for other power actors to control and restrain each other. Their fulfilment is crucially dependent on what constitutes the premise of accountability – namely, that each and every power exercise, as well as each and every measure, must be accountable – in the sense that the actor performing it must be prepared to communicate/report on the measures taken and demonstrate their legality and expediency. Accountability is further linked to the implementation of the principle of representative democracy, in the sense that the political representatives are obliged to report on their actions to the sovereign (as discussed in more detail below) as well as to the institutions of direct democracy, which sometimes seek to enforce accountability for the incompatibility of the exercise of functions with the will of the represented – in particular the recall referendum and the people's veto. Although these institutions aim at negating the actions of the representatives – either as objection to a specific legislative action or refusal of confidence *ad personam* – it is inconceivable that they can be implemented without prior obligation to report on the actions and to justify them by the subject whose authority is being challenged in this way in the first place. The accountability of power is therefore primarily associated with elections and the refusal to continue to accept the exercise of power,[31]

30 Harlow, 199–201.

31 Michael Dowdle, "Public Accountability: Conceptual, Historical, and Epistemic Mappings", in *Public Accountability: Designs, Dilemmas and Experiences* (see note 6), 1–29, 4.

although any limitations on the application of this particular category to the electoral process have been recognised rather well over the years.[32]

Still, since it is already apparent that this concept is ambiguous, takes on different tones in different contexts and is so similar to other concepts (as discussed below), is it even worth distinguishing it? And – if we answer in the affirmative – what is the criterion that makes accountability distinguishable?

In our view, accountability has its place in reflecting on the system, power and the conditions under which it is exercised – both politically and legally – and the reason for its distinction is the unique element of reporting on the entrusted power.[33] This is the only account of its kind within public policy and cannot be equated with any other. Hence, we will now proceed to highlight more precisely what, in our view, deserves attention in the analysis of accountability and gives meaning to its distinction.

Nature and core of accountability

Accountability connotes the meaning of its root word, i.e. to account, to give an account; this is also the origin of the term, which derives from the Latin and then the Old French *aconter*, meaning to count, to account. As Jens Steffek observes, the use of the term can be traced as far back as the Middle Ages,[34] but the English wording hardly lends itself to translation outside the context of bookkeeping[35] and in many languages has no equivalent and is equated with responsibility.[36] The concept of accountability is closely related to responsibility, transparency, answerability and responsiveness, and these terms are often used interchangeably.[37]

Therefore, accountability literally means the obligation to hold an account – to give an account (or report) on the performance of certain activities or functions that have been designated.[38] The entity that is obliged to report – to give an account of its activity, the performance of certain tasks, does so towards the person who has entrusted these tasks – this person in turn is

32 For example: Robert A. Dahl, *Democracy and Its Critics* (Yale University Press, 1991); Joseph A. Schumpeter, *Capitalism, Socialism and Democracy* (Routledge, 2010).

33 Lindberg, 205–8.

34 Steffek, 64.

35 Melvin J. Dubnick, "Situating Accountability: Seeking Salvation for the Core Concept of Modern Governance" (manuscript, University of New Hampshire, 2007); available at mjdubnick.dubnick.net/papers/2007/Situacct031307.pdf (accessed 24.11.2023).

36 Steffek quotes terms: *responsabilidad* in Spanish, *responsabilité* in French, *Verantwortung* in German, 64.

37 Dawn Oliver, *Government in the United Kingdom: The Search for Accountability, Effectiveness, and Citizenship* (Open University Press, 1991), 22; Anthomny Arnull, "Introduction: The European Union's Accountability and Legitimacy Deficit", in *Accountability and Legitimacy in the European Union*, ed. A. Arnull and D. Wincott, Oxford Studies in European Law (Oxford University Press, 2002), 2.

38 Lindberg calls the sphere from which the report is made "Domain", Lindberg, 210.

entitled to demand such an account or report. It is therefore the function of the superior – the entrusting party, called in this relationship the Principal (or: the forum), to judge the actions of the person to whom the task has been entrusted, called an Agent,[39] since accountability is usually considered precisely within the framework of Principal-Agent Theory. The obligation to be accountable is therefore incumbent on the person to whom a certain activity has been delegated and who is carrying out the activity or is to perform certain tasks. However, accountability does not exhaust itself by merely reporting on the tasks performed – its meaning is somewhat broader and denotes a situation in which there is an expectation that one may be called upon to justify one's beliefs and actions to others, expressed implicitly or explicitly, and the extent to which a person's behaviours are observed and evaluated by others.[40] In the public domain, public accountability could involve "the means by which public agencies and their workers manage the diverse expectations generated within and outside the organization".[41]

This way, as Bovens points out, accountability is a relationship between an actor and a forum, in which the actor has an obligation to explain and to justify his or her conduct, the forum can pose questions and pass judgment, and the actor may face consequences.[42]

At this point it is worth making a first important distinction – we assume that accountability in its core sense should be defined as the obligation to be called "to account". This presentation of the report is intended firstly to provide information and secondly to enable the one to whom the report is submitted to check the Agents' activities.[43] This duty to provide an account relates to the exercise of entrusted activities within one's competence or purpose, a duty of "giving and demanding of reasons for conduct".[44] To put it

39 Christopher Achen and Larry Bartels, "Blind Retrospection: Electoral Responses to Droughts, Flu, and Shark Attacks" [online]. Boston: APSA Annual Meeting, 2002, available from https://ethz.ch/content/dam/ethz/special-interest/gess/cis/international-relations-dam/Teaching/pwgrundlagenopenaccess/Weitere/AchenBartels.pdf; Gabriel Lenz, *Follow the Leader? How Voters Respond to Politicians' Performance and Policies* (University of Chicago Press, 2012); Sean Gailmard, "Accountability and Principal-Agent Theory", in *The Oxford Handbook of Public Accountability* (see note 29), 90–105.

40 Yousueng Han and Mehmet Akif Demircioglu, "Accountability, Politics, and Power", in *Global Encyclopaedia of Public Administration, Public Policy, and Governance*, ed. A. Farazmand (Springer International Publishing AG, 2016), 1–8. These authors also add an element of consequence applied to the Agent – as they write, observance and evaluation is connected with important rewards and punishments.

41 Barbara Romzek and Melvin Dubnick, "Accountability in the Public Sector: Lessons from the Challenger Tragedy", *Public Administration Review* 47, no. 3 (1987): 227–38, 228.

42 Mark Bovens, "Analysing and Assessing Public Accountability: A Conceptual Framework", *European Governance Papers* No C-06-01 (2006), 1–37, 9.

43 This is also how Richard Mulgan puts it: *Holding Power to Account: Accountability in Modern Democracies* (Basingstoke: Palgrave Macmillan, 2003), 1.

44 Steffek, 47.

simply, and in the most general terms, accountability can be defined as the ability to give an account of an action and to answer for that action (conduct or performance of an obligation). Accountability is therefore a type of reporting, a feature not of an entity – but of a system, consisting in the ability of the entrusting entity to account for a particular action or sequence of actions. Being accountable means being obliged to report or provide an explanation for one's actions.

However, this relationship is usually directly associated with the imposition of sanctions for the misappropriation of entrusted powers, especially in the context of legal considerations. The second element of accountability is thus the possible incurrence of consequences – either a penalty or an obligation to make changes if such a report reveals misconduct. This element of accountability is highlighted by Mark Bovens, among others,[45] and also Dawn Oliver, who points out that accountability means "being liable to be required to give an account or explanation of actions and, where appropriate, to suffer the consequences, take the blame or undertake to put matter right if it should appear that errors have been made". According to Oliver then, it is an explanatory and corrective action.[46] Likewise, Jonathan Koppell points out five dimensions of public accountability: "transparency, liability (consequences for performance), responsibility (conformity of rule), responsiveness, and controllability".[47] This element of accountability means that it is often equated with responsibility – enforcing the consequences of an action that fails to meet the expectations of the one doing the holding to account. This often echoes the phrase "the need to hold accountable", which is characteristic of the contemporary public debate, naturally associated with the assumption of a negative evaluation of actions and the application of sanctions in the form of withdrawal of the mandate to hold office, as well as with legal accountability. ABut in its primary and most basic sense, accountability literally does not have to include this element at all and is distinctly different from responsibility for the actions of a public authority – for they have somewhat different functions and effects. Existence of an audience observing the Agent – which is a key element of the concept of accountability – is not a condition of responsibility and it does not include the expectation of judgment, which lies at the core of the accountability relationship.[48] Admittedly, there is some overlap between responsibility and accountability in practice – as Yousueng points out, responsibility can be a necessary component of the process of holding individuals accountable for their conduct, although they are separate processes for several

45 Lindberg, 206.

46 Dawn Oliver, *Constitutional Reform in the UK* (Oxford, 2003), 48.

47 Jonathan G. S. Koppell, "Pathologies of Accountability: ICANN and the Challenge of 'Multiple Accountabilities Disorder'", *Public Administration Review* 65, no. 1 (2005): 94–108, 96.

48 Barry Schlenker, Thomas Britt, John Pennington, Rodolfo Murphy and Kevin Doherty, "The Triangle Model of Responsibility", *Psychological Review* 101, no. 4 (1994): 632–52, 634.

reasons. Firstly, responsibility seeks to apply sanctions for exceeding or failing to meet certain requirements,[49] while the function of accountability is simply to obtain an account of the exercised authority.[50] It does not directly aim to apply sanctions for incorrect or unsatisfactory actions. It therefore has a much broader, narrative character – it aims to fill the gap between action and expectation.[51] In essence, accountability can be a relationship where there is no confrontation between Principal and Agent, no restriction or sanction on the latter – it can even be convivial.

Secondly, one very interesting difference between accountability and responsibility is that responsibility can be relatively easily avoided. The bureaucratic system, as well as the political system, provides for many guarantees and instruments to assert responsibility, but at the same time, the system equips whoever is to be held accountable with many excuses, exceptions and procedures in which responsibility may prove impossible to fulfil.[52] Meanwhile, it must be stressed that accountability should be a permanent and condition-independent element of the power entrustment relationship.

Finally, responsibility is often exercised under triadic conditions – i.e. a judicial trial that requires an impartial adjudicator to the parties presenting their positions and arguments – while accountability is played out between two parties and its meaning and purpose is exhausted in this relationship.[53] In an accountability relationship the Agent is required to reveal, to explain and to justify what he/she does[54] and this, in essence, can be considered not only his duty but also his privilege – whereas the element of punishment for actions that do not comply with the expectations of the Principal is no longer directly inherent in accountability.

Similarly, accountability cannot be equated with control, either. The latter rarely involves only knowing the auditee's account of what has been done. The

49 Jeremy Waldron proposes the term "forensic accountability" to describe such forms, as opposed to Agent accountability, meaning the Agent's duty to the Principal to give an account of his or her actions. Jeremy Waldron, "Accountability: Fundamental to Democracy", *NYU School of Law, Public Law Research Paper* no. 14-13 (2014), https://ssrn.com/abstract=2410812.

50 A similar distinction is made by Brian C. Smith, *Judges and Democratization. Judicial Independence in New Democracies* (Routledge, 2017), 186, highlighting two dimensions of accountability: answerability, as the obligation on the part of an Agent to provide an account of activities and achievements; and enforcement, or the power of the Principal to deploy sanctions when the account is deemed unsatisfactory.

51 Mark Bovens, Thomas Schillemans and Robert. E. Goodin, "Public Accountability", in *The Oxford Handbook of Public Accountability* (see note 29), 1–33, 4.

52 This difference is pointed out by John Gardner, "The Mark of Responsibility (with the Postscript on Accountability)", in *Public Accountability: Designs, Dilemmas and Experiences* (see note 6), 220–42, at 228, 237.

53 It is recalled by Morgan, 246–8.

54 Colin Scott, "Accountability in the Regulatory State", *Journal of Law and Society* 27 (2000), 38–60, 38.

criteria and scope of scrutiny are usually very rigorously defined, and it typically takes place during – *ex ante*, as P. Birkinshaw points out – whereas accountability, by its very nature, concerns actions already completed and therefore takes place *ex post*.[55] An audit, on the other hand, has a completely different function and character. Its function is not to give an account of the actions carried out, but to check whether the actions were performed in accordance with the presumed standards; the report of the controlled person is only auxiliary. Nor does auditing presuppose any reporting rooted in the entrustment of power to be exercised. It can be carried out by a superior, but it can equally well be carried out by an entity that is completely independent and outside the hierarchical relationship.The difference between accountability and responsiveness is much more subtle. In both of these relations, there is a certain bond between the two actors, which consists in entrusting the performance of certain actions. There is also an expectation that the one to whom the task has been entrusted will accomplish it in accordance with the entrustor's expectations. However, as far as accountability is concerned, this entrustment and performance takes place within the framework of discretionary power. It is not the action of an Agent totally committed to the intentions and will of its Principal. It is an independent action, and the executor is fully responsible for it: as to the decisions taken, the directions, the actions and the results.[56] As Lindberg illustratively puts it,[57]

> a puppet acting as an extension of someone else's will is not a legitimate object of accountability. That is why accountability is different from "responsiveness". Only actors with some discretion to make authoritative decisions can be the objects of accountability relationships (…). Accountability hence is associated with the act of discretionary governing, typically understood as the authoritative allocation of resources and exercising control and coordination.[58]

55 Patrick Birkinshaw, "Decision-making and Its Control in the Adminsitrative Process – An Overview", in *Law, Legitimacy and the Constitution*, ed. P. McAuslan and J. McEldowney (London: Sweet and Maxwell, 1985), 151–69, 152. It is worth adding that the unreliability of this particular criterion of distinction was demonstrated by Scott, 39.

56 Thomas Christiano, *The Rule of the Many* (Boulder, CO: Westview, 1996), 219; Goran Hyden, "Governance and the Study of Politics", in *Governance and Politics in Africa,* ed. G. Hyden and M. Bratton (Boulder, CO: Lynne Rienner 1992), 3–19.

57 Lindberg, 208.

58 The examples cited by Lindberg: Robert Dahl, *Polyarchy: Participation and Opposition* (New Haven, CT: Yale University Press, 1971); Jan Kooiman, "Social-Political Governance. Introduction", in *Modern Governance, New Government-Society Interactions,* ed. Jan Kooiman (London: Sage, 1993), 1–6.

Accountability in constitutional law

In an attempt to present a model of public accountability within the framework of constitutional law, that is, the science and practice of the field, it is imperative first to outline the model features of this function of the system, or the feature of power relations and entrustment of power, and then to link the category of accountability to principles fundamental to constitutional thought. Since it has been possible to separate accountability from other relations such as the traditionally recognised political, legal responsibility, control and oversight, it is necessary to outline some assumptions of this concept within the constitutional order.

Accountability as a category may be used to instrumentalise the assumption of entrustment of power and the role of both parties in this relationship. The subject obliged to report on the performance of certain tasks (the Agent) does so vis-à-vis the subject who has entrusted these tasks (the Principal). This implies that accountability – if one uses the term consistently and consciously within the framework of legal science – requires that the relationship concerning the exercise of power in the Principal-Agent model be distinguished. Thus, the first assumption to be recognised in the use of the term "accountability" is the idea of a contractual or fiduciary relationship between two social actors, one of whom has the right to demand reporting due to the fact that it is by its will and power that the other actor (Agent) is to perform certain tasks, in the manner and to the extent determined by the Principal. The entrustment is thus the source of accountability and it justifies the demand for an account and the obligation to give it.

There can be many of these entrustment relationships; the people are the first entrustor and Principal. But the people's elected representatives can make further entrustments, the best example being, of course, the government, elected as a result of parliamentary endorsement. Regardless of the levels of entrustment structure and intermediaries, however, as Michael Dowdle puts it, "the idea of public accountability seems to express a belief that persons with public responsibilities should be answerable to 'the people' for the performance of their duties".[59] And the question of accountability must always begin with determining the relation of entrustment of power and identifying the circle of those who are the Principal or Agent, and looking closely at who is entitled to receive an account of the exercise of power, how and on whose authority.

Secondly, there is the question of what the Principal can require an account of, i.e. what such an account can be expected to cover. Is the account supposed to concern the outcome achieved by the Agent within the framework of the powers entrusted, or the manner in which the Agent operated? At its core, democratic governance has procedures for selection and decision-making; the

59 Dowdle, 3.

constitutional system provides for a complex web of relations and mechanisms in which governance takes place. All this leads us to adopt a procedural perspective, assessing compliance with all procedural and institutional restraints. That being said, the Principal also expects to see results; in fact, public accountability can be much more concerned with substantial outcomes than with procedures.[60] This generates considerable tension towards shaping accounts of the power exercised, especially its reception and evaluation. Moreover, as pointed out by Steffek, the goals of public policy-making are manifold and often contradictory, and the preferences of the Principal (citizens) may change rapidly – this is particularly evident in the case of electoral accountability. Rarely is the Principal willing to remember what was expected a few years earlier, and even more rarely are they willing to accept an explanation of what objective circumstances, including procedural ones (e.g. coalition constraints), have led to failure to achieve the expected results. The ephemeral nature of the expectations of the Principal – the citizens – and above all the Principal's vague subjectivity has resulted in a turn to a purely managerial concept of stakeholders, who are supposed to be the recipients of accounts under public accountability.[61] This kind of relationship is easier to imagine and much more practical. In our opinion, however, it dangerously segments the Principal, and further, it can lead to turning citizens into clients rather than those who are the subject of the original authority. Thus, insofar as the government consults stakeholders before making a legislative decision, or as to the effects of this pre-established regulation, it can manipulate the selection of this group and treat its indications quite arbitrarily, if only by formulating the matters to be consulted. This is also because state institutions, equipped with a pool of competences and a mandate, are unquestionable in exercising them, as opposed to a vaguely defined group of those who are interested in the effects of its activities. This purely business-like approach to the accountability relationship seems to detract from the importance of entrustment and makes accountability illusory. Accordingly, we believe that in constitutional law terms, the term "accountability" must be reserved for those forms of receiving accounts that reach, or are likely to reach, the first Principal – the democratic community. We can then refer to such accountability as democratic, or – as in our view – public.[62]

60 Steffek, 48–9.

61 Steffek, 50.

62 On the notion of publicness: Steffek, 47 and the literature cited there in the "publicness" of public accountability and its implications for democracy: Jane Broadbent and Richard Laughlin, "Control and Legitimation in Government Accountability Processes: The Private Finance Initiative in the UK", *Critical Perspectives on Accounting* 14, nos. 1–2 (2003): 23–48; Tero Erkkila, "Governance and Accountability: A Shift in Conceptualisation", *Public Administration Quarterly* 31, no. 1 (2007): 1–38; M. Shamsul Haque, "The Diminishing Publicness of Public Service under the Current Mode of Governance", *Public Administration Review* 61, no. 1 (2001): 65–82; Donald F. Kettl, "The Global Revolution in Public Management: Driving Themes, Missing Links", *Journal of Policy Analysis and Management* 16, no. 3 (1997):

Finally, there is a third problem that needs to be addressed and which we will discuss later more broadly. Accountability, if one takes this concept seriously within constitutional law, does not consist of clear, strict criteria which would make it possible to assess the exercise of power.[63] Standards of proper conduct involve only the forms of reporting – not the actions being reported. This also points to the difference between responsibility and accountability in its "pure form" (what we call "narrative" accountability).

Instead, it should employ concrete instruments for obtaining a report on the exercise of power as well as criteria for this accountability. Reporting must presuppose certain conditions for this process, guaranteeing its fairness and impartiality. At the same time, it should be remembered that this is a bilateral – and not a tripartite – account, and there is no objective entity capable of judging which side is right. All the more so, the environment in which the account is received should satisfy the requirements of objectivity, and the account should also be given in confidence in said environment.

In order to search for instruments and paths of accountability within constitutional systems, it is necessary to recapitulate the observations made so far. Accountability appears to be a category based on three assumptions:

1) It is a relationship between the Principal and the Agent, involving the entrustment of a certain scope of authority, of competence, to be exercised. This relationship lies at the heart of the demand and, on the other side, of the Agent's obligation to give an account of the tasks so entrusted;
2) Accountability for the exercise of tasks and authority must take place under conditions of objective reporting, with the opportunity for both sides of this relation to refer to their positions. This involves the presentation of information and follow-up questions. This is possible when there are clear standards in place for this accountability, concerning the extent to which the account is to be given and the resulting effective accountability;
3) The third element is the consideration of the account given and the formulation of conclusions by the forum requiring the account (the Principal) – also as to the consequences for the Agent.[64] This last step causes aforementioned confusion with the concept of responsibility, but it is just one element of our category, where the first two are of key importance and constitute a distinctive feature.

Of course, it is difficult to find institutions in constitutional law that exactly correspond to such conditions. None of the classical instruments for exercising

446–62; and Paul G. Thomas, "The Changing Nature of Accountability", in *Taking Stock: Assessing Public Sector Reforms*, ed. B. Guy Peters and Donald Savoie (Montreal: McGill-Queen's University Press, 1998), 348–93.

63 In contrast: Lindberg, 211.

64 Bovens, 12.

and controlling power has such an origin or such a distinctive feature explicitly enshrined in its genealogy. On the contrary: when using their constitutional toolbox, lawyers used to sort it into the compartments of responsibility, control or legal accountability. However, we will try to trace the paths of accountability in those instruments that are known and used. This task can be accomplished by compiling and carefully analysing the functions of certain instruments and processes in the constitutional practice and regulation of modern democratic states that lead to obtaining an account (report) of the exercise of power.

Thus, it is necessary to first identify those features that distinguish accountability from other forms of control or enforcement of accountability for the exercise of power.

Firstly, the genesis of the approach to them is different; while control (audit) is a well-established institution within constitutional law that originated from financial and administrative law, and political responsibility is one of the oldest institutions of constitutional law closely related to the separation of powers,[65] accountability is a contemporary category developed through transplantation from other fields of social sciences, in particular management science. The institutions of political responsibility – as well as of constitutional (legal) responsibility – have their source in constitutional regulations and old, often centuries-long practice, the institutions of audit. Control has an almost equally rich tradition, especially the control of state finances. On the contrary, accountability is quite new in this framework concept, based on the observation of relations known in the state and concerning the exercise of power, and proposes to put them in a specific paradigm, i.e. the Principal–Agent model (superior, orderer–subordinate, executor) of power functions.

However, this is a purely conceptual difference. After all, accounts of the exercise of power – although not yet called accountability – have been present since the beginning of constitutionalism.

Above all, the standards used to define and evaluate the actions taken vary. Political responsibility has no clearly defined standards for its enforcement. They are determined *ad hoc* and *ex post*. Constitutional responsibility, on the other hand, is based on a well-defined standard derived from the applicable

65 In English, accountability is used to describe the relationship between ministers and parliament and the capacity of parliament to dismiss the government. Dicey, however, writes about responsibility in this context.

"Ministerial responsibility means two utterly different things. It means in ordinary parlance the responsibility of Ministers to Parliament, or, the liability of Ministers to lose their offices if they cannot retain the confidence of the House of Commons. This is the matter depending on the conventions of the constitution with which law has no direct concern. It means, when used in its strict sense, the legal responsibility of every Minister for every act of the Crown in which he takes part". Albert V. Dicey, "Chapter IX Ministerial Responsibility", in *An Introduction to the Study of the Law of the Constitution*, 10 edition (Macmillan Universal Law Publishing 1959), 325.

law. Its enforcement consists in examining whether the responsible entity has violated certain legal norms. Audit, on the other hand, employs specific, clearly defined criteria – it consists of a detailed, often quantitatively based examination of their conduct.

Accountability, on the other hand, should use explicit, clearly defined instruments to obtain an account of the exercise of power – although it does not generate predetermined requirements to be fulfilled by the party held accountable in its exercise which are derived from constitutional powers and duties. The initiation and procedure of the indicated forms of action against the subject of control or accountability also differ. Political responsibility is initiated on an *ad hoc* basis, at the request of specific political bodies, especially in the situation of a loss of parliamentary majority support for the actions of the executive. Auditing, on the other hand, is carried out either on a permanent or periodic basis, by specialised bodies equipped with the attribute of impartiality, appropriate competences and meeting specific procedural requirements regarding its conduct.

Another noteworthy difference between responsibility or liability and accountability is how they are enforced and possibly avoided. As we noted earlier citing John Gardner, liability can be avoided, or at least an attempt can be made to avoid it.[66] This is made possible by the system of procedures and circumstances under which it is borne, including exceptions and possible defences that can be raised – this happens even within the framework of political parliamentary responsibility.[67] The inherently repressive nature of liability guarantees the subject who is to bear it a standard of conduct, deadlines and the possibility of various methods and means of defence. Accountability in the sense of pure narrative, on the other hand, if viewed first as an obligation to give an account, does not require such forms of guarantees of rights of the reporting party; on the contrary, it requires the environment and conditions of objectivity and impartiality when listening to the Agent's account, creating conditions for disclosure, explanation and justification of the actions.[68] If viewed in this way, accountability actually becomes a privilege of the Agent and not a necessity or a defence against attack, much less a restriction or sanction.[69] Simply put, such accountability is not confrontational in nature, which is immanently linked to responsibility.

Therefore, the pursuit of accountability does not require such a set of guarantees, nor an entity capable of ruling on the effects, especially legal effects. It is also worth emphasising that accountability happens between two actors: the one entrusting the power and the one exercising it, and therefore, in principle,

66 Gardner, 228, 237.

67 For example, in Poland, during the 25 years of the Constitution of 2 April 1997 (despite more than a hundred attempts), not a single minister has been held parliamentarily accountable.

68 Scott, 38.

69 Morgan, 243.

without the triadic model, i.e. an independent body (court) being a third party to the relationship, which is the model associated with the adjudication on responsibility and in many systems – including constitutional accountability functions.[70]

What is most striking, however, yet quite easy to overlook when comparing accountability and other institutions related to being held accountable for actions taken in the exercise of public power, is the difference in effect and purpose of the institutions used. Political responsibility aims directly at the revocation of the mandate, a function of power. Constitutional responsibility intends to apply sanctions for the violation of legal norms, usually with the objective of removing the holder from office. Auditing is directed at obtaining an acknowledgement of the fulfilment of duties, approval or denial of the actions under scrutiny. However, to different degrees and with very different means, all these institutions aim to determine the scope and basis of the responsibility of the entity being audited and to enforce the designated forms of accountability. Their diversity and richness of varieties resulting from such different legal regulations, legal-political context and established practice cannot overshadow the fact that they have one thing in common, which can be described as a quasi-judicial, investigative character. Meanwhile, accountability as a separate category is oriented rather differently. Its purpose is just to obtain an account, a report of the power exercised and only then, as a consequence, to impose possible sanctions. First of all, these sanctions may be linked to an unreliable report (which does not correspond to the actual state of affairs) and only in the next step to the reported activities. As such, accountability is not meant to enforce penalties for inadequate performance. Therefore, despite its confrontational-sounding name, it is a set of institutions aimed at obtaining knowledge of past and present actions, with the possibility of their further use (also for the purpose of other forms of accountability) – and not at assessing (approving or rejecting placet) the conduct of a subject of authority.

Although the picture above is simplified, as is often the case with model depictions, it may be concluded, without avoiding considerable generalisations and omissions, that there are major differences between the forms of responsibility and control currently described in the constitutional studies and the presented category of accountability, introduction of which to the world of constitutional law science is beginning to be demanded with increasing frequency. Moreover, there is a need to carefully abstract it from other known categories.

Features and types of constitutional accountability

As such, accountability's conceptual scope is broad both in constitutional theory and practice. As stated by Steffek, public accountability can be viewed

70 Morgan, 246–8.

as an umbrella concept under which manifold instruments or mechanisms can be subsumed,[71] and as Bovens points out "public accountability comes in many guises". As a result, there are many classifications of public accountability; and these have been reviewed by Yousueng Han and Demircioglu,[72] starting with the split into two types (horizontal and vertical accountability). Another classification was proposed by Dubnick and Frederickson, who classified accountability as three general types – input, process and outcome – and as six particular types – control, integrity, ethical behaviour, legitimacy, performance and justice.[73]

Robert Behn, in turn, sorted accountability into four types – accountability for power, performance, justice and finance.[74] Romzek and Dubnick divided accountability into four categories, taking into account the standards of control source: political, bureaucratic, legal and professional.[75] Mark Bovens distinguishes five types of accountability: political, legal, administrative, professional (to peers) and social (to societal stakeholders).[76] Grant and Keohane indicated seven types of it: hierarchical accountability, supervisory accountability, fiscal, legal, market accountability and peer accountability as well as public reputational accountability.[77] Finally, Lindberg, the author of the last classification indicated here, identifies as many as 12 types using the standards of control source, degree of control and its direction.[78]

However, it is hard to argue with the authors themselves that in most of these classifications multiple activities and relations may belong to several groups at the same time, so the division is not integral and nominal in logical sense. The number of variations of accountability confirms the conclusion that the concept is a broad one, with features that are difficult to distinguish from other accounts known in public law, in particular in the realities of constitutional systems. The difficulty in distinguishing accountability relations is also linked to the aforementioned issue of the innovative nature of the term in the classical framework of constitutional law and generally: public law. Thus, instead of creating a classification of types of accountability, we propose to

71 Steffek, 51.

72 Han and Demircioglu, 3–6.

73 Melvin Dubnick and George Frederickson, "Accountable Agents: Federal Performance Measurement and Third-Party Government", *Journal of Public Administration Research and Theory* 20 (Supplement 1, 2009): i143–i159.

74 Robert Behn, *Rethinking Democratic Accountability* (Washington, DC: Brookings Institution Press, 2001).

75 Barbara Romzek and Melvin Dubnick, "Accountability in the Public Sector: Lessons from the Challenger Tragedy", *Public Administration Review* 47, no. 3 (1987): 227–38.

76 Mark Bovens, "Analyzing and Assessing Accountability: A Conceptual Framework", *European Law Journal* 13, no. 4 (2007): 447–68, at 454, 455–7.

77 Ruth Grant and Robert Keohane, "Accountability and Abuses of Power in World Politics", *American Political Science Review* 99, no. 1 (2005): 29–43. 10.1017/S0003055405051476 at 36.

78 Lindberg, 213.

first demonstrate its designators in constitutional practice and regulation in democratic states, looking for common features that allow us to discern a kind of pure accountability from other relations similar to it in either method or function. We study the mechanisms of accountability within a classic system of separation of powers, using the traditional tools of constitutional law and conceptual apparatus. This research starts from contemporary principles of power relationships, where the Principal is seen as a political community and there are forms of holding those in power accountable for the power entrusted to them. Using this research perspective, we analyse the accountability of public authorities within good, old constitutional order – whilst also taking into account the new instruments used therein. In order to conduct such a study, we need to make certain assumptions based on which we trace the accountability relationship, consistent with what has been established so far. In doing so, we are looking not only for features, but also for the minimal core of this relation.

To recap what has been established so far: accountability is, on the one hand, the possibility of receiving an account and, on the other hand, the obligation to report on the entrusted power. It consists of three steps: information provision, discussion and (potentially) consequence between accountability actors and accountability Principals (Forums).[79] In its premise, accountability entails a clear relationship between the one entrusting the power and the one to whom it is entrusted. These entities must be easily identifiable, as must the sphere of competence within this domain; in addition, these competences must be exercised independently and under the Agent's own responsibility. The second assumption that predetermines the sense of distinguishing accountability in constitutional law concerns the existence of clearly regulated paths and instruments for obtaining accounts of entrusted power.

However, both in the science and in the practice of constitutional law, these assumptions raise quite a few doubts and require some adaptation to the needs of seeking accountability in entrusted power relations.

First of all, these doubts concern whether the classical understanding of the Principal-Agent relationship is adequate to describe and analyse the relations between the subjects of power in constitutional law. They are raised for at least two reasons. The first is the issue of the subjectivity of the Principal – his or her ability to be held accountable as a collective subject, the Sovereign, and therefore by whose mandate power is exercised in a democratic state. The problem of the so-called collective Principal emerges specifically within electoral accountability and the accountability exercised by the representatives of the sovereign. However, according to the theory of democratically exercised power (and this is the assumption we make in order to sidestep the issue of the legitimacy of power in modern democratic states), the axiom of the original origin of power from the governed collectivity – the citizens, or the political

79 Mulgan, 9.

community, depending on the ideologically oriented terminology – cannot be undermined.[80] However, the collective Principal thus personified – the Forum for reporting – is present only in the case of appointment to power and when giving the account for it under general election. At the same time, it is the most problematic relation in this respect[81] (which is discussed at length in the following chapter). The remaining authorities, i.e. the government, as well as the judges, are not entrusted with power by the Principal understood in this way, but indirectly, through bodies already benefiting from the delegation of power. However, in our opinion that does not mean that accountability to the Principal, being citizens in general, is excluded. On the contrary: we believe that the ultimate Principal in all relations of power and in the relationship of entrustment is the people, although it is extremely complicated to define this Forum in theory and to apply it in practice.[82] It should also be noted that vertical character is immanent to the classical Principal-Agent relationship – and it is not always present in constitutional law. Accountability often takes on a diagonal (network) or horizontal form.[83] Accounts of the exercise of power are given to other actors of power (government accountability to parliament), or within it – these are typically the cases of judicial and internal governmental accountability. This brings us closer to adopting a contractual approach, according to which the Principal-Agent relationship was originally conceived as a contract under which one or more social actors (the Principal) engage another one (the Agent) to perform some limited and well-specified tasks within the framework of the entrusted authority.[84] Moreover, the complex interactions between public and political life give rise to diverse and networked Principal-Agent relations, where a player may be a Principal in one interaction and an Agent in another.[85]

However, as we see it, "horizontal" or "internal" accountability constitutes a different category – precisely because of the absence of a vertical reporting and the reflection of a relationship of entrustment of power, and therefore the ability to receive an account of how it has been exercised. There is no doubt that internal bodies that decide when to prosecute or to investigate fraud and other violations of the law play an indispensable role and constitute

80 Ginsburg and Huq, 130–1.

81 See also Simon Tormey, *The End of Representative Politics* (Cambridge: Polity Press, 2015), 130.

82 This issue is precisely the source of the constitutional conflict in Poland (the so-called rule of law dispute). Some participants in political and legal relations (both domestic and foreign) have challenged the parliamentary empowerment of the judiciary by having the Sejm (the first chamber of parliament) elect judges who are part of the Judicial Council as the body guarding the independence of judges and the independence of the courts.

83 Jose Maria Maravall and Adam Przeworski, *Democracy and the Rule of Law* (Cambridge, 2003), 9.

84 Steffek, 51.

85 Benveniste and Shlomo, 244.

an important support to the governance mechanisms,[86] and their demise often heralds the erosion of democracy.[87] However, both structurally and functionally they do not correspond to the assumptions of accountability, which, again, has originally involved entrustment of power and the vertical relationship.

Also the second assumption, according to which accountability is only possible when clear criteria and tools for reporting are in place, is rather troublesome, especially in relation to electoral accountability, whose criteria are still completely unclear (if such a priori criteria do exist at all) and whose instruments are hardly effective.

The proposed application of the category of accountability for the description and analysis of certain instruments and relations known to constitutional law therefore requires a cautious approach to classical assumptions and their adaptation in the conditions of the specific nature of the Principal, as well as taking into account the complex and diverse nature of the relations between the subjects of power, especially with regard to the entrusted power – the tasks or competences and the nature of the mandate that this entrustment gives rise to. This is why we explicitly distinguish electoral accountability – often simply equated with the issue of accountability in constitutional law – and we subject it to an in-depth analysis in terms of the subjectivity of the Principal, the giving and receiving of an account of entrusted power, as well as answering the question of whether elections can be considered an instrument of accountability at all, that is, whether such an account of power is given and received in this process. Our analysis leads to the conclusion that – despite the widely proclaimed slogan of electoral accountability – it should be taken with a pinch of salt – as the founding myth, useful from the point of view of the conscious complicity in the exercise of power, but with no factual grounds. We share the scepticism towards the accountability function of elections with a number of authors[88] and provide additional arguments in this regard.

In the following chapters, we address the formal mechanisms that, in our view, serve the basic assumptions of accountability. We therefore consider only those methods, processes and institutions as pathways and instruments of accountability that are explicitly linked in constitutional law to the relationship of entrustment of power and, in doing so, are used by way of an obligation to give an account of the activities undertaken, to present the rationale behind

86 Guillermo A. O'Donnell, "Horizontal Accountability in New Democracies", *Journal of Democracy* 9, no. 3 (1998): 112–26.

87 Ginsburg and Huq, 150.

88 James Fearon, "Electoral Accountability and the Control of Politicians: Selecting Good Types versus Sanctioning Poor Performance", in *Democracy, Accountability, and Representation*, ed. Adam Przeworski, Susan C. Stokes and Bernard Manin (New York, 1999): 55–97; John Ferejohn, "Accountability and Authority: Toward a Theory of Political Accountability", in *Democracy, Accountability, and Representation*, 131–53; Edward Rubin, "The Myth of Non-Bureaucratic Accountability and the Anti-Administrative Impulses", in *Public Accountability: Designs, Dilemmas and Experiences* (see note 6), 68–71; Benveniste and Shlomo, 242–55.

them and to report on the effects of the activities so undertaken in the area of entrusted power. In our assessment, such pathways do exist, although they often operate on the margins of constitutional law. Alternatively, the function of receiving an account plays a secondary role.

We therefore look at those procedures and instruments that are found in the relationship between the exerciser of power and the entrustor of power in order to locate in them the element of giving and receiving an account of power. The constitutional law studies classically place the exercise of power in the chain of entrustment, and thus the Principal-Agent relationship.[89] The people delegate authority through elections to representatives in parliament, who in turn delegate part of it (drafting laws, administering, running day-to-day policy-making) to the government. Ministers, in turn, delegate the execution of their assigned tasks to thousands of civil servants, and part of the power goes to other agencies and bodies. Each entrustee can and should know what their trustees are doing – so they have instruments to monitor the execution of the delegated public tasks by calling the Agent to account. Such accountability is based on institutional forms of reporting and providing explanation of what has happened, and it rests in the relations arising from the separation of powers – balancing them and their mutual inhibition, i.e. networked (diagonal) interconnectedness – and less on hierarchy and subordination. And this is where the point of considering accountability and its separation from other mechanisms and processes becomes evident. Attempts at analysing these instruments of mutual control and accountability between subjects of power are much less frequent in legal literature. Meanwhile, as della Porta remarks, not only electoral accountability, but also – and perhaps especially – the challenges to procedural democracy should bring our attention back to other democratic qualities.[90] Therefore, verifying the extent to which the paradigm of narrative accountability, i.e. one whose function is to obtain an account of the process or accomplishments without the application of sanctions or consequences, works in this practice may bring a partial answer to the question of the quality of procedural democracy.

To what extent, then, do public power actors give an account of the power they exercise? In the following chapters we try to answer the questions of reporting by the actors entrusted with the exercise of specific branches of power: the legislature, the executive and the judiciary.

These are most easily found in the duties of the executive branch – such instruments include the right to demand a hearing, the interpellation procedures, as well as the parliamentary procedures preceding the discharge decision

89 Kaare Strøm, "Delegation and Accountability in Parliamentary Democracies", *European Journal of Political Research* 37 (2000): 261–90; Bovens, 2006: 9.

90 Donatella della Porta, "Democratic Models in Europe", in *Routledge Handbook of Contemporary European Social Movements: Protest in Turbulent Times*, ed. Cristina Flesher Fominaya and Ramon Feenstra (Routledge, 2020), 73–88, at 75.

and serving to receive the budget execution report. The purpose of these institutions is to receive and analyse (or evaluate) the accounts, the report on the exercise of power in a specific area. Such institutions also include parliamentary committees of inquiry, whose task is to examine a specific matter as part of the scrutiny of the activities of a given public authority, particularly to determine the extent and causes of irregularities in its functioning. Proceedings before a commission of inquiry are thus precisely the implementation of accountability – understood as the taking away of an account of power actions, a necessary stage for the enforcement of forms of responsibility. However, one of the problems of the distinction of public accountability emerges very clearly in this area, namely the issue of duplicate accountability.[91] Parliament (its bodies) receives an account of the power and performance entrusted to the government – but Parliament itself is the Agent of those who elected it, the original Principal. This dual role of MPs means that the accounts received from the executive often serve purposes other than holding the government accountable. At times, they form part of the construction of the MPs' own reports about their departments, which makes it decidedly difficult to be objective in reporting and assessing the government's accounts.

By contrast, legislative action (both by the government and by parliament) can serve as a good example of the lack of accountability. Legislation is not usually subject to accountability within the framework of power relations. The increasingly used *ex post* Regulatory Impact Assessment mechanism, a systemic and authoritative approach to assessing the accomplishments and both desired and side effects of the resulting legislation, could be considered one such instrument. It is a derivative of the *ex ante* Regulatory Impact Assessment, i.e. the estimation of the effects of ongoing legislative activities, which is a specific element of law-making work, consisting in determining the anticipated economic, social and legal consequences of the proposed legal solutions. Although the examination of the effects of a law following its entry into force seems to be a rational, necessary and even obvious element of law-making activities, it has only recently taken a formalised shape at the state level, and is rarely regulated as an obligation of the legislator. As regards legislative action, as we will try to demonstrate in Chapter 3, accountability is negligible.

In turn, introducing the category of accountability into the relations of entrustment of the judicial power may make it possible to reveal a new dimension of its functioning. To date, the forms of control over the judicial power have been viewed mainly within the framework of instance control (implemented in court proceedings). The literature also emphasises the importance of internal accountability based on the trust placed in the holders of this power,[92]

91 The idea of highlighting accountability deformities: deficiency, lack of and duplicate accountability following Benveniste and Shlomo, 245–6.

92 Jane Mansbridge, "A Contingency Theory of Accountability", in *The Oxford Handbook of Public Accountability* (see note 29), 58–9.

also from the perspective of the procedures for the appointment and administration of the judiciary.[93] However, the issue (also in the public debate) is usually viewed in the context of the lack of this accountability – that is, the inability to respond to unethical or illegal behaviour by a judge (some judges).[94] However, in the sense we have adopted, i.e. if accountability is understood as giving an account of the exercise of power, such accountability is practised quite differently within the judiciary. For it is not a question of imposing sanctions on judges: disciplinary or criminal liability, or administrative removal or relocation of judges. Such forms of sanctions against the holders of judicial power reflect their responsibility in relation to the exercise of their office and require proof of the acts that may give rise to such sanctions. However, accountability in its purest form, i.e. giving an account of the exercise of power and justifying the actions taken within its scope, can be implemented in the judicial power most comprehensively compared to other branches of power. This is because the form of accounting for the exercise of power is the justification of a judicial decision, in other words, giving an account of the power entrusted to its wielders. Judicial reasoning is designed to perform precisely this function; at the very heart of the exercise of judicial power lies its immanent accountability. It is, however, realised through the judicial justification of a decision insofar as the conditions for giving an account to those who entrust the power are met. In this respect, there is a unique risk of public accountability being replaced in the relationship between Agent and Principal by so-called internal accountability and, consequently, leading to a serious deficit in the accountability of judicial power.

The following chapters of our book are devoted to these issues. At this point it is still worth stressing what is not going to be discussed in our book. We are only concerned with the formal mechanisms of receiving and giving accounts and not with assessing the exercise of power through the extent of public trust. For this reason, we do not include in the pathways of accountability the workings of the media – neither traditional nor social media replacing them.[95] Openness of governance is an environment in which the Principals can

93 Marco Fabri, Philip M. Langbroek and Helen Pauliat, *The Administration of Justice in Europe: Towards the Development of Quality Standards* (Lo Scarabeo, Bologna, 2003).

94 See e.g. International Principles on the Independence and Accountability of Judges, Lawyers and Prosecutors, International Commission of Jurists, Geneva, 2007.

95 Already in 2016, when the *New York Times* reported a 19% fall for the one quarter print ad revenue, Facebook announced that its digital advertising revenue rose by 59%. Derek Thompson, "The Print Apocalypse and How to Survive It", *The Atlantic*, November 3, 2016), https://www.theatlantic.com/business/archive/2016/11/the-print-apocalypse-and-how-to-survive-it/506429/. As UNESCO Report 2022 points out, between 2016 and 2021, the market for ads in the traditional press was halved; Google and Meta own half of the ad market. Television viewing figures in countries like the United Kingdom and the United States have declined by 3 to 4% per year on average since 2012. Rasmus Kleis Nielson and Richard Sambrook, "What Is Happening to Television News?", *Reuters Institute for the Study of Journalism* 3 (2016), https://reutersinstitute.politics.ox.ac.uk/sites/default/files/2017-06/What%20is

engage in accountability and it is a condition of democracy and public scrutiny – these are truths that do not need to be proven, and social media is becoming the most important element of these processes, becoming the primary source of information and the new gatekeepers.[96] There is an excellent and extensive body of literature devoted to the new media environment, including as regards the accountability of public power. However, in our opinion, obtaining information about the actions of power from the media can hardly be considered as satisfying the criteria of the Principal-Agent relationship and the conditions for objective giving and receiving an account of power for several reasons. Firstly, the issue of the changing manner of media coverage has become highly noticeable in recent decades. The contemporary media world, which makes everyone, including any holder of public office, a daily broadcaster, informer and commentator of their own and others' actions – i.e. his or her own medium – results in the phenomenon of contemporary power being overnarrated, with overabundance of stories about the exercise of power functions. This phenomenon is not only egregious, but also particularly dangerous from the point of view of the quality of power exercised – the setting of long-term goals and their implementation. If it is better to campaign incessantly rather than to govern effectively, this is the rational choice of those in office then.[97]

Such trends are accompanied by the reduced role of the traditional media, or at least of the media functioning under the hitherto accepted model, as a source of factual knowledge objectivised by pluralistic communication, polarisation and the creation of media bubbles and information cascades,[98] which result in a change in the rank of content posted on social media and a drastic decline in the cognitive quality of messages about governance. At the same time, there is a growing epistemic mobilisation associated with observing the actions of public authorities, increasingly fictionalised – both by its subjects and the media world. The media provide a "contemporary illusion of a direct

%20Happening%20to%20Television%20News.pdf (accessed 24.11.2023). These trends are set to increase, as the audience for traditional media consists largely of older people.

96 According to the UNESCO Report "World Trends in Freedom of Expression and Media Development: 2021/2022": "The digital ecosystem has unleashed a flood of competing content and turned large internet companies into the new gatekeepers". The number of social media users increased to 4.2 billion people in 2021.

97 The study was conducted by Daley and Snowberg: Brendan Daley and Erik Snowberg, "Even If It Is Not Bribery: The Case for Campaign Finance Reform," *Journal of Law, Economics, and Organization* 27, no. 2 (2011): 324–49.

98 Timur Kuran, "The Unthinkable and the Unthought", *Rationality and Society* 5, no. 4 (1993): 473–505. https://doi.org/10.1177/1043463193005004005; Cass R. Sunstein and Timur Kuran, "Availability Cascades and Risk Regulation", *Stanford Law Review* 51 (1999): 683–763. Cass R. Sunstein, *#Republic* (Princeton, NJ: Princeton University Press, 2001); Elizabeth C. Connors, "Social Desirability and Affective Polarization", *Public Opinion Quarterly* 87, no. 4 (Winter, 2023): 911–34.

democracy".[99] This activity so vigorously pursued and directed towards the constant reporting of what appears to be the world of power creates the perfect conditions for pseudoaccountability – the transmission and reception of a heavily distorted or even fictionalised version of public power activities. The media world becomes an illusionary space of justice, a true space of democratic verity.[100] Such coverage in public debate actually blurs the standards of governance, creating an environment in which authentic accountability can easily be forgotten or neglected, which can give rise to frustration-induced anti-system movements, populism, and authoritarianism, caused by the crisis of confidence towards classical democratic institutions and the traditional governance model. Due to the spontaneously received, fictionalised and unverified account of governance, the rank of accountability is diminished. Furthermore, there may be a neglect of the standards of the very reception of the report on the exercise of power and a confusion of its essential distinct institutions and procedures: accountability regarding the compliance with the requirements of the process of exercising power or its effects, electoral accountability, as well as that carried out in the exercise and mutual relations of public authorities.

Holding authoritarian regimes accountable, or accountability for violating basic democratic standards under restorative justice, constitutes a separate issue and requires independent reflection.[101] Mechanisms of transitional justice, i.e. how the new state structures deal with a negative past, often take the form of seeking out and describing the facts and causes of the phenomenon, including by fact-finding bodies, working through special parliamentary bodies or with mixed composition, often involving experts.[102] Mechanisms such as special parliamentary committees or specific bodies with pluralist membership, such as truth and reconciliation commissions, of which there are already many, above all in Latin American and African countries as well as some European countries, deserve special consideration, since their key function is to give an account, or rather to demand an account, of those in power or responsible for crimes, repression, etc. This type of measure is expressed in the language of accountability.

99 Antoine Garapon, "La justice est-elle deloacalisable dans le medias?" *Droit et Société* 26 (1994): 73–89; Ramona Coman and Daniela Piana, "A New Triad: Media, Justice and Politics in Political Science", in *Handbook of Judicial Politics*, ed. Ramona Coman and Cristina Dallara (Institutul European, 2010), 259–78 at 263.

100 Coman and Piana, 274.

101 The rank of accountability within restorative justice, among others: John Braithwate, "Accountability and Responsibility through Restorative Justice", in *Public Accountability: Designs, Dilemmas and Experiences* (see note 6), 33–51.

102 T. Lachowski, "Truth commissions as a mechanism of transitional justice in Bosnia and Herzegovina and other states of former Yugoslavia", in: *Bałkany Zachodnie: między przeszłością a przyszłością*, ed. P. Chmielewski (Łódź 2013), 330; cf. also the typology contained in the work of M. Krotoszyński, *Modele sprawiedliwości tranzycyjnej* (Poznań 2017), 235–43.

Nowadays, instruments of accountability of a similar nature are appearing in a somewhat different context of being accountable, i.e. knowing the facts and analysing them after the particularly devastating financial crisis that has affected many countries in the last decade; thus, in the United States, a Congressional committee investigating the causes of the crisis after 2007 was set up, and in Spain, too, special committees have emerged at the level of regional parliaments to investigate the causes of the financial crisis (tireless efforts to set up such a committee were effectively blocked at the central level).[103]

However, in the abovementioned situations, the relationship between the one entrusting power and the one exercising it (the Agent) is more difficult to identify – these are rather attempts to demonstrate the difference of the new order vis-à-vis the old (dis)order or the crimes of the previous regime. The instrumentation and functions of such accountability mechanisms are fundamentally different, typical of a situation of transition and not of the normal functioning of a democratic state, which is the main focus of our work. In our publication we seek to trace and define the instruments of accountability and how they function, trying to verify to what extent they fulfil their assumptions, allow to give and receive an account of the power entrusted to them and whether they fulfil – or negate – the postulates of communication in deliberative democracy.[104]

The significance and risks of accountability

The modern concept of accountability is rooted in the Anglo-Saxon model of entrustment of power and the Weberian model of bureaucracy and efficient governance, albeit based on the assumption of a clear separation of powers and separation between private and public and a single centre. Meanwhile, contemporary governance is significantly different and accountability is divorcing itself from power in the context of complexity, multicentricity, ambiguity, privatisation of power, of goals and objectives, competences, cartelisation of political parties, increasing role of experts whose job is to absolve and give rationale, but who are lobbyists in disguise. So it is not that difficult to notice that accountability has so far been referred to in constitutional-legal contexts, as well as in public debate, mostly when it is alleged to be deficient. This applies both to the ability to hold those in power accountable within the electoral process and at many levels and structures of governance, especially at the transnational level, in the European Union's organisation of power, but also in non-governmental organisations, especially the QUANGOs – quasi

103 https://accountabilityaftereconomiccrisis.com/assets/uploads/Policy-Report-Spain-Eng.pdf) (accessed 24.11.2023).

104 More on the conditions of deliberative democracy and the rank of accountability: Steffen Ganghof, "Reconciling Representation and Accountability: Three Visions of Democracy Compared", Populism In Europe, *Government and Opposition* 51, no. 2 (2016): 209–33, https://.doi.org/10.1017/gov.2015.15

non-governmental organisations acting as Agents of power with entrusted functions and resources.[105]

The phenomenon of accountability is relatively rarely acknowledged in constitutionalists' studies. The crises in contemporary democratic states prompt us to look at this phenomenon and the function of the system of governance a little more closely, from a slightly different perspective than political science and sociological studies tend to do. The relevance of verifiable communication in a democratic system regarding what happens with the entrusted power is fundamental – this is a relatively uncontentious assumption of constitutionalism, but it is too often equated with the paradigm of legal or political accountability – both in terms of electoral accountability and between actors of power. In fact, the latter paradigm is oriented towards sanctions – punishment or removal from office – whereas the category of accountability allows one to look at the accountability itself – the conditions for this type of report, the possibilities of its verification by the one who entrusted the exercise of power and its evaluation. Still, is this not a scientifically worthless endeavour, applying new names to long-established institutions of constitutional law – pouring old wine into new bottles, to use the biblical metaphor used by Noam Chomsky to describe similar activities?[106] If we decide to follow this metaphor, it is worth engaging in this experiment in order to check whether the category of accountability does affect the understanding and evaluation of the established and already rather unreflective model of political control over the government exercised by parliament, or the control function of elections. These forms of control are put in place in order to trigger certain sanctions through a specific decision, to enforce accountability, usually in the most severe form seen in political life, i.e. removal from power. However, they are exercised under the dictates of the majority, in the atmosphere of confrontation and mutual manifestations and accusations, which first of all reduces their significance in the sphere of real control over the exercise of power, and second, makes it difficult, if not impossible, to give an authentic and verifiable account of the entrusted functions of power or mandate. By contrast, the category of accountability dictates that the focus should shift to giving an account and verifying it in a way that is oriented towards the content and scope of the power entrusted, for which several conditions need to be met, among which the decoupling of the decision on sanctions from the accountability framework, and consequently decoupling it from the requirement of a majority vote, the non-confrontational nature and the assumed impartiality of the process seem to be paramount. Thus, if

105 See further: Matthew Flinders, *The Politics of Accountability in the Modern State* (Aldershot: Ashgate, 2001); Matthew Flinders and H.W.McConnell, "Maybe Minister: Quangos and Accountability", in *How to Make Quangos Democratic*, ed. I. Harden and D. Marquand (London Charter 88, 1997).

106 Noam Chomsky, "Old Wine in New Bottles: A Bitter Taste", *Electronic Journal of Radical Organization Theory*, June 1996, https://chomsky.info/199606__/.

we return to the metaphor cited, accountability would be old wine in new bottles. Indeed, constitutionalism requires more than electoral confrontation and parliamentary upheaval. Redefining the manner of giving and receiving an account of entrusted power in the hitherto defined categories of accountability by the science of constitutional law within the framework of the electoral process and parliamentary scrutiny may become bitter in taste.

2 On the illusory nature of political representation and the illusion of its accountability

Multilevel delusion of representation

Regardless of the particular form of government, an overwhelming majority of modern states proclaim the adoption of the regime of representative democracy. It is founded on the universally shared axiom that is taken for granted and which states that the source of all public power in the state is the will of the people as sovereign. It is treated as an indisputable achievement of enlightened reason, a timeless, constitutionally unalterable value. Alluding to the findings of Joseph A. Schumpeter, elections are regarded as the primary and most important indicator of democracy. It is so because of their specific properties in the form of their presumed ability to guarantee citizens' participation in political relations, competitiveness and legitimacy, which in turn are crucial for democratic transition and the consolidation of the political system.[1]

In turn, political representation is crucial for the establishment of democratic practices.[2] The question of political representation can be traced back centuries. It engages the most eminent minds and yet, or perhaps precisely for this very reason, it fails to lead to unambiguous conclusions unchallenged by scholars. The very notion of political representation is controversial. As Hanna F. Pitkin demonstrates in her classical work on representation theory, the publication that also sets the canons of contemporary thinking on the essence of political representation, and whose insights remain unrefuted, there is no single understanding of representation.[3] The issues that have not been agreed upon include: the subject of representation, the representing subject, the object of representation, the manner in which representation is carried out and the effects of representation. The state of understanding of what parliamentarism

1 J. Shola Omotola, "The AU Promoting Democratic Values: An Electoral Perspective", in *African Accountability: What Works and What Doesn't,* ed. Steven Gruzd and Yarik Turianskyi (Johannesburg: South African Institute of International Affairs, 2015), 71.

2 Hélène Landemore, *Open Democracy: Reinventing Popular Rule for the Twenty-First Century* (Princeton, NJ: Princeton University Press, 2020), 66.

3 Hanna F. Pitkin, *The Concept of Representation* (Los Angeles: University of California Press, 1967).

DOI: 10.4324/9781003493419-2

is – as a basic category of political relations analysis – allowed Kaare Strøm to state that parliamentarism is more widely admired than understood.[4]

Is the represented entity an abstract one (the nation, the people, the sovereign, the citizens, the electorate, the constituency) or is it the specific individuals who elect and the non-voters who are not represented? Is the parliament (its chamber in multi-chamber parliaments) the representative, or is it a specific member of parliament (MP)? What does the representative actually represent? The represented, their will, their interests? Is the representative bound by the will and interests of the represented? Do the representatives aggregate the already existing will of the represented or do they create it themselves? What happens when the represented is dissatisfied with the results of the representative's activity? Can they dismiss him/her, replace him/her? What is the relationship between the representative's relationship with the represented and the relationship between the representative and the political party of which he/she is a member and the entities that finance his/her political activities? What are the consequences of a mismatch between the will of the represented and the acts of the representative? Is the represented party bound by them in that situation? Do representatives have the power to annul, to revoke negative consequences for themselves? Is the representative responsible and if so, in what form (constitutionally, criminally, civilly, politically, morally) for the decisions taken? This is not about adding to doubts, creating a myriad of questions. Something different is important: the contentiousness of the rudiments of representative government. The designator of the term "political representation" is difficult to establish irrefutably. It is given a variety of meanings.[5] The assertions made in this regard are being contested together with the dogmas of the democratic regime regarded as the quintessential wisdom of political modernity. The lack of consensus among scholars can be considered an enduring feature of the understanding of political representation. In other words, the concept fundamental to grasping the essence of democratic power relations is conflicting, which also makes the conclusions derived from it about the desired arrangement of power relations questionable. The difficulty in determining what the political representation of the people is stems from the legal fiction: treating the people as a collective entity with a will of its own. In turn, from the fictitious assumption that the nation has a will of some sort comes the equally illusory assertion that this will can be represented,[6] i.e.

4 Kaare Strøm, "Delegation and Accountability in Parliamentary Democracies", in *Political Accountability*, ed. Richard Bellamy and Antonino Palumbo (Farnham: Ashgate, 2010), 114.

5 David Runciman, "The Paradox of Political Representation", *Journal of Political Philosophy* 1 (2007): 93 et seq.; Jarosław Szymanek, "Reprezentacja polityczna: interpretacja pojęcia", in *Ustroje: historia i współczesność. Polska – Europa – Ameryka Łacińska. Księga jubileuszowa dedykowana profesorowi Jackowi Czajowskiemu*, ed. Marian Grzybowski, Grzegorz Kuca and Piotr Mikuli (Krakow, 2013), 433 et seq.

6 James Hogan, *Election and Representation* (Cork: Cork University Press, 1945), 114; Jarosław Szymanek, „Reprezentacja polityczna w ujęciu doktryny francuskiej", *Studia Iuridica Lublinensia* 22 (2014): 135 et seq.

that it is possible to represent something that does not exist, something that does not have its referent. Therefore, legal fictions underlie the systems of modern states, giving legitimacy, no longer fictitious, to actual acts of power.

This interpretation of representation echoes an important dilemma raised by Edmund Burke in his speech to the electors in Bristol in 1774. He drew a distinction between a congress and a parliament. By congress, Burke meant an assembly of representatives with differing and conflicting interests, which parliamentarians, like ambassadors, had to uphold and work towards achieving. Congress people, just like ambassadors, are bound by the will of those they represent. Parliament is quite different. It is not an assembly of the representatives of those who elected it, but a deliberative assembly of the people with a common interest – the interest of the entire community, which should be guided not by partisan aims and not by partisan prejudices, but by the common good, defined by the common understanding of all those assembled.[7] Despite all the years that passed, the dilemma observed by E. Burke has not lost its relevance.[8] Burke's distinction, together with the related difference in understanding the meaning of representation, into congress and parliament, is referred to by Philip A. Gibbons' regime of delegation and representation[9] and the distinction between imperative mandate and representative mandate resulting from their difference. Given the fact that, during an election period, neither the elected nor the electors can predict what actions will be taken, the former should be given leeway to do what they think is right. As P. Gibbons adds, while it may be convenient for them to listen to the opinions of their constituents in order to attach more weight to their opinions, they are nevertheless under no obligation to report on their actions. And, as E. Burke reminds us, parliament is not a congress.[10]

Quite a different view prevails in contemporary literature, and Burke's dichotomy of parliament versus congress is sometimes referred to as false polarisation.[11] It is generally accepted that, by means of elections, the people, in their capacity as sovereign, delegate their power to the public authorities which exercise it in their name and on their behalf. Parliament is the representative body of the people and is created to adopt legal regulations that are

7 Edmund Burke, Speech to the Electors of Bristol 3 November 1774, in *The Works of the Right Honourable Edmund Burke*, 6 vols. (London: Henry G. Bohn, 1854–56). For a comprehensive account of the theory of political representation in Edmund Burke, see Pitkin, in particular 168 et seq.

8 See James S. Fishkin, *The Voice of the People: Public Opinion and Democracy* (New Haven, CT: Yale University Press, 1995), 32–3; Wojciech Włoch, Anna Tarnowska and Agnieszka Bień-Kacała, *Asymetria władzy, czyli delegacja prawodawcza w demokracji reprezentatywnej. Studium filozoficzno-prawne* (Toruń: Publishing house "Dom Organizatora", 2022), 15 et seq.

9 Philip A. Gibbons, *Ideas of Political Representation in Parliament 1660–1832* (Oxford: B.H. Blackwell, 1914), 20 et seq.

10 Gibbons, 20–1.

11 Iris Marion Young, *Inclusion and Democracy* (Oxford: Oxford University Press, 2000), 129.

binding on all participants in legal relations.[12] This is the case regardless of whether the electors support or do not identify with these decisions. With this being said, and it needs to be pointed out, political representation does not mean the same thing as parliamentary representativeness.[13] A distinction is drawn between the electability of representatives and their representativeness in relation to views shared by large sections of society. A parliament elected in free and fair elections does not necessarily have to be representative: neither upon the constitution of the parliament of a new term (as a result of the electoral law and the conduct of the participants in the electoral process), nor during the parliamentary term (as a result of the changing electoral preferences of large social groups or the political views of the deputies).

The legal binding by decisions, regardless of the degree of approval for them, is a consequence of the legal effect of the elections held. The resulting arrangement of political relations (often ambiguous at the time of the announcement of the election results, as in Belgium, Israel or the Netherlands) constitutes the legal basis for the authorisation of the parliament to act and the obligation to submit to its will. This obligation to submit is accompanied by a presumption that acts of parliament are compatible with the constitution and that, in the event of incompatibility (determined by an authority competent to do so), they lose their validity. In modern states' practice, matters become more complicated. The assumption put forward, fundamental to the whole construct of democratic power, turns out to be a pipe dream. Parliaments enact resolutions or laws that are incompatible with the constitution in force, but which are nevertheless enforceable and not repealed by the courts and as such are binding on citizens.

Nowadays, democracy is considered a system of governance in which citizens delegate their power to representatives and those in power are held accountable for their public activities by citizens acting indirectly through the competition and cooperation of their elected representatives.[14] Accountability is intended to influence the conduct of those in power.[15] Regardless of how it is arranged, it is supposed to lead to a correlation of the position of the representatives and the represented, because it is precisely that which defines the

12 Tímea Drinóczi and Agnieszka Bień-Kacała, *Illiberal Constitutionalism in Poland and Hungary: The Deterioration of Democracy, Misuse of Human Rights and Abuse of the Rule of Law* (London: Routledge, 2022), 108; Jarosław Szymanek, *Wstęp do prawa wyborczego* (Lublin: Wydawnictwo Naukowe Episteme, Wydawnictwo Szkoły Wyższej Wymiaru Sprawiedliwości, 2021), 16 et seq.

13 Pitkin, 76.

14 Philippe C. Schmitter and Terry Lynn Karl, "What Democracy Is … and Is Not", *Journal of Democracy* 2, no. 3 (1991): 76; Philip Pettit, "Three Conceptions of Democratic Control", in *Political Accountability*, 30; Marios Costa, *The Accountability Gap in EU Law* (Milton Park: Routledge, 2017), 8.

15 Mark Bovens, Thomas Schillemans and Robert E. Goodin, "Public Accountability", in *The Oxford Handbook of Public Accountability*, ed. Mark Bovens, Thomas Schillemans and Robert E. Goodin (Oxford: Oxford University Press, 2014), 9.

representative relationship.[16] As Scott Mainwaring points out, without accountability there can be no democracy.[17] Antonino Palumbo states unequivocally: political accountability is the cornerstone of representative democracy.[18] It is the core value in a democracy, argues Anne C.L. Davies.[19] This is because the existence of a "vertical linkage" between voters and representatives allows citizens to hold governments accountable for their actions, and provides governments with the opportunity to make the account of their decisions and actions available to the public.[20] Let us add here that these are not incontestable statements. Indeed, it can be argued that democracy means power derived from elections, irrespectively by whom it is exercised and regardless of for whom it is exercised. Democracy understood in this way does not even need to be defined by the stipulation that it is about free and fairly conducted elections in which the participants in political relations freely present their views, the mass media present them in a reliable and objective manner, and the voters can familiarise themselves with the full spectrum of information and opinions on politically relevant issues objectively presented to them. In this sense, as we discuss it in more detail below, there are no free, fair elections in countries nowadays referred to as democracies. To a greater or lesser extent, they are deformed by the mass media and other organised participants in political relations (vested interest groups).

Will of the sovereign and its perplexing features

Irrespective of how individual scholars understand democracy (procedural versus substantive understandings of democracy), the central assertion in each of these interpretations is that the voice of the people is the primary source of political power. At the same time, this is an assumption that is crucial for the understanding of vertical political accountability. It is an important assumption because it serves as the basis for the conviction that the one who transfers power by election has the right to hold accountable those who have been elected and to whom power has been transferred. For if, by means of elections, there was no transfer of power, then the premise of accountability for its

16 Jarosław Szymanek, *Reprezentacja i mandat parlamentarny* (Warsaw: Wydawnictwo Sejmowe, 2013), 27.

17 Scott Mainwaring, "Introduction: Democratic Accountability", in *Democratic Accountability in Latin America*, ed. Scott Mainwaring and Christoper Welna (Oxford: Oxford University Press, 2005), 29.

18 Antonino Palumbo, "Introduction", in *Political Accountability*, xi. Similarly Nicholas Bamforth, "Accountability of and to the Legislature", in *Accountability in the Contemporary Constitution*, ed. Nicholas Bamforth and Peter Leyland (Oxford: Oxford University Press, 2013), 259.

19 Anne C.L. Davies, *Accountability: A Public Law Analysis of Government by Contract* (Oxford, Oxford University Press, 2001), 76.

20 Andrea Fumarola, "The Contexts of Electoral Accountability: Electoral Integrity Performance Voting in 23 Democracies", *Government and Opposition* 55 (2018): 41.

implementation would cease to be valid. The fictitious chain of interdependence between elections and the activity of public authorities and the admissibility of accounting for it would thus be broken.

However, the assumption that the people enjoy certain power and, through elections, transfer it to public authorities is not a reliable assumption. A commonly accepted legal fiction is that of the sovereignty of the people and their will. It is a theoretical construct devised to justify the phenomenon of power in a situation where the religious legitimacy of the monarch's authority has been deconstructed[21] and in place – as it happened in France – of the beheaded monarch, the people were put on the pedestal, sugarcoating them that – in place of the usurpers who had hitherto usurped them – from now on they were the sovereign, the source of supreme power, and that all public authorities were appointed to carry out their will and were held politically accountable by them. This is why Charles Maurras explicitly wrote that the sovereignty of the people does not exist. Its proclamation only means that there is no longer a real sovereign and that sovereign functions are exercised by someone unknown, perhaps by the first sovereign, perhaps by the last sovereign, and most probably by no one.[22] However, and this is telling, irrespective of the proclamation of the sovereignty of the nation, whether in the convention system (France), the council system (USSR) or parliamentary systems, we can easily recognise the problematic nature of the actual influence of the people on the functioning of the governing bodies, on the political decisions taken in the state. It is symptomatic that while, for example, Maximilien de Robespierre initially questioned the legitimacy of the monarch's action by claiming that the people were the sovereign, shortly after the monarch was overthrown he argued that it was he – Maximilien de Robespierre – who represented the will of the people. Following the beheading of the king and the annihilation of self-governing communities and others, there was no reduction of central power, but rather a strengthening of its arbitrariness. As Fareed Zakaria notes, freedom began to depend on the whims of the "citizens", represented by the leaders of the resolution.[23] Similar metamorphoses are not unusual in the history of political representation and its contemporary applications.

The question of the nature of representation was a key dilemma to be resolved by the Founding Fathers as they worked towards the enactment of the US Constitution. Is representation a reflection, a reproduction of commonly held views in parliament, or is representation merely the selection of those views, similar to representation in sporting competitions? Is representation a mirror reflecting the views of those who are represented (anti-federalists), or

21 For more on the subject see Artur Ławniczak, *Geneza Konstytucji* (Wrocław, 2015).

22 Charles Maurras, *Przyszłość inteligencji i inne pisma* (Dębogóra: Wydawnictwo Dębogóra, 2020), 471–2.

23 Fareed Zakaria, *Przyszłość wolności. Nieliberalna demokracja w Stanach Zjednoczonych i na świecie* (Warsaw: Fundacja Kultura Liberalna, 2018), 44.

are representatives independent of those who elected them and thus bestowed confidence on the representatives to express their own views (federalists)?[24] In the United States, the answer to this question is de facto secondary in relation to the answer to another question. It depends on the answer about the essence of the desired state system: democracy or republic? Does a good polity rest on the findings of reason, on primary truths, or does a good political system consist of the rule of public opinion? This, among other things, was one of the manifestations of the dispute between the federalists and the anti-federalists.

The founders of the 1787 Constitution, as well-educated people, familiar with political and legal doctrines, the history of the system of ancient Rome or the First Republic of Poland, were not democrats. Federalists shared Plato's or Aristotle's findings on the nature of democracy. They had no illusions about its self-destructive nature and the essence of majority rule based on equality, that it is a violation of reason, freedoms and human rights. Democracy, Aristotle wrote, means non-government. To give the demos the ability to decide public affairs is to consent to the destruction of all that is crucial to the preservation of social order. For this reason they opted for a republican system, drawing profusely on the achievements of the past. By means of political representation, there is to be a selection, filtering out everything that is rash, violent, lined with emotions, crowned with envy and greed. The political system of the state is to be based on the will of the citizens, but it is their will and on their behalf that the representatives of the sovereign are meant to decide – a political elite with the competence to conceptualise the common good and articulate it in the decision-making process.

From the late 18th century, when the principle of the sovereignty of the nation became embedded in the doctrine of law, throughout the 19th and 20th centuries, and into the present, the question of the feasibility of the principle of the sovereignty of the nation remains relevant: is it really a constitutive principle of the political order of the state and, through the states, of global constitutionalism, or is it, as Joseph de Maistre notes, a view that offends common sense,[25] a principle imbued with fiction, intended to obscure what is crucial, namely the actual mechanisms of political power exercised by the oligarchy for the pursuit of oligarchic ends, as Robert Michels put it in 1911 in the form of the iron law of oligarchy, and as Vladimir Lenin expressed it with the apt observation that an organised minority rules over an unorganised majority, which for the majority is the natural state of affairs?

The will of the people as the collective subject of supreme law, the existence of which precedes the activity of parliament, is an ontologically empty entity;

24 Bernard Manin, *The Principles of Representative Government* (Cambridge: Cambridge University Press, 1997), 109.

25 Joseph de Maistre, „Studium suwerenności", in *O rewolucji, suwerenności i konstytucji politycznej. Wybór pism* (Krakow: Ośrodek Myśli Politycznej, 2019), 444.

it does not exist.[26] What is claimed to be the will of the people is freely determined by parliament through voting. It is only the will of parliament expressed in its acts of action (such as an act of law or other forms of resolutions adopted by it) that becomes law universally and – what is key – binding on the people. Parliament, by passing a law, becomes not so much the expression of the *volonté générale* as it itself becomes the *volonté générale*.[27] Thus, the parliament replaces the fictious sovereign that is the people. "The sovereignty of a fictitious people having a fictitious general will takes on the real shape of a real sovereign, having as real a will as possible, except that it is not universal but, on the contrary, particularistic, often separate and sectional".[28] Meanwhile, nowadays, in the age of global constitutionalism or, as in Europe, also regional constitutionalisms, it would be a gross oversimplification to call the parliament the real sovereign. Even leaving aside the all-important theme of supra-state institutionalised decision-making, the case of Cyprus in 2013, for example, in which, contrary to the provisions of the constitution, without a statutory basis (and at the same time with the opposition of parliament, which rejected the enactment of such a statutory basis), under pressure from the European Commission, the government confiscated part of the funds comprising bank deposits in order to satisfy the financial claims of creditors of the national debt, shows that also parliament may not be the representative of the will of the people. In the state considered to be democratic, decisions contradicting both the constitution in force and the will of the people can be taken and ruthlessly enforced against the will of the people, under the inspiration of the European Union (EU), which is considered to be democratic. As David Runciman notes, this kind of coup takes place without tanks, soldiers or arrests.[29]

Following the rejection of the Constitution for Europe by a majority of the French on 29 May 2005 and three days later by the Dutch through a referendum, similar regulations were introduced into the Lisbon Treaty and, without resorting to referenda, were approved by the parliaments of the EU countries, without the involvement of the people.[30] Ireland was the only state to hold an approval referendum, and when the people voted against being bound by the Lisbon Treaty, another referendum was held, recognising that the Irish would keep voting until they understood what was good for them. When, in 2015, in a referendum, the Greek population rejected the programme of substantial public spending cuts and tax increases imposed on them by the so-called Troika (European Commission, European Central Bank and International Monetary Fund), the Greek government went along with the will of the sov-

26 See Szymanek, „Reprezentacja polityczna w ujęciu", 136.

27 Szymanek, „Reprezentacja polityczna w ujęciu", 139.

28 Szymanek, „Reprezentacja polityczna w ujęciu", 140–1.

29 David Runciman, *How Democracy Ends* (London, Profile Books, 2018), 43–4.

30 Roger Eatwell and Matthew Goodwin, *National Populism: The Revolt against Liberal Democracy* (London, Pelican Books, 2018), 123.

ereign and, a few days later, implemented an even more restrictive package of public spending cuts and tax increases than the one that had not been approved by the people.[31] When citizens walked the streets in Canada during the Covid regime to protest against the government's infringement of their freedom and property, the government responded by imposing the state of emergency, blocking the protesters' bank accounts and sending in the police.

Citizens vote according to their own interests, but the aggregate vote of individuals is presumed to reflect or promote the general interest and materialise the principle of the public good.[32] If we assume that the people delegate their power to parliament, the outcome of this process is parliament determining and expressing the will of the people. But parliament's determination of the will of the people is arbitrary, as perceived by the parliamentary majority at any given time. Significantly, this will changes not only in the context of the passing of the parliamentary term and the formation of a new political majority after the elections, different from the previous one. It also changes during the parliamentary term, just as the political preferences of the parliamentary majority change, whether as a result of changes in the inter-fractional configuration or re-evaluation within the fractionally identical parliamentary majority. In turn, as the examples of the Polish Sejm of the 8th term (2015–19) and the 9th term (2019–23) illustrate, in key systemic issues (such as the system of the constitutional court, common courts, the prosecutor's office or the electoral procedure) the will of the parliamentary majority may be subject to permanent change (the so-called repair or improvement bills), the change that sometimes takes the proponents of the change and other MPs voting for these changes by surprise with its content and effects.[33] In this type of situation, one might ask what is the will of the parliamentary majority? At the level of formal and legal considerations, there is no doubt: the will of parliament is what parliament has expressed in a law. If, on the other hand, the parliamentary majority articulates something different in the law but intended to include something different therein, a separation can be made between the will directly articulated in the law and the implicit will of parliament, which it intended to express in the law but, for whatever reason, failed to do so.

31 Jacek Zaleśny, "Democracy versus the Rule of Law in Conditions of Disturbed Political Balance", *ASEJ* 26, no. 3 (2022): 56, https://doi.org/10.19192/wsfip.sj3.2022.9.

32 David Oliver, "Accountability and the Foundations of British Democracy – the Public Interest and Public Service Principles", in *Accountability in the Contemporary Constitution* (see note 18), 291.

33 In 2020, in Poland, the Sejm repealed the legislation on the additional care allowance, much to the surprise of MPs who voted for it, claiming en masse that they did not want to repeal the legislation. Amendments to the electoral law can serve here as an example. The deputies representing the parliamentary majority repealed the provisions of the electoral law on the election of the President of the Republic of Poland, allowing correspondence elections to be held to a narrow extent, arguing that correspondence elections serve to commit crimes against elections to a broad extent. Subsequently, the same deputies of the parliamentary majority enacted the conduct of the election of the President of the Republic of Poland exclusively by postal voting.

In a situation where the will of the parliamentary majority is subject to permanent change with regard to a given issue, the question can be posed as to whether this is really how the will of the people is conceptualised. Is it really the case that the instability, the unpredictability of parliamentary decision-making mirrors the instability, the unpredictability of the nation's decision-making? Is it true that on key systemic issues the people are tossing and turning between different legal solutions and constantly changing their stance on the matter? Is it really the case, as it is in Poland, that one day the people want to use postal voting, then do not want to resort to it at all, only to wish to use it again the next moment?[34] This type of extreme instability in political preferences of the nation is not demonstrated by opinion polls. The hypothesis that parliament's decision-making vacillation in determining the will of the people is a reflection of the decision-making vacillation of the people themselves has not been confirmed by opinion polls, either. Therefore, it can be concluded that the parliament does not represent the will of the people, because the people do not possess their will and, consequently, do not transfer it to the parliament, nor does the parliament determine their will by an act of its own action on behalf of the people.

Parliament is an organisation alienated from the people and is not linked to them by any legal relationship, and the political relationship that takes place is episodic. It happens once every few years through the act of voting and it is exhausted, terminated, through this act. Just as the act of voting comes to an end, so does the bond between the electors and the elected. When a representative takes up his or her mandate, there is nothing left in common between him or her and the elected, apart from belonging to the same national community, but not necessarily the same political community. Through elections, there is not so much a change in those who represent the electors as in those who govern them. As Yascha Mounk writes, voters experience a sense of alienation from politics. They do not see themselves in the politicians, and they do not see their preferences reflected in the decisions they make.[35] The representatives have less and less in common with the represented. They are subject to social alienation in relation to the represented. Elected by the people to represent their views,[36] they form a closed group with their own particular interests, distinct from those of the larger social groups. Hence, Anne M. Goetz and Rob Jenkins note that elections seem to discipline politicians less

34 Here, we are referring to the subsequent laws regulating the procedure for presidential elections during the Covid pandemic in 2020.

35 Yascha Mounk, *The People vs. Democracy: Why Our Freedom Is in Danger and How to Save It* (Cambridge, Harvard University Press, 2018),80.

36 Yascha Mounk, *The People vs. Democracy: Why Our Freedom Is in Danger and How to Save It* (Harvard University Press, 2018), 101. Similarly: Marek Migalski, *Koniec demokracji* (Warsaw: The Facto, 2015), 24.

than we would like them to.[37] Large social groups are valuable to them in so far as they are providers of votes in elections. Special interest ties, on the other hand, associate them with organised interest groups.

The erosion of political ties is accompanied by the erosion of political accountability. MPs act in their own interests but only indirectly, incidentally and sometimes by chance in the interests of those who voted for them. As Kathlena Walther writes in the context of South African MPs, they become an elite that loses its relationship with the people and does not represent their interests.[38]

The theoretical answer to the non-dependence of the representative on the represented is the "modern formula of the representative mandate".[39] According to it, the representative mandate is free, which means that the representative is not bound by the will of the represented, while the represented are bound by the will of their representatives. The citizens are required to accept the decisions taken by the parliament as their own and to implement them unconditionally. By reorienting the relationship between the representatives and the represented in this fashion, an attempt is being made to offset the existing cognitive dissonance. An effort is made to rationalise and explain why the elected do not carry out the will of the electors, why the expectations of the electors are irrational in this respect. This is precisely because this is not what modern representation is about; MPs are not elected to implement the expectations of the electorate, but in order to set the electorate up with patterns of expected conduct.

As an act of parliament, the law is (depending on the state), if not the exclusive, then the primary regulator of social relations. As a rule, the legislative function in modern states concentrates in parliament. In states based on a parliamentary-cabinet system of government, regulations with universal validity are to be anchored in the law.[40] Normative acts enacted by executive authorities merely concretise and specify what has been stipulated in a given law. Any fragment of social relations can be regulated by a law, for example: issues of the system of public authority bodies, course of proceedings before them, levying of taxes, granting of tax exemptions, as well as financing of selected economic entities, a set of compulsory vaccinations, rules of riding a scooter. By covering any fragment of social relations with a law, it is possible to regulate it in an arbitrary manner. It is possible – as in Poland – to subject the sale of water to 23% value-added tax (VAT), but potato crisps to 8% VAT, although the VAT on corn crisps is again at 23%. Depending on the

37 Anne Marie Goetz and Rob Jenkins, *Reinventing Accountability: Making Democracy Work for Human Development* (London, Palgrave Macmillan, 2005), 18.

38 See Kathlena Walther, *Electoral Systems and Accountability: Challenges and Considerations for South Africa* (Sandton, KMM Review Publishing Company, 2017), 60.

39 Szymanek, *Reprezentacja i mandat parlamentarny*, 84–5.

40 Adam Krzywoń, „Konstytucyjna zasada wyłączności ustawy wobec możliwości jej realizacji we współczesnym systemie źródeł prawa", *Przegląd Legislacyjny* 2 (2014): 26.

characteristics of the product, there may be three VAT rates (23%, 8% and 5%) on bread and confectionery, depending on whether it is frozen, chilled, pre-baked, etc. Mustard may be subject to 23% VAT and mustard sauce to 8% VAT. Spring water – 23% VAT and mineral water – 8% VAT. These are not necessarily regulations designed to meet the needs of large social groups. They can instead be regulations serving particularistic needs, articulated neither in the election campaign nor in parliament.

The parliament's competence to enact legal regulations of arbitrary content includes not only substance that serves the public interest to the fullest extent. This may also include content contrary to the public interest or the preferences of citizens, but instead aligned with the interests of lobbyists or detrimental to all large social groups, such as, for example, the Act of 6 April 2020 on special principles for the conduct of general elections for the President of the Republic of Poland ordered in 2020, adopted in Poland during the presidential election campaign,[41] impossible to execute for technical reasons, resulting in the failure to elect the President of the Republic within the constitutionally prescribed time limit and adversely affecting the constitutional stability of the state as such.

In doctrine, it is often taken a priori, without requiring proof, just as Bernard Manin, Adam Przeworski and Susan C. Stokes do, for instance, that – equipped with the power to act – public authorities act in the best interests of others, citizens or the majority of citizens. In power relationships, representation is understood as acting in the best interests of the public.[42] They believe that a government is representative when it fulfils the wishes of the electorate, when it does what it believes to be in the best interest of the people. Those in government understand the interest of the represented as much as the represented understand it. They equate the will of the representatives with the will of the represented,[43] but it does not have to be so and in fact in some countries, as discussed below, it is not so.

Philippe C. Schmitter points to another circumstance relevant to the representative node in the form of misperception. The elected may sincerely believe that they have done their best to respond to citizens' preferences, only to discover that the citizens had not actually wanted what they claimed. Another situation is when voters change their minds;[44] when the elected have fulfilled the voters' demand and the voters no longer want it, instead they want the opposite. This is hardly an unusual situation. Today's voters are chimerical.

41 Dz. U. poz. 827.

42 Bernard Manin, Adam Przeworski and Susan C. Stokes, "Introduction", in *Democracy, Accountability and Representation*, ed. Adam Przeworski, Susan C. Stokes and Bernard Manin (Cambridge, Cambridge University Press, 1999), 2 et seq.

43 Manin, Przeworski and Stokes, 2.

44 Philippe C. Schmitter, "The Ambiguous Virtues of Accountability", in *Assessing the Quality of Democracy*, ed. Larry Diamond and Leonardo Morlino (Baltimore, Johns Hopkins University Press, 2005), 27.

As the dynamics of electoral preferences show, in different spheres of social relations voters change their stance, and do so multidirectionally. They often do so motivated by specific one-off events. Influenced by an argumentation they have heard, they express their view on a given issue, but when exposed to another argumentation, they change their view. Making the ability to realise voters' expectations even more complicated, and such expectations are not necessarily internally consistent. The same social groups may, for example, demand the simultaneous pursuit of the demand for low taxes and a rich social policy of the state – things which are impossible to combine for objective reasons beyond the control of those in power. They may demand the implementation of the EU's *Green Deal* programme in the form of a ban on coal burning in cookers and cheap coal; the elimination of coal and gas burning in cookers and stable supplies of cheap heat in winter. The failure of those in power to meet impossible social needs makes them accountable for not doing what could not have been done.

Shaping political representation

Since the late 18th century, the structure of political representation has been based on three assumptions. Firstly, those in power are elected (subject to selection) through an election procedure. Secondly, citizens can discuss, criticise and formulate demands at any time, but have no power to give legally binding instructions to the government. Thirdly, those in power are subject to periodic elections.[45] It is generally acknowledged that in democratic states a general consensus, shared by large sections of society, has developed on these three assumptions. The political dispute, however, concerns the implementation of the first two assumptions. Governing parties are elected through an electoral procedure, but in what way is it shaped? And the second group of contentious issues: citizens have the right to discuss, criticise and formulate demands against those in power, but in what form and with what intensity? Is every manifestation of discussing, criticising and formulating demands against those in power permissible, or are some of them subject to rationing? The discrepancy between the consensus on the theoretical Principals of political representation and the controversy over specifically arranged legal solutions highlights the uncertainties surrounding the institutions of representative democracy.[46] People know what they want to achieve, but there is no universally shared confidence in how to achieve these goals, whether the means of action chosen serve to reach them, or whether, on the contrary, they are loosely connected with them or, alternatively, deform the political representation of the nation. In the 19th and early 20th centuries, the construction of representative government was to be facilitated by the prevalence of electoral

45 Manin, Przeworski and Stokes, 3.
46 Manin, Przeworski and Stokes, 3.

law, in the 20th century – the introduction of proportional redistribution of parliamentary seats, the broadening and deepening of democracy; although – remarkably – these occurrences are not matched by the conviction shared by large sections of society that governments are becoming increasingly representative, that those in power are conceptualising and pursuing the public interest to an ever greater extent and with ever greater intensity. The social contestation, as not being empirically grounded, succumbs to the cited statement of B. Manin, A. Przeworski and S.C. Stokes that those in power act in the best interests of the public. This statement is of a global character. It is relevant for citizens of European, African or American countries. As the study on the representative mandate carried out in Poland shows, even members of parliament lack the conviction that they conceptualise and realise the public interest, that it is the basis for their political action.[47]

While the editors of the monograph *Democracy, Accountability and Representation* refrain from carrying out a proof for the theoretical assumption they make that those in power act to serve the best interests of the public, they do justify why governments can represent the interests of the people. In their view, this happens for four reasons. Firstly, only those persons who are public-spirited offer themselves for public service and while holding office remain uncorrupted by power while in office. Secondly, when those entering public service have different priorities, motivations and competences, citizens effectively use their right to vote to select either those candidates whose interests are the same as those of the voters, or those candidates who have remained committed to public service while in office. Thirdly, in situations where those in office may wish to pursue certain interests or values that are disparate and costly to the people, then citizens effectively use their vote to threaten those who deviate from the path of virtue with expulsion from office. Finally, mechanisms for dividing and balancing authorities are essential. Separate authorities mutually check and balance each other in such a way that together they work towards the best interests of the people.[48]

Let us remark that each of the four assumptions given is a product of theoretical reasoning and requires empirical verification, which was not performed by the authors. They do not reveal how the concept of representative authority is realised in contemporary states, whether it is achieved in any of them and, if so, through which acts of law. They clearly have a problem in defining what contemporary political regimes really are. How can they be classified, using the classical, Aristotelian criteria of political regimes? On the one hand, they call modern democracies "elitist systems" or, in the words of Bernard Manin, "aristocratic systems"; and according to the Aristotelian classification, they have no doubt that these are oligarchies. At the same time, however, they

47 Maria Kruk et al., *Representational Mandate in the Polish Deputies' Practice* (Warsaw, 2013), 156 et seq.

48 Manin, Przeworski and Stokes, 3–4.

point out that these are the kind of oligarchies in which citizens are ruled by others, whom they choose for themselves and replace with others through voting. This is a distinctive feature of democracy: those in power are subjected to selection through elections.[49]

Therefore, it can be concluded that by using democratic procedures in the election mode, the people do not establish democratic, but oligarchic rule. Elections change not so much those who represent the people, but those who acquire the right to rule the nation. They establish the reign of a ruling elite for the benefit not of those who elect them, but of their own.[50] Under such conditions, the accountability of those in power loses its raison d'être. There is no rational justification for it. Nor is there any sound reason why *demos* should hold those in power accountable for their exercise of power, because those in power do not exercise it for the common good, but for their own benefit. Accordingly, they themselves know best what is good for them, and there is no need for an outsider to confirm or contradict their objective. In contemporary democracy defined in this way, the basis of governance is not the common good as the constitutive value of the state order, but the good of those in power. Adopting after B. Manin, A. Przeworski, S.C. Stokes that in modern democracies elections are a mechanism for establishing oligarchy denies the essence of representation. A representative acting for his or her particular interest rather than the interest of the Principal constitutes contestation of representation. To recognise this assumption is also to render accountability meaningless as a fundamental category of a system of government and its sui generis punchline – the accountability of those in power for the political decisions they make. In turn, it would serve as a recognition that, just as the principle of political representation is a systemic fiction, so, in effect, democratic governance is a fantasy.

If we employ the Aristotelian typology of political systems, contemporary political regimes are oligarchies established by the demos, which once every few years has the right to elect (in some states people are obliged to do so through electoral coercion) their rulers. The political reality, however, is more complex than the one clearly outlined by B. Manin, A. Przeworski, S.C. Stokes. They neither carry out the proof for the statement they formulate themselves, nor is it confirmed by the results of research by other researchers, including a team of Polish constitutionalists who conducted an empirical study of the representative mandate that remains unique worldwide.[51] In the practice of the majority of contemporary states considered (based on the so-called democratic indexes) to be democratic or not fully democratic (with exceptions including countries such as Ukraine, Moldova or the United States, where the leading feature is an oligarchic inclination), there is a clash of different, opposing, systemic

49 Manin, Przeworski and Stokes, 4–5.
50 See Diamond and Morlino, ix.
51 Kruk et al., 119 et seq.

tendencies: democratic and oligarchic tendencies. We see the implementation of the Aristotelian model of a democracy based on the principle of equality as the basic principle of the system, with priority in its application to what is right and just, which we can associate with the republican system according to Aristotle's typology. At the same time, we note the intensification of oligarchic tendencies in political systems.[52] These are manifested in the promotion of monopolies and rationing in economic relations. The idea of the rule of law, on the other hand, is losing ground, and this is a trend that is as prevalent at the level of contemporary states as it is in regional organisations (such as the EU), in foreign relations or in global constitutionalism.

The illusion of electoral accountability

Similarly to Craig T. Borowiak, the doctrine optimistically assumes that elections are an accountability vehicle in representative government[53] or, as Dawn Oliver points out, accountability moments.[54] They help develop the dependence and sympathy of those in power towards the people. Hence, it is written about voting "for" or "against" a government endowed with the power to shape public policies.[55] Voters express their approval or disapproval of a democratic government through the ballot box, and for this reason, elections are one of the key accountability mechanisms.[56] John M. Carey proves that accountability is as much about holding parliamentarians accountable to the preferences and demands of their Principal(s), that information about parliamentarians' activities is available to the Principal(s) and that Principals can punish parliamentarians for being unresponsive.[57] In relation to these statements, the results of the study by Martin Gilens and Benjamin I. Page are significant. The researchers investigated whose policy preferences are reflected in US legislation. They considered four hypotheses: 1) legislation reflects the preferences of large social groups (*Majoritarian Electoral Democracy*); 2) legislation reflects the preferences of economic elites (*Economic-Elite Domination*); 3) legislation reflects the preferences of mass interest groups (*Majoritarian Pluralism*); 4) legislation reflects the preferences of narrow interest groups

52 On the importance of oligarchic influence in Indonesia – Garry Rodan and Caroline Hughes, *The Politics of Accountability in Southeast Asia: The Dominance of Moral Ideologies* (Oxford, Oxford University Press, 2014), 29 et seq.

53 Craig T. Borowiak, *Accountability and Democracy: The Pitfalls and Promise of Popular Control* (Oxford, Oxford University Press, 2011), 35–6.

54 Oliver, 291.

55 G. Bingham Powell Jr, *Elections as Instruments of Democracy: Majoritarian and Proportional Visions* (New Haven, Yale University Press, 2000), 14.

56 Davies, 76–7.

57 John M. Carey, *Legislative Voting and Accountability* (Cambridge University Press, 2009), 3. Similarly, Andreas Schedler, Larry Diamond and Marc E. Plattner, eds., *The Self-restraining State: Power and Accountability in New Democracies* (Lynne Rienner Publishers, 1999), 14; Strøm, 119.

(*Biased Pluralism*). In order to verify the research hypotheses, they analysed 1,779 cases taken up by the US Congress over a 20-year period (1981–2002). As a result of their study, M. Gilens and B.I. Page found that economic elites and narrow interest groups have a key influence on parliamentary decisions in the United States. Mass interest groups have little influence. In contrast, large social groups have virtually no influence on parliamentary decisions at all. Statistically, their views have zero bearing on the decisions taken by MPs. When the majority of citizens disagree with economic elites or organised interest groups, they usually lose. This confirms the oligarchic nature of the American political system.[58]

The results of the study by M. Gilens and B.I. Page falsify the rationality of the theoretical arguments put forward by scholars such as J.M. Carey, who argue that voters have the (ability) to reward and punish individual parliamentarians directly, whether because primary elections determine appointments or because of open party lists, whereby individual voters' choices determine who gets a parliamentary seat, or because there are no party lists at all. Due to the circumstances under which MPs are elected, voters are their direct Principal.[59] But: what kind of a parliamentarian's direct Principal is this if his or her interests are not relevant to the representative? What kind of Principal is it whose will the parliamentarian does not exercise, while at the same time exercising the will of other actors, often in conflict with the will of this "direct Principal"? In other words, the juxtaposition of the theoretical deductions of J.M. Carey and scholars of similar insight with parliamentary practice in fact falsifies these deductions as an expression of ideas about the desirable state of the relationship taking place between electors and electees, rather than a description of parliamentary reality.

The mechanism of misperception of the relationship linking electors and electees described by B.I. Page, the voter-monopoly illusion vis-à-vis parliamentarians, is not a phenomenon peculiar to the American Congress alone. It is a phenomenon typical of modern states called democratic, such as EU states or the EU Parliament. On the ground of scientific research, we find no justification for the statement formulated by Larry Diamond, Marc F. Plattner and Andreas Schedler that accountability deficits are often more visible, dramatic and urgent in new, rather than in established democracies.[60] Remarkably, despite the far-reaching categorical nature of this statement, the authors do

58 Martin Gilens and Benjamin I. Page, "Testing Theories of American Politics: Elites, Interest Groups, and Average Citizens", *Perspectives on Politics* 12, no. 3 (2014): 575–6. The link between financing an election campaign and buying political influence is contested by Yasmin Dawood. In doing so, she cites empirical research, but – significantly – cites the results of a study published in 1988, i.e. 27 years before she published her research. See more in Yasmin Dawood, "Campaign Finance and American Democracy", *Annual Review of Political Science* 18 (2015): 340–1.

59 Carey, 17.

60 Schedler, Diamond and Plattner, 2.

not provide evidence for its veracity, nor do they cite evidence provided by other scholars. A comparison of the political processes taking place in the so-called established democracies and in the so-called new democracies does not allow us to conclude that they differ substantially in terms of accountability deficits. In our assessment (confirmed on American soil by M. Gilens and B.I. Page), accountability deficits in established democracies are in no way less visible, dramatic and violent than in new democracies such as the democracies of Central European countries. As long as they are not corroborated by scientific research, statements to the contrary in this regard may be the result of misperception or prejudice.

A comparison of the political processes occurring in the so-called established and new democracies does not allow us to conclude that they differ significantly in terms of accountability deficits. In the light of our findings, contrary to the claims of L. Diamond, M.F. Plattner and A. Schedler, it is reasonable to conclude the opposite, i.e. that accountability deficits in established democracies are often more prominent, dramatic and urgent than in new democracies such as the democracies of Central European countries. We make this claim primarily because of the failure of key states in the so-called established democracies to account for crimes against large numbers of their citizens or simply their subjects, such as colonialism, World War II crimes (Germany, Italy) or eugenic crimes (Sweden, Denmark or Norway).[61] A discussion about reckoning with the country's slavery past, the genocide of indigenous people and the descendants of those who managed to survive being locked up in reservations has begun in the United States.[62] In the context of colonialism and war, damage of significant proportions was caused to property, the economic exploitation of indigenous peoples was carried out in a planned and methodical manner and large population groups were subjected to extermination. For instance, before the Germans perfected the technique of exterminating large population groups, there were already British concentration camps in South Africa from the early years of the 20th century, or later German concentration camps in Namibia. In contrast, the wartime experience of World War II concentration camps was further perpetuated by Britain in the 1950s in Kenya. In Congo, some 8 million people were murdered by

61 See e.g. Fernne Brennan and John Packer, eds., *Colonialism, Slavery, Reparations and Trade Remedying the "Past"?* (Milton Park, Routledge, 2012); Pablo de Greiff, ed., *The Handbook of Reparations* (Oxford: Oxford University Press, 2006); Rhoda E. Howard-Hassmann and Anthony P. Lombardo, *Reparations to Africa* (University of Pennsylvania Press, 2008); Antony Anghie, *Imperialism, Sovereignty and the Making of International Law* (Cambridge University Press, 2012); Siba N'Zatioula Grovogui, *Sovereigns, Quasi Sovereigns, and Africans: Race and Self-Determination in International Law* (Minneapolis, University of Minnesota Press, 1996).

62 See e.g. Nikole Hannah-Jones, *The 1619 Project: A New Origin Story* (New York: Random House, 2021); A.L. Araujo, *Reparations for Slavery and the Slave Trade: A Transnational and Comparative History* (Bloomsbury Publishing, 2017).

the Belgians in concentration camps. By comparison, around 11 million people died in German concentration camps during World War II. In 1921 in Sweden, the Riksdag passed an act establishing the State Institute for Racial Biology (*Statens institut för rasbiologi*). This was the first state institution of its kind in the world to deal with racism in an organised manner. One of the results of its activities was a state eugenics programme and forced sterilisation of Swedish women deemed eugenically less valuable, including Roma as an entire ethnic group. The Danish or Norwegian experiences are quite similar.

The failure to account for the totalitarian practices inflicted leads scholars such as L. Diamond, M.F. Plattner and A. Schedler to conclude that the deficits of accountability in the new democracies are more visible, dramatic and urgent than in the established democracies. They are not. In our opinion, lack of accountability of Western colonial states exterminating entire peoples for crimes committed surpasses in both scope and intensity the accountability deficits present in contemporary states and measured in the framework of so-called democratic indices.

Parliamentarians' dependence on economic elites and narrow interest groups corrupts not only them, but above all the entire decision-making process. It means that instead of the promised and proclaimed democracy, the rule of a plutocratic oligarchy takes place. As Pierre Rosanvallon puts it, the voice that resounded at the ballot box somehow dissolves in the backrooms of parliaments, and those in power seem deaf.[63] As a result of the policy carried out between 1986 and 2012, 1% of the increase in wealth went to 90% of US households and 42% to 0.1% of American households.[64] The richest 1% of Americans own about 40% of the national wealth and the bottom 80% own around 7%[65] and over the past few decades this gap has only widened. This was further amplified during the Covid-19 epidemic. While about 90% of American children born in the 1940s earned more than their parents, the ratio dropped to about 50% for children born in the mid-1980s.[66] The deepening of social inequality takes place in the process of economic development, as measured by gross domestic product (GDP) growth. It is not the product of objectively occurring economic processes, but rather the result of

63 Pierre Rosanvallon, *Good Government: Democracy beyond Elections* (Cambridge, Harvard University Press, 2018), 190 et seq.

64 Emmanuel Saez and Gabriel Zucman, *Wealth Inequality in the United States since 1913: Evidence from Capitalized Income Tax Data*, NBER Working Paper Series 2014, https://www.nber.org/papers/w20625.pdf (20.06.2020).

65 Data source: https://en.wikipedia.org/wiki/Wealth_inequality_in_the_United_States (accessed 20.06.2020). When it comes to more recent literature on political oligarchy, see Filip Ilkowski, „Ekonomiczne i polityczne współzależności i sprzeczności koncentracji władzy w kapitalizmie (w kręgu interpretacji myśli Marksa)", *Studia Politologiczne* 55 (2020).

66 Richard V. Reeves and Katherine Guyot, "Fewer Americans Are Making More Than Their Parents Did—Especially If They Grew Up in the Middle Class", https://www.brookings.edu/blog/up-front/2018/07/25/fewer-americans-are-making-more-than-their-parents-did-especially-if-they-grew-up-in-the-middle-class/ (accessed 29.07.2022).

parliament's policies of transferring wealth to the richest and pauperising the middle class. Mounk points to the "conspiracy" of US politicians to reinforce rather than close the divide between the super-rich and ordinary citizens. Tax cuts for the wealthiest were carried out in parallel to the increasing burden on poorer Americans.[67] Tellingly, although addressing American parliamentarism, Mounk's findings are not geographically particularistic and do not apply exclusively to present day. They echo the findings of Wojciech Dzieduszycki made at the turn of the 19th/20th century. In his dissertation *Przesilenie parlamentaryzmu* (*Crisis of Parliamentarism*), published in 1900, he noted that in European countries, more and more burdens were sometimes weighing down on the shoulders of those poorest in society, and that skilful speculators were amassing monstrously large estates, taking advantage of public profligacy.[68] It has turned out that parliament is occasionally the worst enforcer of the most intolerable oppression. In spite of its democratic basis, elected under the influence of the capitalists and dependent on them, it forgets about the poor masses, the labourers or the farmers. It is ready to ruthlessly oppress a particular nationality, to disrupt the religious peace of a minority or even the majority of the electorate, hiding behind meaningless clichés about rape on the justice.[69] Democracy means dual rule: ostensible rule belonging to the parliamentary majority and actual rule, exercised by the oligarchy and money.[70] In theory, it is a system open and accessible to everyone, but in fact it is ruled by the best organised, richest or most fanatical minorities, who look after their own interests[71] at the expense of the general interest, including that of future generations. Courtney Jung writes about political representation as a form of perpetuating exploitation and class rule.[72] Can a government that engages only in what is in the interests of economic elites and narrow interest groups be called representative and accountable to the sovereign?

Since different social groups influence the parliamentary decision-making process with varying degrees of intensity, thus the question must be posed: what does this imply for the accountability of MPs? If, for example, the influence of the American people on the decisions of the federal Congress is close to zero in American conditions, what is the nature and sense of retrospective electoral accountability? What is the point of holding those whose political preferences are not translated into the content of policy decisions and whose

67 Mounk, *The People vs. Democracy*, 265.

68 Wojciech Dzieduszycki, „Przesilenie parlamentaryzmu", in *Wybór pism* (Krakow: Ośrodek Myśli Politycznej, 2017), 501. The findings of Yascha Mounk or W. Dzieduszycki find confirmation in Ferdinand Lassalle's "brazen law of wages". According to it, the capitalist economy reduces wages to the subsistence level in order to maintain the income of capitalists.

69 Dzieduszycki, 501.

70 Maurras, 492.

71 Zakaria, 291.

72 Courtney Jung, "Critical Liberalism", in *Political Representation*, ed. Ian Shapiro et al. (Cambridge, Cambridge University Press, 2009), 156.

opinions do not matter accountable to the decision-makers, regardless of who holds the majority in parliament? Irrespective of the conclusions reached by large sections of society, this is of little relevance to the public policies pursued. For this reason, in some countries, retrospective electoral accountability, if present, may cover issues that are secondary from the point of view of the policies pursued and that do not interfere with the key interests of economic elites and narrow interest groups. In order for this effect of accountability to be achieved, political propaganda is used to distort the balance between different aspects of decision-makers' activities, focusing attention on sub-priorities while diverting attention from Principal issues.

Retrospective electoral accountability carried out by economic elites and narrow interest groups takes on a different meaning. For example, the expenditure reported for the 2018 US Congressional election campaign was $5,725,183,133 billion.[73] As was noticed: "Fundraising has become the most time-consuming activity of US Congress people. They spend more time fundraising than working in Congressional bodies or meeting with voters".[74] For Vincent A. Blasi, this is the critical shortcoming of the political system, the fact that representatives spend too much time soliciting donations when they should instead be focusing on governing.[75] Given the desirability of equivalence of the benefits provided, MPs are required to prove to major benefactors that the expenses they incur have an equivalent in the MPs' legislative activity, that they are translated into the decisions they make. In politics, money drives inequality and political advantage. Through it, the few maintain disproportionate control at the expense of the many, and parliamentarians betray the principle of accountability towards the represented.[76] As Alexander Hamilton noted in the pages of The Federalist Papers: politicians flatter the prejudices of voters in order to betray their interests. This circumstance provides a good explanation for the cited findings of M. Gilens and B.I. Page. Politicians funded by economic elites and narrow interest groups are held accountable by them for implementing the public policies they expect. At the same time, as stressed by Y. Mounk, corporations and pressure groups can spend as much money as they wish on supporting one candidate or attacking another.[77]

73 Data source: *Cost of Election*, https://www.opensecrets.org/overview/cost.php (accessed 20.06.2020).

74 Ezra Klein, "The Most Depressing Graphic for Members of Congress", *Washington Post*, January 14, 2013, https://www.washingtonpost.com/news/wonk/wp/2013/01/14/the-most-depressing-graphic-for-members-of-congress/ (accessed 08.07.2022). Cf. Zakaria, 209–10.

75 Vincent A. Blasi, "Free Speech and the Widening Gyre of Fund-Raising: Why Campaign Spending Limits May Not Violate the First Amendment After All", *Columbia Law Review* 94, no. 4 (1994): 1281 et seq.

76 Mark C. Alexander, "Campaign Finance Reform: Central Meaning and a New Approach", *Washington and Lee Law Review* 60, no. 3 (2003): 804.

77 Mounk, 108.

Negative campaigning, just like public relations (PR), serves to coerce MPs to act accordingly: destroying MPs who harm the vested interests of corporations and pressure groups while promoting MPs who serve the interests of corporations and pressure groups. In the American setting, this process has been thoroughly studied owing to the transparency of the benefactors funding the election campaign and political activities of individual Congress people. The vast majority of them (regardless of party affiliation: Democrat or Republican) have similar benefactors expecting similar policies to be implemented.

In countries such as the United States, the subordination of representatives not to the people (the represented) but to oligarchic groups is official already at the level of public data published in generally available reports and statements. It occurs independently of hidden mechanisms of power, such as "shadow parties" or "dark money". For Heather K. Gerken, these play an important role in the financing of parliamentarians' campaigns.[78] The component that disrupts the ability to hold authorities accountable is the phenomenon described in political science as the "deep state", i.e. the actual arrangement of power realised independently of the formal and legal rules of the decision-making process. An example from the other side of the pond can be the arrangement of power relations created in Poland after 2015, where, irrespective of the constitutional arrangement of relations between the bodies of state power, the key political decisions are made by the chairman of one of the co-ruling parties, Jarosław Kaczyński, who is formally a "rank-and-file parliamentarian", but in fact is recognised as the "centre for political direction", which – in itself – is a reference to the actual mechanisms of power used in communist states, where the highest organ of power was the communist party, typically not mentioned at all within the framework of the constitutional arrangement of state authority. The symbol of the actual arrangement of political forces can be seen in President Andrzej Duda attending night consultations, or Hungarian Prime Minister Viktor Orban paying a visit to party chairman Jarosław Kaczyński, but omitting the meeting with President Andrzej Duda.[79]

A similar process of informal and confidential decision-making mechanisms exists in the European Union. The rationale behind it are the 11,882 organisations accredited as lobbyists to the European Parliament or the European Commission,[80] which are involved in some things and have to somehow justify the legitimacy of using their services. Jürgen Roth writes about the silent

78 Heather K. Gerken, "Boden Lecture: The Real Problem with Citizens United: Campaign Finance, Dark Money, and Shadow Parties", *Marquette Law Review* 97, no. 4 (2014): 905 et seq.

79 For more on the subject see Wojciech Sadurski, *Poland's Constitutional Breakdown* (Oxford: Oxford University Press, 2019), 14 et seq. In US conditions see e.g. Mike Lofgren, *The Deep State: The Fall of the Constitution and the Rise of a Shadow Government* (Penguin, 2016); Jon D. Michaels, "The American Deep State", *Notre Dame Law Review* 93, no. 4 (2018).

80 Data for January 2020, https://www.europarl.europa.eu/news/en/faq/25/accredited-lobbyists (accessed 20.06.2020).

takeover of Europe by secretive economic and political elites.[81] The process of economic elites and narrow interest groups' domination over public policies is also underway in the European Union and EU states. In Italy, this was what underpinned the rule of media tycoon Silvio Berlusconi. In Poland, being the most prominent regional political activist (provincial assembly councillor), Prime Minister Mateusz Morawiecki, with his exclusive knowledge of planned investments, made his fortune in land trading, which he multiplied by working for the international plutocracy. In his capacity of economic advisor to the government, as a banker in opposition to the government, he financed the hostile takeover of Azoty, one of the world's largest producers of fertilisers and one of Poland's largest chemical enterprises, by the Russian oligarchic company Acron. Following his work for the international plutocracy, he became a minister and then the Prime Minister (the so-called revolving door).[82] The pursuit of the economic interests of global transnational corporations,[83] including the largest US companies, is the driving force behind government decisions, as the US ambassador or visiting officials of the US presidential administration tend to remind us regularly.

Reflections on accountability as an analytical category of the representative relationship are further complicated by the ambiguity of the goals set for those in power. In the model approach, taken as it is expressed in political science understood in Aristotelian terms, as the science of good governance, the goal of the activities of public authorities is the pursuit of the common welfare understood as the sum of the individual good and the welfare of various social groups. Alternatively, it may mean the common good understood as the public (state) welfare taking precedence over the welfare of the individual and various social groups. It could be the pursuit of class interest of the "working people" proclaimed in the constitutions of communist regimes. Likewise, the purpose of the activity undertaken was declared by British Prime Minister Edward Heath when he claimed to represent the class interest. It is also necessary to recognise the differences between the proclaimed pattern of

81 Jürgen Roth, *Cichy pucz. Zawłaszczanie Europy przez niejawne elity gospodarczo-polityczne* (Warsaw, 2015).

82 For more on the so-called revolving door and the associated pathologies see e.g. Mirko Draca, *Institutional Corruption? The Revolving Door in American and British Politics*, SMF-CAGE Global Perspectives Series: Paper 1, October 2014, http://www.smf.co.uk/wp-content/uploads/2014/10/Social-Market-FoundationInstitutional-Corruption-the-revolving-door-in-American-and-British-politics.pdf (accessed 08.07.2022); Jordi Blanes i Vidal, Mirko Draca and Christian Fons-Rosen, *Revolving Door Lobbyists*, 2011, https://personal.lse.ac.uk/blanesiv/revolving.pdf (accessed 08.07.2022); Elise S. Brezis and Joël Cariolle, *Measuring Conflicts of Interest: A Revolving Door Indicator*, 2015 EPCS meeting, Groningen, https://ferdi.fr/dl/df-8VhLGpdPRiaiA6D7umRSBVMu/presentation-measuring-conflicts-of-interest-a-revolving-door-indicator.pdf (accessed 08.07.2022).

83 For more on the influence of global corporations on policy decisions see Anna Młynarska-Sobaczewska and Jacek Zaleśny, „GAFAM – globalne korporacje cyfrowe jako uczestnicy procesów politycznych", *Przegląd Prawa Konstytucyjnego* 3 (2022): 225 et seq.

behaviour and its specific form of application in the complex, yet at the same time unique, neither vertical nor horizontal, socio-political conditions.

Singling out criteria for electoral accountability leads to the question about what those in power are to be held accountable for in a situation where national parliaments long ago ceased to have exclusive law-making powers, where the 19th-century English saying that parliament can do everything except turn a woman into a man is a tune of the past. For decades, the parliament has been prevented from doing anything not only by the constraints of the concept of the rule of law, but by the multilevel nature of the political processes taking place along with the law-making processes. This multi-levelness of the decision-making process and its networking make accountability more complicated. Law has shifted from being a product of the exclusive activity of domestic public authorities, including activity carried out with their participation or consent. There has been a successive truncation of parliaments' powers, also by means of acts of application (such as the aforementioned depriving Cypriots of part of their bank deposits against the objections of the House of Representatives) and institutional coercion, such as the jurisprudence of the Court of Justice of the European Union (CJEU). In more and more countries, regulations that arise autonomously from domestic authorities, such as secondary European law, are being applied to a greater extent. What can the members of national parliaments of EU countries be held accountable for in a situation where already several years ago, when the process of European integration was in the phase of coordination of national policies rather than their adoption by EU bodies, a minimum of 60% of the law in force in the EU states was not the product of the activity of these MPs, but of the activity of the EU bodies?[84] Is it possible to draw a line of demarcation in the process of this account between what has been created by national MPs and what has been created independently of them, or have they only been involved in the implementation of European law into the national legal order?

Especially in the process of European integration, one can observe gradually stripping national parliaments of their law-making competences. From the perspective of the principle of political representation, it is significant that having the representative bodies abandon the competence to shape legal relations is carried out by non-democratic, non-accountable, non-formed bodies through decisions of citizens (with the partial exception of the European Parliament). It takes place through a networked, non-transparent decision-making process, with the dominant participation of the European Commission as a bureaucratic authority, elected neither by national parliaments nor by the European Parliament. What is symptomatic of the process of undemocratic unaccountability, the body called "European Parliament" is a parliament only by name. By name alone, it is a body similar to national parliaments as representative

84 Jan Barcz, *Parlament a Unia Europejska. Analiza prawna na przykładzie doświadczeń Austrii (wraz z podstawowymi dokumentami)* (Warsaw: Wydawnictwo Sejmowe, 1999), 11.

bodies and therefore endowed with the competence to shape the behaviour of participants in legal relations. Under the EU's decision-making system, the body called "European Parliament" is not the primary lawmaker, but is only endowed with the capacity to participate in the process, without being the lead participant. Behind its façade, the actual legislator conceals itself. The undemocratic nature of EU decision-making is embedded in the disjointed relationship between the democratic legitimacy of the body and the substance of its participation in the decision-making process, which in turn results in the erosion of accountability and the illusion of its existence, as pointed out by the editors of the monograph *The Illusion of Accountability in the European Union*.[85]

The process of EU member states' parliaments losing their competences was exacerbated during the Covid-19 crisis. They were further marginalised both in terms of their rights to information and scrutiny and in terms of their ability to significantly influence decision-making processes.[86]

What do elections aggregate?

What do elections aggregate, asks Kaare Strøm: preferences or emotions?[87] Electoral accountability rests on the assumption that voters know what is good for them. Following the liberals, it is assumed that citizens are the best judges of their interests.[88] The individual is the only reliable guarantor of his/her own interests. Others are too selfish to safeguard other people's interests[89] or lack an accurate understanding of those interests, or both.[90] This key assumption for electoral accountability, intended to justify its rational character, has at the same time a shaky ontological foundation. Are voters able to rationally assess what is good for them as human beings, what is best for their development, their well-being? Do citizens experience enlightenment, an act of rational cognition, and through it grasp the forms and essence of things? Or do they rely on acts of sensory perception? Perhaps their political decisions are the result of various contradictory tendencies.

In 1996, 91.8% of Italian voters considered corruption a very serious problem. Twelve years later, in 2008, only 0.2% of Italian voters considered

85 Sverker Gustavsson, Christer Karlsson and Thomas Persson, eds., *The Illusion of Accountability in the European Union* (Routledge, 2009).

86 Karolina Borońska-Hryniewiecka and Diane Fromage, "Introduction: Democratic Accountability in the EU Economic Governance Post-Crises: Its Many Faces and Potential Outstanding Gaps", *Journal of Legislative Studies* 28, no. 3 (2022): 10.

87 Strøm, 119–20.

88 Manin, Przeworski and Stokes, 10.

89 An exemplification of this statement can be seen in the frauds committed by board members of public limited companies to the detriment of the company's owners.

90 Pitkin, 198.

corruption a major problem for the government to consider.[91] Although Italy remained a country with an elevated corruption index within the EU,[92] the corruption has become commonplace for the electorate. It went from being an indispensable part of political relations to being tolerated by larger sections of society without evoking interest. Theoretically, each citizen makes his or her own decisions about public relations and his or her private affairs.[93] The idea of electoral accountability assumes that electors have all the relevant knowledge about the activities of MPs and its determinants, and based on this they arrive at a rational decision, a decision which most effectively serves their interests, the sum (aggregate) of which makes up the public interest. However, is this assumption grounded in the facts, under conditions of increasing complexity of legal, economic or social relations, in a situation where there is no consensus even among experts in a given field? Can citizens make a rational evaluation of the government's policy on limiting Covid-19 transmission and mitigating its negative consequences when there is no consensus on the subject among virologists or epidemiologists? Not only is there no *communis opinio*, but the recommendations formulated by the greatest minds in this field are contradictory and, as such, impossible to apply together. In Poland, it was enough for MPs to announce that they would make an interpellation regarding the affiliation of members of the Medical Council under the Prime Minister's Office to pharmaceutical companies, and 13 of the 17 members of the Council submitted their resignations, due to "the lack of impact of their recommendations on actual measures" and "the exhaustion of the previous formula of cooperation". How can those in power be rationally held accountable in such circumstances? The problem of the multiplicity of issues subject to public decision-making by parliamentarians is pointed out by H. Landemore. She believes that for this reason elections are too blunt a sanctioning instrument. Elections are at best a means of eliminating the worst candidates, those who have failed on too many important aspects.[94] When assessing the performance of MPs, one can at best carry out an evaluation of the proceedings, apply a competence criterion, but compliance with these does not prejudge the substantive correctness of the decision made, and whether it took place is a debatable question that is currently impossible to resolve, and in turn, vertical accountability should be now implemented on an ongoing basis.

According to Valdimer O. Key, citizens evaluate retrospectively. They choose prospectively only insofar as they express approval or disapproval of what has come before. Voters may reject what they know or they may approve

91 Alberto Vannucci, "The Controversial Legacy of 'Mani Pulite': A Critical Analysis of Italian Corruption and Anti-Corruption Policies", *Bulletin of Italian Politics* 1, no. 2 (2009): 235.

92 *The Corruption Perception Index 2019: The EU Is the Best Performer in the World*, https://ec.europa.eu/regional_policy/en/newsroom/news/2020/01/27-01-2020-the-corruption-perception-index-2019-the-eu-is-the-best-performer-in-the-world (accessed 20.06.2020).

93 Edward L. Bernays, *Propaganda* (Wrocław, 2020), 20.

94 Hélène Landemore, 103.

of what they know. By contrast, they are unlikely to be attracted in large numbers by promises of novelty or an unknown future.[95] The idea of retrospective electoral accountability is grounded in the assumption that such an account is drawn up, that – following the model of the representation relationship in civil law – the Agent gives certain account to the Principal; the Principal then carefully weighs the rationale and makes electoral decision. This is an illusory assumption for three reasons. Firstly, there is no universal practice of MPs or the government producing a precise report at the end of their term of office on the work that has been done, assessing the impact of the measures taken. Nor has the practice developed of a comprehensive, objectivised evaluation by independent bodies of the work carried out. Secondly, even if individual MPs draw up a report on their activities, these are not subject to a general analysis by the public.[96] Thirdly, the uniqueness of MPs' reporting on their activities means that the citizens who are interested in them do not have at their disposal comprehensive comparative material, which in turn makes it impossible for them to compare MPs' activities, assess them and, as a result, carry out a retrospective electoral reckoning.

Having no empirical support, assuming that voters possess comprehensive knowledge of MPs' activities, are able to quantify and evaluate them and make a rational decision on this basis is an illusion. In this context, the doctrine emphasises the significance of the asymmetric nature of knowledge for the ability to hold the elected accountable.[97] Citizens have insufficient knowledge of what officials actually do,[98] and therefore lack the capacity to assess them comprehensively and competently. While, in essence, they are able to familiarise themselves with the legal conditions of the activities of policy-makers, they are in no position to familiarise themselves with the actual conditions of their activities, with the available decision-making alternatives.[99]

It has been estimated, for example, that 77% of Americans, 47% of Poles and 28% of Swedes are functionally illiterate, unable to understand the content of the simplest instructions or to fill in the most basic forms. Correspondingly, in this group of countries, 2%, 21% and 32% of the population respectively are considered to be linguistically literate.[100] Are citizens with mental dysfunctions, who are unable to check a grocery bill or a bus timetable, competent to properly evaluate the performance of MPs and hold them to account for

95 Valdimer O. Key, *The Responsible Electorate: Rationality in Presidential Voting, 1936–1960* (Cambridge, MA: Harvard University Press, 1968), 61.

96 An objectivised, formal criterion for the coverage of reports is the number of so-called downloads of the report on the internet, i.e. the number of people who have opened the report in question.

97 John Forejohn, "Accountability and Authority: Toward a Theory of Political Accountability", in *Democracy, Accountability and Representation* (see note 42), 132.

98 Borowiak, 12; Mainwaring, 23.

99 Goetz and Jenkins, 18.

100 https://pl.wikipedia.org/wiki/Analfabetyzm (accessed 13.06.2020).

their actions? Can they properly identify those who are performing their representative mandate more effectively and should continue to do so, and those who should be removed from office as a result of a negative evaluation of their performance? Are they competent to assess the alternatives of macroeconomic policies or international alliances implemented in the state? Are citizens, who do not understand the content of simple instructions, competent to determine the weighting of individual forms of action by MPs when there is no consensus about them among experts? And this is, after all, what the idea of retrospective accountability is based on: rewarding some and punishing others, extending the consent to govern or not. Programmers have coined the maxim GIGO – Garbage in, Garbage out. There is hardly any evidence supporting the claim that it does not also apply to political relations. Edgar J. Jung invokes the motif of the "intellectual enslavement of the electorate" as a characteristic feature of electors.[101] In doing so, he notes that the voter is almost always a non-political person,[102] rarely equipped with a sense of responsibility for the community and insufficiently informed about the state of public affairs.[103] Voters political ignorance is a constant variable of electoral processes. Characteristically, as Jason Brennan points out, this is also the case in the age of online means of communication, when political information is cheap and easy to obtain, when the number of people with higher education has increased.[104]

The extent of the demos ignorance in the age of social media is aptly illustrated by the case of George Santos, a Republican, who was representing the people of New York in the federal US House of Representatives from 2022 to 2023. Almost his entire personal and professional CV was falsified. Mr Santos claimed to have obtained degrees from New York University and Baruch College – however, he did not actually graduate from any university. He claimed to have worked at Goldman Sachs and Citigroup, which was untrue. He claimed to be a real estate tycoon, which was again a lie – what was true was that he had to leave flats he rented because he was in arrears with his rent. He claimed to be Jewish and that his grandparents had escaped from the Germans during World War II, which also turned out to be a fiction. His grandparents were born in Brazil. Mr Santos claimed to have a husband (whom no one has seen), but – something he failed to mention – he was married until 2019. Actually, it is not even certain that his real name is George Santos, as he has in the past performed under various names and aliases – George Santos, Anthony Devolder, Anthony Zabrovsky or Kitara Ravache, during his days as a drag

101 Edgar J. Jung, *Władztwo miernot. Jego rozpad i zastąpienie przez Nowe Imperium* (Krakow: Ośrodek Myśli Politycznej, 2019), 228.

102 Broadly on the essence of "politicality" see Mirosław Karwat, „O statusie pojęcia „polityczności", *Studia Politologiczne* 37 (2015).

103 Jung, 228. Similarly, Forejohn, 150.

104 Jason Brennan, *Against Democracy* (Princeton, NJ: Princeton University Press, 2017), 30.

queen in Brazil. It is uncertain whether he is American at all, as he was wanted in Brazil as a Brazilian for forging a cheque.[105]

Due to intellectual deficits and lack of relevant knowledge, large groups of voters are not competent to carry out a rational evaluation of the performance of deputies, yet at the same time they evaluate the performance of deputies during voting; in parts of modern countries they are forced to do so under the threat of sanctions. Therefore, Bryan Caplan writes that the irrationality of the choices made is derived from the irrationality of the voters. Irrational voters vote irrationally.[106] Nor do they have the opportunity to reconstruct the policy-maker's thought process. The informational asymmetry is all the greater because, as Edward L. Bernays rightly points out, public discussion revolves around those pieces of information that politicians and the mass media think are going to become the subject of discussion.[107] Voters are sensitive to the views which political parties and the interest groups standing behind them intend to use to win voters' favour.[108] These do not have to be issues that are of key importance to the formation of public policies and participants in social relations. They may include topics brought forth for other reasons to absorb the attention of participants in social relations, issues that are irrelevant, and that is precisely why they are made the subject of discussion, in order to shift public attention away from what is crucial. The main goals of political parties can remain obscure. Taking advantage of the dexterity of spin doctors and the availability of pro-party mass media lead to bridging of the gap between pre-election promises and party practices.[109] In this process of managing the perception of large segments of society, the mass media play prominent roles as centres of the struggle for public resources and their distribution. People do not read the press to learn about something (cognitive motivation), but to reassert their views (ideological motivation).[110] Meanwhile, according to the researchers' findings, the mass media should act as a watchdog that acts as an entity providing information to the public and enhancing the transparency of the electoral process, revealing any potential distortions.[111] In our opinion, the deforming influence of the mass media on the political consciousness of the participants in political relations is a significant circumstance that interferes

105 Marisa Kabas, "George Santos Was Expelled from Congress. What Did the Media Learn?", https://nbcuacademy.com/george-santos-coverage/ (accessed 21.12.2023).

106 Bryan Caplan, *Myth of the Rational Voter* (Princeton, NJ: Princeton University Press, 2008), 23.

107 Edward L. Bernays, *Propaganda* (Wrocław, 2020), 20.

108 Jung, 228.

109 Jung, 228.

110 Adam Wielomski, *Demokracja nieliberalna* (Warsaw, 2022), 137.

111 See e.g. Elena Costas-Pérez, Albert Solé Ollé and Pilar Sorribas Navarro, "Corruption Scandals, Voter Information and Accountability", *European Journal of Political Economy* 28, no. 4 (2012): 469 et seq.

with the ability to rationally evaluate the public policies carried out and the alternatives formulated to them.

At the same time, which needs to be reiterated, discussion presupposes the existence of common views and the ability to recognise opposing arguments.[112] It assumes that, in the course of the debate, it is possible to change one's position on an issue, to accept the debater's rationale or to seek a common position. Modern "debates", including parliamentary debates, are characterised by rejection of these conditions.[113] They consist in the ritual recitation of stances on a particular issue, most often being a cluster of more or less sophisticated platitudes, prepared by spin doctors or ghostwriters, experts in political narratives. For in the "debate" one does not seek the truth about reality, but, on the contrary, the concealment of the truth regarding the actual assessment of the effects of a proposed policy or regulation, possibly – to gain an advantage, to win the top spot, predestined to enchant other participants in political relations. Parliamentary speeches do not so much serve to discuss and clarify the matter under consideration as to demean the speaker of the opposing party and negate his claims.[114]

Unlike Habermas's ideal speech situation, which assumes that within a free and equal discussion all arguments are considered, neither political debate (like parliamentary debate) nor public debate represent the school of rationality. They are not the school of cognition, of arriving at the truth about the essence of the social processes carried out and the resulting consequences. Truth has become irrelevant as a category of public discourse. Narratives – illusions of artificial consciousness – have effectively replaced truth. Why have a debate, present different rationales, juxtapose and compare them, when the rationale for action is not to establish the legal and factual state of affairs, but to express views both one's own and those spouted by spin doctors?

According to only 0.9% of members of the Polish Parliament, the opposition exerts pressure on MPs during legislative work, voting as well as during work in parliamentary committees.[115] This belief shared by MPs, that the parliamentary opposition does not influence the work of parliament, is accompanied by low attendance at plenary debates and the rationing of MPs' speaking time to one minute. It follows the assumption that since it is irrelevant what MPs say, since it does not affect the substance of decisions made in parliament anyway, there is no point in wasting time on the proceedings of parliament. Parliament should therefore be convened infrequently and for a short time, only to approve what the government has prepared. Diana Woodhouse writes

112 Stanisław Filipowicz, *Demokracja. O władzy iluzji w królestwie rozumu* (Warsaw: Wydawnictwa Akademickie i Profesjonalne, 2007), 189.

113 Filipowicz, 189.

114 Jung, 238.

115 Jacek Zaleśny, „Poseł a partia polityczna", in *Mandat przedstawicielski w teorii, prawie i praktyce poselskiej*, ed. M. Kruk (Warsaw, 2013), 247–8.

about the decline in the frequency and importance of debate in the British House of Commons. In doing so, she adds, parliamentary attention is instead focused on Question Time. It is often used by MPs as an opportunity to score party points and launch personal attacks, rather than to seek and provide information and justification in the parliamentary decision-making process.[116]

Just as in the practice of some contemporary countries parliamentary debate is not central to the decision-making process, so is the evaluation of the effects of work, i.e. legislation, losing its importance. It is being superseded by the procedural punchline of democracy which is the act of voting and obtaining the majority of votes. The role of deputies has been reduced to exactly that. Their primary task is to raise their hand at the right time and press the right button. This is the opinion of half of Polish deputies.[117] In the words of E. Hughes, an MP is similar to Pavlov's dog; all that is required of him is to come to vote when the bell rings.[118] Hence, it is a matter of performing simple, manual tasks, for the performance of which one does not need special qualifications; activities for the performance of which it is easy to replace deputies with new parliamentarians. The expulsion of MPs from the pursuit of the essence of regulated legal relations and the reduction of their role to sui generis operators of voting buttons reduces the significance of their activities. It renders their placement on the electoral list in subsequent parliamentary elections uncertain, which in itself is a source of frustration for MPs. In light of surveys conducted in Poland, this is the reality of approximately half of MPs (primarily of the two largest political parties):[119] awaiting the verdict of the party leader as to the spot on the electoral list. From the perspective of the leaders of the parties, it is of little importance who becomes an MP in a situation in which the leading task of the majority of the members of the parliamentary fraction is to press the right button during voting and to recite what the party gives them to recite in the media outlets as part of the so-called "messages of the day".

According to surveys conducted in Poland, large sections of the population are not interested in politics and have no knowledge of it. Less than 20% of voters follow closely or fairly closely what is happening in politics.[120] Only in the period immediately preceding the vote does the level of interest in politics increase. Citizens only sporadically engage in political processes, and

116 Diana Woodhouse, *Ministers and Parliament: Accountability in Theory and Practice* (Oxford University Press, 1994), 24.

117 Zaleśny, 250 et seq.

118 Emrys Hughes, *Parliament and Mumbo-Jumbo* (London: George Allen and Unwin, 1966), 62 et seq.

119 Zaleśny, 250 et seq.

120 *Monolog, dialog czy kłótnia – Polaków rozmowy o polityce*, Komunikat z badań, CBOS 2017, no. 153, 1, https://www.cbos.pl/SPISKOM.POL/2017/K_153_17.PDF (accessed 20.06.2020). The inability of citizens to monitor the Prime Minister's activities (they merely monitor their effects) is also pointed out by G.J. Miller, "The Political Evolution of PA Models", *Annual Review of Political Science* 8 (2005): 207.

consequently rarely and fragmentarily evaluate the activities of those elected. As J. Brennan remarks, large groups of voters are more ignorant than it appears to observers of political relations: "When it comes to politics, some people know a lot, most people know nothing, and many people know less than nothing".[121] Profound ignorance is an identity trait of a significant proportion of the electorate,[122] but as J. Brennan continues – the political ignorance of non-voters is even greater.[123] As Larry Bartels states, the political ignorance of Americans is one of the best documented features of contemporary politics.[124] B. Caplan concludes: the knowledge voters lack could fill an entire university library.[125] In turn, comparative studies reveal that compulsion to vote has no effect on voters' political sophistication.[126]

Voters have neither the competence nor the desire or the time to monitor the activities of parliaments on a daily basis. The voters' profound ignorance explains well why MPs (like the MPs of the US Congress) do not act to pursue their interests. They do not act because they have no need to. They can easily ignore them.[127] Voters are not competent to press for what they need to demand in order to realise their interests and consequently, as the US studies cited above show, their social needs are not met. In contrast, economic elites and narrow interest groups know how to diagnose their needs, articulate them and compel those in power to implement them.

Unlike citizens, lobbyists and activists are interested in the activities of parliament and, thanks to the openness of its work and the instruments they possess to influence the conduct of MPs, they can ensure that the legislation is favourable to them. Hence, their activities bring the political effectiveness. Thanks to the openness of the vote and thus the information on how individual MPs voted, a mix of means of influence is applied against them, ranging from persuasion and subsidies to provocation, blackmail and black PR. Organised minorities will force either the retention of legislation favourable to them or the introduction of such into the state's legal system. Pressured by organised lobbies on the one hand and noting the lack of interest of large sections of society in an issue on the other, MPs succumb to the former. Profits are accumulated in a narrow interest group, while costs are distributed within

121 Brennan, 24.

122 For more on this see e.g. I. Somin, *Democracy and Political Ignorance: Why Smaller Government Is Smarter* (Stanford University Press, 2013).

123 Brennan, 26–7.

124 Larry Bartels, "Uninformed Votes: Information Effects in Presidential Elections", *American Political Science Review* 40, no. 1 (1996): 194. Similarly: Larry Bartels, "The Irrational Electorate", *Wilson Quarterly* 32, no. 4 (Autumn, 2008).

125 Caplan, 27.

126 See Sarah Birch, *Full Participation. A Comparative Study of Compulsory Voting* (United Nations University Press, 2009); Annabelle Lever, "Compulsory Voting: A Critical Perspective", *British Journal of Political Science* 40, no. 4 (2010).

127 Vincent L. Hutchings, *Public Opinion and Democratic Accountability: How Citizens Learn about Politics* (Princeton, NJ: Princeton University Press, 2003), 2.

large social groups, as Frederic Bastiat explained accurately more than 150 years ago.[128]

Large sections of society are unqualified to make a rational assessment of the activities of the actors in political relations and make a sound electoral decision on that basis. Therefore, they succumb to perverse demagogues, feeding demos with flattery in order to hide their own perverted ambitions[129] and interests. The rule of reason heralded by the Enlightenment turned out to be a fantasy. The promised rule of reason turned out to be a rule of desires, of passions, with which skilful demagogues satiate the sovereign.[130]

It is telling also that social groups with specific professional qualifications necessary for the evaluation of political processes, such as political scientists, economists, lawyers or philosophers, are internally divided when it comes to the perception of political processes. While there is a convergence in terms of the scope of their assessment (e.g. constitutionalists, in principle, have a similar perception of the constitutional changes taking place, and economists of the main parameters of macroeconomic policy), the overall perception is quite different. In other words, the variable in the form of formal education in the area under study is not a determinant of a similar perception of the overall changes taking place during the election period under review.

Since large groups of voters are not familiar with the determinants of the political decision-making process, do not know the key political decisions, they are unable to make a rational assessment of them, and the outcome may be the re-election of politicians who did not do their best. Alternatively, they may reject politicians who did what needed to be done. For this reason, as Hanna F. Pitkin notes, re-election is far from being absolute proof that a politician is a good representative. At most, re-election proves that voters think so,[131] voters who generally are not qualified to judge the correctness of the actions taken by politicians.

In turn, even if some voters are aware of what is best for them, how to most fully achieve their inherent potential, their entelechy, these voters still do not have full knowledge of the essential features of the political processes taking place (on the state, regional or global scale). As a result, they may err in their retrospective assessment of government activity and, based on an erroneous assessment of the government, make an erroneous electoral decision; erroneous in the sense that if they had full knowledge of the relevant aspects of government activity in which they are interested, they would make a different assessment of it and could therefore also make a different electoral decision.

Large groups of voters have no possibility to make a comprehensive assessment of politicians' activities and make a rational, retrospective electoral

128 Frédéric Bastiat, *Co widać i czego nie widać* (Wrocław: Fijor Publishing, 2005).
129 Filipowicz, 9.
130 For all about the reign of demagoguery see: Mirosław Karwat, *O demagogii* (Warsaw, 2006).
131 Pitkin, 165.

decision. A part of the voters not qualified to make a rational electoral decision do not take part in the act of voting. It is no coincidence that the level of voter absenteeism tends to be elevated among the least educated.

Political science recognises the fictitiousness of the assumption that the electoral decision is rational. For this reason, Herbert Simon uses the concept of bounded rationality.[132] Adapting his findings to the ongoing considerations, we can state that due to the limited cognitive capacity of citizens, they do not look for the optimal electoral alternative, instead they are guided by the principle of satisfaction. They choose an electoral solution that satisfies them, whatever the underlying rationale.

As James D. Fearon explains, there is no sound rationale for treating elections as a form of accountability of the elected by electors.[133] For this very reason, re-election does not depend on the economic outcome achieved during a given term of government. In European countries, it makes little difference whether GDP at the time was lower or higher relative to GDP achieved in the previous accounting period or relative to other countries in the region. For large segments of society, elections can serve as a means of selecting the most outstanding individuals. Hence the significance of mass communication, electoral marketing and propaganda as means of creating citizens' political and electoral preferences; the importance of means of widespread and mass stupefaction of citizens, relying not on acts of rational cognition to grasp the forms and essence of things, but on acts of sensory perception, exposing the importance of emotions as motives for human action. This process has intensified along with the development of the internet and the associated networked, democratic nature of political communication. Yascha Mounk emphasises, as long as this communication was based on newspapers, radio stations or television networks, the costs associated with conducting this activity were high, allowing the political establishment to marginalise extreme, nonsensical views[134] and to distinguish, to filter the essential from the marginal.

Meritocracy versus ochlocracy

In democratic regimes, major broadcasters were restrained from spreading false messages. Today, the reality is quite different. In fact, almost two-thirds

132 Herbert A. Simon, "Bounded Rationality and Organizational Learning", *Organization Science* 2, no. 1 (1991). On the concept of "bounded rationality" see also Gustavo Barros, "Herbert A. Simon and the Concept of Rationality: Boundaries and Procedures", *Brazilian Journal of Political Economy* 30, no. 3 (2010).

133 See James D. Fearon, "Electoral Accountability and the Control of Politicians: Selecting Good Types versus Sanctioning Poor Performance", in *Democracy, Accountability and Representation* (see note 42), 57.

134 Mounk, 30–1.

of Americans share the view that “mainstream” news sources are just as full of “fake news”.[135]

The advancement of digital technologies, including social media, has changed the structural conditions of political communication, the relationship between senders and receivers of political communication. It has introduced an egalitarian communication relationship in place of the elitist relationship of sender – social organisations as communication intermediaries – receivers. Everyone can act as a sender and everyone can be a receiver of political communication,[136] where everyone can engage in communication with anyone. Delusions have the same legitimacy of presence as scientific findings. Dilettantes have become equal participants in the public debate and with their mass character have dominated it and brought it down to their level. As David Runciman points out, democracy à la Twitter is not hobbled by personal knowledge of the subject matter.[137] Anything can be communicated. Any fatuity can grow into revealed truth, any delusion can become a pattern of behaviour. Rumours coexist in equal measure with verified messages.[138] Twitter-like democracy takes the form of the democracy depicted in Mike Judge’s *Idiocracy*.

In contrast to so-called traditional media, there are no filters here to prevent false messages from being broadcast. As of 29 May 2020, President Donald Trump has uttered 19,127 false or misleading statements during his 1,226 days in office, which amounts to more than 15 lies per day.[139] Under the traditional media system, relying on vertical communication, it would be difficult for him to expect such distribution. In the time of social media, based on the network rule, i.e. the horizontal rule, he does not need to ask anyone for permission. He can distribute the messages himself. The networked nature of the distribution of messages means that they reach large social groups and influence their perception of reality. As a result of the process described, according to Yascha Mounk, “the provocateurs of instability have gained the upper hand over the forces of order”.[140] The egalitarianism of political communication means the dissemination and appreciation of demagoguery, ignorance, superstition, meanness and everything that can be called mass stupefaction. Mass disinformation coexists with the widespread ignorance of its recipients, who are not competent to evaluate what they read. In North Carolina, a few days after Donald Trump claimed that by endorsing Hillary Clinton, Vermont

135 Tom Ginsburg and Aziz Z. Huq, *How to Save a Constitutional Democracy* (University of Chicago Press, 2018), 230.

136 Landemore, 31.

137 Runciman, 155.

138 Rosanvallon, 176. Similarly, Anne Applebaum, *Zmierzch demokracji. Zwodniczy powab autorytaryzmu* (Warsaw: Wydawnictwo Agora, 2020), 138–9.

139 Michael Tomasky, “Why Does Trump Lie?”, *New York Times*, 11 June 2020 https://www.nytimes.com/2020/06/11/opinion/trump-lies.html (accessed 20.06.2020).

140 Mounk, 31.

Senator Bernie Sanders had "made a deal with the devil", "She (H. Clinton – A. M.-S., J.Z.) is the devil", 41% of his supporters declared that Hillary Clinton really is the devil, 42% disagreed with the statement and 17% were not sure.[141]

The mass production and dissemination of fake news should be added to the spontaneous, dispersed and widespread stupefaction in the form of organised stupefaction. Facebook's calculations show that the majority of accounts created on Facebook are fake. For example, in the first quarter of 2018 2.19 billion accounts were found to be fake and shut down by Facebook.[142] Fake messages are professionally spread using so-called bots. For instance, between February and August 2016, Twitter shut down almost 377,000 accounts that it deemed to be used to promote terrorism.[143] Twitter has blocked more than 170,000 accounts linked to the Chinese government that were spreading false information about the Covid-19 virus and the situation in Hong Kong, among other things. According to Twitter's findings, 23,750 of these accounts showed intense, interrelated activity and published a total of 348,608 tweets. In turn, around 150,000 other accounts were used to amplify and spread the message, for example by sharing posts.[144] Also, Twitter shut down 7,340 accounts of Turkish pro-government "trolls".[145]

Misinformation, delivered through social media (as the primary means of political communication and the formation of political views of large social groups), serves both companies and governments of other countries to manipulate citizens and elicit the making of decisions desired by the manipulators. As Y. Dawood stresses, concerns about this kind of manipulation exceed the usual concerns about the formation of echo chambers in deliberative spaces.[146] This is because the manipulation effected through social media does not concern individual decisions, but is comprehensive in nature. As such, it fosters social polarisation, resulting in the permanent breakdown of a state's political, social, economic or cultural system.

141 Rafi Schwartz, "41% of Trump Supporters in North Carolina Think That Hillary Clinton Is Literally the Devil", https://splinternews.com/41-of-trump-supporters-in-north-carolina-think-that-hi-1793861030 (accessed 20.06.2020).

142 Matylda Grodecka, *Liczba dnia: 2 miliardy. Tyle kont Facebook uznał za fałszywe i skasował w raptem 3 miesiące*, https://spidersweb.pl/2019/05/facebook-skasowal-2-miliardy-falszywych-kont.html (accessed 20.06.2020).

143 Data source: *Twitter zamyka konta promujące terroryzm*, http://www.proto.pl/aktualnosci/twitter-zamyka-konta-promujace-terroryzm (accessed 20.06.2020).

144 Data source: Alicja Podskoczy, *Twitter na wojnie z Chinami. Usunął 170 tys. kont za dezinformację*, https://cyfrowa.rp.pl/globalne-interesy/48985-twitter-na-wojnie-z-chinami-usunal-170-tys-kont-za-dezinformacje (accessed 20.06.2020).

145 Data source: *Twitter zamknął 7340 propagandowych tureckich kont*, https://wolnemedia.net/twitter-zamknal-7-tysiecy-propagandowych-tureckich-kont (accessed 20.06.2020).

146 Yasmin Dawood, "Democratic Theory and Democratic Failure", in *Democratic Failure*, ed. Melissa Schwartzberg and Daniel Viehoff (Cambridge, Harvard University Press, 2020), 151.

As Pierre Rosanvallon puts it, citizens express their opinions in atomised form on social media, manipulated by organised pressure groups according to their particular interests, or in the form of a haze of scattered criticisms.[147] Thanks to online resources, voters know more and more about various aspects of the lives of those in power. They follow their activities, tastes and habits in both their public and private spheres. At the same time, however, they are subject to massive, permanent disinformation. They are often unable to distinguish between a fabricated message and an original one, or a fabricated photograph and a photograph representing an actual event. Technological progress means that crafted messages and photographs have all the characteristics of the originals and in political communication can have a similar effect to the originals. The holistic nature of online communication means that it does not only affect voters' political attitudes and conduct. It affects the political behaviour and attitudes of those in power as well. According to Yascha Mounk, the empowerment of outsiders is accompanied by the destabilisation of ruling elites around the world. Thanks to modern technology, populist demagogues, unfettered by the constraints of the old media system, have gained importance. They have acquired the tools and are using them efficiently to lie, to spin,[148] in short, to manipulate large sections of the population, who are not mentally equipped to evaluate the messages they formulate, on a mass scale. The claims of internet enthusiasts, such as Larry Diamond, who referred to the internet as a "liberation technology" and argued that it strengthens democratic relations, provides opportunities to communicate and exchange views, expose abuses, monitor elections, control government, deepen political participation and broaden the horizons of freedom, have been debunked. The noble assumption was that through the means of online communication, citizens could participate in public debate on an equal basis, exchange views on public affairs, thus forming public opinion based on knowledge and rational argumentation.[149] The author argued that the internet is also an "accountability technology", as it provides efficient and powerful transparency and monitoring tools.[150] The internet has been associated with the development of political participation inherent in ancient direct democracy, a kind of return to a situation where everyone not only has the right, but can actually participate in the political community;[151] in a democratic debate, since it is a universal discourse open to everyone; an inclusive debate from which no one is excluded and in which everyone is called to participate.

147 Rosanvallon, 202.
148 Mounk, 185.
149 Larry Diamond, "Liberation Technology", *Journal of Democracy* 21, no. 3 (2010): 70 et seq.
150 Diamond, 76.
151 Szymanek, *Reprezentacja i mandat parlamentarny*, 33–4.

The actual power relations taking place fail to support this optimism. Instead of the emancipation of reason, mass communication reinforces the emancipation of ignorance. Instead of debate serving accountability, social media brings with it cancel culture and the deprivation of opponents' right to speak (deplatforming).[152]

Internet communication has disseminated and valorised the equalitarian and demagogic potential of democracy and made it the essence of democratic power relations. It is used for "despicable purposes", as noted by L. Diamond, too.[153] Just as in the act of voting every vote is equal, the voice of the taxpayer is equal to the voice of the recipient of social benefits, the voice of the precautionary person is equal to the voice of the wastrel, so it is online: anyone can write about politics and economics as if they had some knowledge of it. Dilettantes have become equal participants in the public debate. Given that statistically they are in the majority, they do dominate it. The internet has reinforced the Aristotelian understanding of democracy as a system in which the principle of equality has been carried out to the fullest, where everything is decided by a majority resolution.[154]

The synthesis of the massive, widespread stupefaction of voters takes shape during the election campaign period. This is when recklessness is considered political maturity and political maturity is considered impossibilism. Prejudice and ignorance are elevated to cardinal virtues. They become the warp of electoral decisions, treated in the process as retrospective accountability.

During the time of election campaigns, in addition to disinformation operations conducted by domestic participants in political relations and being their form of influencing the course of these relations, the implementation of external disinformation campaigns can be recorded. These involve the use of information and psychological means to steer the behaviour of candidates and political parties and to bring about the destabilisation of the state by influencing the behaviour of particular social groups.[155]

In the "Nicomachean Ethics", Aristotle distinguished between negative and positive ways of life.[156] The first negative way of life is linked to a life that is

152 Alan Dershowitz, *Cancel Culture: The Latest Attack on the Free Speech and Due Process* (New York, Hot Books 2020).

153 Diamond, 71.

154 Arystoteles, *Polityka* (Warsaw: Wydawnictwo Naukowe PWN, 2012), 113.

155 On the theory of information-psychological warfare see e.g. Андрей В. МАнойло, АнАтолий И. Петренко, ДМитрий Б. ФролоВ, ГосудАрстВеннАя инФорМАционнАя ПолитикА В услоВиях инФорМАционно-ПсихолоГической Войны, ГорячАя линия –ТелекоМ [Andrey V. Manoylo, Anatoliy I. Petrenko, Dmitriy B. Frolov, Gosudarstvennaya informatsionnaya politika v usloviyakh informatsionno-psikhologicheskoy voyny, Goryachaya liniya –Telekom] (Moscow, 2021). On the practical scope of information and psychological warfare as a means of influencing the course and outcome of elections see e.g. Michael Isikoff and David Corn, *Russian Roulette: The Inside Story of Putin's War on America and the Election of Donald Trump* (New York, Hachette Book Group, 2018).

156 Arystoteles, *Etyka nikomachejska* (Warsaw, 2012), Book One et seq.

subordinated to pleasure and enjoyment. As Aristotle writes, "the uneducated public and the simpletons" are content with a life consisting in consumption. It is a life of slavery. A person is not in control of what he or she does. It is reign of pleasure. The second negative way of life consists in the lust for honours as the goals of human action. They are something superficial, because they depend on those who bestow them rather than on the one who receives them. Life can be about acquiring wealth and for Aristotle this is "in a way a life of compulsion".

The good life, on the other hand, consists of an active life – *vita activa*. It is connected with the political nature of human beings, with the fact that they live and act within the state. It involves cultivating the trait of prudence. The second type of good life is a life dedicated to theoretical contemplation (*vita contemplativa*) – the life of the sage. At the same time, Aristotle recognises that man has to pay attention to the necessities of life, to living together with other people, and therefore – external circumstances affect the correctness of decisions. People are stuck in a tension between the different dimensions of their existence.[157] This dichotomy dating back more than two thousand years remains relevant in contemporary political relations. On the one hand, there is the tendency towards a growing number of citizens who have recourse to rational acts of cognition and are thus able to determine the form and substance of political relations, carry out a retrospective account of those in power and, using this as a reference, make a prospective electoral decision. And the other trend: an increasing number of citizens referring to acts of sensory perception and, on this basis, carrying out a retrospective account of those in power and making a prospective electoral decision (while, and this needs to be emphasised, these need not be disconnected sets).

Therefore, we can consider rational cognition versus sensory perception as a common ground for electoral accountability, as a shared platform for considering the relationship occurring between the electors and the elected, or between the represented and the represented. For this reason, electoral retrospective and prospective evaluation need not be disjoint alternatives. As Morris P. Fiorina writes, it does not have to be a perspective, i.e. looking back versus looking ahead.[158] Voters both look ahead and look back, make judgments about what has happened in the nearer (election campaign) and distant (term of office of the elected body) past.

In our view, widespread and ever-deepening electoral ignorance explains not only the inability of the represented to rationally assess their representatives. It also explains the electoral volatility/vulnerability taking place in parts of contemporary European states, with particular reference to countries such

157 See Marek Drwięga, „Człowiek w filozofii arystotelesowskiej", *Anthropos?* 10–11 (2008), http://www.anthropos.us.edu.pl/anthropos6/texty/drwiega.htm (accessed 20.06.2020).

158 Morris P. Fiorina, *Retrospective Voting in American National Election* (New Haven, CT: Yale University Press, 1981), 196.

as France, Italy or Greece. Referring to the opinions of B. Manin, the identification of voters, their loyalty to a specific party, is becoming a thing of the past. Today, more and more citizens are changing their voting preferences from one election to the next. The number of those voters who reject identification with any existing political party is growing.[159] This is because, and this argumentation is compelling to us, class interests are losing importance and communicative electoral strategies of candidates and political parties are gaining, based on the construction of vague, labile images that expose the personality – or rather the image of it – of political leaders.[160] The public scene has been taken over by wizards in charge of shaping public perceptions, experts in electoral polls and their deformation, journalists-propagandists who can hardly be considered a reflection of society, of its key dilemmas regarding public relations.[161] As in France, from the time of Emmanuel Macron's first presidency onwards, depending on current political needs, convincing that "white is black and black is white", that "unimportant is important and important is unimportant", that – just like in the movie *Idiocracy*: "Brawndo drink is good for everything", they mould politically unsophisticated citizens into voters for particular politicians or political formations.

(Un)accountability versus (un)confidence in democracy

The oligarchisation of parliaments, their orientation towards the pursuit of the interests of the economic elite and narrow interest groups, leads to reduced confidence in democracy and the associated decision-making mechanisms. This process has been widely observed in both the United States and across Europe.[162] Neither Americans nor citizens of Western countries have ever rated their political system as poorly as they do today.[163] Across the United States, a few-odd per cent of Americans declare confidence in Congress. Between 1973 and 2022: 42% (1973), 41% (1986) to 7% (2014, 2022).[164] In Western societies, more voters neither like nor trust their representatives than in previous decades.[165] According to the European Social Survey, only 0.3% of Czechs, 0.9% of Poles, 1.5% of Belgians, 1.6% of Germans, 1.7% of French and 1.8% of Finns declare full confidence in their parliament.[166]

159 Manin, 193.

160 For more on the personalisation of policy see Monika Brenner, "Zjawisko personalizacji politycznej", *Studia Politologiczne* 16 (2010): 117 et seq.

161 See Manin, 193.

162 Mounk, 128 et seq.

163 Zakaria, 23.

164 "Confidence in Institutions", https://news.gallup.com/poll/1597/confidence-institutions.aspx (accessed 08.07.2022).

165 Runciman, 16.

166 The results reported pertain to the eighth round of the survey, for 2016-–17, https://zkarpinski.shinyapps.io/european_social_survey, in: Jarosław Szymanek, "Kryzys demokracji?", *Infos. Biuro Analiz Sejmowych* 7 (2019): 4.

In countries considered democratic in the 1980s and 1990s, such as the United Kingdom, France and Germany, we are seeing growing support for authoritarian governments. Lack of accountability in politics results in an increase in anti-democratic tendencies. The nominal sovereign starts to notice illusions of his sovereignty, illusions of democratic participation. They perceive that, regardless of the election results, the elections are won by the economic elite and narrow interest groups. The Covid-19 epidemic has accelerated this process. It deepened the concentration of capital within global companies, monopolising economic relations (and with them political relations), with the concomitant pauperisation of large sections of society, including the class historically regarded as middle class (highly skilled professionals running sole proprietorships).

Oligarchic democracy, based on the illusion of elections and accountability of the elected, is doomed to failure. As Plato remarked, all excess tends to turn into its opposite.[167] Democracy becomes a castle of false and blasphemous thoughts and opinions. It gives power to the passions that justify every wickedness and every oddity.[168] Flattery and illusory promises become the common creed of democracy, and the demos become slaves to their own preposterousness. The preposterousness and confusion of thought circulating in public are the food with which the oligarchs feed the demos and through which they increase the concentration of power and capital. The public ludicrousness and global confusion of thought of the demos become an instrument for the popular management of the perception of the masses in order to build global monopolies and global governance[169] – a global concentration of political and economic power. So observed Plato or Aristotle, the preposterousness of democracy leads it towards self-destruction. The experience of the city-states of ancient Greece commonly cited as an archetype of good governance, where direct democracy was practised, is quite telling. They all descended into tyranny or chaos, or both at the same time, within a century.[170] Under present-day circumstances remodelled by the proclamation of the global outbreak of Covid-19, these are the global concentration of political and economic power, combined with the widespread application of Chinese techniques for managing human conduct and social relations. And all of this, combined with the widely held declaration of democratic faith that the demos are the sovereign source of power, exercised by public authorities held accountable by them and accountable to them.

167 Platon, *Państwo. Tom II* (Warsaw: Alfa, 1994), 133.

168 Filipowicz, 9.

169 Vitaly Goncharov et al., "The Place of a Person in the Ontological Principles of Global Constitutionalism: Social and Philosophical Analysis", *Wisdom* 2, no. 15 (2020).

170 Zakaria, 292.

Summary

The abovementioned illusions about representation, the expression of will by the sovereign, the competence of the demos to judge the actions of those entrusted with power, and the observed phenomena of increasing epistemic asymmetry between the governed and the governors make it difficult, in fact, to accept the idea of accountability exercised through elections. It is an assumption in the category of myths, not substantiated by easily observable facts. Neither is it customary nor obligatory for those elected to exercise power to give an account of its exercise under conditions of objective and authoritative communication, information about their actions that can be compared, evaluated and elicit rational responses. The ignorance on the part of the demos is a fact.

Instead of a belief in the sovereign power of the people holding their chosen ones accountable, one can assume that elections are not so much a vehicle for electoral accountability as a legitimisation for the succession of power and for governing – an acquiescence to impose a legal order and bind the people to it.[171] As to this, we share Joseph A. Schumpeter's view rejecting the classical doctrine of political representation as the realisation by the elected of the views of those who elect[172] and drawing attention to the legitimising importance of elections. Through regularly held elections, citizens identify those whom they legitimise to make political decisions,[173] without much influence on what follows from this decision-making and what the motives of the representatives are. Despite the democratic ornamentation, Kaare Strøm's arguments about the sovereign's delegation of power to their representatives and the empowerment of others to make public policy decisions on their behalf, binding on them, boil down to the same point.[174]

171 Edward Rubin, "The Myth of Non-Bureaucratic Accountability and the Anti-Administrative Impulse", in *Public Accountability, Designs, Dilemmas and Experiences*, ed. Michael W. Dowdle (Cambridge: Cambridge University Press, 2006), 52–82 at 68.

172 Joseph A. Schumpeter, *Capitalism, Socialism and Democracy* (London: Routledge, 2003), 250 et seq.

173 Schumpeter, 269 et seq.

174 Strøm, 118.

3 Regulatory impact assessment *ex post* as an accountability instrument

Why does it fail to work?

Introduction

In the previous chapter, we demonstrated the illusory nature of accountability in the electoral act. This raises the question as to whether it is at all possible to take an account of the legislative act and evaluate it under conditions that guarantee objectivity and reliability. Theoretically, this ought to be the core of the process of accountability of the exercise of power, and thus the essence of democratic politics. The primary responsibility of the legislator is that the law enacted by him produces the intended social and economic effects: consciously and deliberately conceived situations and relations between people. The public debate is filled with predictions and speculations as to what effects a new regulation produces, particularly one that stirs strong emotions or high hopes, or is pompously adopted as part of fulfilling campaign promises. However, there are numerous examples of regulations producing effects if not counterproductive, at least certainly not intended by the legislator, while a closer and more critical analysis of the effects of a number of legal regulations leads to the general conclusion that people tend to perceive the objectives of legal norms and adapt their situation to them differently from what the legislator would have preferred. Consequently, there is a serious need to report on what effects the law has actually produced, whether they are the same as the effects it was supposed to produce, and then to evaluate both those effects and the law, using reliable criteria and an objective method.

How to hold the legislator accountable not just for his or her intentions and declarations, lest the assessment of the actions of the parliament or the government be based on random and subjective data, political accusations and stories of mutual malice expressed by the opposition and the ruling majority? How to take the account and assess it, based on reliable data, to hold the legislator accountable for what has actually been achieved by the law passed: have the acts of power enacted fulfilled their purpose, and what costs, risks and side effects are involved? Is such an account and subsequent analysis even possible? In order to answer this question in the affirmative, it is essential to find instruments to receive such an account free from the rhetoric of political struggle and independent of the narrative used by the ruling majority. A report

DOI: 10.4324/9781003493419-3

on performance is always a particular kind of narrative; one that is subject to its own rules, its own logic and style, and the choice of content depends on the will of the author and serves a particular purpose. When it comes to the political game, this aim is always the maintenance or acquisition of power, and therefore to convince people of the rightness and legitimacy of the actions taken. So is it possible, by means of the instruments of scrutiny, to set free such an account from this narrative; in other words: to force the legislator to provide an objective and verifiable account of what has been done and what effects it has had? And if the evaluation of the reported effects of the law has been carried out by an external body, can it be treated as an assessment of the effects of the law carried out by the Principal?

It is a challenging, although feasible task, at least in theory. Once again, the consequences of this relationship are not of the utmost importance, that is, in what way the one who enacted the law will be rewarded or penalised; nor is it about sanctions in the form of the repeal of a law assessed negatively. Therefore, this does not constitute a mechanism for the review of constitutionality, and neither the Principal, nor its representative, acts as a veto player. What is significant, is the report on the operation of the law itself: an indication of the purposefulness of the material, social or political resources used as goods at the disposal of the legislator. What the regulation has produced in terms of intended and side effects, what the costs and burdens on the addressees are, what benefits in relation to the expected ones have been gained and whether the implementation itself does not cause problems that were previously downplayed. The literature further emphasises the link between evaluation in terms of the efficiency and appropriateness of the legal measures being applied and the implementation of the principle of proportionality: the use of optimal and therefore not too far-reaching legal measures to achieve the intended effects is, after all, a practical expression of this principle. Finally, evaluation also aims to improve the openness and transparency of law drafting and to learn from solutions previously developed.[1] An incorrect diagnosis is the root cause of an inaccurate prognosis. The key element is therefore giving an account, and reliability and transparency of it. That calls for repeatable practice, authoritative instruments and methods for its submission and reception that are verifiable.

Although from the point of view of the rationality of state decision-making processes the issue seems quite elementary, we must acknowledge that it has been only marginally recognised in constitutional law, either in practice or in theory. As a matter of fact, the existence of the system allowing for the assessment of legislative actions, i.e. the basic task of the legislature, as well as of the executive, which typically is the initiator of regulation, is rare, and if it does exist, it has been (used selectively) so only recently. We are referring

1 Anssi Keinänen, Kati Heikkinen and Laura Rinne, "Lainsäädännön Vaikutusten Jälkikäteinen Seuranta Osana Hyvää Lainvalmistelua: Entä Suomessa?", *Edilex* 15 (2019): 2, www.edilex.fi/artikkelit/19634.

here to the *ex post* Regulatory Impact Assessment (RIA), a specific instrument allowing for the evaluation of legislative acts. According to its premise, *ex post* evaluations of a law refer to the process of assessing the effectiveness and efficiency of regulations once they have entered into force.[2] They are undertaken to ascertain the extent to which the regulations have met their originally intended objectives, do not impose unnecessary costs on citizens and/or businesses and continue to provide positive outcome for the community. The accountability function is secondary here (as opposed to the election function); usually *ex post* evaluation is implemented for completely different reasons and done with a different perspective.[3] However, although neglected in decision-making processes, such *ex post* analysis has the potential to become a policy tool that not only allows for the scrutiny of the effects resulting from legislative action, but also for the transparency of the authorities' performance, permanently and systematically revealing the essence of regulation,[4] pure legislative power in action. We believe that this very instrument can be treated as a tool for assessing legislative actions, including their efficiency and expediency. At the same time, we put forward the claim that it is precisely for this reason that this instrument is so tenuously used in constitutional practice.

Actually, the idea of a reliable assessment of the law in force has virtually no opponents; absolutely everyone is inclined to recognise that legal regulations, the inflation of which has long since exceeded (both at national and European level) the limits of perception of their addressees (both citizens and those specialised in particular areas of legal relations), require all the more reliable an analysis of their actual effects. At the same time, the plurality of interests of the stakeholders of legal regulations needs to be taken into account. Legal solutions have different implications for different addressees. Those ineffective or unfavourable for large social groups or for individual groups may at the same time prove beneficial for certain addressees, who have no legal interest in having the effects of the regulation reviewed.

It is rather difficult to identify satisfactory methods and instruments for conducting reliable studies of the efficiency of legal regulations, both because of the reluctance of the current parliamentary majority, sceptical of attempts aimed at verifying their actions, as well as for purely practical reasons. Regulatory impact assessment has taken a formalised form fairly recently and

2 OECD Recommendation of the Council on Regulatory Policy and Governance 2012, 26, https://www.oecd.org/gov/regulatory-policy/49990817.pdf.

3 In line with the OECD position, the primary objective is to improve the law; however, *ex post* evaluation may be instrumental in increasing transparency and accountability for regulatory outcomes and thus confidence in government action. OECD, "Ex Post Evaluation of Regulation", in *Government at a Glance 2017* (Paris: OECD Publishing, 2017), 166, doi: https://doi.org/10.1787/gov_glance-2017-57-en.

4 Bruno Eustaquio de Carvalho, Rui Cunha Marques and Oscar Cordeiro Netto, "Regulatory Impact Assessment (RIA): An Ex-Post Analysis of Water Services by the Legal Review in Portugal", *Water Resources Management* 32 (2018): 675–99, 676.

in just a handful of states. Regulatory impact assessments are used and analysed mainly at the preliminary stage of legislative work, i.e. they concern the *ex ante* stage. They are therefore a specific component of the methodology of law-making works, involving the determination of anticipated economic, social and legal consequences of proposed solutions.[5] It is a relatively new institution with a varied scope, which makes it difficult to compare its applications, regulations and effects.

The origins of such assessments can be traced back to practices undertaken in the United States in the 1970s. During this period, the US government appointed a number of agencies to address threats to the life, health and safety of citizens.[6] The so-called *Quality of Life Review* was also introduced at that time, to deal primarily with the initial calculation of the costs of adapting businesses to new environmental requirements. A few years later, analysis carried out in accordance with the rules applied in economics (*cost-benefit*) also began to apply to other regulations; in 1974, the *Inflation Impact Assessment* was introduced, which was an *ex ante* assessment of the expected impact of the new regulation's measures on the inflation rate. Such a procedure is considered a prototype for regulatory impact assessment in the United States.[7] In the 1980s, the task to analyse the effects regularly began to be carried out within the structure of the Office of Information and Regulatory Affairs (OIRA), which examines regulations drafted by federal agencies, and is additionally equipped with the power to suspend regulations until the proponent has prepared a satisfactorily thorough and reliable analysis of the benefits and costs of the regulation.[8] The American impact assessment model is considered a benchmark against the others, being a model that guarantees a substantive assessment and clear criteria for cost-benefit analysis, even though it is not free from criticism, regarding in particular the limitations of the adopted methodology. Canada followed the United States towards the end of 1970s. Australia, the United Kingdom and other European countries (Germany, Denmark, the Netherlands, some Scandinavian countries) first adopted RIA instruments in the 1980s.[9] One example of a country with a highly sophisticated and advanced regulatory assessment system is Denmark, where RIA has been practised since the 1980s. There, assessment was initially used for deregulation and

5 Marcin M. Wiszowaty, "Ocena skutków regulacji i procedury konsultacji publicznych w procesie legislacyjnym – analiza prawna", in *Tworzenie i konsultowanie rządowych projektów ustaw*, ed. Grażyna Kopińska et al. (Warsaw: Fundacja Stefana Batorego,2012), 42.

6 These are the institutions:
1) Environmental Protection Agency (EPA);
2) Occupational Safety and Health Administration (OSHA);
3) Consumer Product Safety Commission (CPSC).

7 Andrea Renda, *Impact Assessment in the EU. The State of the Art and the Art of the State* (Brussels: Centre for European Policy Studies, 2006), 9.

8 Renda, 14.

9 Carvalho, Marques and Netto, 115.

simplification in order to improve competitiveness and economic relations.[10] Currently, assessment is carried out there as part of the Better Regulation Strategy (Quality Reform), launched by the government in August 2007 to create a more efficient administration and simplify the regulatory framework, mainly through the cooperation of three bodies: the Coordination Committee, referred to as the "hub for the management of Better Regulation Policy", the Economic Committee and the Steering Group for Cross-National Initiatives (STS), which coordinates activities with local self-governments. Currently, two advisory bodies: Danish Business Forum for Better Regulation and the European Union (EU) Implementation Council were merged into the Danish Business Regulation Forum (DBRF) in 2019 by the secretariat in the Ministry of Industry, Business and Financial Affairs. It advises the government on the development and application of RIA methodologies, particularly with regard to business regulation. At the same time, it conducts in-depth reviews of regulations in various policy areas.[11]

By contrast, in the UK model, assessment began with the evaluation of bills presented for debate before Parliament during the time of Margaret Thatcher under the *Compliance Cost Assessment* (CCA) procedure, implemented as part of the *New Public Management* policy. Its reach, however, was largely limited to assessing the cost of administrative burdens on companies. A decade later, in 1996, the procedure finally took shape as a regulatory appraisal, under which not only the risks and burdens, but also the estimation of profits and the proposed regulation are assessed.[12] Since the Regulatory Reform Act came into force in April 2001, the regulations already in place, which are subject to committee scrutiny in both Houses of Parliament with a view to reducing burdens and increasing the efficiency of the legal system, are also being analysed from a similar angle.[13] Recent decades have seen a proliferation of the assessment practices, with the Better Regulation Task Force periodically preparing reports on the impact of regulation on the functioning of economic sectors.[14]

Some regularities are already noticeable in these two examples. Firstly, the evaluation agenda is either in the government or draws on government data,

10 Indicators of Regulatory Policy Governance Europe 2022, Denmark, 2.

11 OECD Regulatory Policy Outlook 2021, Denmark, available at: https://www.oecd-ilibrary.org/sites/76459155-en/index.html?itemId=/content/component/76459155-en.

12 The administration's deregulation unit (initially the Enterprise and Deregulation Unit in the Ministry of Employment, then the Deregulation Unit in the Department of Trade and Industry) was transformed in 2008 and equipped with functions relating to regulatory assessment, adopting the name *Regulatory Impact Unit* (RIU); within this office, a unit called the *Better Regulation Task Force* (BRTF) was also established as an independent expert group with a strong representation of business professionals as well as consumers, giving recommendations on legislation being drafted in ministries, particularly with a view to reducing the legislative burden. Renda, 26–8.

13 Renda, 32.

14 Justus Kirchhoff and Till Nikolka, "How Evidence-Based Is Regulatory Policy? A Comparison across OECD Governments", *ifo DICE Report* 15, no. 4 (2017).

which is hardly surprising as the government has an extensive bureaucratic apparatus competent to perform this type of task, closely related to the process of initiating legislation. Secondly – the genesis of assessment is related to the need for burden reduction and deregulation. Thirdly, the requirements for the assessment of regulations appeared primarily (and at times exclusively) in relation to the needs of business and competitiveness, taking on other spheres of regulatory impact only gradually and to varying extents.

The weight of impact assessment tools has also been recognised in the law and policy of the European Union and other international bodies. Since 2001, the European Commission has been working towards the introduction of improved regulation standards.[15] As David Keyaerts points out,[16] the assessment of compliance with the principles of proportionality and subsidiarity through impact analysis has already been made not only in documents and recommendations of EU bodies[17] but also in case law, in particular in judgments of the Court of Justice of the European Union – hence in the *Vodafone and others*[18] the consideration of the limits of proportionality of the measures applied was made by reference to the impact assessment of the European Commission.

A very strong drive towards the introduction of *ex post* assessment can be particularly observed in the activities of the Organisation for Economic Co-operation and Development (OECD).[19] According to OECD recommendations, *ex post* assessment should be explicitly and permanently incorporated as an integral part of the regulatory cycle, and reviews should include an assessment of the real outcomes of regulation against their underlying rationale and objectives, as well as include recommendations to address any deficiencies. Such an assessment of existing regulation must identify the extent to which the objectives of the regulation have been achieved in practice, including an assessment not only of the compliance costs, but also of other costs and benefits that relate to the primary objective of the regulation. The analysis of the effects of regulations in force is becoming an increasingly necessary complement to the assessment of proposed acts, leading to the evaluation and possible adjustment of the legal system with a view to creating a system of measures that

15 *Action Plan for Better Regulation* and communications from the European Commission, in particular the communication on impact assessment: *Impact Assessment* (COM(2002)276).

16 David Keyaerts, "The Impact of Better Regulation in the Case Law of the European Court of Justice", *European Journal of Risk Regulation* 3, no. 2 (2012), 241–7; David Keyaerts, "Ex Ante Evaluation of EU Legislation Intertwined with Judicial Review? Comment on Case C-58/08 Vodafone", *European Law Review* 6 (2010): 869–84 at 869.

17 Specifically, cf. "The Impact Assessment Guidelines" (Brussels: EU Commission, 2009), which prescribes the use of qualitative and quantitative arguments to justify EU legislative measures (5, 17, 29).

18 Case C-58/08, Vodafone and others, [2010] ECR 1-4999, §55ff.

19 See e.g. OECD, *Ex Post Assessment of Regulation: Practices and Lessons from OECD Countries* (Paris: OECD Publishing, 2018).

are adequate, consistent within the system and least intrusive into the legal situation of the addressees, significantly influencing the implementation of the legislative function,[20] but above all by limiting the side effects that appear during the application of the act. Let us therefore look more closely at how the assessment is implemented and what its effects are.

Overview – evolution and types of RIA *ex post*

The use of impact assessments varies in form and size across the Member States – the United Kingdom, France, the Netherlands and the Nordic countries (Denmark, Sweden, Finland) have already developed an extensive impact assessment system, while the southern European states (Italy, Spain, Portugal, Greece[21]) are making their first tentative attempts to implement such mechanisms. Germany, Austria and Poland, on the other hand, are somewhat ahead in these efforts – although it is difficult to speak of stabilised and effectively functioning *ex post* impact assessment systems.[22] A breakdown included in the *2015 OECD Government at Glance* report shows that *ex post* regulatory assessment[23] was carried out to varying extents in 17 countries, while in the following 17 it was entirely absent. Of the 16 countries where this instrument has been in use, only 6 reported that it is obligatory for all laws (these are Denmark, Hungary, Japan, Italy, the Netherlands, the United Kingdom) – as it turns out, however, this proves to be a bit of an overstatement as well. Six years later, as reported by the OECD, evaluations are required to assess whether the underlying policy goals have been achieved in only two European countries vis-à-vis primary laws and subordinate laws – these are the United Kingdom and Norway. In relation to primary laws – in the Netherlands,[24] and for certain regulations – Denmark, Estonia, France, Germany, Italy, Latvia, the Netherlands, Poland, Slovenia, Spain. This type of evaluation is also carried

20 Iwona Małajny, "Pojęcie kontroli parlamentarnej", in *Ustroje. Tradycje i porównania. Anniversary Book Dedicated to Prof. Dr. Marian Grzybowski on His 70th Birthday*, ed. Piotr Mikuli et al. (Warsaw: Wydawnictwo Sejmowe, 2015), 544.

21 According to the 2021 OECD report, some mechanisms were introduced to develop *ex post* evaluations in Greece. Ex post evaluations are planned to be conducted by a new body established by Law 4622, the Special Secretariat for Monitoring and Evaluation of the Government Programme. The relevant guidebook and template was published in 2021. OECD Regulatory Policy Outlook 2021, https://www.oecd-ilibrary.org/sites/3022a272-en/index.html?itemId=/content/component/3022a272-en.

22 Renda, 113–15.

23 Hereafter referred to as Regulatory Impact Analysis (instead of Regulatory Impact Assessment, which is done *ex ante*). For terminological notes – see Koen van Aeken, "From Vision to Reality: Ex Post Evaluation of Legislation", *Legisprudence* 5 (2011): 41–68 at 51.

24 Interestingly, the 2018 OECD compilation shows that such evaluations are mandatory and periodically carried out by Austria, Germany and Hungary, as well as Italy and the United Kingdom. OECD 2019, table 4.1, https://www.oecd-ilibrary.org/sites/8f45245f-en/index.html?itemId=/content/component/8f45245f-en.

out with regard to regulations laid down in the EU.[25] It has already become apparent from OECD data that most OECD countries have yet to establish a comprehensive *ex post* evaluation methodology, since the vast majority lack a compulsory and rigorous system of such assessment.

Comparisons of impact assessments across different legal orders face considerable difficulties due to the peculiarities of law-making activities, customs and experience, as well as the relatively scanty normative body of written material on RIA. Differences also concern the very understanding of RIA: whether the issue concerns the entirety of the effects related to a given regulation in their impact on different social groups or – prevailing in practice – narrowly understood effects, reduced to economic or regulatory issues. It can be observed, however, that the idea of introducing an analysis of regulations appeared in the abovementioned examples of countries as an offshoot of impact assessments of proposed regulations, which in turn were related to the policy of deregulation and reduction of bureaucratic burdens and simplification of the legal environment, especially for business entities, that was being introduced. Certain features of these analyses, considered by critics to be its serious deficits, are also related to this; the objections focus primarily on economic methods and evaluation criteria, disregarding other relevant objectives and effects, not measurable in the assessment of gains and losses – such as security, social objectives and equity.[26] This effect of *ex post* assessments is closely linked to their context and origins – it is usually carried out based on deregulatory criteria, from the point of view of entrepreneurs and their legal and social environment and especially on economic impacts.

Two types of regulatory impact assessment can be distinguished. The first is the post-implementation review (PIR), which examines any policy that has undergone an impact assessment and revisits the underlying policy assumptions to verify their validity and relevance. It is conducted usually three to five years after the policy has been implemented. The task of the PIR is to determine whether the chosen policy delivers the desired results; whether the costs and benefits are in line with expectations; and to refine the techniques used to assess the impact of policy interventions. The other form is the post-legislative scrutiny (PLS), which reviews how primary legislation is performing in practice. It serves as a preliminary review of the effectiveness of the legislation, focusing on whether the legislation works in real life.[27] It means a one-time, analytical evaluation concentrating on the key impacts of an action (e.g. legislation), following a checklist, including a comparison of the costs with the

25 OECD, "Ex Post Evaluation", in *Government at a Glance 2015* (Paris: OECD Publishing, 2015), doi: https://doi.org/10.1787/gov_glance-2015-en.

26 With regard to the British system – Renda, 41; with regard to the EU system – Renda, 107.

27 Franklin De Vrieze and Victoria Hasson, *Post-Legislative Scrutiny. Comparative Study of Practices of Post-Legislative Scrutiny in Selected Parliaments and the Rationale for Its Place in Democracy Assistance* (London: Westminster Foundation for Democracy, 2017), 14.

actual benefits and determining the distribution of costs and benefits, against the one projected by the *ex ante* evaluation.

Post-implementation reviews are much more common and are usually conducted by government agencies or bodies appointed by the government to make such assessments. In Australia, for example, the *ex post* evaluation is carried out in accordance with guidelines developed by the Office of Impact Analysis (OIA),[28] a post-implementation review is mandatory if:

- OIA has assessed the proposal as having a substantial or widespread economic impact;
- A Regulatory Impact Statement (RIS),[29] which was subject to final assessment by the OIA for the regulatory change, had not been prepared for final decision and the change was neither minor nor machinery in nature;
- A regulatory change was granted a Prime Minister's exemption from the need to prepare a RIS.[30]

In the United Kingdom, a number of *ex post* evaluation procedures have been developed over time and can be classified as both post-implementation review and post-legislative scrutiny. The requirement for government departments to complete a PIR can be embedded in a statutory review clause or in an administrative obligation to conduct a review. The statutory review is usually completed within five years of the regulatory measure coming into force, and then on a recurring five-year cycle thereafter.[31] To support *ex post* evaluation, the ministries have appointed so-called Better Regulation Units.[32] The Regulatory Policy Committee (RPC), an independent expert body, is responsible for scrutinising the evidence and analyses supporting new regulatory proposals in the

28 Formerly, until November 2022 the Office of Best Practice Regulation (OBPR). This body is responsible for gathering information and consulting stakeholders both during and after implementation. The evaluations completed in the ministries are forwarded to the OIA for review.

29 Every government proposal for regulation must be accompanied by the RIS (Regulatory Impact Statement) addressing the objectives and need for regulation, alternative options, gains and costs, and consultation. See: *Australian Government Guide to Regulatory Impact Analysis* 2020, https://oia.pmc.gov.au/sites/default/files/2021-06/australian-government-guide-to-regulatory-impact-analysis.pdf.

30 "Post-implementation Reviews. Guidance Note", March 2020, Australian Government, Department of Prime Minister, https://oia.pmc.gov.au/sites/default/files/2021-09/post-implementation-reviews.pdf.

31 "Producing Post-implementation Reviews: Principles of Best Practice", Updated 6 August 2021, https://www.gov.uk/government/publications/business-regulation-producing-post-implementation-reviews/producing-post-implementation-reviews-principles-of-best-practice.

32 "Better Regulation Framework Interim Guidance" (London: Department for Business, Energy and Industrial Strategy, 2020), 6, available at: https://assets.publishing.service.gov.uk/government/uploads/system/uploads/attachment_data/file/916918/better-regulation-guidance.pdf.

RIAs, as well as for verifying the quality of *ex post* evaluations of legislation. In turn, the National Audit Office reports on the effectiveness of the regulatory policy framework as a whole by conducting value-for-money studies. The assessments are sent to the Government's Sub-Committee on Reductive Regulations and a post-evaluation report is presented as a Command Paper before the competent parliamentary committee on whose final assessment is published. The scope focuses primarily on the UK business impact.[33] UK government departments conduct post-implementation reviews, with a particular focus on all measures affecting business following the introduction of the Small Business, Enterprise and Employment Act 2015. The government also established the Business Impact Target programme and the Cutting Red Tape reviews programme to reduce regulatory costs for businesses.

Meanwhile, when it comes to post-legislative scrutiny, such an assessment was formally introduced in the United Kingdom in March 2008 as a supplementary and more systematic procedure for assessing the functioning of an act within the legal system.[34] Post-legislative scrutiny is defined by the Law Commission of England and Wales as: "A broad form of review, the purpose of which is to address the effects of legislation in terms of whether intended policy objectives have been met by the legislation and, if so, how effectively".[35] It may apply to all public laws; after three to five years from the entry into force of the law, the relevant ministry prepares an initial assessment of how the law is performing in practice, especially an assessment of the achievement of the objectives that motivated its enactment. A post-legislative scrutiny Memorandum is published by the competent Department and is submitted to the relevant House of Commons Select Committee that decides whether further inquiry is needed. Other Committees may also take an interest;[36] in the House of Lords, it can be undertaken by *ad hoc* committees.

The Committee that reviews the Memorandum may decide whether further scrutiny or inquiry is needed and determines the body that should carry out other reviews, collecting data or the involvement of external experts. The Commons committees may decide also to conduct further PLS.[37] What is

33 Precisely: Trade and Investment Impacts, Commitments under Free Trade Agreements, International Impacts and Regulatory Cooperation, "Retained EU legislation", Small and Micro Businesses, Assessment of compliance and enforcement, Market structure impacts and Innovation Impacts, available at: https://www.gov.uk/government/publications/business-regulation-producing-post-implementation-reviews/producing-post-implementation-reviews-principles-of-best-practice.

34 Lydia Clapinska, "Post-Legislative Scrutiny of Acts of Parliament"," *Commonwealth Law Bulletin* 32, no. 2 (2006): 191–204, at 192; Anna Michalak, "Kontrola post-legislacyjna w Westminsterze", *Przegląd Prawa Konstytucyjnego* 5 (2018): 11–30, at 19.

35 After: Tom Caygill, "Post-Legislative Scrutiny in the UK Parliament", *The Post-Legislative Scrutiny Series no. 1*, Nottingham Trent University. November 2021, 7.

36 Caygill, 14.

37 Such studies are taking place – for instance, the post-legislative scrutiny of The Gambling Act 2005 where the committee examined the effects and effectiveness of the introduced solutions,

important, however, is that the scrutiny is entirely in the hands of MPs; as the authors of the Comparative Study note: "There is freedom for all Committees, in both the House of Commons and the House of Lords, to conduct Post-Legislative Scrutiny work". In the House of Commons scrutiny is occasional, while in the House of Lords it is limited yet consistent. However, it is not extensive in either case.[38] Between 2008 and 2019, 23 PLS inquiries took place in the UK Parliament. Fourteen were initiated in the House of Commons, eight in the House of Lords and one was carried by a joint committee of both Houses[39].

Since 2016, in Ireland, under Standing Orders of Parliament, the Minister responsible for implementing a law must present an *ex post* assessment of its operation within a year. Certain sector departments have also begun to review individual regulations, which is required at least once every seven years, under the 2013 Policy Statement on Economic Regulation. Evaluation is entrusted to ministries, in particular the Department of the Taoiseach (Prime Minister) and the Department of Public Expenditure and Reform (DPER). As can be seen from this procedure, therefore, evaluation in Ireland operates only as a variant of PIR and only insofar as it relates to business.

Having watched the UK system, it is justifiable to conclude that *ex post* evaluation in practice takes the form of yet another instrument of control of the government. It is quite clear in the case of PIR, since it is the government that is responsible for the implementation and execution of the law passed by parliament. On the other hand, although PLS – if exercised – concerns the content and efficiency and efficacy of the regulation, it is done by receiving and assessing a report from the government (departments) – such *ex post* evaluation in the United Kingdom is explicitly recognised in the literature as

---

the financial impact of the Act on the activities of entrepreneurs in this service sector, the effectiveness of the Gambling Commission established by the Act. To this end, the House of Commons committee interviewed 49 witnesses, collected a large number of expert reports, visited places where gambling is deregulated (Australía, Macau), among others. Finally, it presented a very comprehensive report urging the government to take a number of measures. Michalak, 23–4. Report: House of Commons Culture, Media and Sport Committee, "The Gambling Act 2005: A Bet Worth Taking?", First Report of Session 2012–13, www.parliament.uk (accessed 22.05.2017).

38 Franklin De Vrieze and Philip Norton, "The Significance of Post-Legislative Scrutiny", *Journal of Legislative Studies* 26, no. 3 (2020): 349–61, at: https://www.tandfonline.com/doi/full/10.1080/13572334.2020.1780008.

39 Available at:https://www.wfd.org/sites/default/files/2021-12/2021-10-18-PLS-in-the-UK-Parliament-Dr-Thomas-Caygill-FINAL.pdf.

one form of parliamentary oversight of the government,[40] but it needs to be acknowledged that it continues to perform rather disappointingly.[41]

Looking closer at French evaluation might prompt a similar remark. In France, during the constitutional reform of 23 July 2008, the impact assessment procedure was given constitutional status; parliament was granted the right to evaluate public policies under Article 24 of the Constitution,[42] and therefore post-legislative scrutiny, having appeared in practice earlier, has become virtually a systemic element.[43] This task is entrusted in the first instance to the parliament's standing committees, which assess public policies (Article 51-2 in conjunction with Article 24 of the Constitution).[44] The procedure and the body that conducts it indicate that it is in fact an assessment of implementation – the pursuit of policy, and therefore an instrument of scrutiny of the government, much less of the law itself. Thus, the parliament is not so much assessing itself, whether it has enacted a good law, but rather whether the law enacted by the parliament has been correctly implemented by the government; correctly meaning in accordance with the applicable legislation. The scrutiny is carried out in the following way: six months after the law enters into force, the implementation of which requires secondary legislation, two MPs (one of whom is from the opposition party and the other acts as rapporteur for the bill) report to a parliamentary committee on the implementation of the law's entry into force. Standing committees may also refer to the so-called impact studies (*les études d'impact*) that are appended to bills, and request any information necessary in the process of assessing the application of the law from the ministry. It is therefore an implementation control – PIR, not a post-legislative scrutiny – and an instrument for parliamentary scrutiny of the executive by examining the implementation of laws, not their content. It should be added that evaluations are also carried out by specialised parliamentary bodies, including the Committee for Monitoring and Evaluation of

40 Michalak, 25: Franklin De Vrieze and Victoria Hasson, *Post-Legislative Scrutiny: Comparative Study of Practices of Post-Legislative Scrutiny in Selected Parliaments and the Rationale for Its Place in Democracy Assistance* (London: Westminster Foundation for Democracy 2017), 15 (available at:https://www.wfd.org/what-we-do/resources/comparative-study-post-legislative-scrutiny).

41 More on deficits: Tom Caygill, "The UK Post-Legislative Scrutiny Gap", *Journal of Legislative Studies* 26, no. 1 (2020): 387–404.

42 Art. 10 Loi constitutionnelle no. 2008–724 du 23 juillet 2008 de modernisation des institutions de la V-ème République, "Journal Officiel de la République Française", 0171 of 24 July 2008.

43 Jarosław Szymanek, "Francuski model parlamentarnej kontroli polegislacyjnej", *Przegląd Prawa Konstytucyjnego* 3 (2018): 77–102. Cited there: Jacque Chevallier, "L'évaluation légslative: un enjeu politique", in *Contrôle parlementaire et évaluation*, ed. Alain Delcamp, Jean.-Louis Bergel and Alain Dupas (Paris: Institut national du service public, 1995), 15.

44 Szymanek, 84. Cited there: Pauline Türk, *Le contrôle parlementaire en France*, LGDJ 2011, 145 et seq.; Pauline Türk, *Les commissions permanentes et le renouveau du Parlement* (Paris: Dalloz, 2005), 83.

Public Policies (CEC – *Comité d'évaluation et de contrôle des politiques publiques*), which assesses the implementation of public policies that go beyond the powers of a single standing committee of the chamber, MEC (*Mission d'évaluation et de contrôle*) – a body within the National Assembly's finance committee responsible for assessing the impact of implementing certain public policies, and MECSS (*Mission d'évaluation et de contrôle des lois de financement de la sécurité sociale*) – a body set up by the Social Affairs Committee of the National Assembly and the Senate, which assesses and supervises social security financing acts. However, this complex and dispersed system of parliamentary control is rather limited in scope and consequences. Insofar as it is implemented, it is again a tool for controlling the executive, and to a very limited extent, it does, however, monitor the work of parliament itself in terms of its legislative function. The law-monitoring function is in fact implemented according to the political demand.[45]

In Switzerland, the analysis of the functioning of a regulation was also given constitutional status in 2000; according to Article 170 the Federal Assembly shall ensure that federal measures are evaluated with regard to their effectiveness. Switzerland also reformed its regulatory policy framework in 2019, when the Federal Council implemented new directives on regulatory impact assessment. All regulations have to undergo a preliminary RIA to check whether a regulation should be subject to a simplified or full RIA. The State Secretariat for Economic Affairs (SECO) operating within the Federal Department of

45 For example, there is no indication that any of these bodies carried out a preliminary evaluation of the draft reform on the retirement age (raising it from 62 to 64), which triggered an unprecedented wave of mass protests and great outrage also in legal circles in the spring of 2023 – the reform was introduced under the procedure set out in Article 49.3 of the Constitution of the Fifth Republic. According to this: "The Prime Minister may, after deliberation by the Council of Ministers, make the passing of a Finance Bill or Social Security Financing Bill an issue of a vote of confidence before the National Assembly. In that event, the Bill shall be considered passed unless a resolution of no-confidence, tabled within the subsequent twenty-four hours, is carried as provided for in the foregoing paragraph. In addition, the Prime Minister may use the said procedure for one other Government or Private Members' Bill per session. The Prime Minister may ask the Senate to approve a statement of general policy".

This way, one of the issues of key importance for the functioning of members of society, i.e. the issue of their benefits on the basis of having earned a certain length of service or having reached the retirement age, was decided not only without evaluation, but outside the approval of the National Assembly at all – following the rejection of referendum proposals on the issue in the National Assembly (6 February) and the Senate (6 March). This is a prime example of the subordination of political mechanisms to political realities: mechanisms are designed, but they only work when whoever makes the decision is willing to use them. In this case, President Macron and Prime Minister Élisabeth Borne had no such desire.

In contrast, such evaluations of the state of social security in France had taken place before – for example, in 2015, an extensive report and discussion in the Senate (see: session extraordinaire de 2014–2015 No 624, Enregistré à la Présidence du Sénat le 15 juillet 2015, rapport d'information fait au nom de la mission d'évaluation et de contrôle de la sécurité sociale (1) et de la commission des affaires sociales (2) sur la situation du régime de retraites par M. Gérard Roche, https://www.senat.fr/rap/r14-624/r14-6241.pdf).

Economic Affairs, Education and Research is responsible for guidelines on conducting RIAs, reviewing selected RIAs and reporting on the level of regulatory costs and the results of surveys on business perceptions of administrative burdens. The Federal Office of Justice and the Legal and Central Language Services of the Federal Chancellery are responsible for scrutinising the legal quality of draft regulations and providing advice on stakeholder engagement – including on *ex post* evaluations. Although the requirement for policy evaluation is enshrined in the Swiss Constitution, according to the OECD's Regulatory Outlook 2021 report,[46] *ex post* evaluation of regulations is mandatory only for certain regulations and there are no standardised evaluation techniques to be used when conducting evaluations.

Similarly, the *ex post* RIA in Belgium has been conducted irregularly and in a fragmented manner; although a joint committee of both chambers of the federal parliament was set up in 2007 to evaluate legislation *ex post*, the work of this body failed to resume after the 2014 elections, mostly due to a dispute over the participation of the Senate committee in the proceedings of this body.[47] As the OECD report indicates:

> Belgium has not improved its institutional and policy framework for regulatory quality at the federal level over the last years. (…) Periodic ex post review of legislation is mandatory for some legislation and sunsetting clauses are sometimes used. The Court of Audit is involved in undertaking ad hoc "in-depth" reviews on specific regulatory areas such as agriculture, energy or youth.[48]

In Flanders, on the other hand, *ex post* analysis is carried out by one particular department within the state administration.

A completely different solution was adopted in Germany. The Committee of State Secretaries of Germany introduced a systematic *ex post* evaluation procedure in 2013 under its programme to reduce bureaucracy; it was decided that within three to five years of the entry into force of regulations whose annual cost of applicability exceeds one million Euros, an evaluation of the achievement of its objectives and the most important consequences, i.e. efficiency and effectiveness, should be carried out. Carrying it out is left to the discretion of the competent ministry. The report is forwarded to the Federal Government Coordinator for Bureaucracy Reduction and Better Regulation and the National Regulatory Control Council. The *ex post* evaluation instrument is therefore primarily used (just like the German RIA *ex ante*) to reduce

46 https://www.oecd-ilibrary.org/sites/c2a2e50a-en/index.html?itemId=/content/component/c2a2e50a-en.

47 Michalak, 26.

48 OECD Regulatory Policy Outlook 2021, https://www.oecd-ilibrary.org/sites/32067bc3-en/index.html?itemId=/content/component/32067bc3-en.

bureaucracy and burdens on entrepreneurs (in 2015 SME-test guidelines and the One-In, One-Out rule were introduced). Still, there are no data on ongoing, methodical studies of legal regulations. Furthermore – the procedure involves only government action and is therefore a self-monitoring process, and the external body comes in the form of the National Regulatory Control Council, established in 2006 as a one-arm's-length body, which reviews the quality of RIAs and is responsible for burden reduction and administrative simplification.[49] New requirements for *ex post* evaluations were introduced by the government in 2019. But the process of analysis is conducted selectively and practically excludes the participation of the federal parliament,[50] as well as a broader, systemic assessment of the content of existing regulations.

Similarly, *ex post* evaluations in Italy have become more common and transparent recently. Italy also introduced new guidelines for *ex post* evaluations and RIAs in 2018, but these are of a non-binding nature. The Department of Legal and Legislative Affairs (DAGL) under the Presidency of the Council of Ministers is responsible for quality reviews of *ex post* evaluations prepared by ministries.[51] DAGL also approves planned *ex post* evaluations to be carried out by ministries, provides technical guidance and reports annually to parliament on regulatory quality tools. It is supported by the Impact Assessment Independent Unit (Nucleo AIR), which is composed of external experts serving a four-year term. However, as reported in the OECD document, there are numerous gaps in the system: many RIAs lack sufficient quantification of impacts and the number of people affected, so the evidence they are based on is not of the best quality. There are no tools to ensure that *ex post* evaluations do indeed always proceed as planned in practice, consultation processes are not regular and consistent, with more systematic incorporation and consideration of feedback from consultations.[52]

The practice of assessments in Poland is progressing in a similar direction, albeit extremely anaemically – here, too, evaluations are initiated by members of the government and within it. *Ex post* evaluations, which were introduced in 2014 by the Rules of Procedure of the Council of Ministers,[53] shall be made

49 https://www.normenkontrollrat.bund.de/Webs/NKR/DE/der-nkr/aufgabe/aufgabe_node.html.

50 Except Parliamentary Advisory Council on Sustainable Development which reviews RIAs from the sustainability perspective. Germany. Overview and recent developments, OECD 2022, https://www.oecd.org/gov/regulatory-policy/Germany-country-profile-EU-report-2022.pdf.

51 Italy. OECD Regulatory Policy Outlook 2018, 202, available at: https://www.oecd.org/gov/regulatory-policy/italy-country-note-regulatory-policy-2018.pdf.

52 Italy. OECD Regulatory Policy Outlook 2021, https://www.oecd-ilibrary.org/sites/51192a94-en/index.html?itemId=/content/component/51192a94-en.

53 See Resolution No. 190 of the Council of Ministers of 29 October 2013. – Rules of Procedure of the Council of Ministers (official gazette *Monitor Polski* of 2013, item 979).

by the minister responsible for the matters regulated by the act in question,[54] when requested by a member of the governmental or the SME Envoy or the Centre for Strategic Analysis; it may concern a normative act or parts thereof.[55] Practice is negligible: for five years, between 2014 and 2019, 13 *ex post* impact assessments were published, 121 of which are laws, which means that this instrument is used sporadically and typically for reasons related to the fiscal impact of regulations. For comparison, only in the 8th term (2015–19) the parliament passed 923 laws.[56] What is more, such assessments are not carried out on a periodic basis.[57]

Although the Nordic countries are renowned for implementing extensive evaluation systems, *ex post* legislative assessment is also fragmented there. In Sweden, despite the fact that *ex ante* evaluation is mandatory, and the Swedish Council for Better Regulation is tasked with reviewing the quality of impact assessments of legislative proposals, *ex post* assessments are not obligatory. They are carried out on an *ad hoc* basis by a ministry, government agency or a committee of inquiry when these bodies decide that assessments are required. Individuals or interest groups can suggest evaluations by submitting a request to the relevant ministry or government agency.[58]

In Estonia, where, according to a domestic report published by the OECD, *ex post* evaluation has been mandatory for certain regulations since 2012 (although first evaluations were conducted in 2018), the regulatory oversight procedure is in place within the Legislative Quality Division of the Ministry of Justice, which plays the central role in regulatory oversight in the country. Each year, the Minister of Justice presents a report to parliament on the application of Better Regulation principles, including the compliance of RIAs and stakeholder engagement practices with formal requirements. In general, *ex post* assessments have addressed issues of competition, administrative burden and regulatory overlap. The publication of evaluations remains the responsibility of the relevant minister.[59]

54 See § 152(1) of Resolution No. 190 of the Council of Ministers of 29 October 2013. – Rules of Procedure of the Council of Ministers (M.P. of 2016, item 1006, as amended).

55 See § 152(3) of Resolution No. 190 of the Council of Ministers of 29 October 2013. – Rules of Procedure of the Council of Ministers (M.P. of 2016, item 1006, as amended).

56 https://www.sejm.gov.pl/sejm8.nsf/page.xsp/prace_sejmu (available 5 June 2023).

57 On the need for periodic impact assessments: Por. Janusz Paczocha and Wojciech Rogowski, "Ocena skutków przepisów a perspektywa wdrożenia reformy regulacji", in *Ocena skutków regulacji – poradnik OSR, doświadczenia, perspektywy*, ed. Włodzimierz Szpringer and Wojciech Rogowski (Warsaw: C.H. Beck, 2007), 197–9.

58 Sweden. Overview and recent developments, *OECD Indicators of Regulatory Policy and Governance* 2022, https://www.oecd.org/gov/regulatory-policy/Sweden-country-profile-EU-report-2022.pdf.

59 Estonia. Overview and recent developments, OECD Regulatory Policy Outlook 2021, at: https://www.oecd-ilibrary.org/sites/06899687-en/index.html?itemId=/content/component/06899687-en.

Some countries have separate institutions performing RIAs and RIAs *ex post*. For example, in Denmark, *ex post* evaluation is done in certain policy areas only, especially with regard to business regulation and the overlapping of local, regional and federal regulations. The Danish Business Forum conducts periodic in-depth reviews of regulations, marked as having a significant impact. There is also a special independent advisory body: Danish Business Regulation Forum, which is committed to reviewing existing regulations;[60] it cooperates with the government on the RIA's methodology, the implementation of EU law and, at the Minister for Industry, Business and Financial Affairs' request, looks into specific areas in which the rules are perceived as unnecessarily burdensome or where the dialogue between businesses and public authorities is needed. What is noticeable, therefore, is the considerably limited scope of the evaluations carried out and the particular perspective in which they are prepared. The evaluation includes a compulsory analysis of legislation in several areas of impact: on competition law, the environment and relations with the European Union.

The situation is quite similar in Norway. The Norwegian Better Regulation Council is an independent body under the Ministry of Trade, Industry and Fisheries. Its aim is to contribute to the reduction of the regulatory burden on businesses and overall more efficient regulation by issuing advisory statements to proposals for new regulation of the business sector at the stage of public consultation. The Council serves as a body that influences the reduction of burdens on business and facilitates the implementation and application of the law,[61] but it is a very narrowly defined scope and a very specific group of stakeholders.

As in the other countries mentioned here, also in Finland there is a strong emphasis on the development of impact assessments when drafting an act.[62] The Finnish Council for Regulatory Impact Analysis (FCRIA), an independent body established in 2007, reviews selected RIAs (based on relevance and representativeness) before the final version of the regulation is approved and provides advice as well as a formal opinion on the quality of the RIA; that being said, the FCRIA's assessments have no sanctioning power. In terms of *ex post* evaluation, the Council also has a mandate to review *ex post* evaluations done by other bodies, but has never taken this opportunity. The *ex post* evaluation process is neither complete nor sufficient.[63] As was declared

60 See: Denmark. Overview and recent developments in: OECD Regulatory Policy Outlook 2021, https://doi.org/10.1787/38b0fdb1-en.

61 https://regelradet.no/nbrc/.

62 Parliament's website: http://lainvalmistelu.finlex.fi/en/2b-perusvalmistelu-valmisteluelin/#esittely.

63 Anssi Keinänen, A study on the subject for the parliament, https://www.eduskunta.fi/FI/naineduskuntatoimii/julkaisut/Documents/trvj_1+2020.pdf. Author writes: based on the guidelines, one gets the impression that subsequent impact monitoring is not actually an integral part of the law-making process (9).

in an extensive and thoroughly insightful report by Anssi Keinänen, there are numerous shortcomings of the *ex post* evaluation system in Finland; among others the Council should be given more powers to express the requirements for impact assessments, be more involved in the preparatory stage, planning and steering the impact assessments carried out in the course of the project. The Council's analyses are not binding on ministries.[64] Furthermore, only a third of government evaluation proposals specify a deadline for their implementation, and equally rarely does it specify a catalogue of elements to be evaluated.[65] Current guidelines (the Impact Assessment Guidelines) are still too generic to be of much use when working on the implementation of *ex post* evaluations: who is to do them, what should be examined, when and how. They also provide little indication of the necessity to use external data (outside the ministries, expert opinions),[66] and data are treated in significantly different way within particular regulatory areas. The differences are triggered by political impulses and simply produce different results; for political reasons, the solutions proposed by *ex post* evaluations may not be implemented in practice. The Finnish Council also stresses the need to clearly define the objectives of the regulation,[67] to plan the *ex post* evaluation activities carefully, to eliminate the inadequacy of certain metrics and the narrow scope of the evaluations, as well as to improve the checklist of issues that should be taken into consideration when preparing *ex post* evaluation reports.[68]

In many countries *ex post* evaluation is carried out by dedicated bodies. Such a model has been adopted in the Netherlands; both *ex ante* and *ex post* evaluation are conducted partly by the body established in 2000, called Actal (The Dutch Advisory Board on Administrative Burden, since 2017 – ATR – the Dutch Advisory Board on Regulatory Burden). The Board acts as an independent and external advisory body to the government and parliament,[69] it

64 Keinänen, 17.

65 As Keinänen points out, in total, only six government proposals (7% of proposals where monitoring is mentioned and 2% of all government proposals submitted in 2016) included all the elements related to monitoring in the study. In other words, they clarified what is being monitored, what entity is being monitored, what schedule is used for monitoring and what information the monitoring has to be based on.

66 Anssi Keinänen and Jusssi Pajuoja, "Miten Vaikutusten Arviointia Voitaisiin Parantaa? Vaikutusarviointi Ja Sen kehittämistarpeet suomalaisessa lainvalmistelussa", *Eduskunnan tarkastusvaliokunnan julkaisu* 1 (2020): 15–17, https://www.eduskunta.fi/FI/naineduskuntatoimii/julkaisut/Documents/trvj_1+2020.pdf.

67 https://julkaisut.valtioneuvosto.fi/bitstream/handle/10024/164159/VNK_2022_15.pdf?sequence=1&isAllowed=y, 30.

68 https://julkaisut.valtioneuvosto.fi/bitstream/handle/10024/164159/VNK_2022_15.pdf?sequence=1&isAllowed=y, 31. Also: Kati Rantala et al., *Lakien toimivuuden seuranta ja jälkiarviointi Nykytilan kuvauksesta kehittämisehdotuksiin* (*Ex-post Evaluation of Regulation State-of-the-Art Analysis and Recommendations: Publications of the Government's Analysis, Assessment and Research Activities* 2021: 28), https://julkaisut.valtioneuvosto.fi/bitstream/handle/10024/163043/VNTEAS_2021_28.pdf?sequence=1&isAllowed=y.

69 ACTAL currently operates on the basis of Instellingsbesluit Actal 2011 of 16 June 2011.

makes recommendations to the government and parliament on how to reduce the regulatory burden. It is composed of a chairperson and just three members, appointed from among legislative experts, in particular academics and economic or political representatives. ATR does not carry out evaluations, but only monitors the *ex ante* analysis of regulatory burdens made in the relevant government departments.[70] In turn, the ATR advises ministries on the quality of the burden assessment during the elaboration of the proposal and may recommend improvements to the assessment if it is deemed inadequate. Following approval by the Cabinet, the Council of State issues a formal opinion on the overall legal quality of the legislative proposal. Such an opinion is not binding, but means that the explanatory note needs to be reworked by the relevant ministry. However, the Council is primarily concerned with *ex ante* evaluation;[71] *ex post* analyses are primarily carried out in government departments, auditing particular areas of regulation. This evaluation is therefore dispersed across a number of organisational units, drawing on the instrument of the Better Regulation Initiative (Integraal Afwegingskader – IAK), a checklist-based analysis of regulatory and legislative proposals that combines existing requirements and instructions for *ex ante* impact assessment. The *ex post* assessment of regulatory effectiveness and efficiency now includes an assessment of regulatory burden and is complemented by reviews of administrative burdens and compliance costs in specific sectors. However, such assessment is carried out only in the context of processing new bills and amendments – not on a regular basis.

To sum up the rather complicated overview of the Dutch system, although the ATR is an independent body involved in the RIA process, it would be a bit of a stretch to call it the body responsible for *ex post* evaluation; instead, it is one of the advisory bodies, cooperating with governmental agencies, that does not engage in its own impact studies, but only examines the validity of the assessment already made, and *ex post* evaluation itself is carried out only on an *ad hoc* basis, in the event of changes to existing regulations.[72] It is fragmentary and of little relevance for assessing the quality of the law passed by the Dutch parliament.

The model of carrying out *ex post* analyses of regulations is therefore rather a complex and non-uniform one. However, it can be concluded that such evaluation in all the systems mentioned above is of a fragmentary nature and, in general, of little significance from the point of view of the effectiveness of the legal regulations enacted by parliaments. Particularly noteworthy is the

70 Mainly: IPAL within the Department of Finance, the Unit for Judicial Affairs and Better Regulation Policy in the Ministry of Justice and Security, and the Unit for Regulatory Reform and ICT-policy in the Ministry of Economic Affairs.

71 Renda, 63.

72 Interview with Suzanne van Melis, Strategic Legal Advisor, Deputy Head, Section Legal Affairs and Regulatory Policy, Department of Legislation and Legal Affairs, Ministry of Justice and Security in June 2023.

diversity of the positioning of this evaluation and the choice of the entity that is expected to carry it out. The issue of the selection of the body responsible for the preparation of *ex post* evaluation is addressed in different ways: in several countries (France, Belgium, United Kingdom) parliamentary committees or specially appointed bodies are entrusted with this task, in which case the analysis of *ex post* regulations takes the form of an instrument of executive oversight, which means that in essence the analysis is transferred from the legislator to the body responsible for the draft of the act, or just for its implementation and enforcement.

In other countries (Germany, Italy), *ex post* evaluation is carried out outside parliament, internally by ministries or by bodies set up within the government, so it becomes more of an instrument of self-control, with all the shortcomings of such a process, resulting in a poor chance of obtaining a reliable and completely impartial report on the negative and positive outcomes of legislation. The predominant solution, however, is to establish the units carrying out the analyses within the government administration, equipped with appropriate structures of qualified bureaucracy and experts in a given field. This arrangement makes it possible to report on the effectiveness of an act by developing a uniform methodology and ensures consistency of actions and policies, but in turn leaves such bodies and the analyses themselves exposed to a greater risk of being dominated by politics and the ruling majority. Such a model, however, works significantly better for *ex ante* evaluations than for evaluations already carried out during the course of legislation. Under such conditions, the value of the impartiality of the prepared analysis depends on the status of public administration personnel; there should be a "Chinese Wall" between the authors preparing *ex post* analyses and the political authorities of the ministries, guaranteeing that the authors prepare analyses that are reliable, fully objective and supported by verifiable data, as well as independent of the intentions of the political authorities of the ministries or the parliament. However, political factors tend to corrode such a model and the bodies performing the analyses tend to self-censor their reports or modify them under the influence of the superior political forces responsible for the process of enacting, designing and implementing the law.

In certain countries (the Netherlands, Denmark, Finland), there are one-arm's-length bodies involved in carrying out evaluations. There is a fairly widespread consensus in literature that a body endowed with such a competence should be guaranteed independence from political bodies and public authorities.[73] Reg Watch Europe, the umbrella organisation of its European

73 On the need to ensure the independence of the assessing body: Anne Meuwese, "Regulatory Scrutiny in Transition", *European Journal of Risk Regulation* 6, no. 3 (2015): 359–80, at 359; see also Renda, 61–2.

sister bodies,[74] at the very start of its work in summer 2016 was focusing on influencing the work done in the EU and cooperating with the OECD.[75] A closer look at the functioning of such arm's-length bodies, however, reveals that they serve mainly a consultative or monitoring function in the evaluation process carried out elsewhere, i.e. in government ministries, and are rarely tasked with preparing analyses on the functioning of legal regulations themselves. Their recommendations are not binding.

A brief review of practice shows that, despite the commitment declared by countries in OECD reports to the design and development of *ex post* evaluation mechanisms, there is a wide variety of different types of assessment under this designation, carried out by different bodies; above all by government agencies, sometimes only controlled or assisted by independent bodies. As Radaelli rightly points out, despite the grand announcements, RIA practice may exist only on paper, and differences among practice and politics may bring different effects – with the central one perhaps being the will to increase the legitimacy of the government,[76] rather than actually accounting for the effects of the law adopted and implemented. The approaches, methods and scopes of *ex post* evaluation also vary considerably. Regarding the approach to *ex post* reviews, three main categories can be distinguished:[77]

1. Programmed review mechanisms (failsafe mechanisms). In this approach, *ex post* reviews in new regulations are designed to assess the outcomes due to uncertainty, particularly used in acts with a potentially important impact on society or the economy, where their effectiveness is uncertain. This is especially true with regard to the risk of undesirable effects, the potential damage the regulation may cause – such mechanisms are especially used in lower-tier acts: secondary or subordinate regulations, rather than primary legislation. A similar mechanism is known as "Sunset rules", which means that regulations automatically expire after a certain period of time, with the exception of cases where they have been reintroduced.
2. In the second type, called "stocktake reviews" (or stock management), assessments are used to identify cumulative regulatory burdens or to

74 RegWatchEurope Members: Advisory Board on Regulatory Burden (ATR, Netherlands), Danish Business Regulation Forum (DBRF), Finnish Council of Regulatory Impact Analysis (FCRIA), National Regulatory Control Council (NKR, Germany), Norwegian Better Regulation Council (NBRC), Regulatory Impact Assessment Board (RIAB, Czech Republic), Regulatory Policy Committee (RPC, United Kingdom), Swedish Better Regulation Council (SBRC).

75 An observation of the network is the need for extensive *ex post* evaluation support – https://julkaisut.valtioneuvosto.fi/bitstream/handle/10024/164159/VNK_2022_15.pdf?sequence=1&isAllowed=y, 22.

76 Claudio M. Radaelli, "Diffusion without Convergence: How Political Context Shapes the Adoption of Regulatory Impact Assessment", *Journal of European Public Policy* 12, no. 5 (2005): 924–43, doi: 10.1080/13501760500161621, 924–5.

77 OECD 2018, 37–8.

detect adverse interactions between different regulations and to gather public opinions on current regulatory problems. Such approaches often employ the "one-in, one-out" principle, as well as bureaucracy reduction objectives. As is clear from the very premise, they are set to reduce administrative burdens and compliance costs borne by addressees. Such approaches have been widely used across the OECD.
3. In addition, approaches based on a principle-based method that focuses on a specific objective (e.g. elimination of competitive constraints, greener policies) or in-depth reviews: assessing key areas of regulation with wide-ranging implications for stakeholders.[78]

As the OECD points out, most countries have not established a comprehensive methodology for *ex post* evaluation as of now. Among all OECD countries (34 plus the EU states), the principle-based method is the most commonly used in *ad hoc* reviews of regulations (in 28 countries), followed by the public stock-take method (24 cases), with significantly fewer countries opting for in-depth reviews (15). The methodology of *ex post* analyses also varies. Among the multiple methods of regulatory impact assessment, the most popular include benefit analysis (88% of OECD countries), risk assessment (60%) and cost-benefit analysis (29%).[79] It should be acknowledged, however, that methods defined in such a general way, coupled with the rather narrowly defined areas where the impact of regulation is examined, provide a great deal of technical and methodological freedom in carrying out *ex post* evaluations. The evaluation can thus be limited by the degree of regulation, the scope of regulation (e.g. expenditure) and the area regulated, as well as the purpose of the regulation (target).[80] As Carvalho and Marques point out, "under the umbrella of impact assessment, a number of specific forms have developed since 1960s based on scientific analysis derived from analytic tools with a wide variety of different types."[81]

There is also no data on the close connection between *ex ante* and *ex post* assessment. It should be close, as not only would it testify to the effects of the law, but also to the ability of the drafter and the legislator to introduce a regulation, the effects of which were foreseen and planned. *Ex post* evaluations should refer to the process of assessing the effectiveness and efficiency of regulations after they have entered into force. These are usually undertaken to assess the extent to which regulations have met their original intended

78 OECD 2015, similarly: OECD 2021, 14–17.
79 OECD 2015, similarly: OECD 2021, 14–17.
80 Michael A. Crew and David Parker, eds., *International Handbook on Economic Regulation* (Elgar, 2006), 233.
81 Carvalho, Marques and Netto, 115.

objectives, costs imposed on citizens and/or businesses and outcome for the society.[82]

Most countries also focus on reducing administrative burdens, simplifying regulations (Germany, Italy) or promoting competition (Netherlands, Denmark).[83] The remark made 20 years ago by Claudio Radaelli is still relevant here, as he pointed out that "RIA can be seen as a solution to different problems."[84] However, there is still no effort for a more strategic and systematic evaluation to examine or even assess the cumulative impact of the regulatory framework in the sector as a whole, paying particular attention to the performance of legislation. Therefore, the mandatory mode and scope of the study is severely limited. A conspicuous pattern emerges here: most often it concerns the impact on specific sectors of economic life, specifically on the operation and burdens of businesses, especially administrative burdens, and often also with regard to environmental protection and the state budget. This is also how their original and primary function can often be perceived: protection against excessive regulatory burdens – although it must be admitted that this perspective is extremely narrow and it certainly is not the only criterion for the need and effectiveness of regulation and its actual effects, including side effects. Remarkably, at the same time, it is the perspective only of the organised participants in legal relations, which finds confirmation in the findings of Martin Gilens and Benjamin I. Page, referred to previously, stating that just like in the United States, also in European countries economic elites and narrow interest groups play the key role on influencing the parliamentary decisions. In the first instance, the pursuit of their interests is taken into account in the *ex post* impact assessment. It is noteworthy that it is not oriented towards verifying the efficiency of the law in force from the point of view of the interests of the sovereign as the formal source of power in the state, whose power – by means of an electoral act – should be exercised by parliament.

The more astute reader will also note that it poses a real challenge to actually identify the key to carrying them out; they are not mandatory, even in countries that do report it (Denmark, Italy and the United States),[85] but, as indicated earlier, these are somewhat overstated claims.

It is difficult to identify those evaluation systems that comprehensively assess the political, social, economic and other impacts of regulations – an extremely complex, but at the same time feasible, task.

Still, as the OECD acknowledges in its reports, the implementation of *ex post* evaluation seems to be of lower priority than *ex ante* regulatory analysis in many countries. There is no single systematic approach to *ex post* evaluation

82 OECD 2021, 152.
83 OECD 2017.
84 Radaelli, 929.
85 Radaelli, 929; OECD 2015 table 8.8.

and the methodologies used vary considerably.[86] Many countries still lack standardised evaluation procedures, and only about a third of OECD countries regularly assess whether the underlying policy objectives have been met when conducting *ex post* evaluations.[87] Very few countries have mechanisms in place to ensure stakeholders' engagement and consequences in the event that planned assessments are not actually carried out, such as public reporting of non-compliance.[88]

Moreover, there is little indication that this state of affairs is about to change. As the OECD admits, the number of countries that have a formal requirement for systematic evaluations of existing regulations in place has remained essentially unchanged since 2014.[89] The systemic adoption of *ex post* evaluation to ensure effective implementation is still underdeveloped and at a very early stage, remaining the weakest element of the regulatory cycle.[90]

We have not been able to identify a single European country in which a comprehensive *ex post* impact assessment is carried out for every piece of legislation. This is an important manifestation of the lack of accountability of the legislature for its implementation of its representative mandate and, simultaneously, as a formal premise for legislative dysfunctions.

Relevance of *ex post* evaluation for public accountability

Ex post evaluation serves an important function from an institutional point of view in its capacity as a criterion for political and democratic control. Since power is based on delegation, the legislature also has a duty to report on how it is exercised, as indicated by "the first logic of RIA adoption is based on delegation. The main political dimension of RIA lies with power relationship between the principal and the agent".[91] This happens not only in the case of legislation delegated to agencies or ministries, but also when power is vested in parliament for the first time.

86 For instance, in 2015 the OECD survey indicated that public stocktakes to invite businesses and citizens to provide information on the effectiveness, efficiency and burdens imposed by regulation was carried out only in nine OECD European countries. Table 8.7 Regulatory Governance, at 167, available at: https://www.oecd-ilibrary.org/docserver/gov_glance-2017-57- :en.pdf.expires=1687413075&id=id&accname=guest&checksum=E9C84F262880DCE9168684A461AD8B83.

87 OECD 2017.

88 See: *Measuring Regulatory Performance. Closing the Regulatory Cycle: Effective Ex Post Evaluation for Improved Policy Outcomes, Key Findings and Conference Proceedings*, note 27, 12, available at: https://betteregulation.lumsa.it/sites/default/files/sites/default/files/publications/Proceedings-9th-Conference-MRP.pdf.

89 OECD 2021, 152.

90 OECD 2018, 10.

91 Claudio M. Radaelli and Fabrizio De Francesco, "Regulatory impact assessment", in *The Oxford Handbook of Regulation*, ed. R. Baldwin, M. Cave and M. Lodge, Oxford Handbooks in Business and Management (Oxford University Press, 2010), 281.

It is this context and the importance of *ex post* evaluation that interest us. Analyses of legal regulations are also much more broadly anchored in the axiological order of contemporary democracies, as they are related to the transparency of power exercising, including legislative actions, as well as to the verification of these actions and subsequent accountability, i.e. indicating the relations between intentions and expectations and the effects achieved through the implementation of legislative authority.[92] With regard to the legislative authority, such actions are an important complement to the existing checks and balances system (understood as a formal mechanism acting to balance relations within the political authority as a necessary condition for the protection of individuals' rights), constituting a powerful instrument of accountability and of control of the legislature and the executive authority, usually responsible for drafting legal regulations. In addition to its functions, such as efficiency, proportionality, reduction of burdens, searching for optimal solutions, it offers an opportunity to receive and evaluate a report on the activities carried out in this sphere of power. And it does so in two areas – firstly, that of the drafter, and secondly, that of the legislator, and therefore also that of the parliament, as long as *ex post* RIA of laws is involved. The evaluation of the law in force can serve as an instrument to hold the legislator, or perhaps only the drafter, accountable for the legislative action taken, and it seems that this instrument is perfect.

This also allows to set a problem from the perspective of the implementation of other constitutional values. Since the assessment of the law in force fails, the sense of its validity in a given formulation becomes problematic as well, including its coherence with the constitution. What is at stake here is not so much the issue of the unconstitutionality of the created law, since the procedures of reviewing the constitutionality of the law are applied in such circumstances, but precisely the constitutional coherence of the law. Do the laws in force actually comply with the provisions of the constitution, the values and goals proclaimed as supreme in public life, or do they merely avoid direct contradiction? These two planes of reference: representative (electoral) accountability and constitutional accountability should be filled in by *ex post* evaluations of the impact of regulations.

However, three conditions need to be met for this to happen. Firstly, in order to fulfil such a function, RIA should be carried out obligatorily against all laws, on a systematic basis, with a clearly defined scope and procedure for carrying out such an impact assessment of acts. The more comprehensive the scope and obligation to carry it out, the better the chances of holding the legislator accountable for the work performed. Meanwhile, as the OECD report indicates, the majority of EU Member States lack a systematic approach

92 This effect is highlighted by, among others, David Parker and Colin Kirkpatrick, "Measuring Regulatory Performance. The Economic Impact of Regulatory Policy: A Literature Review of Quantitative Evidence", *OECD Expert Paper* no. 3 (2012): 32.

towards *ex post* evaluation of regulations: fewer than one-fifth of Member States make a systematic assessment of whether laws and regulations achieve their policy goals as expected. Several countries have reported the introduction of an *ex post* evaluation system in recent years; these include Austria, Denmark, France, Italy, Japan, Korea and the United States. In this way the number of countries with formal requirements for *ex post* evaluation has slightly increased, yet in most countries where such a requirement exists, it is not applied systematically, be it to all or just major regulations. Moreover, even when it is carried out, it appears that it typically applies only to selected policy areas,[93] which is notable from the point of view of accountability relations, as the very substantive selection of the assessed effects of the regulation points to a Principal genuinely interested in the effects of the law. It is also worth noting that the OECD draws the greatest attention to the introduction of RIA *ex post*, even insists on introducing it,[94] and it is an intergovernmental organisation of 38 member states established to stimulate economic progress and global trade. It is only natural for the OECD to highlight economic, deregulatory issues and underestimate social, political or cultural impacts. The question therefore arises: whose interests are exposed in this way, and can this group be equated with the sovereign entrusting the power of legislation? In most countries, the areas where evaluations are carried out do not give any indication that the relationship of the entrustment of this power and the guarantee of the transparency of the legislative process and its effectiveness are generally noticed at all, except in specific areas. Meanwhile, from the perspective of constitutionalism, the entire decision-making process and everything that accompanies it (*ex ante* and *ex post* evaluation) should be conducted according to the logic of democratic values and the conditions of governance. This viewpoint aims at safeguarding the rationality of the law being drafted and protecting against statutory dysfunction. Unfortunately, it is not implemented, and examples of controversial pieces of legislation, including those concerning the most vital interests of citizens, such as retirement age reforms (French reform of retirement age 2023), or issues strongly interfering with the existing political order (the reform of the judiciary in Poland 2015–20) are carried out outside the *ex ante* evaluation processes, and *ex post* evaluation was replaced by mass protests in the streets.

Secondly, in order to achieve the effect of accountability, namely a report on the entrusted power, the evaluation of the legislation must be carried out

93 OECD Better Regulation Practices across the European Union, 2019, Ex post review of laws and regulations across the European Union, https://doi.org/10.1787/9789264311732-en.

94 For example, the OECD in 2012 called on governments to "conduct systematic programme reviews of the stock of significant regulation against clearly defined policy goals, including consideration of costs and benefits, to ensure that regulations remain up to date, cost justified, cost effective and consistent, and deliver the intended policy objectives". – OECD, *Recommendation of the Council on Regulatory Policy and Governance* (Paris: OECD Publishing, 2012), http://dx.doi.org/10.1787/9789264209022-en.

according to authoritative and objective criteria with the use of a consistent methodology, so that both the account of the effects of the legislative action and its evaluation are credible.[95] Its primary objective is to verify and improve the quality of legal regulations. It plays an important role in verifying the rationality of the legislator's actions and the rationality of policy-making.[96] It is this kind of transparency in legislative preparation that would allow drawing conclusions from decisions made, learning from successful and unsuccessful legislative projects and the functionality of different regulatory options.[97] However, it is impossible without reliable, quantitative reference data. An evaluation based solely on general indicators fails to produce reliable insight.

The scope of assessment also needs to be clearly defined – not everyone can be held accountable for everything. So – in the case of the EU states, which have ceded the vast majority of their legislative competences to EU bodies,[98] their only job is to apply it correctly and, in this respect, they can report back to the Principal, i.e. to the public – citizens of the EU. RIAs concerning those acts that are secondary legislation implementing EU laws should verify the thoroughness of the national parliament's compliance with EU law. On the other hand, the issue of the rationality and efficiency of the adopted national regulations as regulations implementing EU law and thus not being an expression of the will of the domestic parliament should recede into the background. The reason for this is that domestic parliaments should not be held accountable for issues external to them, i.e. issues over which they have no influence. Being mere executors in a given area, they can only be held accountable with regard to the quality of the implementation of the will of the EU legislator, i.e. exactly with regard to whether they have comprehensively and accurately implemented its will.

95 Kirchhoff and Nikolka, passim.

96 Claudio M. Radaelli and Fabrizio De Francesco, "Introduction", in *The Elgar Companion to the OECD*, ed. Fabrizio De Francesco and Claudio M. Radaelli (London: Edward Elgar Publishing, 2023), 5.

97 Keinänen, 19.

98 According to rough estimates, several tens of percent of legislation has passed from national parliaments to EU bodies. As cited by Ton van den Brink, in 1988, the Commission President, Jacques Delors, made a famous prediction on the impact of EU legislation on the Member States. He claimed that in 10 years' time, 80% of economic and perhaps also of social and fiscal policy-making would be of EU origin (the assumption behind it was – Ton van der Brink, "The Impact of EU Legislation on National Legal Systems: Towards a New Approach to EU – Member State Relations", *Cambridge Yearbook of European Legal Studies*, 19 (2017): 211–35 at 213).

J. Barcz reports that, on entering the EU in 1995, Austria ceded about 60% of its legislative competences to EU bodies and about 80% with regard to economic law issues. J. Barcz, *Parlament a Unia Europejska. Analiza prawna na przykładzie doświadczeń Austrii* (Warsaw: Wydawnictwo Sejmowe, 1999), 11. Given that European integration intensified after 1995 (e.g. through the Lisbon Treaty, entry into the euro area), these ratios are now higher.

The outcome of the evaluation should come in the form of an opinion based on sound evidence, including the results of quantitative and qualitative research carried out under predefined conditions, as well as – where possible – a study of the effects of the regulation through an analysis of case law and other instruments of law application. Such analysis must therefore meet the condition of having its conclusions verifiable. This, in turn, requires it to be conducted under conditions of objectivity and legibility of criteria and research methods, in a manner similar to scientific analysis. This does not mean, however, that evaluation is to address only financial, accounting effects. As Stijn Smismans accurately notes, although accountability is often identified as the key objective of *ex post* evaluation, as long as such evaluation is mainly about auditing and financial and legal compliance, it is more about "accounting" than "accounting for".[99] This is because financial or accounting effects (with differentiation between them for the individual social groups directly or indirectly affected by the legal regulation) represent one of several groups of social effects, alongside such effects as political, social, environmental or cultural, and are distinguished by the fact that they are easier to quantify.

This objective implies positioning of the task of preparing analyses in a way that allows for the greatest possible degree of expert judgment and depoliticisation of the process. The objectivity of the analysis is a key condition for it to serve its role in the law-making system, as well as to influence the implementation of the principle of transparency and the oversight of legislative bodies. The *ex post* impact assessment should also be open, i.e. it should be carried out in conditions that guarantee clear and transparent criteria, the participation of specific stakeholders and the publication of its results. A process of analysing the impact of regulations and subsequent publication may result in the proposals for amending (or repealing) the scrutinised provisions being subject to verification in terms of their rationality, i.e. their compliance with the effects of the analyses and their purposefulness in terms of the assumed or achieved objectives of the regulation. In turn, not only would this make it possible to improve the quality of legislative work and base it on authoritative premises, but also to increase the degree of conviction about the rationality of the legislative process, and consequently to legitimise this process in the institutional and social sense.

That brings us to the third condition: positioning of the entity doing the analysis. As we have observed earlier, this entity is sometimes situated in a number of places: as a parliamentary committee, a ministry, a governmental agenda or an independent body, with generally limited competences. It is noticeable, however, that it is relatively difficult to unambiguously determine who reports on the law in force, as well as its effects, and who is to verify

99 Stijn Smismans, "Policy Evaluation in the EU: The Challenges of Linking Ex Ante and Ex Post Appraisal Symposium on Policy Evaluation in the EU", *European Journal of Risk Regulation* 11 (2015): 6–26, at 20.

and analyse this report. The relationship between those entrusting authority and those to whom it is entrusted is therefore difficult to retrace here. The effort to scrutinise the effects of the law, and therefore the *ex post* evaluation, is therefore not a part of the accountability relationship. The relationship between the Principal and the Agent is not at all the determining factor here, especially the role of the Principal, the one entrusted with power, is exercised indirectly and, as it were, *per procura*. Nor does the report on the effects of the legislation itself necessarily and wholly originate from the Agent, i.e. the legislator, or the lawmaker. It is even more complicated to properly identify the entity that verifies this report, since the mechanisms for such verification are sporadic and not particularly binding. Meanwhile, it is precisely this kind of assessment, based on the Agent's own and independent research into the economic, social effects, that would provide an opportunity to account for the sovereign actions taken. The data on the impact of the law should therefore be collected and compared in a way that is free from the intentions of whoever is responsible for its content, while at the same time it should be available to the public. Public access should include not only the results of the evaluations, but also data on the methodology used therein, the empirical data used and the inferences made.

It is difficult to meet all these conditions, yet it is surprising how rarely it happens in practice. As a result, accountability through existing regulation reviews is negligible. It is puzzling why the idea of examining the effects of regulation, which has such great potential to improve the quality of the law, to make it fit in with prevailing social relations and the lives of citizens, and which is of great importance in holding whoever exercises the power to legislate accountable, is so poorly practised and its contribution to accountability is less than negligible.

It is therefore worth looking at the actual reasons for this state of affairs.

Ex post evaluation – conditions that cannot be met?

There are at least three underlying reasons. The first is of an objective nature: it is very hard to find suitable approaches, methods and techniques for collecting data and analysing in order to reliably assess what impact the law is making. Regulatory impact analysis is a discipline in which the research domains of lawyers, political scientists, sociologists and economists, as well as specialists in other fields of knowledge come together, making it extremely difficult, if not impossible, to synthesise research results. For they employ radically different research methods, and to a certain extent their objectives determining their scope and research questions are also somewhat distinct.[100] Therefore, it is

100 On the difficulties of using empirical research methods in regulatory impact analyses – see Richard W. Parker, "The Empirical Roots of the Regulatory Reform Movement: A Critical Appraisal", *Administrative Law Review* 58(359), no. 2 (2006): 359–400. This issue is also discussed by K. van Aeken, 57.

necessary for the document to be prepared by teams made up of people having different expertise, competences and skills. Such a combined set of research tools must be linked to the observation and evaluation of the overall effects of the regulation – both financial and social in the broadest sense, i.e. covering the widest possible spectrum of systemic consequences in economic, political and social life, both from the individual perspective of the addressee, as well as groups and society as a whole – the intended effects as well as potential side effects. The primary objective is to indicate to what extent the analysed regulation fulfils its purpose, is effective and leads to the intended outcomes in an optimal manner and as such realises the constitutional values relevant to the state in question to the fullest extent. In this context, the criterion of the rationality of the regulation is frequently also invoked as a form of synthesis of the criteria for the analysis of the regulation. In doing so, the rationality of regulation should be viewed through the prism of legal structure of the rational legislator as a component of the constitutional principle of the rule of law. There is a consensus in the jurisprudence of constitutional courts and in constitutional law doctrine that an irrational law cannot be considered to be properly created (principle of correct legislation) and hence compliant with the constitution. The irrationality of a law is sometimes regarded by constitutional courts as an intrinsic premise of its unconstitutionality. Studying such effects requires extensive use of quantitative and qualitative methods, including surveys, consultations, focus studies (this is the case, for example, in the Danish impact analysis system).[101] At the same time, they must allow for an evaluation of the efficiency, appropriateness of the legal measures applied as well as their potential for application, system coherence, clarity and transparency.[102] They therefore require a study of case law, but also of administrative acts of law enforcement, as well as in-depth studies related to the legal context of the regulation under consideration, especially its systemic coherence.

In principle, the evaluation of any phenomenon, not just regulation effects, consists of three elements: data collection, analysis and the formulation of conclusions. Naturally, the validity of the conclusions depends on the reliability of the first two stages. Unfortunately, as far as the evaluation of *ex post* regulation is concerned, both of these stages are questionable. Firstly, the collection of qualitative and quantitative data on the effects of regulation is far from easy and yet it is absolutely crucial in order to achieve a meaningful report.[103] When it comes to acquiring reliable data in significant quantities, there is obviously a strong temptation to stop with the opinion of selected stakeholders, or to

101 Renda, 114.

102 As Andrea Renda notes, a pilot programme on indicators of regulatory quality was implemented at EU level, in the final report of the 2004 programme, three groups of indicators were suggested: 1) macro and *ex ante*, indicating the instruments developed and the policies to be implemented through them, 2) micro and *ex post* focused on effects and the situation of the addressees, 3) qualitative indicators on legislative technique. Renda, 110.

103 Kirchhoff and Nikolka, 46.

entrust them with the task of gathering information. The lack of independent data and substituting it with consultation with selected stakeholders definitely reduces the credibility and relevance of *ex post* evaluations. This risk has been highlighted by the OECD, among others.[104] There is always the risk of missing data, or omitted data concerning certain issues that are not very convenient from the point of view of the author of the regulation, or the agency that is commissioned by the author to perform such an assessment. There is a huge risk of so-called shadow costs, the enormity and variety of costs.[105] Nor is it obvious what this data should be compared with and how it should be examined – in other words, how to determine the projected and desired effects of the regulation to be assessed. It refers to the problems associated with comparing effects of different kinds and confronting them with constitutional values. As is well known, constitutional values may stand in opposition to each other and require moderation (establishing rules of priority for the application of protected goods and the application of the principle of proportionality). As a result, although the RIA procedure could produce a broad stock of evidence, it does not automatically lead to evidence-based policy-making.[106] The data problem has also been flagged by the OECD, which states that standard datasets may not have sufficient granularity or specificity within government to assess all relevant impacts of regulation.[107] This deficiency is also identified as the first cause of poor performance of RIA mechanisms.[108]

Secondly, the choice of the method of studying the effects of the law and the transparency of the process causes serious problems. There is no single precisely defined theory nor method on how to carry out the study, not to mention how to proceed with consultations, surveys regarding the regulation under evaluation.[109] The approach based on cost-benefit analysis, or cost-effectiveness analysis, or risk assessment, which allows the benefits and costs of regulation to be estimated using methods rooted in economic science, is of the greatest importance in regulatory impact analysis.[110] Also this method is favoured and brought to the fore in documents of the European Commission

104 OECD 2018.
105 Parker and Kirkpatrick, 27, 38.
106 Kirchoff and Nikolka, 45; Claudio M. Radaelli, "Evidence-Based Policy and Political Control: What Does Regulatory Impact Assessment Tell Us?", 2008 Paper delivered to the ECPR Joint Sessions of Workshops, University of Rennes 2008, Workshop on The Politics of Evidence-Based Policy, 2, available at: https://citeseerx.ist.psu.edu/document?repid=rep1&type=pdf&doi=296e82c73514a3fe02fc7eeb76609e63f73fb8dc.
107 OECD 2018, 42.
108 Carvalho, Marques and Netto, 119.
109 Parker and Kilkpatrick, 10.
110 Włodzimierz Szpringer and Wojciech Rogowski, "Problemy metodologiczne oceny skutków regulacji w Polsce – czy powstają nowe perspektywy ekonomicznej analizy prawa", in *Ocena skutków regulacji* (see note 57), 3–18.

and EU expert groups,[111] although, as has already been mentioned, it faces legitimate criticism regarding the limited scope of the analysis so performed.[112] Despite the development of the methods used in this approach and the expansion of the range of goods to be estimated,[113] the deficits of this method in the evaluation of intrinsically non-quantifiable goods, like demographic changes, a sense of security, environmental values, social trust, coherence of legal order, nature conservation are highlighted.[114] The aforementioned criticism of the narrow and limited scope of the gain and loss analysis relates to the failure of *ex post* analyses to cover social effects in the sphere of social relations and with respect to such tasks of the state as ensuring security and a sense of justice. The problem, however, is that these scopes are extremely difficult to cover with objective criteria as well as hard to measure, especially when using the method of indicating measurable and quantifiable gains and losses. Indeed, one important approach to risk analysis within the framework of the effects of the law should also be the examination of the case law and administrative acts, as results of law application, and demonstrating the problems, controversies and risks of error that the regulation under review creates.

As regards the analysis itself, the cost-benefit method is all the more difficult because it has to be done by way of a comparison of new options with the existing "baseline" scenario[115] since this requires the development of a hypothetical image of reality, which by its very nature is hardly verifiable. Such comparisons are usually made using regulatory tests, specifically compliance or performance tests – though these can lead to quite different results. Another method, designed to apply a broader analytical perspective, is the functional test, including an audit of how regulations are applied within an administration, including surveys of changes in behaviour and legal culture – this has been done in countries considered to be the most advanced in their use of evaluation.[116]

According to the OECD,[117] four questions for such an assessment should normally be applied. The first is appropriateness, which means that it should be determined whether the original politics that justifies it still makes sense

111 Mandelkern Group on Better Regulation, Final Report, 13 November 2001, Communication on Better Regulation in 2005, Action Programme for Reducing Administrative Burdens in the European Union, Communication from the Commission, "Better Regulation for Better Results – An EU Agenda", 19 May 2015, COM (2015).

112 Kai P. Purnhagen and Peter. H. Feindt, "Better Regulatory Impact Assessment: Making Behavioural Insights Work for the Commission's New Better Regulation Strategy", *European Journal of Risk Regulation* 6, no. 3 (2015): 361–8, at 361.

113 Matthew D. Adler and Eric A. Posner, *Cost-Benefit Analysis: Legal, Economic, and Philosophical Perspectives* (Chicago: University of Chicago Press, 2001), passim.

114 Radaelli, "The Diffusion", 925.

115 Kirchhoff and Nikolka, passim.

116 Renda, 110. As pointed out by this author, such tests are being introduced in Denmark, New Zealand and Canada, among others.

117 OECD 2018, 40–2.

given changes in the political framework, the economy or society. This therefore requires defining, or rather: redefining the purpose of regulation under current circumstances, the reasons for legislative intervention. It is needed to determine whether the regulation actually achieves the purposes for which it was introduced. This can prove to be an extremely difficult task – precisely because of the multiplicity and diversity of factors and certain unquantifiable values to be achieved, such as the state of public health, the level of education or environmental protection. As we pointed out in the previous chapter, the regulations adopted by parliament reflect the views shared by the parliamentary majority. Irrespective of parliamentary elections and the associated alternation of power, even during the parliamentary term, the parliamentary majority has the right to deviate from the view held at the time the legal regulation was adopted. The political preferences of citizens also tend to change. Changes in the external circumstances of parliamentary decision-making, such as new expectations of key players (such as the EU vis-à-vis the EU Member States), natural disasters or demographic changes are also important.

The second issue is effectiveness; the evaluation should determine whether the regulation actually achieves the objectives set for it. It is here that the problem of reproducing what would have happened had it not been for the regulation in force, thus building some far-reaching hypotheses about economic and social life, is most fully revealed; after all, legislation is not created in a vacuum. During the period of its validity, the external environment of the binding normative act is subject to change, including to an extent and intensity that could not have been foreseen by a rational legislator.

The next matter to be examined is efficiency: this is where the costs and unintended consequences are compared with the objectives pursued by the regulations. It is not difficult to notice that this is where the cost-benefit method, considered the mother and reference point of *ex post* evaluation methodologies, becomes useful. However, it should be remembered that this is only one of the criteria for a reliable assessment.

Finally, the evaluation should analyse alternatives: other competing instruments, which could be used to achieve similar or identical goals, comparing their costs and effects.

As can be seen, the evaluation process is quite complex, requires considerable research and – in fact, the *ex post* assessment of regulations is in certain respects more demanding and less straightforward than the assessments carried out at the proposal stage. Collecting reliable data as well as methodology requires considerable effort and dedication, and the requirements for transparency of the process, its availability to policy-makers and the public are difficult to meet.[118]

That is why the method of evaluation itself, i.e. the method of collecting and aggregating data on the effects of the law, is an important issue. These are

118 Kirchhoff and Nikolka, 46.

quantitative methods, which may include a number of qualitative methodologies and techniques, including but not limited to: in-depth interviews, focus groups, panels, surveys, regulatory implementation analysis, process mapping, problem trees, data analysis, etc. Of course, the most challenging issue is the selection of data and its quality. The key questions for evaluating existing regulations are: What are the effects of the regulations? What relevance do they have for stakeholders? What are the mechanisms that have produced these outcomes? What is the context in which the impact was developed?[119] There are plenty of ways to collect data[120] and just as many methods of analysing it, and it is baffling that very few are being used. Almost every OECD report comments on the lack of a methodical approach to *ex post* evaluation.

It needs to be stressed that irrespective of the chosen methods, especially in qualitative research, the crucial aspect is the appropriate selection of data, including the stakeholders under study. After all, they can be – and are – variously identified by the evaluator. This means that the selection of the stakeholder group determines the scope of the evaluation. There are some areas prioritised in the specific evaluation: the sphere of competition law, the impact on public finances, SMEs – this indirectly indicates which group of stakeholders the legislators are *really* interested in, while ignoring or downplaying the opinions of others. The lack of impact analysis in a broader social well-being context is also highlighted in the OECD 2021 report.[121]

Let us briefly summarise the observations made so far with regard to the *ex post* impact assessment. First of all, the very low rank of the legal acts used to regulate these institutions is notable. Secondly – the narrow scope and assessments are performed *ad hoc*, or only to a certain extent, which allows the stakeholders to assess – or comment on – the impact of the regulation on their performance – incidentally, these are usually business representatives. Thirdly – regulatory impact assessment (both *ex ante* and *ex post*) is characterised by a considerable degree of generality. Phrases about the impact on the "labour market, competitiveness of the economy and entrepreneurship, including the functioning of entrepreneurs" cause, in practice, a great deal of freedom when formulating the assessments included in the evaluation. The arbitrariness of the conclusions formulated in *ex post* evaluations is also attributable to the lack of a verification mode for this type of analysis and considerable freedom in demonstrating evidence and research to support the conclusions reached. The scarcity of methodology compared to RIAs is also striking, especially since, after all, it is easier to evaluate something that works than something that is yet

119 OECD 2018.

120 On data collection methods and impact studies, see Carvalho, Marques and Netto, 111–26. These authors also point out that scientific uncertainty can occur at each stage of the RIA process.

121 OECD 2021, 42, 53–4.

to come; as the OECD points out, it is experimental in nature and depends on judgments about causal relationships and responses.[122]

Past experience of *ex post* impact assessments clearly shows that they are prepared only for a limited number of pieces of legislation, and that the initiation of the process depends on the political body (or its subsidiary body), or on whoever was the drafter of the law – this kind of positioning of the analysis process is doomed to make the analysis, but also its outcome, dependent on the will of the body interested in reaching a particular conclusion. Also, there is no introduction of factors or guarantees of the independence of the evaluators from the influence of political influences. Although the evaluation process is usually parameterised, it has not been provided with an expert and authoritative character. Finally, impact analyses are not produced under conditions that allow them to be verified. Lack of verification procedures, and sometimes lack of transparency, allow them to be superficial and perfunctory in their conclusions on the effects of the act itself. If impact assessments of the operation of a law are prepared within the government, i.e. by the bureaucratic apparatus of the ministry involved in the law-making process, they are therefore often sectoral in nature and their substantive verification is of a very limited and non-expert nature.

Another reason for the failure of the *ex post* RIA to perform successfully reveals itself through the aforementioned inconsistencies and difficulties with the institutional positioning of this procedure. In regulatory evaluation, provided that it is to have a dimension of accountability for the exercise of legislative authority, there is a strong need to delegate the evaluation of the report to someone else.[123] Yet, on the other hand, the entity deemed responsible for the content of regulation is reluctant to relinquish its information monopoly – its influence over what data will be used and for what purpose. It is only natural for the government to be in this position.

This brings us to the final reason for the low popularity of the instrument of *ex post* regulatory assessment. This reason comes directly from the world of real politics. The problems described previously regarding the positioning of the independent body as responsible for carrying out evaluation, or rather participating in it, also point to a fundamental problem – political and bureaucratic reluctance to report on the application of the enacted law in a way that would make it possible to evaluate it – as indicated, *inter alia*, by the OECD 2018 report,[124] as well as Claudio Radaelli and Fabrizio De Francesco.[125] If the decision-makers are allowed not to report on the effects of their action – then they

122 OECD 2018, 10.

123 Carvalho, Marques and Netto, 119–20.

124 There may also be more political or bureaucratic resistance to scrutiny of regulations in place than for those in prospect. This is perhaps understandable, in light of the possibility of a review finding that certain regulations have been unduly costly or failed to achieve their objectives (OECD 2018, 10).

125 Radaelli and De Francesco, "Introduction",12.

will probably take this opportunity, mitigating political and bureaucratic risks. Indeed, the evaluation of the effects of a law falls between the bureaucratic and the political process – and while there is room in each for the Agent's accountability for the power entrusted, this perspective is almost entirely invisible.

We remarked earlier that parliament can scrutinise the government through *ex post* RIA, with regard to both the execution of laws and the legislative initiative process. Alternatively, evaluation can be seen as a kind of legislative self-monitoring, particularly in those cases where the government engages in a process of examination, or appoints agencies to assist this process. RIA as administrative procedure solves the Principal's problem of controlling bureaucracies. But this raises several troublesome issues. Firstly – a lot of Principals and Agents appear within the executive itself,[126] questions arise as to who wanted what, what the alternatives were. It turns out that there are no people willing to take on such explicit roles; who is to do the accounting, i.e. become the Principal and how the agency responds. The accountability process can easily be taken over by professional scientific or technical personnel.[127] The victim is the transparency of the process; formal procedures effectively dilute the accountability for both the adopted law and opponents. Thus, even if we reduce *ex post* evaluation to the process of government legislation and execution of laws, the question arises as to who is to carry it out and it is a question to which the constitutional systems have been unable to find a clear and satisfactory answer yet – should it be entrusted to state control bodies, experts, or given to leaders, responsible for something? These are the dilemmas the OECD highlights, recognising the needs of both sides.[128]

Systemic and political differences, including the system of governance, together with their coalition nature in many European countries, make intra- and inter-ministerial accounts face further difficulties.[129] Furthermore, a change of government results in a change of leaders (ministers), but not of apparatus. Senior officials have an institutional memory, but also remain in a delicate relationship with their superiors.

Naturally, it is even more difficult to find an independent body in the system that could verify the *ex post* evaluation. Such verification is replaced by the transparency of the process – this seems to indicate that everyone, civil society, can verify such a report itself. But does it actually do so, or: does it have sufficiently comprehensive data and a reliable report to do so? And can the report be supplemented in any way, can the supplement be requested? Does it do so

126 Gary Miller, "The Political Evolution of Principals-Agent Models", *Annual Review of Political Science* 8 (2005): 203–25, cited in: Radaelli and De Francesco, " "Introduction",8.

127 Miller, 203–25.

128 OECD 2018, 48. OECD recommends the participation of senior officials – as the most appropriate choice (49–50).

129 Radaelli and De Francesco, "Introduction",13.

entirely on its own account? Evidence in the form of independent reports suggests that it is unlikely to rely solely on data prepared in ministries.

In fact, *ex post* reviews inform the government about regulatory decisions, but out of necessity, systems initially limit discretion, with the findings and recommendations from reviews ultimately having to be agreed at a political level. And even though the change is agreed at a political level – the outcome will be one that justifies it. And so the data and the stakeholders will be carefully selected (perhaps influencing the content, but it will be presented in a way that the author of the report will rationalise). This is thanks to the master-level gate-keeping power of government agencies. As such, the information monopoly allows for manipulation of content – and the institutional conditions allow for limiting the scope of reviews. The OECD report is right when it states:

> Just as *ex ante* assessments have often been found deficient, or merely to have provided "backfill" for decisions already taken, *ex post* reviews may be conducted poorly or, worse, arranged so as to provide support for a preordained position. And there is the ever-present risk of a "tick a box" approach to compliance emerging over time, with form taking precedence over substance.[130]

Basically, *ex post* reviews do not function as a controlling measure for the entire law and legislative process, i.e. also as a review of the relevant legislative authority. This shows unwillingness to cast anyone in the role of Agent and Principal in such a framework.

It is necessary to add that in the EU states, all this takes place within the framework of a system in which neither the parliament nor the government decides on the content of the emerging law, because it is determined elsewhere – in the system of EU bodies. Therefore, mostly within the scope delegated to EU regulation, the relationship concerns the EU bodies and the national body (government, parliament) and focuses on the correctness of the implementation of directives, while in national relations it is rather the correctness of the implementation of directives that is reported. The rationality of an act itself is of secondary importance, because even if the national bodies find the law to be irrational, they do not have the competence to correct it. So *ex post* RIAs drafted in this way are useless to citizens, parliament and government. It is reasonable to prepare full-scale RIAs only on issues not covered by EU law, when their content can actually be relevant to the state's power relations and the public authorities' reporting on the exercise of their powers.

A crucial element concerning the functionality of the legislature is also highlighted by Stephen Laws, who writes that the lack of parliamentary accountability (in the Westminster reality) for the legislation passed is not at

130 OECD 2018, 49.

all paradoxical. In the Westminster system parliament is assumed to be ultimately responsible for every aspect of the legislation it passes. As he puts it: "Parliament must deal with every respect in which the quality of legislation fails short of perfect".[131] However, the recognition of parliament as legislator is a false – albeit common, fundamental and yet silent assumption.[132] The premise that parliament is the nation's legislature and is vested with exclusive legislative power is based on what is manifestly a myth. In practice, neither the parliament nor its members have a decisive say over the shape of the law and its content – they do not draft laws or pass them in isolation from other authorities. It is the government, or more precisely the majority that forms the government, that makes legislative decisions, and parliament's role in relation to legislation is reactive rather than proactive. It responds to legislative proposals brought forward in a fully drafted form by the executive.[133] If something is passed against the will of the government, it only means that the government has lost its majority; perhaps permanently – and then a new government and a newly formed majority will soon appear – and probably take steps to rectify this temporary defeat, or a newly formed parliament. Therefore, without this majority, the parliament has no legislative power. In fact, the enactment of laws may even diminish the political accountability of the government (since it is acting pursuant to the law passed by parliament), shifting the burden of power first to parliament and second to the courts, especially the constitutional courts, which rule on the interpretation of the law and its existence in the system.

This demonstrates the dual nature of the exercise of power in the state fully – politics and law are obviously intertwined, but also the positioning in the system of the law passed by the parliament through a special procedure, a debate involving the representatives of the people gives legitimacy to govern, creates the conditions for the exercise of power, rather than creating a Principal-Agent relationship, which in this case (parliament-government) fails completely, and in the case of the nation-parliament fails for the reasons already discussed.

In our view, these are the reasons why impact assessment is unlikely to fulfil its accountability function. The technical reasons and the poor data collecting and analysis methods as noticed in the literature, as well as the lack of a coherent and efficient model for their execution, are a consequence rather than a root cause. Hence, it is not overly difficult to perform, but inconvenient for all actors to give an account of the operation of a law. If, however, one takes the promise of a democratic form of government seriously, public scrutiny of the actions of the authorities, under conditions of transparency in connection with

131 Stephen Laws, "What Is the Parliamentary Scrutiny of Legislation For?", in *Parliament: Legislation and Accountability*, ed. Alexander Horne and Andrew Le Sueur (Oxford: Hart Publishing, 2016), 19.

132 Laws, 18. This assumption repeatedly calls it a myth, misleading, false assumption (23, 25).

133 Laws, 20.

the assumption that the Agents owe the Principal a proper account – then the absence of a report on the validity of the law prepared by its creators, responsible for its content, as well as its execution constitutes a breach of obligation. Giving an account cannot be substituted with media or court actions. And it is indeed quite intriguing that this does not happen, and even when it does – it does so to such a narrow extent.

4 Parliamentary scrutiny
Toolbox of institutional accountability of government

Introduction

Accountability is inscribed in the genesis of the establishment of parliament and the essence of its activity as a body set up to hold the executive (originally: the monarch) to account. In parliamentary models, such as Westminster or the Chancellor system in Germany, the relationship between the parliament (or its chamber), to which the government is politically accountable, relies on the flow of information and related assessments. It is their stream that shapes the behaviour of political actors. On the one hand, it is the flow of information communicated by the government to parliament, its internal bodies or individual MPs in order to hold the government accountable for the implementation of public policies determined in parliament. If the government is to be representative, parliament must be able to scrutinise, and before that: have the knowledge of what actions are being carried out by the government and why. This is also how parliaments define their own role: for example, the UK Parliament defines its scrutiny as "the close examination and investigation of government policies, actions and spending" as one of its main roles.[1]

On the other hand (something we do not address here), it is a stream of information transmitted in the opposite direction, i.e. from parliament to government, allowing for ongoing verification of the trust placed in parliament and parliamentary approval of particular public policies pursued by the government.

When analysing such systems of government, the government's accountability to parliament is particularly prominent, which means parliament can decide government's fate. There are a number of instruments of accountability in place, established and analysed in constitutional law, specifically instruments expressing confidence or lack thereof in the government (vote of no confidence and vote of confidence). Usually, authors and practitioners focus on the

1 *UK Parliament, Scrutiny (parliamentary scrutiny)*, 2021; https://www.parliament.uk/site-information/glossary/scrutiny-parliamentary-scrutiny/ after: David Judge, "Walking the Dark Side: Evading Parliamentary Scrutiny", *The Political Quarterly* 92, no. 2 (April–June 2021): 283–92 at 283.

DOI: 10.4324/9781003493419-4

function of sanctions – the right to dismiss or change the government. This is a logical and natural consequence of the entrustment of executive power to the government, and therefore the relationship between the Principal and his Agent, which empowers parliament to decide the fate of the government, endowed with investiture, is clearly delineated here. However, we are interested in the government's accountability towards parliament, understood as the mere giving account of the power exercised. Many authors actually dissociate such reporting and scrutinising the government by demanding information from the function of forming and dismissing the government, and therefore from political responsibility.[2] This function is carried out in various political arenas,[3] while we are interested in three levels: the parliament *in corpore* (its chambers), the internal bodies of the parliament (parliamentary committees) and the deputies. The most valuable and at the same time most comparable observations with regard to the various parliamentary practices are made against the background of the practice of parliamentary committees, especially committees of inquiry, which is why we are going to focus on them in this chapter.

Plenary accountability

Parliament-wide accountability is carried out through debates on the government's policies as a whole (in particular in the vote of confidence/no confidence procedure), individual government policies (such as European Union [EU] governments' reporting on their policies towards the EU or reporting on the state's foreign policy objectives) or specific scopes of its action (such as reporting on specific, individual events). In this respect, with the exception of classified matters, there are no material limitations. The government may be called upon by parliament to report to it on any issue. In some cases, this obligation to give an account may be expressed directly in the applicable law. In the EU Member States, this is the case with regard to reporting on the government's activities in relation to the EU bodies in particular.

The government's accountability for its budgetary policy needs to be singled out. Typically, this is carried out in annual cycles (financial year). The government's report on the implementation of the budget law in the previous year serves as its basis. Its content covers the activities of all entities implementing

2 For example Robert Hazell reports that there are seven classic functions of legislatures. These are: Representation; Legislation; Deliberation; Scrutiny; Budget setting; Making and breaking governments; and Redress of grievances. Robert Hazell, "The Challenges Facing Our Parliaments: How Can We Improve Their Performance?" Australasian Parliamentary Review 16, no. 2 (Spring 2001), 5–26, at 23–4. Parliaments themselves define their functions in various ways – see: Ken Coghill et al., "The Functions of Parliament: Reality Challenges Tradition", *Australasian Parliamentary Review* 27, no. 2 (Spring 2012): 55–70, at 57–8.

3 Kaare Strøm, Wolfgnang C. Müller and Daniel M. Smith, "Parliamentary Control of Coalition Governments", *Annual Review of Political Science* 13 (2010): 517–35, at 522.

the state budget, primarily the government. What is relevant from the point of view of the parliament in its capacity as Principal, the government's account of the implementation of the Budget Act is not the only document used by it to assess the performance of the government as the Agent implementing the state budget. Usually, the government account is supplemented by a report from a supreme audit institution, i.e. a state authority independent of the government, professional and specialised in state audit, conducting it in a continuous fashion.[4] The national audit institutions review the budgetary and legal correctness of the implementation of the financial plans. It determines whether the public accounts include expenditure that should have been incurred and do not include expenditure that could not have been incurred, and include revenue that should have been collected and do not include revenue that could not have been collected. Without the Auditors' report, parliament would not be able to carry out a substantive assessment of the government's budgetary activities.[5] In a number of countries, the state authority, which is independent of the government and conducts the state's monetary policy, also formulates its report. Consequently, in the budget execution (discharge) assessment procedure, parliamentarians are provided with professionally prepared analytical material. Its content makes it possible to hold the government rationally accountable for the conduct of budgetary policy.[6]

At the request of the parliament and to the extent indicated by it, the audit institution also carries out an audit of the government's implementation of

4 There are three kinds of supreme audit institutions (SAI) frameworks:

1) The Anglo-Saxon model, used in the United Kingdom, most Commonwealth countries and some European countries, as well as Latin American countries (Peru and Chile). A National Audit Office is headed by an independent Auditor General or equivalent, which submits audit reports to a committee of Parliament (often the Public Accounts Committee).
2) The Judicial model (in France, many Latin countries in Europe, Turkey, francophone countries in Africa and Asia and several Latin American countries (Brazil and Colombia)). The SAI acts as a Court of Accounts or Cour des Comptes belonging to the judicial system.
3) The Board or Collegiate model used by many Asian countries including Indonesia, Japan and the Republic of Korea, some European countries, including Germany and the Netherlands as well as Poland. In this model SAI acts in a similar way to the Anglo-Saxon model except an audit board or boards produces audit reports and submits these to Parliament. Supreme Audit Institutions, https://sirc.idi.no/about/what-are-sais.

5 Jerzy Kuciński, *Sejmowa kontrola działalności rządu z perspektywy prawnoustrojowej i praktyki politycznej* (Warsaw: Dom Wydawniczy Elipsa, 2017), 190–2.

6 A somewhat different issue is the practice of discharge, by which we mean, firstly, the actual ability of MPs to draw rational conclusions from the analytical material provided to them, and secondly, the consequences of a negative assessment of the government's actions and the political motives for granting/not granting the government discharge on the execution of the state budget. The latter issue, however, is not directly related to the accountability of the government, but to the expression of confidence in it, i.e. an issue not addressed by us in this publication.

particular state policies or specific actions it has taken. In some states, such an audit is carried out at the request of a proportion of MPs. In Austria, for instance, at least one-third of the deputies of the National Council (i.e. a minority of the deputies) have the power to initiate an audit, which is carried out by the Austrian Court of Audit (ACA), the Austrian supreme audit institution.[7] The involvement of state audit bodies allows MPs to learn about the course of the executive's actions and its legal assessment drawn up by a body specialised in drafting such legal documents. This happens independently of the interactions that take place directly between the parliament and the government. It is also the kind of activity that, in principle, the government cannot ignore. It cannot dose information and thus distort parliamentary perception of its policies. It is not its will that determines the scope and content of the information provided, but the will of a third party – the state audit body.

The parliament's instruments of holding accountable those entrusted with power extend to entities other than the government, with regard to which the entrustment relationship is not evident or even non-existent. State bodies appointed with parliamentary participation (e.g. the ombudsman), as well as those completely independent of parliament (including the supreme court), are often required to provide an annual report on their activities. Such accounts are intended to inform parliament of significant issues arising in the practice of these bodies, but to a certain extent they can also function as an accountability of the authority exercised. It is difficult to explain otherwise why such bodies may sometimes avoid submitting this report under conditions of debate (such as the Polish Constitutional Tribunal).[8] However, this sort of information on activities or reports must be regarded more as an instrument of the deliberative function or representation of parliament. This is due to the fact that they primarily serve the purpose of obtaining information on what needs to be rectified in the state, which elements of the law and the decision-making process seem to be malfunctioning.

The plenary accountability of the executive by the legislature is shaped by two streams of relations. Firstly, the relations based on political communication occurring directly between the parliament and the executive. Secondly, there are relations built around clerical communication conducted in a triangle: legislature–state control body(ies)–executive. Plenary accountability incorporates a high probability of efficiency. Essentially, its level of realisation depends not so much on the will of the Agent as on the will of the Principal to seek information of interest from the Agent. This will of the Principal will vary. Its distribution is not politically neutral, instead it depends on the political relations taking place between the Principal and the Agent. The category of

7 Art. 127 sec. 7 Constitution of Austria (German: *Österreichische Bundesverfassung*).

8 For example, in 2020, the President of the Polish Constitutional Tribunal did not appear at the committee meeting nor at the plenary session of the Sejm. https://prawo.gazetaprawna.pl/artykuly/1453486,przylebska-posiedzenie-sejmowej-komisji-dzialalnos-tk.html.

parliamentary majority/minority therefore does apply to accountability. The MPs of the parliamentary majority do not necessarily have an interest in pursuing information through legal channels, as they can obtain it through less formalised channels, i.e. through party interaction. They may, on the other hand, express interest in restricting access to information on the government's activities when it is unfavourable to the government and thus unfavourable also to the MPs of the parliamentary majority. Not only does restricting access to information on government activities for the sake of political protection nullify accountability, but it also undermines the principles of a democratic community that makes public use of its knowledge of the political relations taking place and that continuously evaluates individual political formations or political activists. With a view to building an open society as a *sine qua non* of a democratic state, the rights of the opposition to obtain information on the activities of the government and to spark a parliamentary debate in this regard are legally guaranteed in a number of modern states. Irrespective of the will of the parliamentary majority, the obligation to carry out the activity in question arises at the request of a certain number (percentage) of MPs. In this respect, Article 114(3) of the Portuguese Constitution is instructive; according to which, the political parties represented in the Assembly of the Republic that are not part of the government especially enjoy the right to obtain information regularly and directly from the government regarding the development of matters of public interest. In turn in Austria, according to § 74b of the Rules of Procedure of the National Council, plenary debates are held at least four times a year on topics of interest to the EU.[9] At the written request of at least five MPs, members of government appear in parliament and inform MPs of issues of interest to them (Section 81 of the Rules of Procedure). Similarly, a debate is held in the National Council at the request of at least five MPs on the reply to an MP's written query given by the chancellor or a member of the government. In Bulgaria (Article 90 of the Constitution), at the request of at least one-fifth of the representatives of the people on an interpellation, a parliamentary discussion is held and a resolution is adopted. According to Section 43 of the Finnish Constitution, a group of at least 20 MPs may submit an interpellation to the Government or an individual minister on matters within the competence of the Government or the minister. The interpellation is answered at the plenary session of Parliament within 15 days of its receipt by the Government. The debate on the interpellation is followed by a vote of confidence in parliament regarding the government or minister, unless a motion of no confidence in the government or minister is tabled during the debate. The institutionalisation of the parliamentary opposition, and its associated right to evoke the government's case in the public forum, makes the accountability mechanisms obstructed in this respect, since, notwithstanding

9 https://www.parlament.gv.at/en/explore/making-laws/legal-bases/rules-of-procedure-of-the-austrian-national-council/ (accessed 28.08.2023).

the will of the parliamentary majority, there is a mechanism for obliging the Agent to report on the tasks assigned to him/her. In turn, the circumstances of scrupulousness in seeking information and reporting on public tasks performed remain in the sphere of political practice and its assessment by citizens.

Accountability before committees

At the level of the internal bodies of parliaments (chambers of parliament), accountability of the executive is implemented through a system of parliamentary committees, known as "the poster organisations" of parliamentary scrutiny.[10] Their number and structure correlate with the number and structure of ministries.[11] This way, both accountability and issue-based scrutiny of individual areas of government activity are carried out.

Three classical instruments of government accountability are used in the parliamentary committee system: the right to information, the right to attendance and the right to a hearing.

In some countries, the right to demand information is designed as a cyclical right. In the United Kingdom, members of the Cabinet are required to cooperate with parliamentary committees, including responding to a call from a committee.[12] However, there are times when vague or factually incorrect answers are provided (such as regarding Iraq's possession of nuclear weapons, which was the pretext for the 2003 attack by the United Kingdom and several other states on that country) to answer the questions posed. For the sake of the public interest, members of the Cabinet can refuse to provide answers and indeed this is the practice. Therefore, they are in fact not necessarily bound by the will of the Principal, but they do decide to a considerable extent what information they provide to the committee and how they will use the committee's findings.

The British example should be regarded as an isolated case. The practice in European countries is dominated by the obligation of a government member to appear before a parliamentary committee. In Germany, for instance, the summoning of a minister by a committee of the Bundestag (as well as by the chamber *in corpore*) entails the obligation to appear. Any refusal to appear is

10 David Judge, "Walking the Dark Side: Evading Parliamentary Scrutiny", *The Political Quarterly* 92, no. 1 (2021): 283–92.

11 See e.g. Klaus von Beyme, *Parliamentary Democracy: Democratization, Destabilization, Reconsolidation, 1789–1999* (London: Palgrave Macmillan, 2000), 61; Cristina Leston-Bandeira, *From Legislation to Legitimation: The Role of the Portuguese Parliament* (Routledge, 2004), 46; Donald R. Matthews and Henry Valen, *Parliamentary Representation: The Case of the Norwegian Storting* (Columbus: Ohio State University Press, 1999), 157.

12 There are occasional cases of insubordination – non-appearance of cabinet members – see Hannah White, *Parliamentary Scrutiny of Government*, Institute for Government 2014, 24, available at: https://www.instituteforgovernment.org.uk/sites/default/files/publications/Parliamentary%20scrutiny%20briefing%20note%20final.pdf.

treated as a breach of parliamentary rules. However, similarly to other countries, appearance at a parliamentary committee meeting does not entail an obligation to provide a full and factually correct answer. The extent and factual accuracy of the answers given by members of government reflect their will. Persons summoned are not subject to legal liability for refusing to answer or making false statements. Also in other countries, the practice of ministers being heard by standing committees is common; so, for example, in Romania, in accordance with Article 54 of the Rules of Procedure of the Chamber of Deputies, at each session (session) of the Chamber of Deputies, ministers present to the relevant parliamentary committees a report on the work and strategy of their ministries.[13] Once ministers have presented their policies, MPs can ask questions and hold discussions.

In addition to information obtained directly from the government, parliamentary committees have extensive access to information coming from other public authorities. Among these, it is worth highlighting the information produced by state audit bodies, which also include the government and government administration in their sphere of competence. Typically, this is professionally drafted information on various aspects of government activity, presented both in general terms (characterisation of the implementation of particular state strategies or public policies), as well as on specific actions taken by the government or episodic audits – resulting from an event of interest to the parliamentary committee. In a significant number of countries, parliamentary committees are competent to entrust a state audit body to carry out an audit in the area of interest (e.g. France, Poland).

As part of their right to be heard, parliamentary committees formulate positions, reports or other types of statements addressed to the government and calling for a proper response. In Poland, for example, the relevant minister responds to a report (desideratum) within 30 days of receiving it. If the parliamentary committee finds the response to the report unsatisfactory, or if it has not received it at all, it may formulate a new report, at the same time informing the Speaker of the Sejm of the inappropriate action of a member of the government, which results in the intervention of the Speaker of the Sejm with the competent minister or prime minister. Committee reports also serve as a basis for the future activity of individual committees or of the entire Parliament.[14]

In this context, the British select committees' reports stand out. These are recognised as professionally produced analytical material, often critical of the

13 Regulations of the Chamber of Deputies, https://www.cdep.ro/pls/dic/site.page?den=regcd2_1#s5 (accessed 24.08.2023).

14 Hironori Yamamoto, *Tools for Parliamentary Oversight. A Comparative Study of 88 National Parliaments* (Geneva: Inter-Parliamentary Union, 2007), 34.

government policies described. It is the government's duty to respond to the parliamentary committee's report, a process which usually takes two months.[15]

Committees of inquiry as a particular tool of accountability

The complexity of decision-making processes and government-led policies, and the sometimes spectacular failures or scandals associated with them, means that the competences of parliamentary standing committees may be insufficient to receive and assess a government report. The triad requesting information, attendance and a hearing may prove ineffective from the point of view of the chain of entrustment and accountability. In most countries[16] parliamentary committees of inquiry are programmed for such circumstances. Occasionally, standing parliamentary committees are also equipped with investigative powers, such as the Defence Committee in the German Bundestag.[17] The tradition of their appointment dates back a long time[18] and they are known to the vast majority of political systems in democratic countries.[19]

The committee of inquiry (COI) is a variant of parliamentary committees, meaning it is an internal and subsidiary body of parliament, typically composed only of MPs (exceptions include, for example, the Danish parliamentary committees of inquiry composed of experts), appointed to investigate a specific matter. Its function results in it having competences not exercised by parliament, which extend externally, beyond intra-parliamentary issues and

15 Philip Norton, "Old Institution, New Institutionalism? Parliament and Government in the UK", in *Parliaments and Governments in Western Europe*, ed. Philip Norton (London: Routledge, 1998), 35.

16 These include countries such as: Austria, Belgium, Bulgaria, Croatia, Czech Republic, Denmark, Estonia, France, Germany, Italy, Latvia, lithuania, the Netherlands, Poland, Portugal, Romania, Slovenia, Spain. .

17 E.g. the 2019 case on Defence Minister Ursula von der Leyen's appointment of external consultants to the ministry, receiving exorbitant fees with no equivalent in the work they do. The Defence Committee found, among other things, that the minister deleted text messages that were evidence of this. "Ursula von der Leyen Tries to Contain Fallout over Consultants", *Financial Times*, 14 February 2020.

18 Olivier Rozenberg, "Inquiries by Parliaments. The Political Use of a Democratic Right", Brussels: Policy Department for Citizens' Rights and Constitutional Affairs Directorate-General for Internal Policies, 2020, 15 https://hal.archives-ouvertes.fr/hal-02888751/document (accessed 20.06.2023); Anna Młynarska-Sobaczewska and Piotr Polak, "Komisje śledcze w Polsce międzywojennej", *Przegląd Prawa Konstytucyjnego* 4, no. 62 (2021): 287–99 at 288.

19 In some countries such as the Scandinavian countries (with the exception of Denmark) or the United Kingdom, it is uniquely not possible to set up parliamentary committees of inquiry (with the exception of the House of Lords) or to endow standing committees with investigative powers. In the United Kingdom, political inquiry is carried out by ministries or by royal commissions of inquiry appointed by the government (White, 34–5). In Slovakia, on the other hand, the possibility of setting up a parliamentary committee of inquiry existed until 1996, when the Constitutional Court ruled that their creation was contrary to the principle of a tri-partite government and unconstitutional due to the lack of a legal basis in the constitution.

even beyond the structure of the apparatus of public authorities, consisting in investigative activities such as questioning witnesses or the right to request the files of any case. Another feature that distinguishes committees of inquiry from other parliamentary committees is their legal standing. Due to the extent of their powers (discussed below), this is constitutional in most countries,[20] and in exceptional cases only statutory.[21] Again, their mode of operation depends not only on parliamentary regulations, but also on the provisions of the law and criminal law. At the same time, however, the scope of their application in the work of a committee of inquiry may vary. It may be "appropriate" to the needs of parliamentary proceedings, or it may relate to particular – statutorily designated – aspects of the activity of a committee of inquiry.[22]

Most often, committees of inquiry are set up *ad hoc* to investigate a specific case,[23] and the commencement of their operation is determined by the will of Parliament, which is specified in a resolution of the Chamber. It is permissible to decide in the resolution appointing a committee of inquiry on the date on which it is to submit its report, particularly when the matter is not overly complicated or when it is nearing the end of the parliamentary term, which also brings the committee's work to an end. In some countries, the law limits the duration of a committee of inquiry. In France, it is no more than 6 months. In Austria, a committee of inquiry terminates after 14 months, but it is allowed to extend its activities twice, each time for no more than 3 months, i.e. up to a total of 20 months (unless the end of the parliamentary term is imminent). Furthermore, the parliament, as the body setting up the committee of inquiry and deciding on the ratio of its activities, is empowered to summon the committee to carry out specific actions at any time, or – while it is already functioning – to set a deadline for the submission of its report.

20 It should be added that it was not until the 2008 constitutional reform that such a regulation was introduced in France; according to Article 51-2: "In order to implement the monitoring and assessment missions laid down in the first paragraph of article 24, committees of inquiry may be set up within each House to gather information, according to the conditions provided for by statute. Statutes shall determine their rules of organization and operation. The conditions for their establishment shall be determined by the Rules of Procedure of each House".

21 In Estonia, for example, the appointment of committees of inquiry is allowed under the rules of parliament, not the constitution (Estonia: Riigikogu Rules of Procedure and Internal Rules Act).

22 As in Poland, in the proceedings before the committee of inquiry, the provisions of criminal procedure apply mutatis mutandis with regard to summoning and questioning witnesses, releasing them from the obligation of secrecy to the extent not regulated by the Act on the Parliamentary Committee of Inquiry, the appointment of a representative, including also the procedure for the consideration of a request for the application of a disciplinary penalty and its enforcement against a witness. Also on the basis of the provisions of the Code of Criminal Procedure, the Prosecutor General performs certain activities ordered by the committee.

23 Parliamentary standing committees, permanently endowed with investigative powers, such as the committees of the US Congress or the German Bundestag's Defence Committee, rarely exercise investigative powers.

The exceptional nature of the legal remedies assigned to a committee of inquiry means that it is not an ordinary parliamentary committee. Only when all the tools available to and used by parliament to ascertain and investigate the actions of the government have failed, i.e. failed to achieve the desired objectives, can a committee of inquiry be set up. In this functionally designated sense, a committee of inquiry can be described as an auxiliary body of parliament created precisely to hold the executive to account. The subsidiarity of the committee of inquiry to parliament is of a different measure than the subsidiarity of the other committees to parliament. It is a subsidiarity to all powers held and used by parliament and its internal organs, including parliamentary committees.

To a significant extent, the legal nature of a commission of inquiry is determined by the legally limited application of the rules of criminal procedure in proceedings before it. However, the (limited) application of the rules of criminal procedure by a committee of inquiry does not turn it into a judicial authority, a public prosecutor or a body of similar substance. It is not appointed to formulate an indictment or to adjudicate on culpability or punishment understood in terms of criminal law. It does not have the power to replace the public authorities competent in this respect. The application of the criminal law procedure is intended to make it possible to carry out the parliamentary task of ascertaining the course of events implemented by the executive and assessing them from the point of view of the policy shared by the parliamentary majority.

By investigating certain events using instruments known to criminal procedure, the committee of inquiry does not cease to be a parliamentary body, i.e. a political body *par excellence*, composed of persons engaged in political activities and pursuing political objectives. Although in European countries the parliamentary mandate is *de iure* representative, in reality parliamentarians are bound by party discipline and take the guidelines of their political formation into account, both at the stage of the proceedings and when formulating their conclusions. Thus, the outcome of a committee's work is similar, typical of parliament. Political criteria determine the establishment of a committee of inquiry and the subject and methodology of its work, the content of the recommendations produced, the method and intensity of their implementation. The range of means available to the committee, on the other hand, is to enable it to carry out the mandate assigned to it by the parliamentary chamber.

The appointment of COIs is an independent decision of the chamber of parliament. Typically and naturally, the appointment of committees of inquiry by the parliamentary majority prevails. In Germany and Italy, the appointment of committees requires a simple majority. In turn, according to Polish statutory regulation, a committee is appointed by the Sejm by an absolute majority of votes. The latter solution obviously increases the dependence of the commencement of the parliamentary inquiry on the will of the majority. Spain is a clear example, where 16 commissions of inquiry were proposed in the 2004–8 legislature, but only one was set up.[24]

This logic of the parliamentary majority, which, after all, preconditions the existence of the government but also the possibility of holding it to account, is at times relaxed, though. So in Germany, the Bundestag has the right to set up a COI and in the event of a request by at least a quarter of the members, it is obliged to establish one, according to a rule already laid down in the Basic Law (Grundgesetz).[25] It has been emphasised in the literature that this is a vital minority right, used in particular by the opposition to ensure investigation of cases of alleged misgovernment, maladministration or misconduct on the part of individual politicians.[26]

Similarly, a commission of inquiry must be set up at the request of a certain number of MPs in: Portugal (at least one-fifth of the deputies in the Assembly of the Republic), Austria (at least one-quarter of the total number of deputies in the National Council), Slovenia (at least one-third of one deputy in the State Assembly) or Latvia (at least one-third of the deputies in the Sejm). The obligatory appointment of committees of inquiry at the request of a representative group of opposition MPs (complemented – as in Germany or Austria – by due respect for minority motions also in the course of the work of the committees of inquiry) allows the parliament (Principal) to call the government (Agent) to report on activities, obliging it to give an account. A certain range of governmental affairs ceases to be at the real, exclusive and publicly undisclosed disposal of the government and becomes the subject of information called to the public forum and determined therein. The reaction of the executive to the request to give an account, to its readiness to respond, can be observed openly. Irrespective of the content of the report to be given, and even more so of the legal and political implications of the activity of the committee of inquiry, the compulsory appointment of a committee of inquiry at the request of a representative group of members of a parliamentary minority should be perceived as a mechanism of dependence of the government on parliament, understood not so much as a parliamentary majority, but actually parliament as a public authority in its politically diverse composition, but at the same time uniformly exercising a representative mandate.

24 Manuel Sanchez De Dios, "El Control del Ejecutivo en la Democracia Parlamentaria Europea. Estudio comparado de España, Francia, Reino Unido, Italia y Portugal desde la teoría de la agencia", *Revista De Las Cortes Generales* 78 (2009): 135–74. at 161.

25 Art. 44 sec. 1: (1) The Bundestag shall have the right, and on the motion of one quarter of its Members the duty, to establish a committee of inquiry, which shall take the requisite evidence at public hearings. The public may be excluded.

26 Suzanne Linn and Frank Sobolewski, *The German Bundestag – Functions and Procedures. Organisation and Working Methods: The Legislation of the Federation* (Kurschners Politikkontakte, 2015), 51. However, at this point it should be remarked that this minority right is rarely exercised, especially in recent years due to the substantial size of the governing coalitions and the atomisation of the opposition (Rozenberg, 34).

The method of electing COI members constitutes an essential factor in determining the body's ability to carry out the tasks assigned to it. The composition of the committee determines to a large extent the sense in which the body is established, and often the condition for the desired outcome of the entire investigative project. Interestingly, the legislator tends to regulate the issue of the selection of members of committees of inquiry in a special way – if compared to the formation of the composition of other parliamentary committees. The differences relate to the majority of votes necessary to carry out the above activity in parliament, the setting of the maximum number of committee members and the regulation of the political affiliation of committee members. The sum of the above elements determines the distinctive features of the staffing of the committee of inquiry.[27]

The regulation of the composition of committees of inquiry shows significant similarities. Only deputies may be members of a committee.[28] Mostly, the structure of the committees must reflect the proportion of power in the parliament, so it is in parity (France, Germany, Poland, Italy). Thereby, the customary and generally approved in practice structure of parliamentary committees, expressing the main lines of political divisions articulated in parliament, in relation to the committee of inquiry, has been normatively shaped. In doing so, the formula that each political formation is represented in a committee of inquiry by the same number of MPs is rejected. Italian Rules of Procedure in this matter echo the constitutional regulation, on the composition of COIs.[29] In Germany, under § 4 of the Act, the Bundestag determines the number of members and substitute members of the committee of inquiry, provided that the composition of the committee reflects the composition of Parliament; each faction must be represented. The number of seats for the parliamentary groups is calculated using the mathematical proportion method (St. Lague/Schepers). The members are elected by the parliamentary factions,

27 Similar comments apply to the issue of the selection and composition of select committees (Backbench Business Committee) in the British Parliament, especially under the Wright reforms. Richard Kelly and Lucinda Maer, "Parliamentary Reform and the Accountability of Government to the House of Commons", in ***Parliament: Legislation and Accountability***, ed. Alexander Horne and Andrew Le Sueur (Oxford: Hart Publishing, 2016), 147.

28 Against the background of the cited legal solutions, the Danish regulations are atypical. Under these, a commission of inquiry is composed of experts, including judges.

29 The Constitution of the Italian Republic regulates commissions of inquiry in article 82, according to which: "Each House of Parliament may conduct enquiries on matters of public interest. For this purpose, it shall detail from among its members a Committee formed in such a way so as to represent the proportionality of existing Parliamentary Groups. A Committee of Inquiry may conduct investigations and examination with the same powers and limitations as the judiciary". They are further regulated by the Rules of Procedure of the Chamber of Deputies (Articles 140–2) and Article 162-3of the Rules of Procedure of the Senate. Both regulations provide, essentially echoing the constitutional regulation, that the composition of committees of inquiry must reflect the proportion of parliamentary groups (141.1 and 162.3).

the chairperson and the deputy are appointed by the committee in accordance with the arrangements laid down by the Council of Elders. The Polish Act provides that the composition of the committee should proportionally reflect the composition of the parliamentary clubs and groups – though only those with representatives in the Council of Seniors. This is a classic solution for the rules of parliamentarism, but again it draws attention to subordination to the logic of the parliamentary majority – ensuring parity in composition does not release the majority from supremacy in COIs.[30]

The Polish Act also regulates the number of committee members (Art. 2.2) with the maximum being 11 persons. Limiting the number of committee members is a rather unique solution in parliamentary law. As a rule, the law does not specify the number of committee members. The raison d'être of this standardisation is to make the committee a capable, operational body. Excessively large bodies devolve into discussion forums, consume resources on generating and then resolving internal conflicts and lose their ability to communicate with the outside world by carrying out their originally assigned tasks. French regulation is similar in this respect. In France, where a commission of inquiry may be set up by the National Assembly or the Senate at the request of one or more members of one of the chambers of parliament, it may consist of no more than 30 deputies.

All committees of inquiry in the examined states have extensive investigative power, regulated in quite a similar manner; they may carry out on-the-spot investigations; request documents from the government, national authorities, agencies, any natural or legal persons; seek expert opinions; interview officials as well as any other natural person.[31] The specificity of the work of COIs requires particular procedural rules. On one hand, they are parliamentary bodies, by their nature internal and auxiliary to parliament *in pleno* – and on the other hand, investigative committees conduct investigations, gathering evidence and establishing facts, therefore they operate under a strictly defined procedure, fulfilling the obligations of revealing the truth and guaranteeing the rights of persons interviewed by committees. Therefore, references to court procedures appear in the regulations. For example the Italian Rules

30 It is worth noting that in Poland in February 2022 a draft was presented for a commission of inquiry in the controversial case of wiretapping and tracking of citizens, including opposition politicians, by the authorities with the Pegasus system – the application was submitted by independent deputies, and the proposed composition differs slightly from the assumptions of the Act: 5 seats each for the government majority and the opposition and 11 seats for the chairperson for an independent MP. The draft was not approved by the Sejm, but in the next term of office, after a change of ruling majority, in January 2024,such committee has been rapidly and almost unanimously created.

31 *Committees of Inquiry in National Parliaments. Comparative Survey*, Policy Department for Citizens' Rights and Constitutional Affairs Directorate-General for Internal Policies, PE 649.524 – March 2020, Study requested by the AFCO committee, available: https://www.europarl.europa.eu/RegData/etudes/STUD/2020/649524/IPOL_STU(2020)649524_EN.pdf. (accessed 22.09.2023).

of Procedure of both chambers confer the same constraints on parliamentary committees as on judicial authorities (art. 141.2 and 162.5 respectively). The German Act defines the procedure of the commission's work in great detail, paying particular attention to transparency[32] and exhaustively specifies the modes of the committee's activities, the conduct of the inquiry and the obligations of federal authorities, corporations, institutions and foundations in this respect.[33] The Act also contains regulation on the resolution of disputes arising from the functioning of a committee of inquiry – they are resolved by the Federal Court of Justice (§ 36).

In Poland the provisions of the Code of Criminal Procedure apply accordingly to the questioning of persons summoned by the committee; every person summoned by the committee is required to give evidence.[34] It is worth to mention that many of the norms contained in the Polish Act concern the exclusion of members if there are doubts as to their impartiality.[35] In some countries, a committee of inquiry is obliged to take evidence at the request of a certain number of its members, as in Germany, at the request of at least a quarter of the members of a committee. Following such an arrangement enhances the ability of a COI to obtain the information it needs and, at the same time, reduces the risk of it being instrumentalised by the parliamentary majority. It minimises the risk that a majority of committee members will refuse to agree to the necessary evidence, guessing that its provision could result in the establishment of politically unfavourable facts.

A factor that frequently determines the effectiveness of the stated objective of a committee of inquiry is the competence to summon persons and take evidence from them. In essence, a person summoned by a COI is treated as a witness in criminal proceedings. He or she is compelled to appear and give evidence. Giving false testimony or concealing the truth is an offence punishable by imprisonment. Public authorities shall, at the request of the commission, provide written explanations or produce documents at their disposal or the file

32 § 12 of the 2001 Act on Committees of Inquiry (Gesetz zur Regelung des Rechts der Untersuchungsausschüsse des Deutschen Bundestages (Untersuchungsausschussgesetz – PUAG) of 19.06.2001 (BGBl. I S. 1142)): The committee may also appoint its own investigator, conferring on her/him the scope of the investigation (Sec. 10). It is also necessary here to distinguish investigative committees, which the Bundestag establishes to prepare legislative decisions on complex and important issues. They are composed of Members of the Bundestag and external experts, who enjoy the same rights as the parliamentarians and prepare the materials for legislative decision-making (after: Linn and Sobolewski, 50–1).

33 § 12, 13, 18 of the 2001 Act on Committees of Inquiry.

34 This general rule applies to everyone summoned by the committee of inquiry; the Constitutional Tribunal only exempted those holding positions with a legal status independent of other constitutional bodies (e.g. the President of the National Bank of Poland) from the obligation to testify.

35 Articles 4, 4a, 5, 5a and 6 of the 1999 Act of Committee of Inquiry – these provisions were laid down in the amendment of 3 June 2005, following the experience of the first committee of inquiry.

of any case handled by them. The principle of broad access to information is emphasised very clearly in German law and practice.

The Constitutional Court decided that the discretion of government to decide which documents contain relevant information for the Bundestag breaches the investigative powers of COI.[36] The Court also confirmed the COIs' right to request information and its scope in its 2009 and 2016 rulings.[37]

By contrast, one of the bigger practical challenges faced by committees of inquiry set up in European countries is the wording of questions and their admissibility. Occasionally, politically motivated MPs mislead witnesses about facts in order to validate a wrongful act, or formulate questions that include answers, and when they fail to obtain confirmation of the thesis they put forward in such a question, they present it over and over again. We also see questions relating to events that the committee was not appointed to investigate. These actions can be seen as an attempt to force witnesses to testify and prevent them from speaking freely. It also raises the question of the worth of testimony received this way. Often, there is also the issue of disclosure of confidential (professional, business, state or other) information during the hearing. In some countries, consideration of the proper use of classified information by the committee of inquiry leads to the involvement of non-parliamentary bodies. For example, in Austria, the Constitutional Court may rule on the legal classification of information of interest to a committee of inquiry. The Constitutional Court is competent to rule on the inquiry committee's obligation to maintain confidentiality of information. In Poland, on the other hand, to obtain permission to be heard as to facts covered by statutorily protected secrecy, the investigating committee is required to approach a general court.

Presenting a committee with the task of investigating a particular case does not mean that it has to perform all activities directly. It may ask the public prosecutor's office (or, as in Germany, the examining magistrate) to carry out certain activities, including: establishing certain facts, finding documents or confirming their authenticity in situations where there is a need for expertise, technical equipment not available to the commission.

In practice, the question of the investigative nature has raised numerous doubts as to the nature of the relationship with court proceedings, especially pending ones. The concurrent operation of commissions and courts (law enforcement agencies) may disrupt the separation of powers. Specific issues, such as public questioning of witnesses by a commission of inquiry and the impact of this event on the credibility of questioning the same witnesses in

36 The Federal Constitutional Court ruling of 17 June 2009, 2 BvE 3/07.

37 As the Federal Constitutional Court ruled in 2016: "The right of a parliamentary committee of inquiry to collect evidence is subject to limitations; any such limitation, including those set out by ordinary statutory law, must be rooted in constitutional law (cf. Accordingly, obligations arising under international law cannot immediately limit the parliamentary right to collect evidence, given that these obligations do not have constitutional rank", Order of 13 October 2016 – 2 BvE 2/15.

criminal proceedings, are of considerable importance. For this reason, in some countries (e.g. Bulgaria, France, Croatia or Romania[38]) it is prohibited to conduct simultaneous proceedings before a court and a committee of inquiry. In Germany or Poland, on the other hand, the legislator has responded favourably to the question of the concurrent investigation of a particular case by a parliamentary committee of inquiry and another public authority. The conduct of proceedings or their final closing by another public authority does not exclude the possibility of proceedings before the committee. For it is independent of other proceedings and no extra-parliamentary authority may condition its conduct. Nor is the outcome of work carried out before another body of public authority relevant to the proceedings in progress. The activity of the committee of inquiry is not interrupted either by the discontinuation of an investigation, the bringing of an indictment before a court or the suspension of court proceedings. Similarly, the findings of a COI are binding neither on the public prosecutor nor on other public authorities. By way of example, in Germany, according to Article 44 (4) of the Basic Law, the courts are free to evaluate and rule upon the facts that were the subject of the investigation. Permitting the concurrent investigation of a case by a committee and another public authority is being justified by the fact that the activities of a COI and the outcome of its work do not constitute either evidence or guidelines binding on extra-parliamentary entities. These findings serve different purposes. The investigation of the circumstances of the government's actions, or omissions, also falls within the remit of parliament and is intended to hold the executive branch accountable for the tasks entrusted to it by parliament. While the essence of the work carried out by a prosecutor's office or a court is to uphold the rule of law, to ensure that crimes are prosecuted (prosecutor's office) and to administer justice (courts), respectively, then the essence of the establishment of a parliamentary committee is to investigate a specific case in which the government was (possibly: is) involved and to report to parliament on its assessment of the government's actions and the need to take specific measures. Potential requests to prosecute crimes committed or requests for constitutional liability are of secondary importance in the sense that they are not the causes for which parliament appoints a committee of inquiry. Therefore, although there may be a material overlap between the proceedings before a committee of inquiry and criminal procedural proceedings, the purpose of the proceedings, the bodies conducting them and the scope and methods used are different, consequently the outcome of the activity of the proceedings differs. At the same time, a committee of inquiry must take into account the complexity of the situation and the need to respect the independence of the judiciary and the independence of judges. Neither can it express views as to how a case should be decided by a court, nor can it put into question the legitimacy of judicial decisions.

38 *Committees of Inquiry in National Parliaments. Comparative Survey*, European Union, 2020, 15, http://www.europarl.europa.eu/supporting-analyses (accessed 26.08.2023).

This has been made clear by the Italian Constitutional Court defining the limits of judicial authority used by the COI; its task was declared as "not to judge, but only to gather news and data necessary for the exercise of the functions of the Chambers".[39]

Sometimes, however, the question of separating the functions and scope of judicial and commission proceedings raises serious questions of a different nature. In the Italian practice, the committees of inquiry occasionally take on the function of channelling attention and finding out the truth about controversial activities – albeit at the behest of the ruling majority. For this reason, they have even become known in the literature as "dishonest investigations",[40] replacing or overlapping ongoing judicial investigations.

A committee of inquiry acts as an auxiliary body of parliament, and its findings usually do not entail a sanctioning or binding effect. In Germany the report is submitted to the Bundestag (§ 33 of the 2001 Act on Committees of Inquiry) – if the committee does not agree on a joint report, separate opinions may be expressed. In Italy the report of a committee of inquiry is not determined by law – the usual practice is that the report is not discussed by the Italian Chamber. It has been emphasised in the literature that, on the one hand, this is a manifestation of the committee's autonomy, but on the other hand, it leads to reduced Chamber influence on the exercise of the oversight function.[41] The Polish rules on the preparation and presentation of the reports of COIs were quite substantially changed by the amendment to the 2005 Act, which introduced rules on dissenting opinions to the report, its preparation by the committee's chairperson and the right to present amendments, as well as the fact that the parliament does not vote on the committee's report. This was instituted following the bizarre end to the work of Poland's first committee of inquiry, where the report prepared by the committee was rejected by the Sejm in a vote; instead, out of several versions of the report prepared by its members as motions of minority, the chamber accepted only the one that was in radical contrast to the position voted on by the committee majority. It prompted a discussion about the legitimacy of such a "vote over the truth" established by the committee in its report; in consequence the amendment introduced a clear ban on voting on the committee's report.

In certain countries, the government is obliged to provide parliament with a response to the report of the committee of inquiry. This is the case in Finland, where the government must report on the measures it has taken in response to a parliamentary resolution based on the report of the committee of inquiry.

39 Sentenza della Corte Costitutionale n. 231/1975, 22 October 1975, available at: http://www.giurcost.org/decisioni/1975/0231s-75.html (accessed 22.09.2023).

40 "Inchieste canaglia" – see: Andrea Manzella, "Il Parlamento e le inchieste canaglia", *La Repubblica*, 12 August 2003; Eleonora Bardazzi, "Le Commissioni parlamentari d'inchiesta dopo la riforma costituzionale", 2016, 5, available at: https://www.forumcostituzionale.it/wordpress/wp-content/uploads/2016/06/bardazzi.pdf (accessed 20.04.2023).

41 Bardazzi, 5.

In France, on the other hand, six months after the publication of the report of the committee of inquiry, a member of the competent standing committee of parliament reports on the government's implementation of the conclusions contained in the COI's report.

Committees of inquiry are purely parliamentary bodies operating with transparency, and thus they provide the public with access to their investigations of matters of relevance and public importance. Yet it seems to be aptly argued in the literature that the primary objective and focus of the committee's work, especially from the point of view of the transparency of its work and its accountability function, is not the report, meaning a detailed document usually amounting to several hundred pages – but the investigation itself, frequently conducted in the spotlight – as is the case in Poland – or somewhat more discreetly, but still with public access to the evidence (Germany). Sittings, and particularly committee hearings, are usually open to the public, often streamed online or televised. It is on this element – the oral part of parliamentary investigations – that public attention is focused, and which seems to form the centrepiece and to make sense of the appointment of committees.[42] This is the case in Italy, and has also been the case in Poland since the first committee of inquiry, established in 2003.[43] The Polish law explicitly regulates the openness of the committee's work, including the right of the press to record images and sound from the meeting (under Article 16a). Against this background, the first broadcast of the German committee of inquiry meeting took place in 2005. At that time, however, the parties agreed that only the interrogation of ministers and secretaries of state would be broadcast, and not other witnesses. But this, in turn, showed who really runs and decides the work of the committee – not its members, but political parties. It was similar to the decision to terminate the work of the committee in connection with the elections – although the Federal Consitutional Court did not agree to such a solution at that time.[44]

From the point of view of the accountability under scrutiny, however, the most intriguing question is: what can a committee of inquiry – that special body set up solely to investigate, receive and verify an account within the framework of an executive entrustment relationship – investigate? What constitutes a matter of public concern?

The position of a parliamentary body assumes that the subject matter of the committee's proceedings must be a derivative of the parliament's function – as it is rightly argued, the parliament cannot entrust its body with more power

42 Rozenberg, 17.

43 The change occurred during the work of the Sejm Committee of Inquiry to investigate allegations of corruption during amendment of the Broadcasting Act. The case was the first one appointed on the basis of the 1999 Act.

44 BVerfGe, Beschluss vom 15.06.2005, 2 BvQ 18/05, Mehde, "Political Accountability in Germany", in *Political Accountability in Europe: Which Way Forward? A Traditional Concept of Parliamentary Democracy in an EU Context*, ed. Luc Verhey, Hansko Broeksteeg and Ilse Van den Driessche (Groningen: Europa Law Publishing, 2008), 99–119 at 112.

than it holds itself.[45] Thus, the matter that parliament delegates to a committee for investigation must fall within its sphere of competence as set out in the law. The constitutional regulations are rather vague in this respect, failing to indicate literally to what extent proceedings may be conducted in committees of inquiry – the Polish constitution indicates that these are "particular matters" (Art. 111), the Italian Constitution states that these are "matters of public interest" (Art. 82). The motive of public interest is further raised in the laws of Bulgaria, Croatia, the Czech Republic, Estonia, Spain, Latvia and Portugal. The German Basic Law does not determine the scope of the investigation at all. The problem with the committee's scope of action is, however, resolved by the German Act of 2001, according to which the committee may investigate matters within the limits of the constitutional jurisdiction of the Bundestag (Art. 1.3), also envisaging the Federal Constitutional Court's oversight of the limits of this competence. However, the issue of the limits of parliamentary investigations was a controversial and doubtful matter, as the legal norms here left some room for broad interpretation of parliamentary competences, which could lead to the assumption that committee investigations go beyond the function of overseeing the executive.[46]

A more systematic overview of the subject matter of the commissions of inquiry that have been set up in recent years in Poland, Germany and Italy makes it possible to assume that the category of public affairs within the framework of executive scrutiny is at times understood very broadly. The German example may be regarded as illustrative, where committees are set up frequently and regularly in every parliamentary term (63 committees have been appointed to date; on average, the number of committees is 3–4). The committees' scope of work is varied and the rich practice makes it difficult to classify them. However, many of them fall into the following categories:

1) Alleged or exposed abuses or negligence in the exercise of functions in the state administration (e.g. Investigation of abuses in the federal administration, such as "Platow" Committee of Inquiry (1951–2), COI "Visa issuing practice since 1998" (2004–5)),
2) Issues of malpractice in public procurement (e.g. the COI on contracts awarded in the Bonn area (1950–1), the Defence Committee "Case of bribery in the Federal Procurement Office of the Armed Forces in Koblenz" (1957)),

45 Jacek Zaleśny, "Status prawnoustrojowy sejmowej komisji śledczej", *Studia Politologiczne* 18 (2010): 157–205, at 176.

46 Bardazzi, 5; Alessandro Isoni, "Sui limiti del potere di inchiesta nel Parlamento bipolare", 2011, available at: https://www.rivistaaic.it/images/rivista/pdf/Isoni.pdf (accessed 20.04.2023).

3) Controversies surrounding large capital conversions (e.g. allegations of corruption in connection with the question of determining the capital between Bonn and Frankfurt (the so-called Spiegel Committee)),
4) The activities of the special services and state security (e.g. the committee on telephone tapping (1963–4), the COI on "State Security and Counterintelligence" (1968–9), the COI into the "Strauss/Scharnagl wiretapping affair" (1978–80)),
5) Incidental events generating great interest and agitation (e.g. Defence Committee as a Committee of Inquiry "The Rammstein Air Accident" (1988–9), COI on "HIV risk due to exposure to blood and blood products" (1993–4)).

German practice indicated also that most of the committees formed in the 21st century have concentrated on matters of public interest, right from the front pages of the German press; many of them were individual events that shocked public opinion (such as a terrorist attack or even a paedophile scandal), with no significant links to the functioning of the executive.[47] The function of the executive's control gives way here to the parliamentary will to explain matters that outrage the public opinion. In academic debate, disappointment has been expressed regarding their effectiveness,[48] as well as their submission to the reality of political confrontation rather than as an objective tool to get a reaction.[49] Sometimes neither the legal nor the political consequences of parliamentary investigations were significant – a perfect example is the last Wirecard report of the commission, published in April 2021 – it made serious accusations against Angela Markel and, above all, the then Minister of Finance, Olaf Scholz, who soon took the Chancellor's office, though.

Similar conclusions can be drawn from the Italian practice. Committees of inquiry have been appointed in the Italian Parliament on many occasions and have been particularly numerous in recent years.[50] Many of these have operated for multiple terms of office, which is striking given the duty of the committee to resolve the issue and the matter to which it is devoted. Among others, the Italian committees set up after World War II examined the Anti-Mafia matters seven times since 1958 (III, V, XI, XII, XV, XVII and XVIII terms of office), waste cycle – six times (XII, XIII, XIV, XVI, XVII, XVIII (XII term of office as COI of Chamber, after – Senate COI, in next terms: both

47 Rozenberg, 52.
48 Mehde, 112; George A. Wolf, "Die Optimierung von Auskunftspflichten im parlamentischen Untersuchungsverfahren", *Zeitschrift fur Parlamentsfragen* 36, no. 4 (2005): 876–87 at 876.
49 Mehde, 112.
50 Ten committees were appointed during the 14th parliamentary term, seven in the 16th term. The 17th term saw a record number: three parliamentary committees of inquiry were set up in the Senate, six unicameral committees in the House and there were three bicameral committees, making a total of 11 committees.

chambers). The committees of inquiry to investigate both of these matters have been appointed on a cyclical basis during the last decade.

A review of investigative committees in Italy indicates that committees of inquiry are also set up to look into sensitive issues, e.g. administrative fraud and unclear financial transactions, as well as state security (organised crime, terrorist attacks). They often have only an indirect, or even only potential relationship with the actions of the government, particularly those in office at the time of the investigation. As has been pointed out in the literature, the Italian experience shows that committees of inquiry are used as an instrument of the parliamentary majority. A parliamentary enquiry was regularly chosen in a purely political way, often in order to avoid cumbersome judicial investigations.[51]

This kind of practice can also be observed among Polish committees of inquiry. While compared to German and Italian practices, the number of Polish committees of inquiry is relatively small and the practice is fairly new; the COI Act was passed in 1999, with the first committee of inquiry only appearing in 2003. Since then, a maximum of three committees have been appointed in each parliamentary term. In the short practice of Polish committees, two trends regarding the matters of their interest seem to be prevalent. The first one involves a significant predominance of committees which are set up to investigate the circumstances of the involvement of the governmental administration in ownership transformations, including allegations of corruption and abuse occurring at the intersection of political and economic life – both in the process of conducting state affairs and in the preparation of legislative solutions (or their omission). Out of the total of ten committees established so far, eight investigated such affairs.

Moreover, several committees investigated allegations of the abuse of power on the part of members of the government against the special services, and allegations concerning the operation of the police and prosecution authorities. These issues drew the most attention of the parliamentary investigations, and all the committees were set up to investigate matters that stirred up public opinion, made headlines and had a strong impact on voters' opinions and beliefs. The reports of Polish COIs contain a number of motions for prosecution (e.g. in the report of the committee investigating pressure exerted on special services), but very few actual findings. Proposals for proceedings before the courts or the Tribunal of State were also announced and suggested in advance, although none of the committees formulated such a request. This feature of forensic accountability is clearly visible in Polish committees and since 2004 it has essentially consisted of the parliamentary majority demanding

51 Bardazzi cites, among others, examples of such investigations in the "Telekom Serbia" case (XIV term of office of parliament), as well as the "Mitrochin" case (COI appointed in 2002), affairs and scandals related to the activities of foreign intelligence and entering into particularly controversial matters of international interest against officially established foreign policy.

the exposure of the mistakes of their political opponents who held power in the past. One tends to agree with Rozenberg, who referred to Poland as an example of committees acting as "a majority-led procedure against the previous government".[52] In Poland, committees of inquiry have had a distinctly retrospective, perhaps even retaliatory character, often accompanied by the increasing polarisation of the political scene since the early 2000s.

The other noticeable trend is a pronounced reluctance or even failure to appoint committees during a second term, i.e. when the ruling majority wins – this was the case in the 2011–15 term and it has continued during the previous term (2019–23). Almost all committees in Poland were set up in an atmosphere of "restoring justice" after the rule of their predecessors and concerned past actions, that is, before the change of the parliamentary majority. This is exactly what happened after the incumbent opposition took power in the new term – the ruling majority almost immediately initiated the establishment of three committees of inquiry to investigate the alleged illegality and overreach of power in the previous term (the so-called "envelope' election planned and financed partially during the Covid-19 pandemic, the visa scandal and to investigate the operational and investigative activities undertaken with the Pegasus software).[53]

An analysis of the COIs from the point of view of their duty to report on their power shows that, despite the political intentions of the parliamentary factions, the analytical results of the committees of inquiry are impressive. Regardless of whether the issue concerns the Austrian, German, Polish committees or the US Congress committees with investigative powers, they produce extensive findings. The state of knowledge of the issues under investigation following the parliamentary enquiry is significantly deepened compared to the state of knowledge prior to the parliamentary enquiry.

What is significant from the point of view of accountability mechanisms is that the conclusions reached by the Principal after receiving the report, and in particular the consequences of the assessment of the report, must be separated from the passing of this information to the Principal by the Agent: how they affect the change of behaviour of the participants in political relations, the legal or political accountability of the persons whose activities were investigated by the commission of inquiry. Lack of spectacular political consequences of the activities of commissions of inquiry does not prevent them from being an important instrument for gaining knowledge about the activities of the executive. While it is therefore noted in the literature[54] that parliamentarians are rarely keen to clarify the matter under investigation and to identify those

52 Rosenberg, 34.

53 https://www.sejm.gov.pl/Sejm10.nsf/agent.xsp?symbol=KOMISJE_SLEDCZE&Nrkadencji=10 (available 22.02.2024).

54 See e.g. Ryszard M. Małajny, *Parlamentaryzm europejski* (Warsaw: Wydawnictwo Sejmowe, 2019), 430.

responsible for the improper exercise of governmental powers, that they are often concerned with creating media effects, drawing the attention of public opinion to certain issues, it should be emphasised that this does not invalidate the fact that the activity of committees of inquiry provides findings unattainable for a parliament applying typical (non-investigative) means of action, i.e. allows for the investigation of the matters these committees are appointed to investigate. This does not take place in an objective manner – for parliaments are also not an arena for establishing the truth, using an unobjectionable methodology of investigation. Nevertheless, parliamentary enquiries are among the most effective instruments of government's accountability. We share Matthias Keppel's opinion that the effects they achieve are far more momentous than those of any other parliamentary oversight mechanism.[55] Meanwhile, they lead to the most spectacular findings, unattainable under the regime of other parliamentary committees.

In this context, it is worth recalling the extensive findings of the Austrian commissions of inquiry, set up on matters crucial to the government's policies. Such was the nature of the Commission of Inquiry into the procurement of fighter aircraft (Eurofighter) established in 2006, and in subsequent years (2017, 2018) the two Commissions of Inquiry into the investigation of the Eurofighter Typhoon aircraft system. The Committee of Inquiry established in 2015 investigated the circumstances of the collapse of the Hypo Alpe-Adria bank, whose bonds were covered by government guarantees.[56] Two COIs into the so-called Ibizagate (set up in 2020) and into corruption in the government of Sebastian Kurz and the ÖVP party (set up in 2021) have established the occurrence of corrupt incidents of significant proportions in both the government and the ÖVP party, including extensive Russian penetration of the Austrian political elite.

In Belgium, a committee of inquiry was set up by the parliament in November 2001 to investigate the causes and consequences of the bankruptcy of the national airline Sabena and to determine possible liability for it. The committee also made recommendations to improve the control and rules of companies owned or controlled by public authorities.

Although the committee of inquiry appointed in Germany to investigate illegal surveillance of political parties by the secret service (Bundesnachrichtendienst – BND) confirmed the allegations made, it did not lead to a change in practice in this respect.[57] In turn, a committee of inquiry set up in Denmark in 2021 to investigate the issue of the government ordering the culling of all Danish mink

55 Matthias Keppel, "Political Control and Parliamentary Committees of Inquiry: Strengthening the Quality of Democracy", *Journal of the Knowledge Economy* 14, no. 2 (2023): 1298–320, 2, https://doi.org/10.1007/s13132-021-00883-x (accessed 27.06.2023).

56 https://www.parlament.gv.at/dokument/unterlagen/Ablauf_Untersuchungsausschuss.pdf (accessed 20.02.2024).

57 Keppel, 16.

found that the government's action in this matter was unjustified and that the public was being misled.

In Poland, the first commission of inquiry established in 2003 (the so-called Rywin commission) led to the identification of corrupt entanglements of members of the government in connection with the legislative process concerning the regulation of the mass media market, the existence of the deep state negating the mechanisms of democratic and transparent state decision-making process and, ultimately, the fall of the government and the formation of a new configuration of political parties in the parliament. The COI into irregularities in the supervision of the Ministry of the State Treasury over representatives of the State Treasury in the company PKN Orlen SA (the largest fuel concern in Poland) and allegations of illegal pressure on judicial authorities made it possible to establish the scale of Russian special services' penetration of the state energy sector and the prominent public administration officials' entanglement in this activity, dating back to the communist period. The COI investigating the correctness of the privatisation of PZU SA (Poland's largest insurer) established incidents of corruption and nepotism of significant proportions.

There is another remark concerning the effects of the COI's activities. The regulations (and practice) usually pay relatively little attention to committee reports. The preparation of the report, being *de iure* the outcome of the committee's work, as well as any follow-up measures taken in connection with its conclusions for the future, are not as relevant and attractive to the media as an inquiry in the presence of the cameras.[58] This is linked with the character of COIs. The committee's work is primarily performed in sittings, gathering oral testimony from those summoned – this provides a unique opportunity to give and take a report directly from Agents, and instantly. As a process, kind of a *cause celebre*, such enquiries can provide an explanation, even a cathartic effect – but they can also make a real opportunity to account, i.e. to receive the report and to make an assessment as to the accounts, the explanations of those who are obliged to give them.

Parliamentary committees of inquiry are frequently set up in connection with serious events that shock public opinion, although their connection with the actions of the executive is rather vague and remote. Examples of this are the committees of inquiry set up in France on the 2003 heat wave deaths and to investigate the so-called "Outreau affair", to look into the reasons why a group of residents were falsely accused of acts of paedophilia. They are also often appointed to deal with issues regarded as particularly controversial (such as paedophilia, child custody or organised crime) and concerning the activities of special services and law enforcement agencies. The majority of COIs are

58 Rozenberg, 19; Sebastian von Münchow, "Security Agencies and Parliamentary Committees of Inquiry in Germany: Transparency vs. Confidentiality", *The Quarterly Journal* [online] (2013): at 71, available at: http://connections-qj.org/system/files/12.4.03_Munchow.pdf (accessed 11.05.2022).

devoted to seeking links between big business and politics, which shows the socio-economic challenges of modern politics.

However, the evidence of the functioning of committees in the last dozen years, particularly in closer examined practice in Germany, Italy and Poland, shows that committees of inquiry are functionally, yet often indirectly connected with holding ministers or the government accountable for their policies or administration *in corpore*.[59] The German, Italian and Polish committees mainly look into issues related to the operation of state security organs, procedures of drafting legislative proposals, public procurement and more broadly: relations between business and authorities in specific matters, which creates an opportunity to examine things that are usually hidden. There is also a noticeable tendency to steer the interest of the committees towards the functioning of the judiciary, at times leading to concurrent proceedings in committees and in the courts – or parliamentary committees preceding possible court proceedings (Italy) or verifying them *ex post* (Poland).

A COI can therefore provide an excellent environment for accountability, not only of the government as the Agent entrusted with power by parliament, but also of ensuring their Agents give an account directly from the administration, state finances, and law enforcement services, including the special services. Under judicial procedure these are much better and more effective conditions for obtaining information, not only from a direct Agent, i.e. a minister or Prime Minister, but even more essentially, from officials of the entire complex apparatus of state administration, whose actions usually fade away into the secrecy of cabinets, small individual decisions, the "capillaries of power", according to Foucault's notion. At the same time, the committees' interest in such activities is a response to frustration caused by a lack of transparency in their activities, professionalism, as well as a multitude of issues, in which decisions significant from the point of view of governance (and its oversight) are buried. The committees play the role of obtaining and providing information and giving reports on how the authorities operate in depth.

As for their actual significance and the role they play as part of the checks and balances system, two features deserve particular attention, important from the point of view of exercising accountability.

The COI's parliamentarian, but at the same time quasi-judicial proceedings are a perfect environment for exercising the relationship between the Agent (i.e. members of the government or officials organisationally subordinated to them, possibly members of the judiciary) and the Principal, understood here as MPs involved in the committee's works. Such political investigations can also change the meaning of classical instruments of government oversight into tools of involving the media in political life – and lead to a change in the nature of the accountability and Agent-Principal relation in the contemporary legal cultures. This relationship is twofold; the Parliament (its members) hold the

59 Rozeneberg, 32.

government (its administration and subordinate services) accountable – but parliamentarians sitting on the committee are also held accountable for their actions – by their parliamentary factions, and above all: by the voters. Thus, not only the questioned, but also the inquirers and investigators in the committee are the agents who are held directly accountable before their main principal (the leaders and voters) by demonstrating their activity and political attitude. COIs seem to work as the interface between Parliament and the public, offering by their proceedings publicity and advertising. This tendency is enduring – as evidenced by the committees that have been consistently appointed in Poland in order to "deal with past wrongdoing", as well as the subject matter of Italian and German committee proceedings, relating either to public matters from the front pages of the newspapers, or to matters of ongoing concern.

The COIs are designed to be of an explanatory nature, to expose, and in consequence, to blame politicians and officers. Italian practice is full of committees appointed recurrently, in each parliamentary term – which means that the issues investigated still need to be improved, as well as clarified. Even in the German experience, COI reports usually do not bring direct real political or legal outcomes. They are of explanatory nature, but on the other hand strongly linked to parliamentary structure and logic, subordinated to the will of the parliamentary majority and political parties.[60] In consequence, the outcomes of investigations cannot be universally satisfying in such an environment. Contrary to the will of political parties, truth "is seldom pure and never simple", according to the words of Oscar Wilde. This party bias condemns COIs to instrumental use, or at least marginalisation, when their investigations may prove to be inconvenient for the parliamentary majority. At the same time, they are definitely responsive in nature – as evidenced by their appointment after an event or scandal arousing great interest and public outrage. This in turn produces increasing affect-mobilised participation under conditions of decreasing and impoverished access to information.[61] However, even if their activities often give a kind of "illusion of involvement",[62] with a predominant function of blaming rather than learning,[63] they still work as they were designed: to make political bodies accountable for their exercise of entrusted power.

60 von Beyme, 278.

61 George Sartori, *Comparative Constitutional Engineering: An Inquiry into Structures, Incentives and Outcomes* (Basingstoke: Macmillan, 1997), 150.

62 Pierre Bourdieu, *Language and Symbolic Power* (Cambridge, MA: Harvard University Press, 1991), 180.

63 Raanan Sulitzeanu-Kenan, "Reflection in the Shadow of Blame: When Do Politicians Appoint Commissions of Inquiry?", *British Journal of Political Science* 40, no. 3 (2010): 613–34 at 633.

Deputies as Principals in the accountability process

If we are to understand accountability as a process that involves explanation to be given by the responsible actor in a forum which can then scrutinise the information provided,[64] its classical tool is the right of MPs to put questions to members of the government. Questioning procedures are regarded as one of the most distinctive, well-established and at the same time key institutions of parliamentary law.[65] These are activities that extract information, explanations and justifications. In the questioning mechanisms, the nature of the Principal-Agent model between parliaments and cabinets is fully revealed.[66]

In the course of the evolution, taking place primarily under English parliamentarianism and the regime of the French Third Republic – referred to by legal regulations adopted in other countries – questioning procedures have taken on different forms and functions. In England, from the 1880s onwards, we can see the established practice of questioning the MPs for information on the scope of the government or indicating an area of its activity, to which the government would briefly respond, after which the speaker would move on to the next item on the agenda, thus reducing the importance of the questioning as a means of scrutinising executive policy to a minimum. The steady and predictable balance of party power in the House of Commons meant that, regardless of the content of the government's response to an MP's question, there was no change in the balance of power in parliament.

By contrast, in the countries of continental Europe – including France of the Third and Fourth Republics – the interpellation and the subsequent submission of a report by the government (minister) on key issues for the state became a launching pad for political accountability, containing a powerful charge of influencing the composition of government personnel and policies. Since the debate on interpellation could lead to a change in the political composition in parliament, to the downfall of the cabinet, there was a rationalisation – a reduction in the use of this instrument. For this reason, for instance, at the time of the formation of the Fifth French Republic, a deputy submitting an interpellation was obliged to attach to it a motion of no confidence co-signed by at least one-tenth of the members of the National Assembly.[67]

64 Mark Bovens, "Analysing and Assessing Public Accountability: A Conceptual Framework", 16 January 2006. European Governance Papers (EUROGOV) [online], No. C-06-01, 2006 available at: https://www.mzes.uni-mannheim.de/projekte/typo3/site/fileadmin/wp/pdf/egp-connex-C-06-01.pdf

65 See: Maria Kruk, *Funkcja kontrolna Sejmu RP* (Warsaw: Wydawnictwo Sejmowe, 2008), 63; Lech Garlicki, "Uwaga 3 do art. 25", in *Komentarz do Konstytucji Rzeczypospolitej Polskiej. Komentarz, t. 3*, ed. Leszek Garlicki (Warsaw: Wydawnictwo Sejmowe, 1997), 1.

66 Ruxandra Serban, "The Practice of Accountability in Questioning Prime Ministers: Comparative Evidence from Australia, Canada, Ireland, and the United Kingdom", *British Journal of Politics and International Relations* 25, no. 1 (2021): 42–63.

67 Jerzy Stembrowicz, *Rząd w systemie parlamentarnym* (Warsaw: Wydawnictwo PWN, 1982), 215.

Similarly, according to Section 122 of the 1938 Constitution of Lithuania, at least a quarter of the members of the Sejm could put forward a motion to declare the Prime Minister's answer to an interpellation unsatisfactory. If such a motion was supported by at least three-fifths of the MPs, then the President of Lithuania either dismissed the Prime Minister or dissolved the Parliament.[68]

The addressees of the interpellation procedures are the government (as a body of the executive) and its individual members. The Prime Minister is the unique addressee of questions.[69] Their subject matter, in turn, concerns issues falling within the competence of the interpellated bodies – the powers they possess and the manner in which they are exercised. The subject matter of the interpellation procedures depends on the scope of government activity, its members, bodies subordinate to or otherwise connected with government. They can only include matters that are directly or indirectly the responsibility of the government or its agencies.

Formally, as a general rule, MPs – either individually or as a collegiate body – are the sole holders of interpellation instruments. They may use them at their discretion and for a variety of reasons. Neither any public authority nor the citizens can oblige an MP to use the means of address in question, or dissuade him or her from using this instrument.[70] However, this formal freedom to use interpellation procedures must be overlaid with considerations arising from the political organisation of MPs into political factions.[71] For example, in Germany, an interpellation can only be requested by a group of Members in the number required to form a parliamentary group (at least 26 Members). The Government replies to an interpellation during a plenary sitting of the Bundestag. If the number of Members required to form a parliamentary group so requests, the Government's reply is debated.

Given the basic division of Members into parliamentary majority and its opposition, interpellation procedures are instruments of accountability used predominantly by the opposition. They are the means of gathering knowledge about the activities of the government and its agencies in order to verify the regularity and expediency of these activities. One important feature of these

68 Verfassung des Litauischen Staates vom 12. Februar 1938, https://www.verfassungen.eu/lt/verf38-i.htm (accessed 26.08.2023).

69 A comparative study of accountability of primie ministers under questioning – see further: Serban, passim.

70 For more on interpellation procedures as a form of communication between MPs and their constituents, see e.g. Stefanie Bailer, "People's Voice or Information Pool? The Role of, and Reasons for, Parliamentary Questions in the Swiss Parliament", *Journal of Legislative Studies* 17, no. 3 (2011): 302–14.

71 See Lieven de Winter, "Parliament and Government in Belgium: Prisoners of Partitocracy", in *Parliaments and Governments in Western Europe,* ed. Philip Norton (London: Routledge, 2004), 111; Simon Otjes and Tom Louwerse, "Parliamentary Questions as Strategic Party Tools", *West European Politics* 41, no. 2 (2018): 1, doi.org/10.1080/01402382.2017.1358936.

procedures is that they are open to the public, both in terms of what an MP says and the response he/she receives.

What is of interest to MPs in these accounts? In many constitutional systems, in addition to obtaining an account from a member of government of their activities, an element of the questioning procedure involves the exercise of a political function – the articulation of citizens' political preferences. Questions (interpellations) are an instrument to provoke a discussion in parliament about the policy pursued by the government and the right to make an assessment of this policy. This is the case in Bulgaria, among others. According to Article 90 of the Bulgarian Constitution, deputies of the National Assembly have the right to interpellate the Council of Ministers or individual ministers. At the request of at least one-fifth of the deputies, the interpellation is debated and a resolution is adopted.[72] Occasionally, a vote of confidence in the government (respectively: minister) follows the debate over the answer to interpellations. According to § 43 of the Constitution of the Republic of Finland, a group of at least 20 MPs may submit an interpellation to the government or an individual minister on matters falling within their respective competence. The interpellation is answered in the plenary session of the Eduskunta within 15 days of its receipt by the government. The debate on the interpellation shall be followed by a parliamentary vote of confidence in the government or the minister, unless a motion of no confidence in the government or the minister is tabled during the debate.[73] Pursuant to Article 80 of the Constitution of the Slovak Republic, a Member of Parliament may submit an interpellation to the government, a member of the government or the head of another central state administration body on matters falling within their competence. The MP must receive an answer within 30 days. The answer to an interpellation is debated in the National Council of the Slovak Republic, which may be coupled with a vote of confidence.[74]

During the historical development of democratic systems, inquiry procedures have been subject to development and modification. Nowadays, we can aggregate them into written interpellation procedures and interpellation procedures carried out orally – in the forum of parliament (its committees).

The former are typical enquiries of the government (of individual ministers) for information concerning particular, specific areas of government (of individual ministers') activities or action. These are universally applicable. Exceptions include some of the presidential systems of government where there is no provision for MPs to ask questions to the government (Mexico or

72 Конституция на РепублиКа БългаРия в сила от [Konstitutsia na Republika Bulgaria v sila ot], 13 July 1991, https://www.justice.government.bg/home/normdoc/521957377 (accessed 23.08.2023).

73 Suomen perustuslaki, https://www.finlex.fi/fi/laki/ajantasa/1999/19990731 (accessed 28.08.2023).

74 Ústava Slovenskej Republiky, 1 September 1992, https://www.slov-lex.sk/pravne-predpisy/SK/ZZ/1992/460/ (accessed 28.08.2023).

Nicaragua). In the context of enquiries, within a legally stipulated timeframe, members of the government report back to the MPs on a subject of interest to them concerning the competence of the government. At the same time, apart from their informational potential, their capacity to inspire the government to take specific actions, in particular concerning events of a concrete or local nature, is very important, thereby their interventionist character is realised: at the request of citizens or their associations, MPs approach the government on an issue of interest to them and in the reply they get, they receive information about the government's approach to the issue of concern to the citizens or their associations.[75]

A written question from an MP is typically answered in writing. In some countries the form of response (written or oral) is decided by the deputies, and in others by the addressee of the question. In contrast, in isolated cases (Philippines, Lithuania), a member of the government responds orally to a written question. In Bulgaria, on the other hand, a member of the government answers in writing or orally, unless the deputy has requested that the answer be in writing. From the point of view of receiving a report from the Principal, the form in which the answer is given is not irrelevant. By its very nature, the oral form is more ephemeral, non-formalised. It is hard to recall the source material used to provide the response. It is also less effective when there is a disagreement between the Principal and the Agent about the content of the answer given. A written reply is devoid of such inconvenience and, as such, has a higher utility value for MPs than an oral reply.

An interpellation, more often than a question from an MP, represents a collegial right of the MPs or their factions. What most frequently distinguishes it from MPs' questions is the procedure behind it, its content and its implications. An interpellation usually concerns issues of importance to state policy and, more often than in the case of questions, the answer to an interpellation may lead to a parliamentary debate (e.g. Estonia) or, as in Sweden, a parliamentary debate on interpellations is held periodically. This way, the interpellation takes on a partisan meaning. It becomes a form of government reporting not so much to individual MPs, but to parliamentary factions, in their political diversity and different perceptions of government activity.

Formally, responding to an interpellation is not only a political obligation, but also a legal one. If a relevant answer is not provided, it can be concluded that there is inaction on the part of the addressee of the interpellation, resulting in a violation of the law (e.g. in Poland – committing a constitutional tort). However, in practice, such far-reaching consequences are not drawn from the unsatisfactory assessment of the submitted report. The effectiveness of the questions submitted also varies: for example, in the Italian Parliament only 43% of questions received an answer in 2001.[76] More often than not, the

75 De Winter, 111.
76 De Dios, 151.

absence of a written answer to an MP's question allows parliament to demand an oral answer.

A key accountability institution used by MPs in parliament is the so-called "question time" (*Question Time* in the UK Parliament, *Questions au gouvernement* in the French Parliament or *Frågestund* in the Swedish Riksdag), based on English solutions. It is a tool for the day-to-day communication between MPs and the government, generally carried out at each session of parliament, a permanent flow of information necessary for the proper shaping of decision-making processes, both parliamentary and governmental. It is implemented with varying frequency, from once a month (Tunisia) to every working day of parliament (Australia). With that being said, the predominant practice in modern states is to hold the question hour once a week when parliament is in session. As a rule, the question requires an announcement. In the majority of states, the questioner has the right to ask a supplementary question when he or she considers the answer to be incomplete. Holding the government to account requires taking into account the political organisation of MPs. For this reason, it is prevalent to maintain factional parity when asking questions. In parliaments with a tradition of bipartisanship, as in Australia, MPs from both the ruling and opposition parties take turns asking questions.

In the United Kingdom, when a question concerns government policy, the Prime Minister is the one to answer. Other questions are answered by other members of the Cabinet. They typically do this in a rotating fashion; each minister answers MPs' questions at least once a month. In other countries practice in these details may slightly differ. For example, in Bulgaria, the National Assembly hears questions and answers during the last three hours of the session every Friday. The Prime Minister is the first to answer, followed by the deputy prime ministers and ministers, with the ministers' answers subject to rotation. Questions to members of the government are asked in the order in which they are received. The Prime Minister, deputy prime minister or minister who has failed to answer must appear in person before the National Assembly within 10 days and give an explanation for failing to do so. Additionally, pursuant to Rule 107a of the Rules of Procedure for the organisation and activities of the National Assembly,[77] during the last two hours of the session on the first Thursday of every month, the Prime Minister and deputy prime ministers (but not ministers) appear before the National Assembly and give oral answers to topical questions posed by MPs directly in parliament regarding general government policy. The questions asked must not ask for specific figures. Each parliamentary group is entitled to two topical oral questions and MPs who are not members of a parliamentary group are entitled to a total of two questions.

77 ПРавилниК за оРганизацията и дейността на НаРодното събРание в сила от [Pravilnik za organizatsiyata i deynostta na Narodnotosabranie v sila ot], 2 May 2017, https://parliament.bg/bg/rulesoftheorganisations (accessed 28.08.2023).

In order to discuss the day-to-day business of the government, a so-called current affairs hour (in Germany: *Aktuelle Stunde*) is in place. In Austria, it is held at the request of at least five MPs.[78] There is a similar procedure in Poland, called current information. A motion for current information is submitted by 9 p.m. on the day before the beginning of the sitting of the Sejm, together with reasons and the indication of its addressee. The Presidium of the Sejm, having consulted the Council of Seniors, decides which of the proposed information proposals will be taken into account. The Presidium of the Sejm is guided by the relevance and topicality of the proposed question, but also takes into account the size of the fraction proposing it. In the absence of an unanimous opinion of the Council of Seniors, the Sejm decides by a majority of votes (absolute, if there are more than two motions for information). The formula adopted in Poland in no way guarantees the ability of the parliamentary opposition to provoke discussion in the Sejm on key issues of the government's current policy. In a parliament with a stabilised government majority, it is the government that decides not only on the substance of decisions to be made, but also on the space for parliamentary discussion. It has the tools to block information and discussion of phenomena inconvenient to the government. Ninety minutes are devoted to government information and discussion. The extensive time and discussion make current information a convenient platform for the flow of information and its assessment between the government and its parliamentary base and the opposition. Following the British model, it can serve to bipolarise the political scene, with its division into government majority and minority. The procedure for the so-called questions on current affairs is carried out in a similar way, except that they are tabled orally and are not debated. There can be a maximum of 11 such questions. The Presidium of the Sejm decides the order in which questions are asked and which are not (unanswered questions lapse). This competence often limits the ability of the parliamentary minority to ask the government about matters which it finds inconvenient. According to Article 48 of the French Constitution, at least one meeting a week is reserved for questions from members of parliament and replies from the government. These are not accompanied by a vote as an expression of a formal assessment of the answers given.

In practice, there has been a kind of boom in the use of various types of interpellation procedures by MPs. Below we demonstrate the quantitative development of interpellation procedures by juxtaposing two terms of the Sejm of the Republic of Poland: Sejm of the 4th term (2001–5) and Sejm of the 8th term (2015–19). In the Sejm of the 4th term, there were: 10,660

78 In Austria, the so-called "European hour" is convened independently of the "current affairs hour". It is devoted to questions from MEPs on Austria's EU membership and related European policy priorities of the country.

parliamentary interpellations,[79] 4,386 parliamentary questions, 710 questions on current affairs[80] and 57 items of current information submitted.[81] In turn, in the Sejm of the 8th parliamentary term, 34,043 parliamentary interpellations, 9,955 parliamentary questions, 835 questions on current affairs and 76 current information were submitted.[82]

According to De Dios, in a single term at the beginning of the 21st century, some 30,000 questions were tabled (in plenary and committee sessions) in the Spanish Parliament, around 45,000 in the Italian Parliament, 50,000 questions in the French Parliament and over 80,000 in the UK Parliament.[83] Almost 90% of cases in the countries under study see the answers being given, which means that they are very effective in obtaining direct information from the executive. Its importance is lower in Italy and Portugal than in the other cases analysed. A significant increase can be observed in France and Spain. In the United Kingdom, the figure is by far the highest. Similar trends can be noted outside Europe – in the Parliament of the Republic of South Africa, MPs asked 18,823 written questions during a single term (2014–19).[84]

In order to avoid the practice of overusing interpellation procedures, some countries have limited the right of MPs to request information from the government. There, it takes the form of a right exercised collectively rather than by an individual MP. In Austria, a minimum of five members of the National Council may ask the government a question, as is the case in Latvia. In some parliaments, quantitative limits have been adopted for putting questions to the government. In Germany, for example, a member of the Bundestag is entitled to ask the government no more than four questions per month.

79 In Poland, parliamentary interpellations are similar to parliamentary questions. According to the Sejm's rules of procedure, they differ in that parliamentary interpellations are to be tabled on matters of a fundamental nature and relating to problems of state policy, whereas parliamentary questions are to be tabled on other matters relating to the activities of the government or of individual ministers. In practice, the distinction between the subject matter of interpellations and questions is not respected: parliamentary questions on secondary issues are referred to by MPs as "interpellations", and vice versa: questions on issues relevant to government policy are sometimes referred to as "questions". The failure to draw a distinction between "interpellations" and "questions" in practice is of little relevance to the accountability of the government, since in each of these two forms ("parliamentary interpellations" and "parliamentary questions") the same set of actors (members of the Council of Ministers) are asked by the same set of actors (MPs), in the same form (written) and with identical consequences (obligation to reply in writing within 21 days).

80 They are submitted orally by Members during each sitting of the Sejm and require a direct response from a member of the government. They concern current government issues.

81 Current information is presented orally by members of the government at a sitting of the Sejm. A parliamentary debate is held on the information presented. *Sejm Rzeczypospolitej Polskiej. IV kadencja. Informacja o działalności Sejmu (19 października 2001 – 18 października 2005)* (Warsaw, 2006), 35–6.

82 https://www.sejm.gov.pl/sejm8.nsf/page.xsp/prace_sejmu (accessed 02.06.2023).

83 However, the data also includes questions asked in committees. De Dios, 166.

84 https://pmg.org.za/parliament-review/statistics/questions (accessed 28.08.2023).

In Poland, the quantitative development of MPs' interpellations and questions has generated a substantive problem of responding to them in a timely manner. Despite hiring additional staff in ministries and the Prime Minister's Office,[85] it has become common practice not to respond in time. Simultaneously, the multiplicity of parliamentary enquiries became an excuse for some ministers to fail to reply to interpellations and enquiries that were problematic for them, under the pretext of being overloaded with ministerial work. In reaction to such conduct, MPs began to make use of the generally applicable provisions on access to public information and the court action envisaged thereunder for the failure of a public authority to act in providing public information. In this way, the use of specialised mechanisms of accountability of executive bodies (interpellation procedures) and general mechanisms of accountability of public authorities (general access to public information) are mixed in parliamentary practice.

An essential feature of interpellation procedures is to give an account, to provide information on the government's actions. The addressee of the question is obliged to provide an answer and this answer must be complete, i.e. it must take into account the essence of the addressee's knowledge of the issues about which he/she is being asked. In the case of written interventions, if the answer is considered unsatisfactory, the interpellant may request additional explanations in writing, substantiating why the answer has not been accepted.[86] The discussion accompanying the current information allows the Cabinet member to offer additional explanations.

The analysis of the interpellation procedures carried out reveals their extensive and varied nature. To a large extent, they make it possible to receive a report from an Agent. However, the practice of their application is conditioned by the understanding of the role of the majority and the parliamentary opposition and, indeed, by comprehension of the role of the parliament and the debate on the actions taken within the framework of the entrustment of power. It is the political culture and the reflections of that culture that show how much of parliament is a place for debate and obtaining information in a viable way, and how much of this function can be blocked by the majority from which the executive originates.

Summary

In terms of accountability mechanisms, parliamentary procedures are extensive and varied, as well as well established and rooted in each country's

85 A similar process is taking place in the United Kingdom, as indicated by Philip Giddings and Helen Irwin, "Objects and Questions", in *The Future of Parliament: Issues for a New Century*, ed. Philip Giddings (London: Palgrave Macmillan, 2005), 76.

86 In Poland, such a request may be made only once, no later than 30 days after receiving an unsatisfactory reply. Additional explanations shall be provided by the addressee within 21 days of receipt of the request for additional explanations.

constitutional practice.[87] They are subject to implementation at every level of parliamentary activity. Their efficiency is determined not only by the wording of individual provisions, but also by the context of their application through the balance of political forces in parliament and the political relations taking place between parliament and government. Thus, while on a legal level parliament has an elaborate instrument for receiving a report from the Agent, in practice the effectiveness of its application is subject to variation, even though it is still high. In general, we have not found a case where parliament or parliamentary committees requesting information from the government were unable to obtain it. Cases of the Agent failing to report do, however, occur in relation to MPs.

Different practices affect the quality of the information provided. The government has a predisposition to abuse its information advantage vis-à-vis parliament, especially in the area of classified information, either by failing to submit the information requested by parliament or by submitting information that is deficient, misleading parliament about a given area of government activity.

The most general conclusion that follows from the analysis of the implementation of accountability by parliament and its bodies concerns the dependence of the effectiveness of the instruments cited above on the will of the parliamentary majority. The ruling majority may prevent the development of a specific path for obtaining information, as often happens in the case of committees of inquiry or requests for information by MPs, as shown, *inter alia*, by the Polish example of the current information and the French restrictions on asking questions. Moreover, it can manipulate the accountability mechanism through parliamentary committees for its own purposes: to highlight the mistakes of predecessors (the Polish case of committees of inquiry) or to deflect or marginalise law enforcement investigations where public officers are suspected to have committed serious crimes.

Importantly, however, from the point of view of accountability mechanisms, the conclusions reached by the Principal after receiving the account and the possible sanctions against the Agent (being held legally or politically liable) must be separated from the Agent's report to the Principal. The lack of spectacular political consequences of the mechanisms cited in this chapter does not mean that they do not constitute an important instrument of accountability, understood as the acquisition of knowledge about the activities and motives of the executive. Of course, the accountability process does not take place under conditions that are fully objective and impartial. Parliaments are immanently political and so are their debates and questions. On the other hand, the mere

87 On the historical determinants – Anna Młynarska-Sobaczewska, "Committees of Inquiry: Some Remarks on Accountability in Practice", *Oñati Socio-Legal Series* 12, no. 6 (2022): 1589–621, available at: https://opo.iisj.net/index.php/osls/article/view/1434 (accessed 23.02.2024).

articulation of certain rationales for action, activity and, sometimes, mistakes made, ensures that the effect of the Agent's accountability efforts are met.

In this case, as in the others discussed in this thesis, one can also clearly see a certain opposition emerging: the more strongly the mechanism is directed towards sanctions, the more difficult it is to obtain a real report on the actions performed by the Agent. The Agent then adopts a defensive position, trying to avoid giving the report, or manipulating its content. There is also a full political mobilisation of the Principal, especially of the parliamentary majority, which quite frequently nullifies the chances of obtaining an account at all.

5 Judicial accountability – where to look for it and why is it not there?

Introduction – extremely difficult kind of accountability

The issue of accountability for the exercise of judicial power evokes strong reactions, revealing highly divergent expectations. This is because a fundamental premise of a state governed by the rule of law, capable of protecting freedoms and human rights, is the existence of a judiciary that is independent and free from political influence.[1] At the same time, the judiciary constitutes part of the state system,[2] and judges are at the centre of political processes. The politicisation of judicial power is a state of affairs that accompanies this process, as pointed out by W.J. Quirk and R.R. Bridwell in a monograph with the telling title "Judicial Dictatorship".[3] A model in which the judiciary is part of the political system and yet, unlike the other components of that system, remains excluded from the general rules of conduct seems to be irreconcilable with the assumptions of the democratic system and the very essence of the judiciary's power. Those who are called to administer justice cannot do injustice. For this very reason, the power to decide for others in democratic states should be linked to accountability. But how to hold accountable those who are supposed to be autonomous, because their ability to dispense justice depends on this independence?

One of the few unquestioned statements in this regard is that courts can fulfil their function in society if the adjudication process is fair, efficient, expected and not overly costly, and since this is the case, it is necessary to know and be able to verify these qualities.[4] Therefore, accountability seems to be a potential

1 Brian C. Smith, *Judges and Democratization: Judicial Independence in New Democracies* (London: Routledge, 2017), 1.

2 Patricia Pederzoli and Carlo Guarnieri, *The Power of Judges: A Comparative Study of Courts and Democracy* (Oxford: Oxford University Press, 2002), 185.

3 William J. Quirk and Randall R. Bridwell, *Judicial Dictatorship* (London: Routledge, 1995).

4 Shimon Shetreet, "Judicial Accountability: A Comparative Analysis of the Models and the Recent Trends", *International Legal Practitioner* 11 no. 2 (1986): 38–42 at 39; Zoltan Fleck, "A Comparative Analysis of Judicial Power, Organisational Issues in Judicature and the Administration of Courts", *Fair Trial and Judicial Independence: Hungarian Perspectives,* ed. Attila Bado (Cham: Springer International Publishing, 2013), 3–25. See also: The Preamble to

DOI: 10.4324/9781003493419-5

solution to the problem of judicial ideological and political bias.[5] This type of reasoning underpins the attention paid to accountability in international documents as a determinant of judicial independence and impartiality. The preamble to the 2015 UN resolution on the independence and impartiality of the judiciary, jurors and assessors, and the independence of lawyers[6] emphasises the importance of ensuring the accountability, transparency and integrity of the judiciary as a key element of judicial independence and a condition for the rule of law.[7] Accountability also appears in documents on the rule of law and judicial corruption that emerge from the Council of Europe.[8] The importance of this category is given particular prominence in the 2016 Report of the International Commission of Jurists.[9] According to it, the right to trial, that is, to a public and fair hearing by a competent, independent and impartial court established by law, found in all human rights instruments,[10] also implies the right to a court that is held accountable for the exercise of its authority. The Report also highlights that international standards for the independence of the judiciary consider judicial independence and impartiality as impossible to guarantee unless there are effective instruments to respond to the behaviour of judges who do not maintain their requirements within this scope. This is

the UN Human Rights Council Resolution on Independence and Impartiality of the Judiciary, Jurors and Assessors, and the Independence of Lawyers, 29.06.2015; Resolution 19/36 (2012) on Human Rights, Democracy and the Rule of Law, Parliamentary Assembly of the CoE, Resolution 1703 (2010), "Judicial corruption", and Resolution 2098 (2016), "Judicial corruption: urgent need to implement the Assembly's proposals".

5 Smith, 185.

6 The Preamble to the UN Human Rights Council Resolution on Independence and Impartiality of the Judiciary, Jurors and Assessors, and the Independence of Lawyers 19/06 adopted in 2015.

7 "Stressing the importance of ensuring accountability, transparency and integrity in the judiciary as an essential element of judicial independence and a concept inherent to the rule of law, when it is implemented in line with the UN Basic Principles on the Independence of the Judiciary and other relevant human rights norms, principles and standards". The Preamble to the UN Human Rights Council (see note 6).

8 Resolution 19/36 (2012) on Human Rights, Democracy and the Rule of Law. Parliamentary Assembly of the Council of Europe, Resolution 1703 (2010), "Judicial corruption", and Resolution 2098 (2016) (see note 4).

9 In Report of International Commission of Jurists: https://www.icj.org/wp-content/uploads/2016/06/Universal-PG-13-Judicial-Accountability-Publications-Reports-Practitioners-Guide-2016-ENG.pdf (accessed 11.12.2023).

10 International Covenant on Civil and Political Rights, Art. 14, African Charter on Human and Peoples' Rights (1986), Art. 26, and African Commission on Human and Peoples' Rights, Principles and Guidelines on the Right to a Fair Trial and Legal Assistance in Africa ("African Fair Trial Principles") (2005); American Convention on Human Rights (1969), Art. 8, and American Declaration of the Rights and Duties of Man (OAS General Assembly, 1948), Art. XXVI; European Convention for the Protection of Human Rights and Fundamental Freedoms, Art. 6; Arab Charter on Human Rights (2004), Art. 12 and 13; Beijing Statement of Principles of the Independence of the Judiciary in the LAWASIA Region ("Beijing Statement"), Art. 2.

expressed, *inter alia*, by the 1985 Basic Principles on the Independence of the Judiciary[11] and the 2001 Bangalore Principles on the Conduct of Judges,[12] and similarly by ECOSOC Resolution 2006/23.

Like any public authority, the judicial power should therefore be subject to monitoring and evaluation of the performance of the tasks entrusted to it, but, on the other hand, this evaluation must not serve as a pretext for interfering with those tasks. For it must be borne in mind that accountability may become a basis for the appropriation of judicial power by other participants in legal relations. At the same time, guarding against this appropriation can be a clever excuse for being the only public authority that is not subject to accountability – *sui generis* supreme authority. Thus, as can be seen, holding the judiciary to account is like walking a tightrope: seeking a balance between the risk of impunity for judges on the one hand and, on the other, the no less dangerous risk of subordinating the judiciary to other authorities.

Is it at all possible to reconcile the independence of the judiciary with the fundamental democratic principle that whoever exercises power should be held accountable by the political community? Carlo Guarnieri and Patricia Pederzoli ask: on what principle can the power of the judiciary and democracy coexist?[13] This question is discreetly ignored by jurisprudence, and even when noticed, it is dismissed with generalities about the independence, impartiality and apolitical nature of judges. In our view, this is a question still worth examining.

Two observations about the category of accountability are perhaps most evident in this area: its fragmentary nature[14] and the lack of consistency – both in practice and in its description and analysis,[15] as well as invoking the accountability primarily in the context of its deficit[16] or a demand for change or a threat from populists to the independence of the courts.[17] At the same time, when it comes to judicial power, accountability suffers from particular

11 UN Basic Principles on the Independence of the Judiciary 1985, accepted by the Seventh United Nations Congress on the Prevention of Crime and the Treatment of Offenders, implemented, inter alia, by UN General Assembly Resolutions 40/32 and 40/146 (1985). Following these documents, accountability is treated as an element of the right to a court in reports: UN Special Rapporteur on the independence of judges and lawyers ("UNSRIJL"), Report on Judicial Accountability, UN Doc A/HRC/26/32 (2014).

12 Bangalore Principles of Judicial Conduct ("Bangalore Principles"), 2001.

13 Pederzoli and Guarnieri, 158.

14 Joe McIntyre, *The Judicial Function: Fundamental Principles of Contemporary Judging* (Sydney: Springer, 2019), 227.

15 Richard Mulgan, "The Processes of Public Accountability", *Australian Journal of Public Administration* 56 (1997): 25–36 at 26; Gareth Griffith, *Judicial Accountability, Background Paper*, New South Wales Parliamentarian Library, 1998, 14.

16 E.g. Smith, 4.

17 In recent literature see, e.g. Smith (see note 1); Petra Bárd, "In Courts We Trust, or Should We? Judicial Independence as the Precondition for the Effectiveness of EU Law", *European Law Journal* 27 (2021): 185–210 at 190–3.

challenges, unknown or less relevant to the other branches of power for at least four reasons.

Firstly, judges in most systems lack democratic legitimacy. The sovereign simply has no say in who exercises judicial power and the way it is exercised. There are exceptions to this rule, such as the electivity of judges practised in some American states,[18] which due to its political entanglements, susceptibility to dependence on election campaign sponsors is sometimes criticised as not guaranteeing judicial independence.[19] At the same time, the scope of their authority and the immanent characteristic of their independence mean that judges must rely on public confidence. Even more – the sense of their authority depends on public trust.[20] The accountability of judges is crucial in this regard. However, they do not receive this mandate directly. It is also not renewed, and thus the bond between the one entrusted with power and the one to whom it is entrusted is much more difficult to find, let alone enforce.

Secondly, judges exercise power using their pool of knowledge. This is the foundation on which their exercise of power is based – *they know the rules* and this knowledge is virtually unquestionable under usual circumstances. The profound and direct interference in the sphere of the lives of the defendants makes judicial knowledge immensely important and inextricably linked to judicial power. It is a special kind of expert knowledge from which the content of the act of authority is directly derived. This knowledge is practically indisputable, in the sense that it can neither be altered nor challenged (outside the course of the instance, and therefore by submitting the decision to a higher court). The great extent of judicial power is based on knowledge of the law, a difficult and sometimes for this reason considered esoteric area. And this intertwining is always particularly dangerous and gives rise to many potential risks. "The law prescribes", "the law does not allow recognition" are phrases that allow the judge to justify a decision in a way that is difficult to challenge even through intellectual reflection. There is the external source, the authority that the judge knows and interprets – not an independently made decision for which he or she can be held accountable. The judge's authority is based on the interpretation of the law and the facts, making the process of accounting

18 Thirty-eight US states hold popular elections to select judges for their highest courts, and 90% of appellate court judges face some kind of election. *The Problem with Judicial Elections*, Lambda Legal, https://www.lambdalegal.org/justice-out-of-balance/judicial-elections. (accessed 11.12.2023).

19 Zachary J. Siegel, "Recall Me Maybe? The Corrosive Effect of Recall Election on State Legislative Politics", *University of Colorado Law Review* 86 (2015): 307–50 at 342; Arthur G. Sulzberger, "Ouster of Iowa Judges Sends Signal to Bench", *New York Times*, 3 November 2010, citing E. Chemerinsky, https://www.nytimes.com/2010/11/04/us/politics/04judges.html (accessed 28.03.2023).

20 In McIntyre's words: "The judiciary, with its triadic form of dispute resolution and its 'soft' governance techniques, is particularly dependent upon maintaining a broad public confidence in its institutional integrity", 228.

for it extremely challenging, exposing discretionary elements and making it "answerable to society".[21] But in fact, legal science has not developed universally accepted canons of interpretation of the law. When interpreting the law, the judge shares a preference for one understanding of the law and a disapproval of other applications of the law.[22] The application of different canons of interpretation of the law may lead to different interpretative determinations, and the objective of achieving a specific result in the application of the law may determine the application of the relevant interpretative canon.

As to the limits of their authority, courts are left to their own devices, i.e. they broadly decide for themselves what falls within their jurisdiction and how the matter should be resolved. They are, of course, subject to the law, but it is for them to decide what is the law and what, in turn, is not. Their power to decide on the limits of their authority is also practically absolute. In other words, by deeming themselves competent to decide a given issue (despite the objections of other participants to the legal relationship), they can make a final and universally binding judgment about it.

Thirdly, in line with the prevailing rule of law paradigm, courts normally have the power to decide whether other actors of power are exercising power properly, respecting the limits of law and in conformity with it, as well as liability for its breach. As Smith notes:

> the expansion of constitutional and administrative review by the judiciary is inevitably controversial politically. When judges are called upon to decide whether executive and administrative decisions are lawful, there is always the risk that they will substitute their own interpretation of the law's intention for that of legislators. When judicial review extends to constitutional matters, such as whether a legislature has jurisdiction over a particular subject or is entitled to pursue political objectives through legislation, judicial independence enters a potential minefield.[23]

Judicial review is moving into ever wider territory, covering new areas of legislative and administrative decisions, now extending to all spheres of political life – from the issue of abortion and euthanasia to the appointment of judges

21 Shimon Shetreet, "The Limits of Judicial Accountability: A Hard Look at the Judicial Officers Act 1987", *University of New South Wales Law Journal*, 10, no. 1 (1987): 4.

22 For example, Antonin Scalia and Bryan A. Garner counted 57 valid canons of interpretation of the American Constitution. Antonin Scalia and Bryan A. Garnet, *Reading Law. Interpretation of Legal Texts* (St Paul: Thomson/West, 2012), ix.

23 Smith, 160.

themselves,[24] the deprivation of public rights, the legality of political parties,[25] the validity of elections and referendums.[26] It is the judges who play the central role in holding the other actors of power civilly and criminally accountable. In many systems, the judicial power is also involved in the adjudication of constitutional liability.[27] The model for adjudicating the accountability of those holding the state's central political functions actually implies the key role of the courts – as custodians of the confidence resulting from impartiality and competence to guarantee the rule of law.[28]

The courts are responsible for deciding on the validity of major policy decisions made in elections, electoral processes or the conduct of elections in a variety of situations as well – this has been done, for example, by the US Supreme Court in *Bush v. Gore*,[29] by stopping the recount of votes on December 12, 2000, and determining the outcome in the 2000 presidential election between George W. Bush and Al Gore (by 5/4 voting). The UK

24 As Smith cites: "These have included abortion and taxation in Poland, capital punishment and regulation of the tobacco market in Hungary, and access to telecommunications data and civil procedure in the courts (Romania). Judicial interventions have affected government austerity measures, including cuts in civil service pay (Lithuania), education (Indonesia), housing (South Africa), workers' rights (Egypt), and health care (Argentina), all as a consequence of mobilization by civil society organizations in support of social and economic rights. The Brazilian judiciary has been drawn into policy-making on labour conditions, fiscal reforms, wages, taxation, social security, privatization and other aspects of economic policy, once again causing concern about the power of an unelected branch of government. Since 1988, the judiciary has been involved in 'practically all significant reforms encompassing Brazil's social economic and political spheres'", at 169.

25 According to Art. 21(2) of the Basic Law and §§ 43 et seq. of the Federal Constitutional Court Act parties that, by reason of their aims or the behaviour of their adherents, seek to undermine or abolish the free democratic basic order or to endanger the existence of the Federal Republic of Germany must be declared unconstitutional. The Federal Constitutional Court has twice prohibited a party: the Sozialistische Reichspartei (SRP) was prohibited in 1952 and the Kommunistische Partei Deutschlands (KPD) in 1956. Proceedings for the prohibition of the Nationaldemokratische Partei Deutschlands (NPD) initiated in 2001 were discontinued in 2003 on procedural grounds. On 17 January 2017, the Federal Constitutional Court again decided on the prohibition of the NPD. Other examples: Smith, 170.

26 For instance the Constitiutional Court in Spain declared the nullity and unconstitutionality of the Law of Catalonia 19/2017, of 6 September, so-called "on the self-determination referendum" of 17 October 2017. The present judgment was handed down in Madrid, on 17 October 2017. On other examples: Smith, 170.

27 The countries in question include those in which holders of public office are held accountable for illegal actions before special courts (including a constitutional court). This is the case, for example, in Albania, Bulgaria, the Czech Republic or Venezuela.

28 As Jose Maravall explicitly writes: "(judges) become actors in political strategies that alter the rules of democratic competition". Jose Maravall, "The Rule of Law as a Political Weapon", in *Democracy and the Rule of Law*, ed. Jose Maria Maravall and Adam Przeworski (Cambridge: Cambridge University Press, 2003), 262.

29 *Bush v. Gore*, 531 U.S. 98 (2000).

Supreme Court decided that Scotland's 2022 referendum was illegal[30] (did not take place), and the Spanish Constitutional Court on the unconstitutionality of the 2017 referendum in Catalonia[31] (which eventually took place).

The judiciary is becoming increasingly involved in the exercise of power and is more and more often engaged in partisan struggles. Courts represent an instrument in political conflicts and they tend to expand their authority[32] in democratic states. This happens irrespective of the type of system of government adopted in a country. Similarly, in supranational organisations such as the European Union (EU), the courts have played a key role in the political processes taking place within them, with a tendency to expand the competences assigned to them.[33] At the same time, as was noticed by Richard Y. Schauffler, it is easy to observe the growing politicisation of the judicial decision-making.[34]

Judges and courts can also become an instrument of authoritarianism, as shown by the examples of the Republic of South Africa, communist states and, in more recent times, Brazil, Turkey,[35] Belarus or Russia. In this regard, the futility of efforts to hold judges accountable for actions committed in the name of the state, with the hallmarks of serious human rights violations or even crimes, is particularly notable. Accountability and the right to justice of victims and their families[36] in times of transition have had very little effect, as exemplified by efforts in this direction in Latin American countries such

30 The Supreme Court of the United Kingdom in the matter of a reference by the Lord Advocate under para 34 of schedule 6 to the Scotland Act 1998, Case no. 2022/0098.

31 10287 Recurso de inconstitucionalidad n.o 4334-2017, contra la Ley del Parlamento de Cataluña 19/2017, de 6 de septiembre, del Referéndum de Autodeterminación.

32 Maravall, 13–14; Smith, 90, 160.

33 See e.g. Danuta Kabat-Rudnicka, *Konstytucjonalizacja Unii Europejskiej a sądownictwo konstytucyjne. Wielopoziomowa współpraca czy rywalizacja?* (Warsaw: Wolters Kluwer, 2016), 66; Tomasz Koncewicz, *Filozofia europejskiego wymiaru sprawiedliwości. O ewolucji fundamentów unijnego porządku prawnego* (Warsaw: Wolters Kluwer, 2020), 404.

34 Richard Y. Schauffler, "Judicial Accountability in the US State Courts: Measuring Court Performance", *Utrecht Law Review* 3, no. 1 (2007): 112–28 at 112.

35 Thomas Bustamante and Emilio Meyer, "Judicial Accountability", in *Max Planck Encyclopaedia of Comparative Constitutional Law* (MPECCoL) (July 2020), 5; Emilio Meyer, "Judges and Courts Destabilizing Constitutionalism: The Brazilian Judiciary Branch's Political and Authoritarian Character", *German Law Journal* 19 (2018): 727–68 at 727.

36 On the right to truth as an important human right a.o.: ECtHR (Grand Chamber), *El-Masri v. the former Yugoslav Republic of Macedonia*, App. No. 39630/09 (13 December 2012), paras 191–94, IAmCtHR, *Gomes Lund et al. ("Guerrilha do Araguaia") v. Brazil*, Series C No. 219 (24 November 2010), para. 200 and proclaimed by international documents, among others: Human Rights Council, resolutions on the right to truth, 9/11 (2008), 12/12 (2009) and 21/7 (2012); and the General Assembly, resolution 68/165 (2013) on the right to truth, "UN Impunity Principles".

as El Salvador[37] and Chile[38] as well as Uruguay.[39] Similarly, attempts to hold judges accountable in South Africa,[40] Sierra Leone,[41] Kenya[42] and Nigeria.[43] The results were no better in post-national socialist Germany, post-fascist Italy or post-communist countries. In some of them, as in Poland, this accountability has not been carried out, and as a consequence – 30 years after the time of the system change – there are still judges from the communist era sitting in the Supreme Court ruling on political trials, while the rest are retired judges.

The vetting instruments against judges are treated with great distrust. For instance, the Venice Commission suggests in its opinions that lustration can be justified in extreme cases of deep and massive judicial corruption. However, it also warns that such a radical solution as lustration cannot be applied under normal conditions, for it creates great pressure on judges, destabilises their work and causes an increase in distrust towards adjudication, as well as the risk of political authorities taking control of the adjudication process.[44] The Venice Commission's view on the vetting of communist judges is widely shared by the political elites of Central and Eastern European countries.

All these remarks lead to the conclusion that a fundamental challenge is posed by the clash between accountability and judicial independence.[45] This is the crux of the dispute as to the extent of judicial accountability. Proponents of holding judges accountable for their power argue that in a democracy, all authorities, including the judiciary, must be held accountable by the sovereign. They point to the risk of a dictatorship of unaccountable judges,[46] who

37 Report of the El Salvador Commission on Truth, UN Doc S/25500 (1993): 172, 176–9, 181–2.

38 Report of the Chilean National Commission on Truth and Reconciliation (1993), Part Two, Chapter Four "Behaviour of the courts towards the grave human rights violations that occurred between September 11, 1973 and March 11, 1990".

39 In a 2014 report, the UN Special Rapporteur on truth, justice, reparation and guarantees of non-recurrence noted the lack of attention to human rights violations related to the actions of the judiciary (including the Supreme Court) during the years of the military regimes (1970s and 1980s).

40 In its final report, the TRC expressed "great regret that judges refused to appear before the Commission on the basis that this would negatively affect their independence and would harm the institution of the judiciary", and disagreed with the judges. South Africa Truth & Reconciliation Commission, *Final Report* (1998), Vol. 4, Chapter 4, "Institutional Hearing: The Legal Community", Vol. 5, Chapter 5, "Findings and Conclusions", 201, 253–4.

41 Sierra Leone Truth & Reconciliation Commission, *Witness to Truth: Final Report* (2004), Vol. Two, 90–3.

42 Kenya, *Truth, Justice and Reconciliation Commission Final Report* (2013), Vol. I, xiii and Vol. IIA, 598, para. 30.

43 Hakeem O. Yusuf, "Truth, Transition, and Accountability of the Judiciary", in *Transitional Justice, Judicial Accountability and the Rule of Law* (London: Routledge, 2010), 33–40, 45–6.

44 Venice Commission, Final Opinion on the Revised Draft Constitutional Amendments on the Judiciary of Albania, CDL-AD(2016)009 (2016) para. 52, as well as its Interim Opinion, CDL-AD(2015)045, paras 98–100.

45 Smith, 183.

46 See Quirk and Bridwell.

disregard the will of the parliamentary majority that has been democratically elected to govern. They also point out the risk of excessive judicial activism[47] of judges who put their own political views before the will of the majority with a democratic mandate, sometimes even refusing to apply laws passed by parliament.[48] Opponents of accountability thus understood articulate its populist connotations and suggest that it is merely a pretext for interfering with judicial independence.[49] Both sides of the argument therefore appeal to fundamental values: democracy and rule of law.[50] This leads to the disappearance of an element that is barely noticed any more in the discourse conducted in this way, namely the question of internal impartiality, the ability to decide a case without the involvement of a personal worldview and therefore prejudice or preference. This concept, developed in the philosophical and legal literature[51] succumbs to the idea of independence from external factors. The question then arises to what extent can impartiality meant as capacity to judge neutrally towards different ideological, moral attitudes be subject to accountability for the exercise of power at all.

These disputes are particularly intense in new democracies, in post-authoritarian states where the need for lustration and the fight against corruption

47 Smith, 4.

48 This alternative-law position is expressed perfectly in an article written by law professor Paulo Roberto Pereira de Souza, formerly the chancellor of the State University of Maringá: "In our postmodernist society, we are seeing a true revolution in law… The installation of judges with new powers resulting from this process has allowed judges to make advanced decisions going against unjust norms that conflict with public interest. There is no law, no legal norm or statute that justifies fraud of the public interest". Paulo Roberto Pereira de Souza, "Constitutionalism in Brazil", *Florida Journal of International Law* 16 (2004): 155–9, at 155, 158 after: Augusto Zimmermann, "How Brazilian Judges Undermine the Rule of Law: A Critical Appraisal", *International Trade and Business Law Review* 11 (2008): 179–217. See also: Diego Arhuelhes, "Judges Speaking for the People: Judicial Populism beyond Judicial Decisions", Verfassunglobg 2017, https://verfassungsblog.de/judges-speaking-for-the-people-judicial-populism-beyond-judicial-decisions/ (accessed 12.06.2023).

49 Wojciech Sadurski, *Poland's Constitutional Breakdown* (Oxford University Press, 2019), 8 et seq; James E. Moliterno et al., "Independence without Accountability: The Harmful Consequences of EU Policy toward Central and Eastern European Entrants", *Fordham International Law Review* 42, no. 2 (2018): 481–543 at 484, 487–8, 538–40.

50 A review of the positions in this regard is being carried out by John A. Ferejohn and Larry D. Kramer, "Independent Judges, Dependent Judiciary: Institutionalizing Judicial Restraint", *New York University Law Review* 77 (2002): 962–75. Cf. Charlie Geyh, "Judicial Independence, Judicial Accountability, and the Role of Constitutional Norms in Congressional Regulation of the Courts", *Indiana Law Journal*, 78, no. 1 (2003): 153–97 at 160, https://www.repository.law.indiana.edu/ilj/vol78/iss1/7 (28.05.2023). On a collision democracy against rule of law in this context: Maravall, 262.

51 John Rawls, *Theory of Justice* (Harvard University Press, 1999), 514; see also: Brian Barry, *Justice as Impartiality* (Oxford: Oxford University Press, 1995); Susan Mendus, *Impartiality in Moral and Political Philosophy* (Oxford: Oxford University Press, 2002); Paul Kelly, ed., *Impartiality, Neutrality and Justice – ReReading Brian Barry's Justice as Impartiality* (Edinburgh: Edinburgh University Press, 1998).

resonate particularly strongly, but also more broadly: under conditions of increasing judicial activism and the rise of the rule of law,[52] where the law, as the sole and supreme criterion, determines the limits and bases of government action.[53]

If, however, the accountability of judicial power is to be considered outside of political rhetoric, outside of its operation within the framework of current political disputes, then it requires, at the very least, certainty about the terms used and unambiguity of the categories, the definition of its types and the elements used by its participants. Indeed, it is a concept that is often used but hardly ever seriously considered,[54] which stems from either an instrumental use of the term[55] or an overly hasty and simplistic view of accountability itself in this area of governance.

What a judge should be held accountable for

Accountability for the exercise of judicial power is neither uncontested nor uniformly understood.[56] The encyclopaedic definition indicates its effect and scope; accountability is thus defined as "the set of mechanisms aimed at making judges and courts personally or institutionally responsible for behaviours and decisions contrary to constitutional or legal standards".[57] The giving of an account of the entrusted authority itself is highlighted by Louis Seidman; according to him a person may be "accountable" when they are required to give an account of themselves – give reasons or justifications for conduct; a person may also be held accountable for their decisions, i.e. being made responsible for them or being forced to bear the costs of a mistake.[58] In turn, as Antonina Peri points out, the account-giving relationship means that the

52 Smith, 4, 7. See also *Judicial Accountability in Developing Countries. Report of Consultation Meeting Tunis, 8–9 October 2015*, International Commission of Jurists 2016, 1 et seq.

53 Sadurski, *Poland's Constitutional Breakdown*, 8 et seq. On this reasoning see also: Moliterno et al., 484, 487–8, 538–40.

54 McIntyre, 231.

55 McIntyre, 230. As he writes: "In many respects, 'judicial accountability' appears to have become a 'useful buzz-word', filled with whatever content the speaker desires".

56 Andrew Le Sueur, "Developing Mechanisms for Judicial Accountability in the UK", *Legal Studies* 24, no. 1 (2004): 73–98 at 73, 76 points out: In the UK, there are three schools of thought about accountability of judges. "Opponents" argue that the notion of an "accountable judge" is an oxymoron. "Re-conceptualists" point out that courts already engage in a number of practices that make them accountable. The "radical" claim is that new forms of accountability are needed. Re-conceptualists argue the judiciary has long had accountability practices without explicitly labelling them as such, by disciplinary measures, open justice principles and other ways. See also McIntyre, 231.

57 Bustamante and Meyer, "Judicial Accountability".

58 Louis M. Seidman, "Ambivalence and Accountability", *Southern California Law Review* 61, no. 6 (1988): 1571–615 at 1574. On the interchangeable use of accountability and responsibility: Mulgan, 26.

judge should answer not only to written norms, but also to the people and society, and thus to democratic institutions.[59]

As we assume in our work, accountability in public law, also regarding judges and courts, means the obligation to submit an account of the performance of the entrusted activities within the scope of one's competence.[60] It allows to instrumentalise the assumption of the entrustment of power and the necessity to give an account on the manner and effects in which this power has been exercised.[61] This shows that, firstly, accountability can be seen as a platform for account-giving in the power entrustment, and that is founded, even implicitly, on the Principal (Forum)-Agent (entrustor-performer) relation. Accountability makes use of some specific instruments for obtaining an account of the exercise of power, like in the case of the judiciary: the supervision by a higher-level authority, social control of the actions of the judiciary, professional accountability, parliamentary procedures for institutional monitoring of the judiciary, disciplinary responsibility, as well as procedures for the impeachment of judges, criminal liability of judges, civil liability for damages and specific procedures such as truth commissions, *ad hoc* tribunals to try crimes committed by the judiciary set up in times of transition[62] and, finally, anti-corruption instruments. Our analysis will focus on those instruments that have a legal dimension as a factor constructing a constitutional model of entrusting power to an independent judiciary.

The multiplicity of forms and contexts has led to attempts to classify the category of accountability of judges, courts and judicial power as a whole, taking into account the criterion of the subject of accountability,[63] the object

59 Antonina Peri, "Judicial Independence vs. Judicial Accountability. Judicial Selection Models for Constitutional Courts. A Comparative Analysis", *Comparative Law Review* 3, no. 1 (2012): 3.

60 Mark Bovens, "Analysing and Assessing Accountability: A Conceptual Framework", *European Law Journal* 13, no. 4 (2007); Mark Bovens, Thomas Schillemans and Robert Goodin, "Public Accountability", in *The Oxford Handbook of Public Accountability*, ed. Mark Bovens, Robert Goodin and Thomas Schillemans (Oxford University Press, 2014), 9.

61 Gabriel Lenz, *Follow the Leader: How Voters Respond to the Politicians' Performance and Policies* (Chicago University Press, 2012); Sean Gailmard, "Accountability and Principal-Agent Theory", in *The Oxford Handbook of Public Accountability*, 90–3.

62 David Dyzenhaus, *Judging the Judges, Judging Ourselves: Truth, Reconciliation and the Apartheid Legal Order* (Hart Publishing, 1998); Hakeem Yusuf, *Transitional Justice, Judicial Accountability and the Rule of Law* (Routledge, 2010); Hans Peter Graver, *Judges against Justice: On Judges When the Rule of Law Is under Attack* (Springer, 2015).

63 Stephen Colbran identifies: public scrutiny, instance-based scrutiny, accountability for the exercise of judicial power by the legislature and the executive, opinions formulated by legal professionals and academics and oversight exercised by judicial authorities. Stephen Colbran, "The Limits of Judicial Accountability: The Role of Judicial Performance Evaluation", *Legal Ethics* 6, no. 1 (2003):55–72 at 56.

of accountability,[64] the manner of execution[65] or the model in which it is implemented.[66]

The criteria are various, but one question remains central to the above classifications: *for what* should judges (courts) be held accountable for the authority they have been entrusted with?

In our approach, accountability aims at gaining knowledge about the power actions taken and being taken, with the possibility of its further use. This is accomplished in the form of reporting on the actions taken, presenting their reasons and reporting on the effects of the activities so undertaken in the sphere of authority entrusted. We propose the thesis that accountability is realised in this dimension mainly through the justification of the judicial decision – not only in the course of instance control, but also in the direct relation between the court and all those who are interested in the activities of the judicial power. In addition to the basic form of such a relationship, i.e. the grounds for a decision, instruments relating to the transparency of the operation of the courts fall into this category: guarantees of the openness of the hearing, the recording of hearings, the broadcasting of trials of public interest, access to court files and making judgments publicly available – thus, everything that can make whatever happens in court open but also easily understood by the public. The openness of the proceedings to parties other than the parties to the proceedings (the so-called external openness of the judicial proceedings) is a key method for determining how a judge acts in the course of judicial proceedings, whether he or she correctly performs the task entrusted to him or her and, consequently, whether the actions the judge performs and the effect of those actions can be called the administration of justice. In this respect, the role of the mass media and legal science in particular must be acknowledged. As emphasised in case law and jurisprudence, "justice should

64 Charlie Geyh puts forward a distinction between institutional accountability, behavioural accountability and accountability for the decisions made. Charlie G. Geyh, "The Elastic Nature of Judicial Independence and Judicial Accountability", in *The Improvement of the Administration of Justice,* 7th edition (ABA Press, 2002), 167, 168. McIntyre puts it similarly (249). Le Sueur distinguishes accountability for content, process, performance and probity (81).

65 Shimon Shetreet identifies three types of it: 1) legal accountability, in the form of disciplinary responsibility, appellate review and civil and criminal liability, 2) public accountability, exercised through parliamentary and executive scrutiny and 3) informal (social) accountability, exercised by the legal professionals (Shetreet, 38).

66 Mauro Cappelletti proposes to distinguish three models in which accountability can be exercised: a repressive model, an autonomous (corporate) model and a responsive or consumer-oriented mixed model. Mauro Cappelletti, "Who Watches the Watchmen?," in *Judicial Independence: The Contemporary Debate* ed. Shimon Shetreet and Jules Deschêness (Martinus Nijhoff Publishers, 1984), 570–4. Thomas Bustamante and Emilio Meyer put in two main models for securing judicial accountability. Firstly, an internal accountability, which is provided by organs located inside the judiciary structure, composed of members that are normally judges, justices or magistrates. Secondly, there is an external accountability, which is managed by a body that usually does not constitute a part of the judiciary, such as judicial councils and Ministers of Justice (Bustamante and Meyer, 3).

not only be done, but should also be perceived as being done in an obvious and unquestionable manner".[67]

Two directions in the concept of accountability can therefore be seen again: *answerability*, as the obligation on the part of an Agent to provide an account of activities and achievements; and *enforcement*, understood as the power of the Principal to deploy sanctions when the account is deemed unsatisfactory.[68] In practice, however, it is apparent how strongly accountability is linked in meaning and popular perception to the concept of sanctions for behaviour or acts of authority that deviate from the accepted standard or are contrary to the law, as discussed below. In contrast, the assumption that accountability means that an actor (Agent) has to be answerable for his/her actions and decisions to some clearly identified body (Principal, forum) becomes distant, then: who and in which way has a duty of explanation.[69]

It goes without saying that the accountability pertains to the judge's behaviour. However, it is particularly difficult to indicate, whether the judge's behaviour outside the bench affects the exercise of the power entrusted, and on the other hand, how a judge should be held accountable for what she/he has done within the framework of that power in which she/he must remain independent to fulfil the court's functions at all. At this point, in particular, a conflict with independence may arise, and it is a conflict *par excellence* irremovable and immanent, as we will try to demonstrate later. In our view, however, the essence of accountability is not how a judge behaves, but how he or she has exercised that authority. This is not quite the same thing. A judge's conduct that undermines confidence in him or her as a competent, impartial and independent person is part of that accountability, but the key thing is to give an account of the exercise of power, i.e. the handling of cases to their substantive and just resolution under fair trial conditions.

Let us add that the courts should therefore also be held accountable for the efficiency and effectiveness of their performance – the manner in which the power is exercised.[70] This model leads to an accountability of the judiciary for its efficiency, including the time and quality of procedures as well as the outcome of the adjudication of cases in the exercise of its functions. However, this kind of accountability faces difficulties in finding the right parameters. Efficiency and fairness while resolving disputes is hardly measurable.[71] It can

67 *R v. Sussex Justices*, Ex parte McCarthy [1924] 1 KB 256, 259; after: James Spigelman, "Seen to Be Done: The Principle of Open Justice, part I", *Australian Law Journal* 74, no. 5 (1999): 290, at 378, available at SSRN: https://ssrn.com/abstract=1800451 (accessed 11.12.2023).

68 Smith, 186.

69 Patricia Day and Rudolf Klein, *Accountabilities: Five Public Services* (Tavistock, 1987), 5.

70 McIntyre, 282–3.

71 James Spigelman, "Judicial Accountability and Performance Indicators", Paper presented at *1701 Conference: The 300th Anniversary of the Act of Settlement, Vancouver, British Columbia 2001* (also as: James Spigelman, "Judicial Accountability and Performance Indicators", *Civil*

only be judged and not counted,[72] as is possible in many aspects of the public service. This also requires shaping the structures and actors of judicial power and the administration of the courts in such a way that they are autonomous and thus meet the requirement of real entrustment of power.

As a conclusion to the above remarks, the two types of accountability within the judicial power, that is, answerability and "forensic' accountability are particularly distinct, employ quite different tools and, above all, lead to different results. In the following sections, we will try to demonstrate that in the field of judicial power, accountability equated with control or enforcement of sanctions against judges behaving against certain standards may not only fail to exhaust the sense of reporting on the exercise of power, but may also nullify such a possibility.

Let us therefore present some observations on responsibility as part of the accountability of judges. Indeed, the solutions applied in this area seem to replicate certain practical and theoretical problems.

Responsibility versus accountability: recall, impeachment, disciplinary measures

The discussion concerning the application of sanctions for judicial misbehaviour should start with an overview of the instruments aimed at removing a judge from the office. The most prominent example is the institution of recall (removal from office by popular vote). It is applied, for example, to American judges in several states.[73] Such recalls have occurred on a number of occasions; for example, in Iowa in 2010, three judges of the state Supreme Court were recalled through the recall procedure. They were removed – a point made very clearly during the campaign – for issuing a particular ruling (legalising same-sex marriage).[74] Observation of practice, however, leads to the conclusion that the account of governance here has given way to a confrontation of expectations with the image formed during the recall campaign.[75] The example of recall

---

Justice Quarterly 21 (2002): 18–28, available at SSRN: https://ssrn.com/abstract=1802176 (accessed 11.12.2023).

72 "Not everything that counts can be counted. Some results or outcomes are incapable of measurement. They can only be judged in a qualitative manner. Justice, in the sense of fair outcomes arrived at by fair procedures, is, in its essential nature, incapable of measurement. (…) Justice, in the sense of fair outcomes arrived at by fair procedures, can only be judged. It cannot be measured." Spieglman (see note 71).

73 Among others: Arizona, California, Nevada, North Dakota, Oregon, Wisconsin. In: Siegel, 308; Report Recall of State Officials, National Conference of State Legislatives, 15.09.2021, https://www.ncsl.org/elections-and-campaigns/recall-of-state-officials#Laws (accessed 11.12.2023).

74 Siegel, 340.

75 The case of Justice Rose Bird, Chief Justice of the California Supreme Court, whose nomination was not confirmed in the 1986 election, by a majority of 67%, after a campaign attacking her attitude to the death penalty, is often cited in this context (Preble Stolz, *Judging Judges:*

shows the very strong connotation of responsibility for adjudication decisions and implies its direct enforcement, which raises doubts as to the actual independence of the judge under such a "corrosion of the mandate". American jurisprudence, however, presents the line that recall does not constitute a violation of the formulaic mandate entrusted to judges,[76] nor the due process of law,[77] and the principle of equality before the law.[78] It acknowledges that the recall implements the principle of a republican form of government, [79] based on the idea of accountable and responsible governance, in which the attribute of accountability is not only extended to parliamentarians, but also to the depositaries of the other authorities, including the judiciary. These remarks lead to the conclusion that reflection on recall does not concern the question of answerability of judicial power to any extent – but only the consequences of acting against the expectations of the Principal. The account of the exercise of power itself is irrelevant here, and only the effect of exercising the entrusted power, unsatisfactory to the Principal, is of importance.

Of course, these considerations remain irrelevant in a system where judges are not elected by the people. However, the same applies to the relationship between responsibility and accountability in the case of the application of the institution of impeachment against judges, which is allowed in a number of states governed by the common law system (such as Great Britain,[80] the

---

The Investigation of Rose Bird and the California Supreme Court (New York, 1981); Patrick K. Berown, "The Rise and Fall of Rose Bird. A Career Killed by the Death Penalty", California State University, Fullerton, accessed: https://www.cschs.org/wp-content/uploads/2014/03/CSCHS_2007-Brown.pdf (21.05.2023).

76 Iowa Supreme Court decision of 1908, *Eckerson v. City of Des Moines.* More in: "Constitutionality of Local and State Recall Provisons", *American Law Reports* 13, no. 6 (2006): 661.

77 The Supreme Court of the State of Texas, in its decision: *Bonner v. Belesterling,* 104 Tex 432, 138 S.W. 571 (1911).

78 The Supreme Court of California in its ruling *Baertschiger v. Leffler* z 21 XII 1939, 36 Cal. App. 2d 208, 97 P.2d 501 (2d Dist. 1939).

79 In the cited *Bonner v. Belsterling* decision, the Texas court explained that the type of republican form of government guaranteed by Article IV sec. 4 of the US Constitution implies governance by the people, and emphasised that ceding the decision on the election and removal of any elected office holder to the people can hardly be considered a violation of it in any way – for even if it implies a limitation on the mandate of elected persons, this limitation implies a transfer of power directly to the people, i.e. to the subject of sovereign power (after: "Constitutionality of Local and State Recall Provisions", see note 76).

80 The procedure has never been initiated against an English or Welsh judge; it has only been used once against an Irish judge.

United States,[81] India, Australia,[82] Ireland[83] and Japan[84]). According to constitutional regulations or customs, cases of misconduct or unfitness for office provide grounds for impeachment.[85] This first premise has an extremely broad scope and can apply both to the judge's behaviour outside the adjudication process and to behaviour during the exercise of judicial power. Although this form is rarely resorted to, it is important to note individual cases, especially in the United States[86] in the 20th and also in the 21st century.[87] In the case of impeachment, the relationship between the entrustor of power (epitomised by parliament) and the judge exercising power as a result of the entrustment is very much accentuated. However, the element of responsibility completely obscures the essence of accountability, that is, the sentence of an objective account of the power exercised.

In fact, the problem of accountability is quite similar in the model of disciplinary responsibility of judges that is generally adopted in modern states. The first problem in such a system is to define what a judge is to be disciplined for. Immanently vague is the formulation of the basis for such responsibility, which presents an obvious challenge to the principle of judicial independence.

81 Frank Thompson Jr. and Daniel H. Pollitt, "Impeachment of Federal Judges: An Historical Overview", *North California Law Review* 49 (1970): 87–121, available at: http://scholarship.law.unc.edu/nclr/vol49/iss1/9 (accessed 11.12.2023).

82 Article 72 of the Constitution of Australia provides that a judge may not be removed from office except by the Governor-General in Council at the request of both Houses of Parliament, justified by the judge's bad conduct or incompetence ("Shall not be removed except by the Governor-General in council, on an address from both Houses of Parliament in the same session, praying for such removal on the ground of proved misbehaviour or incapacity").

83 Under Article 35 of the Irish Constitution, judges may only be removed from office in cases of established impropriety or incompetence (judges "shall not be removed from office except for stated misbehaviour or incapacity") and exclusively by a resolution of both chambers of parliament.

84 Art. 78 of the Japanese Constitution: Judges shall not be removed except by public impeachment unless judicially declared mentally or physically incompetent to perform official duties. No disciplinary action against judges shall be administered by any executive organ or agency. According to the Judicial Impeachment Act of 1947 anyone may make a complaint to the Judicial Impeachment Committee; made up of members of parliament, the Committee determines whether start the impeachment process at the court or dismiss it. Sarah M. R. Cravens, "Shifting the Balance: Public Perspective and the Japanese Judicial Discipline Process", in *Disciplining Judges*, ed. Richard Devlin and Sheila Wildeman (Cheltenham:Edward Elgar Publishing, 2021), 213.

85 *Judicial Accountability in Developing Countries* ..., 24.

86 Today in the United States, the regime has been dual since 1980 federal statute judicial discipline procedure under Judicial Councils Reform and Judicial Conduct and Disability Act. Impeachments are rare, time-consuming and cumbersome (Bam, 339; see note 87), highly political and a threat for judicial independence.

87 Proceedings concern sexual harassment, fraudulent conduct, viewing pornography, see: Dmitry Bam, "Legal Process Theory and Judicial Discipline in the United States", in *Disciplining Judges*, ed. Richard Devlin and Sheila Wilderman (hereinafter: Devlin and Wilderman), 336 (see note 84).

So Piotr Mikuli and Maciej Pach, for example, do not narrow it down to unlawful acts (that are not common offences), but include acts incompatible with judicial ethics that are not subject to judicial challenge.[88] The definition of the acts for which a judge bears disciplinary responsibility is a sensitive element of accountability, and various regulatory strategies are adopted in this respect.[89] We also face the fundamental question from the point of view of accountability: whether an act committed on the bench can be qualified as misconduct, as is the case in several countries, such as Australia,[90] Canada,[91] Italy[92] and Croatia.[93] Another solution, although not a competing one, is that a judge can be held accountable for conduct outside this sphere, in private life – as is the case in many legal regimes (United States, Canada, England and Wales,[94] Italy,[95] Australia,[96] Japan).[97] However, from the point of view of accountability, the problem is rather critical, because it concerns the relationship between accountability for exercising the power of a judge and accountability for being a judge. Can a judgment, that is, an act of judicial power endowed with the value of being issued by an independent subject, be subject to disciplinary responsibility in the face of the principle of independence? And on the other hand: with the exclusion of such behaviour from the sphere of responsibility, does it make any substantial sense at all from the point of view of accountability for the exercise of power? As the authors of the Report on Judicial Accountability point out,[98] the premise of misconduct cannot relate to

88 Piotr Mikuli and Maciej Pach, "Disciplinary Liability of Judges. The Polish Case", *Accountability and the Law Rights, Authority and Transparency of Public Power*, ed. Piotr Mikuli and Grzegorz Kuca (London: Routledge, 2022), 63.

89 Daniela Cavallini, "Judicial Discipline: Different Approaches in Five EU Member States", *Handbook of Judicial Politics*, ed. Cristina Dallara and Ramona Coman (IAŞI Institutui European, 2010), 125–55.

90 Suzanne Le Mire, "Regulation of Judicial Misconduct in Australia: Why, How and Where Next?", Devlin and Wilderman, 30.

91 E.g. Landreville case, see: William Kaplan, *Bad Judgment: The Case of Mr Justice Leo A. Landreville* (University of Toronto Press, 1996), after: Devlin and Wildeman, 53.

92 Devlin and Wildeman, 16.

93 Art. 62 (2) on the SJC says it shall be considered that a judge has committed a disciplinary offence when:

> without a justified reason, fails to draft and dispatch court decisions,
> his performance has been negatively evaluated by the council of judges,
> without justified reason, the number of decisions that a judge has rendered within a period of one year is significantly below the average in the Republic of Croatia (see: Dubravka Aksamovic and Sanja Misevic, "Fighting with the Ghosts of the Past: The Discipline Process for Judges in Croatian Law", in Devlin and Wilderman, 121).

94 Courts Act 1971 sec. 17, see: Graham Gee, "Judicial Conduct, Complaints and Discipline in England and Wales: Assessing the New Approach", in Devlin and Wilderman, 131.

95 Devlin and Wilderman, 6.

96 Le Mire, 26.

97 Devlin and Wilderman, 6.

98 Devlin and Wilderman, 6.

bona fide errors or the interpretation of norms – although these too, of course, are concepts that are subject to a considerable degree of relativity. The various solutions used in this area indicate that there is no unequivocally correct answer to this question.

It involves the issue of determining the level of regulation and the precision of defining what judicial misconduct means. The literature perceives vague, unarticulated standards of judicial conduct (Australia, China, England and Wales, India, Italy, Japan, the Netherlands),[99] in several systems (Anglo-Saxon countries, the Netherlands, Republic of South Africa till 2013[100]). These standards take the form of guidelines, suggestions rather than a catalogue of requirements. Japan has rejected the idea of cataloguing judicial duties in a code of conduct at all.[101] On the other side we have systems with a well-defined catalogue of behaviours (Italy,[102] Croatia,[103] Netherlands, Hungary, Bulgaria, Slovenia, South Africa) – but here, in turn, the analysis of practice brings the conclusion that such a system is too descriptive.[104] In order to judge misconduct, a standard of appropriate conduct to the judge must be developed, as emphasised, *inter alia*, by the Bangalore Principles,[105] which call for judicial behaviour to be catalogued and specified by judicial bodies, guaranteeing independency and impartiality of proceeding.[106] Also, other international documents, including many produced by judicial bodies,[107] stress the

99 Devlin and Wilderman, 7, 14.

100 The Code of Judicial Conduct for Judges was adopted by Parliament on 18 October 2013, although it is still described as "a thoroughly laudable set of guidelines for ethical behaviour by judges (...) retaining a degree of flexibility". See: Hugh Corder and Calli Solik, "Judge and Be Judged: Judicial Discipline in South Africa", in Devlin and Wilderman, 319.

101 Devlin and Wilderman, 17; Cravens in Devlin and Wilderman, 212.

102 The Code of Discipline 2006 consists of 37 disciplinary violations divided into three categories: violations in office, violations beyond official duties and violations as criminal offences in: Daniela Cavallini, "Why Is the Complaints Procedure Still Lacking in Italy? The Difficult Pathway towards a More Transparent, Inclusive and Effective Disciplinary System", in Devlin and Wilderman, 187.

103 Art. 62 on the State Judiciary Council. See: Aksamovic and Misevic, 121.

104 Devlin and Wilderman, 15.

105 The Bangalore Principles of Judicial Conduct (2006) ECOSOC 2006/23, UN Doc E/RES/2006/23.

106 Bangalore Principles of Judicial Conduct, Bangalore Implementation Measures, art. 15.5; 56 B.

107 E.g. International Association of Judicial Independence and World Peace, New Delhi Code of Minimum Standards of Judicial Independence 1982, Universal Declaration on the Independence of Justice (Montreal Declaration) of the First World Conference on the Independence of Justice (Montreal, Canada 1983), Beijing Statement of Principles on the Independence of the Judiciary in the LAWASIA Region, 1995, amended in 1997 (Manila), The Universal Charter of the Judge, International Association of Judges 1999 (updated 2017), Magna Carta of Judges Consultative Council of European Judges Strasbourg 2010, International Association of Judicial Independence and World Peace, Bologna and Milan Global Code of Judicial Ethics 2015.

importance of careful delineation of judicial rights and duties.[108] Without clear standards, it can be overly easy to present charges and the judgment can easily become subjective and biased; or vice versa: it can be impossible to present charges, thus blocking a fair judgment.

Another challenge is to define the procedure for adjudicating on disciplinary responsibility. A number of their conditions emerge from the international documents indicated, concerning, among others: ensuring the independence of investigatory bodies (preferred to be judicial council or commission, dominantly composed of judges), and the procedure itself: procedural fairness, proceeding in camera, proportionality of sanctions, judgments to be published.[109] Together, these conditions and previous observations lead us to identify another issue relevant to the accountability function. The implementation of the procedure to enforce the deposition of a judge determines the course of these proceedings, the rhetoric of the efforts of the accusers, as well as the judges defending themselves against the charges.[110] In this type of proceeding, therefore, there is no room for an impartial account of the authority exercised; on the contrary: the relationship is already directed towards the defence of the position. The weight of procedural issues (i.a. the principle of procedural fairness, including the equality of the parties to the proceedings) also points to this nature of the relationship arising in the procedure for the dismissal of a judge. It is thus an accountability already aimed directly at the application of sanctions, i.e. accountability with a negligible function of obtaining an account of the exercise of judicial power. One phenomenon which is very characteristic of the disciplinary responsibility of judges is the issue of the use of argumentation reduced to a defence by law. If the allegations against a judge relate to the improper administration of justice, the judge's response and account consists of an argumentation amounting to an indication of the law which, in the judge's opinion, directed the actions for which he or she is to be held responsible. In the most elementary sense, which reduces the administration of justice to the adjudication of a case, disregarding the principle of *non omne quod licet honestum est* – what is not unlawful cannot be judged wrong, and according to this line of argumentation, although it is logically beyond reproach, it remains in the rhetoric and plane of responsibility rather than accountability.[111]

108 UN Basic Principles on the Independence of the Judiciary GA Res 40/32 and GA Res 40/146, UNGAOR UN Doc A/CPNF.121.22/Rev.1 (1985), Council of Europe European Charter on the Statute of Judges (1998) DAJ/DOC (98) 23.

109 Devlin and Wilderman, 11.

110 Colbran, 60.

111 Moliterno et al., 540. From a point of view of the aforementioned feature (defence through the argument of a legal order), the first case of an attempt to apply impeachment against a federal Supreme Court judge; Samuel Chase, accused by the Republicans of violating the law in his ruling, is characteristic. The House of Representatives voted in favour of impeachment. During his trial in the Senate, Chase argued that he could not be removed from office

It would be difficult to overlook another fundamental problem from the perspective of the accountability model: who adjudicates on disciplinary responsibility. In the model adopted in most countries and proclaimed in international documents, there is no doubt that such a body must stand independent of the executive, of political influence and have its composition dominated by judges. It is noteworthy, however, that the model quite commonly used today, namely the enforcement of disciplinary responsibility by the judges themselves, abandons the link between the Principal altogether, entrusting the judicial power, and the one who exercises it. As Brian Smith points out,[112] "In Principal-Agent terms, judicial self-management appears to require accountability to a separate Principal rather than to some members of the Agent itself, but it is not clear which external Principal is consistent with judicial independence". In effect, this nullifies the effect of accountability and, as a consequence, reduces, rather than increases, public trust in judicial power. The problem is somewhat insoluble, because a judge is entitled under disciplinary responsibility to the right to fair trial, as the European Court of Human Rights (ECtHR) has repeatedly confirmed in recent years,[113] especially in the Polish cases of recent years, as discussed below. This in turn means that only the court can rule on the judge's misconduct – a situation reminiscent

---

for either an error in judgment or misconduct in adjudication, but only for a crime. While approving this position, the Senate in 1805 did not vote to remove the judge from office.

112 Smith, 199.

113 The Grand Chamber of the Court in the case of *Guðmundur Andri Ástráðsson v. Iceland* [GC], no. 26374/18, 1 December 2020 clarified the scope of, and meaning of the concept of a "tribunal established by law" against the context of disciplinary process of judges. The Court reiterated that the purpose of the requirement that the "tribunal" be "established by law" was to ensure "that the judicial organisation in a democratic society did not depend on the discretion of the executive, but that it was regulated by law emanating from Parliament" (§ 214). In following paragraphs the Court defined the meaning of the notions of "tribunal", "established" and "by law":

217. As regards the notion of a "tribunal", in addition to the requirements stemming from the Court's settled case-law, it was also inherent in its very notion that a "tribunal" be composed of judges selected on the basis of merit – that is, judges who fulfilled the requirements of technical competence and moral integrity. The Court noted that the higher a tribunal was placed in the judicial hierarchy, the more demanding the applicable selection criteria should be.

218. As regards the term "established", the Court referred to the purpose of that requirement, which was to protect the judiciary against unlawful external influence, in particular from the executive, but also from the legislature or from within the judiciary itself. In this connection, it found that the process of appointing judges necessarily constituted an inherent element of the concept "established by law" and that it called for strict scrutiny. Breaches of the law regulating the judicial appointment process might render the participation of the relevant judge in the examination of a case "irregular".

219. As regards the phrase "by law", the Court clarified that the third component also meant a "tribunal established in accordance with the law". It observed that the relevant domestic law on judicial appointments should be couched in unequivocal terms, to the extent possible, so as not to allow arbitrary interferences in the appointment process.

of Baron Munchhausen's, who pulled himself and the horse on which he was sitting out of the mud by his own hair.

It does not do so very effectively. A study by the ENCJ [114] carried out in 2022 indicates that judges, while satisfied in principle with their level of independence, are more critical of accountability for misconduct.[115] The country average is 6% of respondents disagreeing with the proposition that judges adhere to the ethical standards. But over 10% of respondents felt that it was inappropriate to respond to these behaviours. The rate is higher in Spain, Portugal and Bosnia and Herzegovina, where many respondents feel that the authorities do not act appropriately to judicial conduct (38%, 23% and 23%, respectively).[116]

It is possible to make this challenge less relevant by recognising that the entrusting authority has not so much the right to judge the judge's conduct as merely to report the judge's misbehaviour and submit it to the judgment of an independent body (court). What matters, therefore, is not the adjudication itself, but the right to prosecute for judicial misconduct. However, the figures for filing complaints and subjecting them to filtering processes are also striking. Here a key procedural issue arises: who is responsible for gatekeeping? Is it the judicial bodies, or the representatives of the Attorney General (Italy) or independent bureaucratic agencies (England and Wales)?[117] This last distinction yields instructive knowledge – when the vast majority (90–95% of complaints) are filtered out, in England and Wales this rate is significantly lower (70%).[118] But since such a significant proportion of complaints do not reach adjudication at all, it appears that the role of the Principal, even if limited to the right to complain, is minor and the accountability of judges itself illusory.

Who is to hold accountable and whom – a list of challenges

Let us now address accountability understood as answerability – the relationship of reporting on entrusted authority. While we are relieved to leave behind all the dilemmas of sanctioning judges and trying them on indictment, the latter type quickly leads us to another perplexing question – who can hold judges to account? As with the other types of systemic accountability discussed herein, it would indeed amount to a trivialisation of this phenomenon to frame it solely in terms of the dual relationship between the Agent and the Forum

114 European Network of Councils for the Judiciary (ENCJ) – organisation of councils for the judiciary in Europe.

115 he Netherlands Council for the Judiciary; Frans van Dijk (B. Diephuis, S. Koolen), *Data ENCJ Survey among Judges* 2019, 4, available at: www.encj.eu. Poland was not included in the study, as its membership in the Network has been suspended since 2018. In 2021, Poland was excluded from the Network.

116 van Dijk, 39, 40.

117 Devlin and Wilderman, 16.

118 Devlin and Wilderman, 16.

(the Principal). The judicial accountability relationship makes even more use of intermediaries and instruments that neutralise this inherently hierarchical relationship than the others discussed here. Nevertheless, there has to be some kind of connection between the one who exercises authority and the one who entrusts it and the conditions and procedure under which this entrustment takes place. In a democratic state, where the origin of power lies in the political community, represented by elected representatives, this relationship is fundamental. This axiom, however, is subject to exceptionally strong contestation in the case of judges, and the problem of identifying to whom judges are to report is not insignificant and even worse: rarely resolved. As Brian Smith accurately points out, the problem of accountability has been approached so far by the formulation of principles[119] of judges' behaviour rather than specifying to whom judges should be held accountable and through what rules and relationships.[120] In turn, Mark Bovens calls this issue "the problem of many eyes".[121]

If one focuses on pointing out the types of accountability due to the subject that identifies the recipient of the report of authority, the first problem appears immediately. The chain of delegation/trust of authority disappears here. With the exception of a handful of American states and countries, judicial power is entrusted by bodies set up for that purpose, having a preponderance of judges and little to do with the will of, or even the approval of, the electorate. Therefore, the doctrinal assumption of entrustment of power and accountability for its exercise by the sovereign is here no longer de facto demystified, as in the case of electoral accountability, but non-existent at all.

While recognising the need for intermediaries and proxies in this relationship, we make use of the classification of types of accountability based on the entity that receives the accountability. When writing about public accountability, Mark Bovens distinguishes between, firstly, legal accountability,[122] in which the subject receiving and assessing the account of the authority exercised is the court. Its scope usually relates to the violation of the law in the process of appellate review of decisions, i.e. by higher courts. However, it still has nothing to do with an account of the entrustment of power, nor with the receipt of an account of the exercise of power by the forum-entrustor. The problem is that the forum that carries out the accountability is precisely the judges, so it is not only a horizontal accountability in this case, but an internal

119 Devlin and Wilderman, 3–5.

120 Smith, 186.

121 Bovens, 18, see also: Mark Bovens, *Analysing and Assessing Public Accountability. A Conceptual Framework*, European Governance Papers (EUROGOV) No. C-06-01 (2006), available at: http://www.connex-network.org/eurogov/pdf/egp-connex-C-06-01.pdf. (accessed 11.12.2023).

122 Lawrence M. Friedman, *Total Justice* (New York, 1985); Robert D. Behn, *Rethinking Democratic Accountability* (Washington, DC: Brookings Institution Press, 2001), 56–8; Bovens, 16.

one. Nor is it an accountability of the judge or the court in the functional sense. The purpose is to control the judgment from a legal point of view. Finding a violation of the law to the extent that justifies any reaction against the judge personally may only be an incidental and extremely rare outcome.

The second type of accountability is called "administrative". It is carried out by auditors, inspectors and controllers, and concerns the effectiveness of the resources spent and the action taken. It is relatively uncontroversial. This is because it does not relate to the sphere of adjudication, but rather to the management of the courts, although it is worth noting that usually, in the event of a dispute between an auditor/inspector and an Agent (a court in this case), the dispute is submitted to the court for resolution.

Besides, there are two more forms, distinguished by Mark Bovens, which seem to be of the greatest importance in terms of judicial power. The first is professional accountability exercised by peers: professional associations and disciplinary tribunals, according to standards for acceptable practice binding for all members on the basis of peer review.[123] Again, however, the fundamental problem is that it is difficult for the forum not to be identified with the accountability actor. In a systemic sense, it is the same group all the time and the risks involved are quite evident in practice.

Finally, the last type of accountability is social accountability, carried out by observers and addressees of the actions taken within the framework of the entrusted power. In our opinion, this is where the accountability of the exercised power can be truly taken away, especially through the justification of judicial decisions, both during the trial and in the ruling issued by the court. The public nature of the trial, the openness of the rulings, the justification of the verdict and the monitoring and commentary on the administration of justice are essential elements of accountability for the exercise of judicial power. The forum that receives this account may also have "many eyes". These may include the defendants, lawyers – usually the most diligent and insightful recipients of judicial justifications, public agencies, the general public, interest groups, non-governmental organisations (NGOs) and other stakeholders. Although central in our opinion, this type of accountability is subject to particular risks, especially in relation to the transmission of the very content of accounts of power and the fragmented reception of it. Here, however, let us indicate just one of them: this forum can be ignored by the Agent, i.e. the court. The reason is quite natural: the judge is usually subject to the evaluation of the court of second instance. This court is also the one where accounts are given by the judges. It is this entity that has to be convinced about the rightness, the fairness of the action, its legality. The forum in the form of the parties to the trial or the public in the judge's mind is a subjudicial or ephemeral entity, and not the entity to which one has to explain one's exercise of power. This hazard is, of course, consciously exaggerated here – but it must be borne

123 Bovens, 19.

in mind that the notion of observers of judicial action may be particularly ambiguous here and may influence the nature and addressee of the account of the exercise of judicial power.

It is somewhat simpler to indicate who is to give an account of the exercise of the entrusted power. Two entities can be distinguished in this respect which are obliged to give this account. The first is the judicial power understood institutionally, namely the courts. They are obliged to give an account for the organisation of the exercise of the power entrusted to them, including self-regulation and enforcement of the standards of adjudication set within its framework, and in the most literal, accounting sense – of the costs that have been incurred towards the operation of the courts. This is institutional accountability and in practice it is primarily concerned with efficiency of operation, which on the other hand is extremely hard to value.

The second Agent in the accountability relationship of judicial power is the judge, exercising power in the adjudication process. The judge is required to give an account of the adjudication of the case and the motives that determined the decision. Judicial behaviour outside the process of adjudication therefore does not fall within this scope – it should be assessed and judged within the framework of disciplinary and professional responsibility. However, they can hardly be expected to become the subject of answerability, a classic account of the exercise of entrusted power, as this category should only concern the acts of exercising that power: that is, judgments and proceedings in the administration of justice.

The presentation of the entities that are parties to the judicial power relationship raises further questions and concerns. Let us indicate just two of them at this point.

First: the diversity of the actors receiving the account of the exercise of power does not render them effective enforcers and does not offer the possibility of a real, and not just a façade, reception of this account, let alone drawing sanctions. Parliament and government are severely limited or eliminated in this relationship due to the protection of the independence of judges. As the Consultative Council of European Judges emphatically states in its 2015 opinion:

> "Accountable" does not mean that the judiciary is responsible to or subordinate to another power of the state, because that would betray its constitutional role of being an independent body of people whose function is to decide cases impartially and according to law.[124]

124 "The position of the judiciary and its relation with the other powers of state in a modern democracy"; Opinion n°18 on the position of the judiciary and its relation with the other powers of state in a modern democracy, Consultative Council of European Judges London 2015, para 20, available at: https://www.coe.int/en/web/ccje/opinion-n-18-on-the-position-of-the-judiciary-and-its-relation-with-the-other-powers-of-state-in-a-modern-democracy (24.04.2023).

By contrast, citizens functioning within the framework of social accountability are background audience. They are spectators, constrained by the prohibition to step onto the pitch, rather than decision-makers who determine who is on the pitch. The lack of an instrumentality to hold judicial power accountable and the impotence of actors inevitably subordinated to the power of the courts at the end gives rise to considerable social frustrations. These are expressed, among other things, by the grassroot action of organisations monitoring the operation of the courts.[125]

Consequently, most of the accountability instruments are left to the judges themselves. This results in the accountability being addressed to the judges. Accountability is inherent in nature, which very much affects its content and the character of the account given. It is directed not to the one who has constitutionally entrusted the power, but to the one who has actually made the entrustment of that power, i.e. the body of judges who fulfil the de facto role of the Principal, namely the superiors and the "tribal elders" who decide on judicial appointments. This problem can be seen quite well in the observation of the judicial councils. At the same time, the accountability of judges before other judges, and not through democratic procedures, is essential to preserve the autonomy of judges and their political independence.

Councils for the judiciary – who is the Principal in practice?

The remarks we have made so far regarding the difficulty of identifying the relationship between the entrustor and the exerciser of judicial power point to the elementary problem of entrustment – the delegation of power. Here, the requirement of democratic empowerment of judges is intertwined with the meritocratic criterion, which remains in the hands of the judges themselves. Looking from the perspective of systemic practice, the conflict between corporatism and political dependence, implying a limitation of judicial independence and impartiality, is far more serious. Therefore, a key issue in terms of accountability, as Emilio Meyer and Thomas Bustamante note, is the creation of independent bodies equipped with the competence to hold judges accountable. The councils for the judiciary are such bodies.

They have become a widely used solution; a survey in the Constitute Project, using the term "establishment of judicial council" demonstrates that around 140 countries have in their constitutions devices for judicial accountability. As many as 93 countries among 121 examining mention directly

125 These include the national civic activism network Court Watch. They also include organisations such as the National Forum on Judicial Accountability (NYC) and other state organisations of this kind, including Montana Citizens Council on Judicial Accountability, https://www.mtscoja.org as well as Forum for Judicial Accountability in India, see e.g. http://images.assettype.com/barandbench/import/2011/08/Various-Representations-Against-Justice-Dinakaran.pdf (24.04.2023).

judicial councils.[126] However, not all judicial councils have the same status and composition. In the ENCJ functioning in Europe, there are 20 members[127] (several countries have separate councils for administrative justice – Greece and Italy) and three observers (councils from England and Wales, Scotland and Northern Ireland).[128] ENCJ Compendium on Councils for the Judiciary adopted on 29 October 2021 takes the view that councils for the judiciary should be independent not only from the executive and legislative powers (external independence) and should be free from undue influence from within the judiciary (internal independence).

The councils can be composed either exclusively of members of the judiciary or mixed, consisting of members and non-members of the judiciary.[129] The most successful models appear to be those with representation from a combination of judges and lay members elected from the ranks of legal, academic or civil society.[130] When the composition is mixed, the council should be composed of a majority of members of the judiciary. As was added by the General Assembly in Vilnius on 29 October 2021, all judicial members should be elected by their peers and a majority of judicial members should be guaranteed in the composition of all panels of the council. The councils for the judiciary, according to the ENCJ memorandum, are to be responsible for the appointment of judges, judicial training and ethics, disciplining judges, processing of complaints of litigants, as well as the management of the courts.[131]

126 Nuno Garoupa and Tom Ginsburg, *Judicial Reputation: A Comparative Theory* (University of Chicago Press, 2015), 129.

127 Belgium: Conseil Supérieur de la Justice / Hoge Raad voor de Justitie, Bulgaria ВИСШ СЪДЕБЕН СЪВЕТ / Supreme Judicial Council, Croatia Državno sudbeno vijeće / State Judicial Council, Denmark: Domstolsstyrelsen, Finland Tuomioistuinvirasto/ Domstolsverket / National Courts Administration, France: Conseil Superieur de la Magistrature, Greece ΑνωΤαΤο ΔικασΤικο ΣυμΒουλιο / Supreme Judicial Council of Civil and Criminal Justice and ΑνώΤαΤο ΔικασΤικό ΣυμΒούλιο ΔιοικηΤικήσ Δικαιοσύνησ / Supreme Judicial Council for Administrative Justice, Hungary: Országos Bírói Tanács / National Judicial Council, Ireland: Courts' Service, Italy: Consiglio Superiore della Magistratura, Consiglio di Presidenza della giustizia amministrativa, Latvia:Tieslietu padome, Lithuania: Teisėjų Taryba, Malta: Commission for the Administration of Justice, the Netherlands: Raad voor de rechspraak, Portugal: Conselho Superior da Magistratura, Romania: Consiliul Superior al Magistraturii, Slovakia: Súdna rada Slovenskej republiky, Slovenia: Republika Slovenija Sodni Svet, Spain: Consejo general del Poder Judicial.

128 By decision of the General Assembly of 10 June 2020 the Councils for the Judiciary from the United Kingdom were granted Observer status: Judges' Council of England and Wales; Northern Ireland: Judges' Council; Scotland: Judicial Council.

129 ENCJ Resolution of Budapest on Self-Governance for the Judiciary: Balancing Independence and Accountability of Budapest 2008, https://www.encj.eu/images/stories/pdf/opinions/budapestresolution.pdf (accessed 24.04.2023).

130 ENCJ report on Councils for the Judiciary 2010–11, https://www.encj.eu/images/stories/pdf/workinggroups/report_project_team_councils_for_the_judiciary_2010_2011.pdf (accessed 24.04.2023).

131 All or part of the following tasks should fall under the authority of a council for the judiciary or of one or more independent and autonomous bodies:

It is therefore a (model) body representing the judges, or at least with a majority of judges, and as to the decisions made by the judges. These councils play a key role in the process of appointing judges,[132] shaping ethical rules, and often influence the composition and adjudication process of disciplinary responsibility cases. They therefore exercise many of the instruments classically included in the accountability of judicial power. Their positioning within the constitutional system is supposed to guarantee their independence from political power. Much less emphasis appears to be placed on guaranteeing their internal independence, that is, the absence of any external influence from the judicial community on the course of their work and the decisions they take.

In such a model, there is concern about the formation of a guild mentality.[133] This fear is quite intense, given that judges usually tend to be part of a small, familiarised, homogeneous group of society, and they try to preserve their exclusive character and their own customs,[134] which does not always fit with social expectations and above all: principles of accountability. These are not just hypothetical risks. In some countries, the mastery of the council for the judiciary by the presidents of key courts has reinforced the subordination of judges to superiors in key decisions about appointments, promotions and positions. Empirical research by Garoup and Ginsburg also indicated that importing judicial councils does not imply increasing of quality of the judiciary nor does having more judges in the composition of the council produce more independence.[135]

- the appointment and the promotion of judges,
- the training of judges,
- the discipline and judicial ethics,
- the administration of the courts,
- the finances of the judiciary,
- the performance management of the judiciary,
- the processing of complaints from litigants,
- the protection of the image of justice,
- the formulation of opinions on judicial policies of the State,
- setting up a system for evaluating the judicial system,
- drafting or proposing legislation concerning the administration of the judiciary/the judiciary and/or courts.

The ENCJ Compendium on Councils for the Judiciary, 9; available at: https://pgwrk-websitemedia.s3.eu-west-1.amazonaws.com/production/pwk-web-encj2017-p/ReportsThe%20ENCJ%20Compendium%20on%20Councils%20for%20the%20Judiciary%20-%20adopted%20EGA%2029%20October%20Vilnius%20coverpage.pdf (24.04.2023).

132 However, it should be mentioned that there are two systems for the appointment of judges. As Bustamante and Meyer point out: "career judiciary", in which judges are selected in hierarchical bureaucracies (existing in European countries, civil law tradition), and a "recognition judiciary", which recruits judges from legal careers that span over a lifetime (system linked to common law jurisdictions and the United States (Meyer and Bustamante, 2).

133 DmitryBam, 346–50, with many examples of "guild mentality in action".

134 Devlin and Wilderman, 12–13.

135 Garoupa and Ginsburg, 129.

Owing to this mechanism, trends and reforms to limit self-government within judicial power are evident in many parts of the world. Smith gives the example of Bulgaria, where reforms in 2007 took place to provide a better balance between independence and accountability in favour of the latter by the reducing the autonomy of the Supreme Judicial Council.[136] Also in the Czech Republic the system of discipline was reformed in 2008 by requiring the judicial disciplinary board to draw half its members from lawyers who are not judges, selected by the chief state attorney, the chair of the Bar Association and the deans of law faculties.[137] The Swedish and Finnish models are also worth noting, where the Parliamentary Ombudsman is responsible for prosecuting public servants including judges, who are subject to criminal liability for the performance of their official responsibilities[138] and is entitled to intervene if it appears there were faults or malpractices during the proceedings of the trial such as if the parties or witnesses were mistreated in the court – also by supervision of the decisions of the courts, when an obvious error has been committed.[139]

However, let us leave aside the disputes and controversies about corporationism and political dependence, or lack thereof, and the questions of the effectiveness of the judicial governance model, in which the judicial council plays the decisive role of both decision-maker and controller. Instead, consider the positioning of the councils in the context of accountability and the relationship between the Principal and the Agent. Are the councils a representative of the Agent or an intermediary or do they simply serve as the sole forum performing accountability?

The model solution proposes that, to a large extent, councils for the judiciary are independent of actors other than judges and that their composition is completely independent of the electoral process, i.e. that the political Agent has no influence over them. Lay members are in a minority under the ENCJ's requirements and are therefore virtually deprived of any influence on the final decisions of the councils as to the appointment of judges, the shaping of the judicial ethics and disciplinary process. In the name of judicial independence,

136 So the chairs of the Supreme Administrative Court and the Supreme Court of Cassation now have to report directly to Parliament on the management of the courts. An inspectorate elected by Parliament monitors the performance of magistrates. Members of the Supreme Judicial Council no longer act as judges during their tenure on the Council; Smith, 190.

137 Smith, 192.

138 Walter Gellhorn, *Ombudsmen and Others* (Harvard University Press, 1966), 201.

139 Griffith, 42–5. The author states that The Parliamentary Ombudsman's Annual Report, covering the period 1 July 1996 to 30 June 1997, shows that the total number of cases concerning the courts was 390 (326 of these had reference to courts of law and 64 to administrative courts). In six of these cases the Ombudsman decided to start a preliminary criminal investigation, and 39 of the cases were finished by a decision including admonitions or other criticism. More in: Kristina Boutz, "The Supervisory Function of the Parliamentary Ombudsman in Relation to the Swedish Courts", Office of the Swedish Parliamentary Ombudsman 1992 in: Griffith, Appendix C.

the councils consciously detach the instruments of entrusting and giving an account of governance from the original Principal. The judicial councils themselves become the embodiment of the forum that entrusts the power of judging, evaluates its exercise, decides on promotions, and thus performs the very accountability. This creates a pastoral model, exclusive and at odds with the concept of an accountability relationship to an external entity entrusting power. Under such circumstances, reconstructing the role and position of the entrusting authority proves extremely difficult. The solution to this problem is subject to numerous compromises, trying to reconcile, for better or worse, the independence with the accountability understood in this way. The attempt to reduce the dominant position of judges in the judicial council carried out in the name of judicial accountability, which took place between 2017 and 2023 in Poland, is an enlightening experience that the search for deepening accountability may result in its reduction. It led to a spectacular disaster and the undoing not only of judicial independence, but also of judicial accountability.

Case study – Polish struggles with judicial accountability. How to reinvent and bury it with one reform

The issues discussed above have become the subject of paradigmatic changes in Poland in recent years, introduced under the banner of repairing the system of judicial accountability and improving the quality of the Polish judiciary. The controversies related to the accountability of judges, which make up the process of the so-called democratic backsliding, resonate particularly strongly here.[140] At the same time, this provides a special opportunity to observe and analyse the features and conditions for judicial accountability in the context of a certain systemic experiment. Hence, using this example, we will demonstrate the wrong leads and dead ends where judicial accountability has been lost.

The first problem is the staffing of the Principal. To begin with, following the example of many other countries, the constitutional system in Poland provides for the existence of a council for the judiciary. According to the Constitution (Art. 186), the National Council of the Judiciary (NCJ) protects

140 For an extensive discussion regarding Poland and Hungary as illiberal democracies, see: Timea Drinóczi and Agnieszka Bień-Kacała, *Illiberal Constitutionalism in Poland and Hungary: The Deterioration of Democracy, Misuse of Human Rights and Abuse of the Rule of Law* (Routledge, 2022); Zsolt Körtvélyesi, “The Illiberal Challenge in the EU: Exploring the Parallel with Illiberal Minorities and the Example of Hungary”, *European Constitutional Law Review* 16, no. 4 (2020): 561–600 at 571 et seq.; Rosalind Dixon and David Landau, “1989–2019: From Democratic to Abusive Constitutional Borrowing”, *International Journal of Constitutional Law* 17, no. 2 (2019): 489–96 at 490 et seq.; Wojciech Sadurski, “Constitutional Democracy in the Time of Elected Authoritarians”, *International Journal of Constitutional Law* 18, no. 2 (2020): 324–33; Anna Gora and Pieter de Wilde, “The Essence of Democratic Backsliding in the European Union: Deliberation and Rule of Law”, *Journal of European Public Policy* 29, no. 3 (2022): 342–62 at 345.

the independence of the judiciary and the autonomy of judges, and as regards the appointment process, is the gatekeeper to the judiciary. NCJ plays a key role in the process appointing judges – according to Art. 179 judges shall be appointed by the President of the Republic on the motion of this body.

The Constitution predetermines that the vast majority (17 of 25 members) of Council members are judges. Pursuant to the law that was in force until 2017, a majority of Council members was also appointed by judges, but in December 2017 the Sejm decided that the 15 judge members of the NCJ should be elected by the Sejm from among candidates proposed by at least 2,000 citizens or at least 25 judges. The amended law terminated the terms of office of the 15 existing members of the NCJ.[141] This literally preserves the constitutional requirement, but the judges have been drastically restricted in shaping the composition of the NCJ.[142]

The reform of the way judges are appointed to the NCJ has triggered a strong international reaction. The Grand Chamber of the CJEU of 19 November 2019[143] stated that the position of the NCJ thus shaped "may become relevant when ascertaining whether the judges which it selects will be capable of meeting the requirements of independence and impartiality arising from Article 47 of the Charter" (par. 139). At the same time, the CJEU reserved that it is up to the national court of reference to determine whether or not such process of appointing offers sufficient guarantees of independence, having regard to all of the relevant points of law and facts relating both to the circumstances in which the members of that body are appointed and the way in which that body actually exercises its role (par. 140).[144]

Two months after this verdict, on 23 January 2020,[145] the Polish Supreme Court, composed of the combined Civil, Criminal and Labour and Social Security Chambers, ruled that if the composition of the court includes a person appointed to the office of a judge of the Supreme Court at the request of the new NCJ, this could mean that the court is unduly formed and unlawful according to the provisions of civil and criminal procedure (Art. 439(1)(2) of the Code of Criminal Procedure, and Art. 379(4) of the Code of Civil Procedure, respectively). The Court stipulated that such a conclusion depends

141 And this was accepted by the (defectively staffed) Polish Constitutional Tribunal in its judgment of 25 March 2019, ref. K 12/18.

142 This reform led to the situation in September 2018, when the ENCJ suspended the membership of the NCJ, then on 28 October 2021 found that the NCJ did not comply with a condition of being independent of the executive and legislature and ensure the final responsibility for the support of the judiciary in the independent delivery of justice body and expelled the Polish NCJ from the Association.

143 Cases: C-585/18, C-624/18 and C-625/181.

144 http://curia.europa.eu/juris/document/document.jsf?text=&docid=220- 770&pageIndex=0&doclang=PL&mode=req&dir=&occ=first&part=1&cid=264338 6#Footnote (22.05.2023).

145 BSA Act I–4110–1/20.

on an examination of whether the defect in the appointment process led, in specific circumstances, to a violation of the standard of independence and impartiality (within the meaning of Art. 45(1) of the Constitution, Art. 47 of the Charter of Fundamental Rights of the European Union, and Art. 6(1) of the European Convention on Human Rights [ECHR]).[146]

In turn, the ECtHR ruled[147] in 2022 that a procedure for appointing judges that contained undue influence of the legislative and executive powers was per se incompatible with Art. 6(1) and, as such, amounted to a fundamental irregularity adversely affecting the whole process and compromising the legitimacy of a court composed of judges so appointed – thus, the breaches in the procedure for the appointment of judges to the Civil Chamber were of such gravity that they impaired the very essence of the right to a "court established by law".[148]

The reaction described above was clear, understandable and justified. However, these decisions deserve particular attention from the point of view of accountability. The result of the NCJ reform, the subsequent appointment of judges with NCJ participation and the rulings of the CJEU, ECtHR and the Supreme Court cited, was the emergence of two categories of judges: those appointed at the request of the NCJ in its old composition, and new judges "tainted with the original sin" of having been appointed by a body deemed politically dependent (referred to in Polish parlance as "neo-judges"). As the effect, the door was thus left wide open to the status of the new judges being questioned. Because they were appointed with the participation of the defectively formed NCJ, the presumption of the independence and impartiality of persons holding the office of judge was undermined, and this has created the need to assess whether the standard of independence and impartiality normally required of a judge had been breached by having them improperly appointed. This has led to confusion and uncertainty concerning judgments handed down, and has resulted in a lack of guarantee of the right to a court hearing to an even greater extent than before. The circumstances of a judge's appointment need not, and usually do not have a demonstrable effect on the course of the trial or the judgment by which it is concluded. At present, however, such rulings may be challenged on the grounds that the judge was appointed at the request of the new NCJ.

146 This resolution of the Supreme Court was commented on by the Polish Constitutional Tribunal (acting *ultra vires*, as the Tribunal has no jurisdiction to review acts of the application of the law), which ruled on 20 April 2020 that it was unconstitutional. See: Adam Płoszka, "It Never Rains but It Pours. The Polish Constitutional Tribunal Declares the European Convention on Human Rights Unconstitutional", *Hague Journal on the Rule of Law* 2022, https://doi.org/10.1007/s40803-022-00174-w (22.05.2023).

147 *Advance Pharma v. Poland* ECtHR judgment of 3 February 2022, app. No. 1469/20.

148 The issue of appointing and the status of judges to the Disciplinary Chamber of the Supreme Court was analysed in similar manner in previous ECtHR judgments (*Reczkowicz v. Poland*, app. No. 43447/19, *Dolińska-Ficek and Ozimek v. Poland* app. Nos. 49868/19, 57511/19).

The decisions of the CJEU and the Supreme Court led to the implementation of a mechanism called the "judge independence test", first in case law and then in legal regulation. The Act amending the Act on the Supreme Court enacted on 9 June 2022[149] provides that it is permissible to examine a judge's compliance with the requirements of independence and impartiality taking into account the circumstances surrounding their appointment and their conduct following the appointment, bearing in mind the circumstances of the litigant and the nature of the case at hand. The rationale is still vague ("if under the circumstances of the particular case it may lead to a breach of the standard of independence or impartiality influencing the outcome of the case") and the procedure inconvenient (the request for an examination must be made within seven days of the notification of the panel hearing the case), yet the consequences are severe. A judge is no longer held accountable simply for the process of adjudication, but for his/her nomination procedure, and for the body making the appointment, a circumstance over which the judge (with the exception of their consent to stand for judicial office) has no control. It is simplistic to assume that the appointment process alone causes a judge to be biased or dependent on the body that makes the appointment; this simplification is only partly nuanced by an examination whether this may have "led to a breach of the standard of independent court affecting the outcome of the case". Indeed, the criteria for this test are unclear, meaning that any decision by a court staffed with a new judge can be challenged, and the judges are presumed not to be independent. Finally, this "original sin" of appointment is irremovable, accompanying the judge forever, and so "neo-judges" must continually explain and account for who appointed them.

This outcome contradicts the true idea of accountability, for it calls into question the very relationship of entrusting power. Since it is assumed that the judges are to be held accountable for the process under which they were appointed, the entire chain of entrustment is called into question. The judge is held accountable for the actions of the constitutional public authorities (the NCJ and the President) in the procedure they followed and the criteria they applied in assessing candidates for the office of judge, which is beyond judicial power and *ex ante*, when true accountability should pertain to verifying and giving an account of what was done within the framework of the power entrusted, not of its having been entrusted by other entities.[150]

Under regulations of 2022, the systemic presumption of impartiality and appointment to the office of judge may be verified in successive, repeated vetting procedures. The legal mechanism adopted in Poland diminishes the

149 Act of 9 June 2022 amending the Act on the Supreme Court and certain other acts, Journal of Laws, item 1259.

150 Patrick Birkinshaw, "Decision-Making and Its Control in the Administrative Process – An Overview", in *Law, Legitimacy and the Constitution*, ed. Patrick McAuslan and John McEldowney (Oxford University Press, 1985), 152.

legitimacy of judges in public perception by questioning the belief that those appointed to the office of judge are worthy of holding that office, since it must be verified whether a given judge is independent and impartial. As a consequence, the accountability mechanism adopted undermines public confidence, not only in specific individuals, but in judges and the courts in general.

The problem of accountability understood as disciplinary responsibility was also changed in radical and remarkable manner. Up until 2015, the disciplinary responsibility of Polish judges was regulated in the general way; a judge was subject to disciplinary action for official misconduct, including a manifest and flagrant violation of the law or for breaching the dignity of office.[151] The disciplinary courts for disciplinary cases of judges were the courts of appeal and the Supreme Court. The system was designed in line with the principles of guaranteeing judicial independence – the disadvantage was that it did not work effectively.[152] This led to a major change in 2017, when a Disciplinary Chamber of the Supreme Court was created to rule on disciplinary cases concerning Supreme Court judges and as an appellate court for common court judges.[153] It was composed of "neo-judges" only.[154] The Minister of Justice (who is at the same time the Prosecutor General) selects both the disciplinary officers (from among the judges) and assigns the composition of the disciplinary court adjudicating at first instance.

Thus, the primary issue in terms of disciplinary proceedings, namely who is to hold a judge accountable, was resolved in such a fashion that, firstly, the judges of the disciplinary court were appointed by a body of the executive, and secondly, the Disciplinary Chamber of the Supreme Court, composed entirely of judges appointed by the new NCJ shaped in significant part by the ruling majority. Hence, the solutions adopted departed drastically from the model of judicial independence and impartiality. Even though decisions on accountability were made by formally independent judges, it was the Minister of Justice-Prosecutor General who selected the disciplinary officers and the disciplinary court judges, and the court adjudicating at second instance was composed of judges, whose appointment was doubtful.

151 For the entirety of this discussion, see Michał Laskowski, *Uchybienie godności urzędu sędziego jako podstawa odpowiedzialności dyscyplinarnej* (Wolters Kluwer, 2019).

152 The number of cases was strikingly small – around 50 out of 11,000 of judges annually in 2010–13 (data delivered by Ministry of Justice in 2014 in a reply to interpellation No. 25438 on disciplinary proceedings).

153 Act on the Supreme Court of 8 December 2017, Journal of Laws, 2018, item 5 as amended.

154 Agnieszka Bień-Kacała, "Illiberal Judicialisation of Politics in Poland", *Comparative Law Review* 25 (2019): 197–215; Sławomir Patyra, "Sądownictwo dyscyplinarne w kontekście ograniczeń konstytucyjnych", *Przegląd Prawa Konstytucyjnego* 4 (2020): 109–22; Anna Rytel-Warzocha, "Contemporary Problems of the Judicial Power in Poland", *Gdańskie Studia Prawnicze* 24, no. 4 (2020): 90–105.

On 19 November 2019[155] the CJEU stated in the judgment cited above, that the circumstances under which the system was set up and its characteristics gave rise to reasonable doubts as to its independence from external factors, in particular from the influence of the legislative and executive branches, as well as its neutrality. Following this judgment, the Chamber of Labour and Social Security of the Supreme Court ruled, in judgments of 5 December 2019 and 15 January 2020, that, in view of the circumstances of its creation and its appointment by the neo-NCJ, the Disciplinary Chamber could not be considered a court either under EU law or Polish law.[156]

The issue of the functioning of the Disciplinary Chamber of the Supreme Court was also addressed by the ECtHR in a judgment of 22 July 2021, in *Reczkowicz v. Poland*.[157] In the context of evaluation of the appointment process, the ECtHR confirmed that the NCJ did not provide sufficient guarantees regarding its independence from the legislative and executive powers. In assessing the irregularities in the establishment and staffing of the Disciplinary Chamber, the ECtHR determined that these nullified its legitimacy by being inconsistent with the requirements of independence and impartiality.

The consequences of these rulings for judicial accountability are serious. Judges who are deprived of the attribute of impartiality are no longer afforded the authority necessary to judge as they are lacking public trust. They are perceived not as independent and impartial arbitrators, but as parties to a political conflict – in the case under discussion, as ministerial vassals implementing a certain policy in the courts. Simultaneously, the undermining of trust in the Principal alters the legal and factual position of the Agent; in the absence of a properly empowered Principal, the Agent does not have to report on their activities. Under the pretext of strengthening the accountability of judges, a nullification of the meaning and function of disciplinary responsibility occurred, along with a reduction in the systemic accountability of judges.

The new regulations have fully confirmed this view. Following the CJEU judgment of 19 November 2019, which questioned the ability of the Disciplinary Chambef of the Supreme Court to act independently, the First President of the Supreme Court called on the judges of the Disciplinary

155 CJEU judgment of 19 November 2019 (the joined cases: C-585/18, C-624/18 and C-625/18, EU:C:2019:982, paras 149–51, 153).

156 See more in: Małgorzata Szuleka and Maciej Kalisz, *Disciplinary Proceedings against Judges and Prosecutors* Helsinki Foundation for Human Rights (Warsaw, 2019); *The Disciplinary System for Judges in Poland. The Case for Infringement Proceedings, The Opinion Accompanying the ESI Report "Under Siege: Why Polish Courts Matter for Europe"*, 22 March 2019; "Poland: the Judges Who Defend the Rule of Law", Index, EUR 37/9800/2019, Amnesty International, 2019.

157 App. No. 43447/19. In order to assess the violation of the Convention, the ECtHR applied the three-stage test adopted in its judgment of 1 December 2020 in *Ástráðsson v. Iceland* (manifest breach of national law, breach of standard fundamental to the procedure for the appointment of judges, and whether the breach could be effectively assessed and remedied by a domestic court).

Chamber on 10 December 2019 to refrain from all adjudicatory activities in ongoing cases, as she pointed out: to ensure the protection of the rights of participants in judicial proceedings, and to avoid worsening the legal chaos. At the level of the court of appeal, disciplinary responsibility ceased to function at all, so final judgments in this regard were discontinued. Instead of the promised tightening and increased efficiency, there has been chaos, lack of recognition and, ultimately, an annihilation of this form of accountability.

This chaos was further exacerbated by an Amendment Act passed on 20 December 2019 (popularly known as the "Muzzle Act")[158] which, among other things, introduced new definitions of disciplinary offences, expanding the catalogue of "actions or omissions which may prevent or significantly impede the functioning of the judiciary", "actions questioning the existence of an official relationship of judges, the effectiveness of a judge's appointment or the legitimacy of a constitutional organ of the Republic of Poland", and "public activities incompatible with the principles of judicial independence and the independence of judges". The introduction of judicial offences so defined was motivated by two reasons. The first was the external reaction, primarily of the CJEU, questioning the status of the new NCJ and the creation of the Disciplinary Chamber,[159] which happened primarily because of preliminary questions from Polish courts concerning the legal status of the newly established NCJ in the context of the courts' application of EU law. The new regulation meant that submitting a question for a preliminary ruling to the CJEU could be regarded as an action "preventing or obstructing the administration of justice". This is clearly contrary to Art. 267 TFEU, which provides for the possibility of submitting such a question, and of the second subparagraph of Art. 19(1) TEU, which obliges EU Member States to establish measures necessary to ensure effective legal protection in areas governed by Union law.

The second new offence, i.e. "actions calling into question the existence of an official relationship of judges, the effectiveness of a judge's appointment or the legitimacy of a constitutional organ of the Republic of Poland", was the legislature's reaction to the behaviour of those judges who had begun to refuse to adjudicate in compositions that included judges appointed by the new NCJ – whom they viewed as being of illegitimate provenance without the status of independent judges, and who denied the authority of the NCJ.[160] Similarly, the third new offence: "public activity incompatible with

158 Act of 20 December 2019 amending the Act – Law on the System of Common Courts, the Act on the Supreme Court and certain other acts.

159 On 23 January 2020, the EC asked the CJEU to suspend the operation of the Disciplinary Chamber. On 7 April 2020 the request was granted.

160 Court decisions questioning the NCJ's ability to act and appoint judges have also emerged. One example is a ruling by Judge Paweł Juszczyszyn, who, in November 2019, while hearing an appeal, found it necessary to decide whether a judge nominated by the new NCJ was entitled to adjudicate at first instance and asked the Chancellery of the Sejm to submit lists of support for candidates for the new National Council of the Judiciary. Disciplinary

the principles of judicial independence and the independence of judges", was introduced to exclude judges from participating in political protests related to judicial reforms.

Disciplinary proceedings shaped in the manner outlined above became the subject of a ruling by the CJEU. In its judgment of 15 July 2021,[161] the CJEU found that Poland had failed to ensure the independence and impartiality of the Disciplinary Chamber of the Supreme Court, had allowed the content of judicial decisions to be classified as disciplinary misconduct and had failed to ensure that disciplinary cases were decided by the court "established pursuant to the statute". The ECtHR also expressed doubts about the newly formed body, issuing interim measures in numerous cases of complaints from Polish judges.[162]

The main criticism voiced against the new offences introduced by the Amendment Act of 2019 concerned the attack on judicial independence.[163] At least two of the new offences concern the entrustment of judicial power relating to the process and administration of justice – the first involving the obstruction of justice, and the second challenging the mandate of a judge. From the point of view of accountability, the latter act is of greater interest. Its genesis and purpose are related to the emergence of the phenomenon of new judges being denied tenure in Poland, essentially by other judges. A judge was no longer held accountable only for the exercise of their authority, but for the manner in which they were appointed, and therefore the manner in which that authority was entrusted to him/her. In this way, a judge becomes accountable to the other Agents to whom power has been entrusted. The ruling majority, equated with the Principal, has desperately tried to block any legal assessment of the effects of its activities by introducing an *ad hoc* offence clearly aimed against just such judicial decisions. In turn, the casuistic characteristics of the new offence compromise the entire system of disciplinary responsibility and

proceedings were initiated against him, and he was suspended for almost three years (in May 2022 the Disciplinary Chamber overturned this decision). Krystian Markiewicz, "Iustitia", *European Law Journal* 27, no. 1–3 (2021): 312–47 at 326.

161 Case C-791/19, https://curia.europa.eu/juris/liste.jsf?num=C-791/19 (22.05.2023).

162 The cases of Polish judges have also been communicated to the Polish government; among others, these include complaints by judges: *P. Gąciarek, A. Synakiewicz, M. Piekarska-Drążek v. Poland.*

163 The Act is the subject of a complaint procedure by the CJEU in case C 204-21, in which interim measures were ordered that suspended some of its provisions. On 23 June 2023 the CJEU ruled (i.a.) that by adopting and maintaining in force points 2 and 3 of Article 107(1) of the Law relating to the organisation of the ordinary courts of 27 July 2001, as amended by the Act of 20 December 2019, which allow the examination of compliance with the EU requirements relating to an independent and impartial tribunal previously established by law to be classified as a disciplinary offence, the Republic of Poland has failed to fulfil its obligations under the second subparagraph of Article 19(1) TEU, read in conjunction with Article 47 of the Charter of Fundamental Rights of the European Union, and under Article 267 TFEU.

deny its essence, revealing the obvious intentions of the Principal and thus depriving it of its mandate to exercise accountability.

Pressured by the European Commission, which is withholding funds from the Reconstruction Fund for Poland on account of the judicial reforms, in June 2022 the Sejm amended once again the recently enacted legislation. While the disciplinary offences introduced in 2019 have not been abandoned, under the provisions introduced in 2022 they now exclude the issuance of a ruling that is vitiated by an error in the interpretation and application of national or European Union law, in the establishment of facts or the assessment of evidence, a request to the CJEU for a preliminary ruling on a question as referred to in Art. 267 TFEU or an examination of whether a judge is duly independent and impartial. The Supreme Court's Disciplinary Chamber has been replaced by a Chamber of Professional Responsibility composed of judges appointed by the President of the Republic of Poland from among judges of the Supreme Court drawn by lot – including judges whose legal status has been challenged by the CJEU, ECtHR and domestic judges.

Thus, two of the most serious and obvious flashpoints have been eliminated – the new disciplinary body is no longer fully appointed by the new NCJ, and therefore not burdened with the stigma of a lack of independence, and those offences which were directly within the sphere of judicial power, and therefore affected by autonomy, have been excluded. Nonetheless, the NCJ continues to be predominantly formed by politicians, and the Minister of Justice has retained considerable influence over the formation of those bodies that decide on disciplinary responsibility. It is hard to accept that the disciplinary responsibility system, understood as an important element of accountability, can meet the condition of giving an objective, bias-free account of possible abuses of power. This discrediting of the Polish system of disciplinary responsibility has also been to the detriment of accountability. The lack of independence of the disciplinary court and the circumstances of how judges are appointed have nullified the disciplinary bodies' true function – namely, to give an account of the exercise of judicial power and tenure of office in conditions which enable these to be objectively and factually assessed.

There is one more significant change in the scope of the accountability about efficiency of performing agencies. The activities of the common courts in Poland are subject to administrative supervision by the Minister of Justice and presidents of courts. In practice, court presidents are chiefly responsible for managing the operation of the courts, and court directors are directly involved. It is therefore crucial for an understanding of accountability in this sphere to regulate the manner in which these people are appointed and how the administration entrusted to the presidents of courts is accounted for. In this respect, there has also been one particularly notable reform in Poland in recent years.

Prior to July 2017, the presidents of appellate and regional courts were appointed by the Minister of Justice after consultation with the general assembly of judges of the relevant courts. In turn, the presidents of lower (district) courts were appointed by the president of a court of appeal after obtaining the opinion of the assembly of judges of the district court concerned. In the case of a negative opinion by the assembly of judges, the Minister of Justice could appoint the president of the court after receiving a positive opinion from the NCJ. A negative opinion by the NCJ, however, was binding on the Minister.

An amendment to the Law on the System of Common Courts in 2017[164] introduced discretionary power of the Minister of Justice in the appointment of presidents of courts. According to the amended Law on the System of Common Courts, the president of a court is appointed by the Minister of Justice from among the judges of that or a superior court. Once the president of a court has been appointed, the Minister of Justice presents him to the relevant general assembly of judges. Accordingly, the amendment removed the obligation to consult general assemblies or meetings of judges, leaving the Minister of Justice with the exclusive right to appoint the courts' authorities.

It also made the courts' directors fully subordinate to the Minister of Justice, who was given unfettered power of appointment and dismissal.[165] The draft's explanatory memorandum also argued that the proposed regulations would bring certain benefits: "they reduce the scope of duties of presidents of courts in the area of internal administrative supervision of court presidents".

According to new provisions, the function of the president was held for the duration of the term of office, yet presidents may be dismissed by the Minister for discretionary reasons, *inter alia*, "when the continuation of the function cannot be reconciled for other reasons with the good of the administration of justice" and when "it is ascertained that the effectiveness of actions in terms of the administrative supervision exercised or the organization of work in the court or lower courts is particularly low", although the criteria for such effectiveness are not measurable. The dismissal of a president or vice-president takes place after obtaining the opinion of the board of the relevant court (i.e. a body composed of the president of the court in question and the presidents of subordinate courts). If the opinion is negative, the Minister of Justice may submit the intention to dismiss to the NCJ. Only a negative opinion by the NCJ, adopted by a majority of at least two-thirds of the votes, does not allow the Minister to dismiss the president.[166]

164 Act of 12 July 2017 (date of entry into force: 12 August 2017).

165 It is particularly noteworthy that the amendment in this respect ignores the findings of the Constitutional Tribunal's judgment of 7 November 2013 (ref. K 31/12), according to which the provision regulating the status of the court director (Article 32b § 3 of the Act on ordinary courts system) is unconstitutional since it does not specify the consequences of a court president's request to the Minister of Justice to dismiss a court director. As indicated by the Court, "if the actions or omissions of the court director had an adverse effect on the functioning of the court and, as a result, significantly impeded the performance of the tasks of the administration of justice and legal protection, the judicial authorities would have no effective means of counteracting such a state of affairs".

166 Additionally, transitional provisions contained a competence of the Minister of Justice to dismiss court presidents solely on the basis of a discretionary decision for six months after

As a result of these changes, the Minister has been given unique powers to arbitrarily appoint and remove judges responsible for the functioning of the institutions in which judicial power is exercised. The involvement of the Minister of Justice in the appointment of presidents of courts without the participation of judges or their committees is unprecedented in Europe.[167] The strengthening of the Minister's supervisory measures over the courts has met with a strong reaction from Council of Europe bodies[168] and the EU.[169] In its judgment of 29 June 2021 in *Broda and Bojara v. Poland*,[170] the ECtHR considered the arbitrary dismissal of vice-presidents of courts from their posts before the expiry of their term of office to be a violation of Art. 6 of the Convention, questioned the compliance of the provision of the law permitting this with the requirements of the rule of law and criticised the deprivation of the right of appeal to a court, as well as the lack of justification for the decisions on dismissal.

The new draft of the Act on the System of Common Courts of 2022 similarly entrusted the Minister of Justice with the exclusive competence of appointing presidents of courts,[171] and ceases the terms of office of existing presi-

the entry of the Act into force. During this six-month transitional period, the Minister dismissed a total of 158 court presidents and vice-presidents, often by fax, email or letter signed by the Deputy Minister of Justice, without providing any justification. The dismissals affected around 21% of the 730 presidents of Polish courts. Report of the Council of Europe Commissioner for Human Rights following the visit to Poland in March 2019 (CommDH(2019)17).

167 Opinion on the Draft Act amending the Act on the National Council of the Judiciary, on the Draft Act amending the Act on the Supreme Court, proposed by the President of Poland, and on the Act on the Organization of Ordinary Courts, adopted by the Commission at its 113th Plenary Session (Venice, 8–9 December 2017), available at: http://www.venice.coe.int/webforms/documents/?pdf=CDL--AD(2017)031 (22.05.2023).

168 Parliamentary Assembly of the Council of Europe: resolution "New threats to the rule of law in Council of Europe member States: selected examples" of 11 October 2017 (resolution 2188 (2017)), decision of 28 January 2020 to initiate a procedure to monitor the functioning of democratic institutions and the rule of law against Poland, "Functioning of democratic institutions in Poland" (resolution 2316 (2020). In a subsequent resolution of 26 January 2021, "Judges must remain independent" (resolution 2359 (2021)) the Assembly explicitly stated that the power of the Minister of Justice to appoint and dismiss court presidents remains excessive.

169 When initiating the procedure on 20 December 2017 under Art. 7(1) of the Treaty on the Functioning of the European Union, the European Commission referred, *inter alia*, to the risk of the independence of common courts being undermined through statutes shaping the structure of the Polish judicial system, which are linked by the fact that they systematically allow the executive or legislative authority to significantly interfere in the composition, competences, management and functioning of these authorities and bodies. In the comments made in paragraphs 152–3 of the Commission's proposal, reference is made to the power granted to the Minister of Justice to dismiss presidents of courts during the transitional period.

170 Application Nos. 26691/18 and 27367/18.

171 Draft law by the Ministry of Justice of 15 March 2022, available at: https://legislacja.rcl.gov.pl/projekt/12359104/katalog/12874355#12874355 (22.05.2023).

dents and vice-presidents of common courts at all levels.[172] The employment relationships of all court directors were also to expire. Furthermore, according to the new draft, all proceedings in respect of identified deficiencies in court proceedings or management not concluded by the date of entry into force of the new were to be discontinued by virtue of law.

Nevertheless, the issue of the appointment and dismissal of presidents by the Minister should not overshadow another problem related to the management of the courts. Court directors, i.e. those in charge of the economic and organisational matters of a court, are direct subordinates of the Minister of Justice. This "relieving judges of administrative duties" actually means that the presidents are deprived of the competence to perform the tasks for which they are responsible, i.e. to actually manage their court.

The changes outlined here have led to a situation where judges have been stripped of their influence over the appointment of presidents of courts, and presidents have become largely incapacitated and completely dependent on the Minister of Justice. They were not held accountable for their authority – in the sense that they were deprived of the capacity to report on their assignments. Their activities were not subjected to any evaluation carried out on the basis of previously known performance evaluation criteria. They had no real opportunity to defend themselves against dismissal for vaguely defined reasons and without justification for the decision to dismiss them, or from being appointed at the discretion of the Minister following an opinion by a politicised NCJ. This negates the independence of these functions, or even their real entrustment for a certain period and under certain conditions.

If the Minister has virtually completely assumed the competences indicated here and has subordinated the organisation and finances of the courts to himself, court presidents simply have nothing to be accountable for. Their sole concern is not to fall into the Minister's disfavour. And this is not a relationship of real accountability in a system of entrustment and separation of powers, which presupposes independence in self-regulation and administration and must therefore be firmly and clearly separated from political power.

Decisions by the legislature in Poland between 2015 and 2022 and the events that accompanied them lead us to the conclusion that, along with the reduction of judicial independence, there has also been a significant decrease in the accountability of courts and judges. Accountability was falling victim to the reforms, which is ironic given that the reforms were introduced under the slogan of implementing mechanisms for accountability.

This allows us to experimentally trace what elements are necessary for judicial accountability. It demonstrates that not only is the accountability of judicial power not in conflict with judicial independence, but the two values are mutually necessary for each other's existence: an independent judge must

172 Draft law introducing the Law on the System of Ordinary Courts, available at: https://legislacja.rcl.gov.pl/projekt/12359104 (accessed 11.12.2023).

be held accountable, yet a judge can only be held accountable if he or she is independent. The relationship is much more "complementary rather than antithetical".[173]

In the Polish reforms discussed here, the Principal has been falsely positioned, for it is not the Minister of Justice who entrusts the exercise of judicial power. For the Minister of Justice to usurp so much influence over the enforcement of the accountability of judges and the appointment of their authorities is not only an assault on their independence, it is also a nullification of the relationship fundamental to accountability (i.e. the proper staffing of the Principal) and an annihilation of the Principal-Agent relationship.

Another consequence of this situation is to bring about extreme bias. Under such conditions, in turn, there can be no impartial accountability of entrusted power. This kind of accountability is controversial, and makes it difficult to identify the right evaluation criteria. Since it is carried out by nominees of political power, it has parallels with political accountability. The appointment of judges was carried out by a new council of the judiciary, formed by the ruling majority. This has led to an unprecedented and destructive situation for the operation of judicial power, in which some judges deny the newly appointed judges the legitimacy to adjudicate and their judgments are stigmatised as invalid. This, in turn, has led to the creation of new definitions of the acts for which judges are to be held disciplinarily responsible.

Under such circumstances, no objective and impartial account of the authority vested in the judiciary or of the acts and omissions performed within their framework can be made. Judge are obliged to give an account not of the exercise of power, i.e. of the outcome of a case and the motives that determined the outcome. Case studies of Polish reforms regarding the process of appointing judges and disciplinary liability show that not only independence, but also impartiality, are necessary for proper judicial accountability. Judges suspected of being dependent are immediately labelled as being biased; a division into "our" judges and "foreign" ones occurs, and confrontation replaces reporting on the entrusted authority. The regulation of the judge's independence test does not remove the bias – on the contrary, it deepens and perpetuates it.

Finally, the removal of real power from presidents of courts causes a diminishment of accountability for management; if there is no competence, there is nothing to be accounted for. The bill on the new System of the Courts Act,

173 Robert D. Nicholson, "Judicial Independence and Accountability: Can They Co-exist?", *Australian Law Journal* 67, no. 6 (1993): 404–26, at 414; McIntyre, 142. Bustamante and Meyer take a similar view, pointing out that the alleged conflict of accountability and independence is based on the "false dilemma", As Bustamante and Meyer wrote: "I . "Independence is pointless without responsibility, and with responsibility comes accountability. The only reason why judicial independence is meaningful and valuable is that it is a constitutive aspect of judicial responsibility: "meaning comes with responsibility and through responsibility", as argues Joseph Raz, *Value, Respect and Attachment* (Cambridge University Press, 2001), at 20. Bustamante, Meyer, 4.

removing this responsibility, is also a cursory example of the arbitrariness of the decisions taken by the political authorities in this regard.

But looking at these reforms and the disaster they triggered[174] raises a question of a more general nature: whether it is feasible at all to cast the role of the Principal under the reality of the political system and whether judicial accountability should be sought in the instruments of appointment, accountability and other sanctions. Perhaps Poland's unsuccessful reforms reveal, as if through a lens, the pitfalls and errors to which such attempts are prone.

And if so – where can judicial accountability be sought in that case?

So, where is judicial accountability?

Traps of accountability outlined so far, understood as the power of the Principal to deploy sanctions when the account is deemed unsatisfactory made by external actors[175] prompt a closer look at the concept of accountability meant as a pure answerability, as the obligation on the part of an Agent to provide an account of activities and achievements. Within its framework, the only way of pure accountability is to justify the judicial decision. As Brian Smith puts it: "it is much easier to specify how the answerability dimension of accountability works than the enforcement dimension when considering to whom the judiciary is accountable. Indeed, it has been argued that answerability is the only dimension consistent with judicial independence. Accountability can only mean giving reasons for judicial decisions".[176] In such a situation, however, sanctions only apply if the explanations given are not satisfactory and are therefore primarily incurred under internal accountability, when judges are held accountable by a system of appeals and judicial decisions are verified on points of fact or law in higher courts and may be corrected.[177]

In accountability understood in this way, it is the acts of the authorities that are subject to accountability, not the judges, which allows for the preservation of judicial independence.[178] This position brings us closer to the reconceptualists,[179] as defined by Le Souer. We believe that judicial power is

174 Even PM Mateusz Morawiecki, the creator of the judicial changes carried out, called the current state of the Polish judiciary: "chaos and disarray", https://tvn24.pl/polska/projekt-zmian-w-ustawie-o-sadzie-najwyzszym-i-innych-sadach-premier-mateusz-morawiecki-i-wiceminister-michal-wos-komentuja-6543172 (22.12.2022). At the same time, however, what is striking is that the factual assessment of one's own involvement in the destruction of the judiciary is not matched by a reflection on what is the cause of this corruption and its outcome.

175 Smith, 186.

176 Smith, 187.

177 Smith, 188.

178 Tien Dung, *Judicial Independence in Transitional Countries* (Oslo, Norway: UNDP Governance Centre, 2003), 16.

179 Le Sueur, 76. Le Sueur argues that, like Molière's Monsieur Jourdain who talked prose without knowing it, to the re-conceptualists the judiciary has long had accountability practices

made accountable in a much broader and more serious way than any of the others, and the primary instrument of this category in terms of answerability is the obligation of judges to conduct hearings in public; and to give reasons for their decisions.[180]

Giving reasons for a judicial decision makes it possible to review its correctness. It allows internal accountability to be exercised as a check within the framework of the instances of proceedings, a process of identifying and correcting errors in the adjudication of cases. Within this framework, the court articulates its position in order to present the motivation of its decisions to the defendants and other interested parties. At this point, the problem of the addressee of the statement of reasons arises. It is usually drafted with the intention of justifying the position taken (decision) to the appellate court. Appellate review is aimed at the correctness of the judicial decision taken. In its procedural effects, however, it does not refer to the accountability of the judges who reached the reviewed decision. A negative assessment of a judicial decision results in its annulment or modification – it refers only to that decision. It does not, however, relate to the assessment of the judge who made it, nor does it involve his or her legal responsibility for the decision. In addition, an interlocutory review does not constitute a relationship with the Principal, and so there is a risk that the appellate court becomes the primary recipient in place of those who entrusted the power.

This is why it is necessary to see the other facet of the justification of a judicial decision: the function of accounting for the exercise of entrusted power. In our view, it is the justification of decisions that lies at the heart of judicial accountability as answerability is to the community in formal and informal ways.[181]

Its second element is transparency of judicial process in all ways: public hearings, the publication of court decisions, public scrutiny of the judiciary by the media and civil society, annual reports to parliament, information on the judiciary's website and the right to know and comment on judicial decisions.[182] Stating that the openness of the trial and the public announcement of decisions is a necessary standard for a fair trial as an element of the right to a court is a truism. Such a position has been repeatedly confirmed also in the ECtHR case law. The Court has repeatedly stated that judges are a fundamental apparatus of power and both they and their rulings may be subject to criticism not only in theory, but also in general,[183] which, however, does not

without explicitly labelling them as such. See also: McIntyre, 232.

180 Murray Gleeson, "Judicial Accountability" *The Judicial Review* 2 (1995): 122–23, after Griffith, 16.

181 Griffith, 16.

182 Smith, 197.

183 "Save in the case of gravely damaging attacks that are essentially unfounded – bearing in mind that judges form part of a fundamental institution of the State, they may as such be subject to personal criticism within the permissible limits, and not only in a theoretical and

exhaust the problem from the point of view of the accountability function. What is at stake here, however, is not only the right to a court, but also the possibility of receiving an account of how judicial power is exercised.

If we look closely at the implementation and effects of this instrumentality from this perspective, giving a detailed account of how the entrusted power is exercised and assessing this account is subject to two risks. The first is related to those who are supposed to receive this account, the embodiment of the Principal (the Forum), i.e. the citizens.

In such a situation of communication, the Forum can be identified with the one to whom the court addresses itself in justifying its decision, that is, the audience. The judge is empowered to make choices, weigh values for the decision to be fair and legally correct and then: to demonstrate these values and make them justified as intersubjectively acceptable.[184] The key problem in legal reasoning is still how to identify who is to be convinced by the argument. Convincing someone requires contact of minds – and this in turn requires recognition of the characteristics of the audience. Legal reasoning means organising argumentation, but also – and above all – turning towards the legal audience.[185] Each court has its own concept of this audience, dependent on historical, cultural and social factors.[186] This is different for international courts,[187] for national courts and for constitutional courts. Nonetheless, it is always the court's responsibility to explain the rationality and rightness of its ruling decision by means of a statement of reasons – this is in fact the source of its legitimacy and therefore the conviction of the legitimacy of its decision and authority. Thus, the Forum has many more eyes than it might think. Yet it uses them to a very narrow extent. The assumption that citizens can observe how justice is administered is, in practice, implemented in a limited way. Usually, the observers are the parties to the judicial proceedings and

---

general manner. When acting in their official capacity they may thus be subject to wider limits of acceptable criticism than ordinary citizens", ECtHR (Grand Chamber), *Morice v. France*, App. No. 29369/10 (23 April 2015), para. 131, ECtHR, *July and SARL Libération v. France*, App. No. 20893/03 (14 February 2008), ECtHR, *Mustafa Erdoğan and Others v. Turkey*, App. Nos 346/04 and 39779/04 (27 May 2014).

184 Eveline Feteris and Harm Kloosterhuis, *Law and Argumentation Theory: Theoretical Approaches to Legal Justification* (June 21, 2013), available at SSRN: https://ssrn.com/abstract=2283092 or http://dx.doi.org/10.2139/ssrn.2283092, p. 9 (accessed 11.12.2023).

185 Michael H. Frost, *Introduction to Classical Legal Rhetoric: A Lost Heritage* (Ashgate, 2005), 57 et seq.

186 Feteris, Kloosterhuis, 8.

187 George Letsas, *A Theory of Interpretation of the European Convention on Human Rights* (Oxford University Press, 2009), 10; Samantha Besson, "European Human Rights, Supranational Judicial Review and Democracy – Thinking Outside the Judicial Box", *Human Rights Protection in the European Legal Order: The Interaction between the European and the National Courts*, ed. Patricia Popelier et al. (Intersentia' 2011), 107; Alain Zysset, *The ECHR and Human Rights Theory: Reconciling the Moral and Political Conceptions* (Routledge, 2016), 11; Janneke Gerards, "The Prism of Fundamental Rights", *European Constitutional Law Review* 8 (2012): 173–202, at 173.

those with an indirect interest in the outcome, and therefore hardly objective in their view and unaware of their role as entrustors of power. NGOs have a certain function in this respect, being observers,[188] and sometimes parties/participants in trials, but this is a negligible proportion of court cases.

The administration of justice *ab casu ad casum*, an essential part of the exercise of judicial power, is observed today peripherally and almost exceptionally through the media. However, due to the change in the status of the media and the struggle for audience attention (viewership) at the price of fictionalisation and subjectivisation of the coverage, the press tends to sharpen the content and form of coverage.[189] It follows the same trend with other mass media, including social media. Statements about courts, judges or the judiciary are no longer an objective report on the exercise of power, but a story with a thesis, often with sensational overtones, as Justice Spigelman puts it, "penetrating populist mythology" and fulfilling a persuasive function, particularly with regard to the appeal of marketable emotions. Furthermore, Thomas Bustamante and Emilio Meyer[190] draw attention to other circumstances that hinder the accountability by taking away the relationship in the reasoning of the judicial decision, which relate to the "information asymmetry", namely the substantive unpreparedness of the audience, the number of rulings made over time and the lack of a reference point, of adequate comparison material. These barriers make answerability done in this way highly illusory.

The second risk is related to the actions of the court, which has a role in the Agent's accountability relationship. This is because it has a lot of resources at its disposal to make its account of the way in which the case was handled and the way in which it was resolved compelling, without always reporting on its actions of authority. The court gives an account, but is in near total control of the message. The institutional author of the account is the narrator who is not only omniscient but also omnipotent as to the management of information and arguments. The conditions of the relationship are also very specific. It is a situation occurring in a particularly formalised environment that determines the form and content of the account. Indeed, in the accountability relationship the application of the law becomes a communicative situation in which the information asymmetry takes a particular form, the predominance of the court as ruler and expert and interpreter of the authority of the law is enormous. As a consequence, the court's persuasive function and instruments can

188 Particularly it is worth to bear in mind organizations' monitoring by residents of the work of their local courts. This popular form of civic activity in North America has over time adopted the name "court watch".

189 See further: Jacek Sobczak, "Dziennikarz sądowy. Dylematy i zasadzki", in *Media i sądy pro bono et malo. Wzajemne relacje w służbie demokratycznego państwa prawa*, ed. Bożena Godlewska-Michalak (Warsaw, 2008), 6 et seq.; Jerzy Bralczyk, Jacek Wasilewski, "Wizerunek sądu i sędziów stan obecny, przyczyny, perspektywy", in: Godlewska-Michalak, 43, 47, 54–6.

190 Bustamante and Meyer, 2.

effectively mask the accounts of the essential elements of the court's authority action.

Moreover, as mentioned above, according to the logic of internal accountability, the justifications of most of the contestable court decisions are produced not only to present the motivation of the decisions made to the defendants and other interested parties, but first of all to defend the court's position before the appellate court. The instantiation of proceedings, as a process of identifying and correcting errors in deciding cases, results in the lower court presenting its position arguing that it is in accordance with the law and logic, moral judgment and life experience, but also with the existing line of jurisprudence. This may result in the true motivations being obscured behind the message that the superior court wants to receive in order to consider the decision as lawful. Thus, the risk arises that it is the appellate court that becomes the primary recipient in place of those who entrusted the authority.

Under these circumstances, the account of the court in its communication with the recipient is fraught with particular semantic noise factors. The sender (court) has the opportunity to make its message seemingly objectified, for example, by making factual determinations or interpreting norms based on circumstances and interpretations of its own choosing, hiding others less appropriate for the selected act of the authority – the ruling. Secondly, the specificity of the legal and juridical language used in the justifications of court decisions, making the account incomprehensible to the reader, may constitute a significant factor. And thirdly, the court, being the author, has, for reasons previously mentioned, a natural tendency to apply an argumentation aimed at demonstrating the syllogism and the consequent legal precept of a particular decision, rather than indicating the actual motives for the act of power performed. "Law made me do this" – and what is lawful cannot be flawed: this is the main basis of judicial reasoning. This is the ultimate argument in such a paradigm, though it is neither the only one nor universal. In doing so, the argument masks the circumstance that adjudication is an individual act of power, requiring justification at the volitional level as well, in order to provide an opportunity not only for persuasion, but also for receiving an authentic and truthful account of what happened in the course of adjudication.

The path of narrative accountability, however, is prepared by the judges and for the judges. Trial rules play a special role in this process: among them, adversarialism, which allows the court of facts to hide behind the activity (or lack thereof) of the trial parties. The formalism of the trial, i.e. the time limits for submitting motions and evidence, certain prohibitions and rules of evidence also avoid many doubts that could reflect judgment. The judge can disguise it as a formal requirement and an adversarial model of process – instead of concluding that "it was not so", it is enough to write "it was not proved".[191]

191 Such activities have been called in the literature "trial by voodoo" – Evan Whitton, *Trial by Voodoo: Why the Law Defeats Justice and Democracy* (Random House, 1994). The argument

At this point, it is worth pausing for a moment to consider the difference in approaches to the process of law application. Chaim Perelman distinguished between two approaches to the process of law application: the French (continental) and the Anglo-Saxon. In the first of these, related to civil law, the priority is to resolve all the problems and uncertainties that may arise in advance in the various situations that the examining authority can imagine. This is the approach of the researcher who tries to formulate a general rule, who develops a legal or ethical doctrine and who proposes a solution to as many such cases as possible that may arise in practice. The logical approach assumes that one can sufficiently explain the concepts one is using, make the rules clear enough to apply them so that the solution itself is merely a deductive operation and any potential problems are of a purely technical nature. This is opposed to the Anglo-Saxon practical approach, in which problems are solved as they arise (and only then) by someone doing the thinking, interpreting the rules in the circumstances of the particular case requiring adjudication. This approach assumes that no one else is bound by one's own construct beyond what is absolutely necessary, freedom to behave according to circumstances and opens one's solution to the judgment of unknown, future experience. It is the approach of a judge who knows that, in passing judgment, he or she creates a precedent. Therefore, the judge seeks its boundaries and gives only those rationales for judgment that are necessary without extending the scope to other hypothetical situations, the complexity of which is unknown after all.[192] It leads to "judicial minimalism",[193] understood as a departure from the search for abstract and universal meanings, instead opting to refer to the realities of a specific dispute and the relevance to the circumstances that may arise in that dispute.

In the logical approach, the court uses the rhetoric of principles and legal constructs of the highest degree of abstraction (dignity, rule of law, morality) and pretends to construct general rules for resolving conflicts between goods and values. It remains in the formalist trend, based on the assumption that law must be understood and analysed as a distinct phenomenon, coherent and completely separate from other objects of social life or morality. This assumption essentially determines the content of the justification. For insofar as we accept that law has an internal system of understanding and an immanent moral rationality,[194] the justification is the discovery and expression of this

is developed in: Evan Whitton, *The Cartel: Lawyers and Their Nine Magic Tricks* (Herwick Pty Ltd, 1998). See also: Griffith, 18.

192 Exhaustively on the dissimilarities in the process of applying the law in continental (French) culture and common law: Chaim Perelman and Lucie Olbrechts-Tyteca, *New Rhetoric: A Treatise on Argumentation* (University of Notre Dame Press, 1969), 197–8.

193 Michael Dorf, "The Supreme Court 1997 Term Foreword: The Limits of Socratic Deliberation", *Harvard Law Review* 112 (1998): 4 at 13.

194 Ernest J. Weinrib, "Legal Formalism: On the Immanent Rationality of Law", *Yale Law Journal of Law* 97 no. 6 (1988): 949–1016 at 952, 957. Compare the text discussed by Wein-

rationality within the law – not the search for the meaning of norms and their effects outside it as well as their explanation. Formalism is sometimes greeted with scepticism.[195] Others, on the other hand, defend it by recognising that it is a remedy for the preponderance of judicial power.[196] It dictates that we stop short of considering and interpreting norms and their interrelationships, dismissing the spectre of instrumental treatment and application of the law.[197] This essentially obvious observation, however, also results in formalism refusing to take into account the effects of the law, including the social effects,[198] and its persuasive value is significantly lower.[199] Consequently, there is also less potential for accountability contained in such justifications. If the justification of judicial decision refers to principles, law, jurisprudence and academia, then, firstly, it becomes less intelligible to those outside the circle of professional lawyers, and secondly, it does not seem to be addressed to them. If one treats the justification of an act of judicial power in terms of giving an account of what has been done and decided, one has to admit that the audience understood more broadly is, unless ignored, at the very least marginalised as an addressee. The people who are believed to be entrusted with the power of judging in a democratic system are limited in their perception of the report and its exercise. Thus, first of all, they have no knowledge of what has actually been done. Secondly, they have no instruments or competences to assess this account. This is the fundamental risk and the fundamental deficit of judicial accountability. It is here that both accountability and – its close relative – judicial legitimacy are buried.

Yet there is a third approach alongside these two, singled out as a novelty by John Merryman in 1969,[200] still highly influential legal tradition of socialist law. As Alan Uzelac demonstrates,[201] socialist law approach already copes perfectly well without socialism. Its three basic features are: 1) the instrumental treatment of law and process as the tool for the protection of the interests

rib by Roberto Unger, "The Critical Legal Studies Movement", *Harvard Law Review* 96 (1983): 561–675, at 561, 563–7, where Unger identifies three features of law in the formal position: distinct rationality (unrelated to political realities), immannence (own rationalising operations) and morality based on normativity (conformity to norms).

195 Weinrib, 950. For a summary of criticisms of the formalist position, see: Frederick Schauer, "Formalism", *Yale Law Journal* 97, no. 4 (1988): 509–48 at 509.

196 Marc Tushnet, "Anti-Formalism in Recent Constitutional Theory", *Michigan Law Review* 83 (1985): 1502–44 at 1506.

197 Morton Morwitz, *The Transformation of American Law* (Harvard University Press, 1977), 254.

198 Unger, 561–2.

199 See further: Aleksandra Mężykowska and Anna Młynarska-Sobaczewska, *Persuasion and Legal Reasoning in the ECtHR Rulings: Balancing Impossible Demands* (Routledge, 2023).

200 John Henry Merryman, *The Civil Law Tradition: An Introduction to the Legal Systems of Western Europe and Latin America* (Stanford University Press, 1969), 3–4.

201 Alan Uzelac, "Survival of the Third Legal Tradition?", *Supreme Court Law Review* 49, no. 2 (2010): 377–96.

of political elites, 2) evading responsibility for decision-making (to pass final judgments as a guiding principle) particularly with use of judicial formalism, which holds that, whenever possible, cases should be decided on mere formal grounds, without entering into their merits and 3) the specific status of judges: not high but convenient, and forming a well-insulated circle from the rest of society. These three characteristics make it even more difficult to receive an account of the power exercised, because the court actually consciously and deliberately avoids passing it, or even avoids doing actual justice at all through formal procedures. It is also perfectly understandable that the court will not be prepared to report on the actual motive, which may be to act for the benefit of the Principal, whom it has itself cast in that role and in whose interests the law and the judgment are being used as instruments. Isolation from other social groups that is inherited both practically and mentally preserves this tradition quite well, thus nullifying the chance to fulfil the first condition of judicial accountability – to give an account of the judicial power exercised. Observation of the practice of post-communist countries provides evidence of the validity of Uzelac's conclusions even today, and the discussed accountability crisis in Poland also has many overlapping elements with it.

Summary

The first and the basic premise of public accountability: the relationship between the Principal, who entrusts power, and the Agent, to whom it is entrusted is hard to instrumentalise in a situation of judicial power. This is not an obvious task from the point of view of guaranteeing judicial independence in a democratic state, where fundamentally power originates from the political community, represented by elected representatives. Hence, the requirement for the democratic election of judges, and the meritocratic criterion, which remains in the hands of the judges themselves, are intertwined here.

Judicial accountability pertains to a judge's action and behaviour. It is particularly difficult to determine whether a judge's behaviour off the bench affects their exercise of the power entrusted to them, or how a judge should be held accountable for what they have done within the framework of that power, in which they must remain independent for the courts to function effectively at all.

Finally, the courts should also be held accountable for the efficiency and effectiveness of their performance – the manner in which they exercise power.[202] This, too, necessitates shaping the structures and actors of judicial power and the administration of the courts in such a way that they are autonomous, and thus meet the requirement of the real entrustment of power.

All three of these nodal issues of judicial accountability are the subject of various systemic solutions. They are considered and practised, with varying

202 McIntyre, 282–3.

degrees of success, not least because of the sensitive interface with the principle of judicial independence. The Polish case study shows how far one can go astray in the search for judicial accountability in almost every aspect of it, leading to chaos and burying judicial independence, the judge's mandate and accountability as well.

It makes no sense to look for judicial accountability in the simple mechanism of liability in the Principal-Agent relationship, in the democratic principles governing the creation of their composition or the ability to dismiss them or punish them for misbehaviour. The source of accountability should therefore be the fruits of their actions – the purpose for which they have been endowed, and the primary instrument should be the receipt of an account, a report on the exercise of power, that is, first and foremost, on the decisions made by the courts. However, it is impossible to limit judicial accountability solely to reporting to judges (national or international), as this inevitably leads to the annihilation of any relationship of democratic entrustment.

What matters most in accountability is the exercise of power and the reporting of its entrustment within the act of power itself, all the more so as it affects human beings in a concrete and direct way. The best, and perhaps the only, form, as we are trying to demonstrate here, is a pure accountability done primarily through justification. Our focus should be directed towards this when speaking of judicial accountability, verifying if the justification does indeed meet such a condition. Firstly, therefore, it must be directed at the audience, the one who is in fact the Principal, and understandable to it. The audience means the people who are directly or indirectly affected by the ruling, not the higher court, other judges (national or international) or the law as such. This predetermines the persuasive power of the statement of reasons, i.e. to explain to each addressee, to each potential reader of the decision, why the court has ruled in this specific way. The way in which the statement of reasons is drafted, its authenticity, that is, the rendering of the true reasons, the language, the communicativeness of the text and, as far as possible, its simplicity, are prerequisites for the effective communication of the message.

The second condition concerns the argumentative layer. The justification must contain arguments that are acceptable to free and equal persons beyond their worldview, appealing to rationality, practical knowledge, a sense of responsibility and freedom and mutual respect, which are constitutive of the political community. The court is required to explain and justify its decisions as grounded in an understanding of the law,[203] referring to values and principles that are shared, uncontested and respectful of other values that members of a particular community may consider important, even though they are not shared by other members of the political community. However, this is not facilitated by the use of large, formal, predetermined structures and doling out

203 John Rawls, *The Political Liberalism* (New York: Columbia University Press, 1993), 215–16, 224–5.

the legal categories too freely.[204] Moreover, principles and abstracts (dignity, morality), as the American authors point out, carry the risk of worldview bias, which always makes it difficult to find compromise and common rationality. A style of legal reasoning based on an appeal to fundamentally defined principles, and then attempting to resolve a dispute through such an appeal, is tainted with the error of tautology. It is self-defeating – rather than conveying the message of what the court has truly done in a way that the audience can comprehend. It has the effect of leaving the reader with the belief that the court has in fact stated: "it is supposed to be this way – because this is how we think it is".

This very mission of the judiciary, namely to find the rationale and persuade it in judgments, is crucial in terms of seeking accountability, as well as the legitimacy of the court's action and existence.

204 Emmanuelle Jouannet, "French and American Perspective on International Law: Legal Cultures and International Law", *Maurie Law Review* 58 (2006): 292–335 at 305. Frederick Schauer, *Playing the Rules: A Philosophical Examination of Rule-Based Decision Making in Law and in Life* (Oxford University Press, 1982).

6 Non-state actors in the constitutional framework

Political impact without public accountability

As we have sought to demonstrate, accountability of public authorities is a permanent and fundamental condition of constitutionalism. Without the ability to obtain an account of the exercise of entrusted power, we cannot speak of its control, nor of the influence of the one who entrusts power on its exercise. As we have also shown, accountability takes on a variety of forms in every sphere of power, and although it faces many obstacles and limitations and is sometimes illusory, it constitutes the core and foundation of any democratic system. The report on the work done is sometimes given by the Agent in a perfunctory manner (legislative action report), reluctantly, taking into account the considerations of the political majority (executive accountability), or in an uncommunicative manner (judicial accountability), but it is nevertheless given, if only in a flawed form.

However, it must be recognised that the system of public power in modern states is not being exhausted under the classical separation of powers (legislature-executive-judiciary); and public power is not exercised exclusively by actors elected and controlled under the constitutional system. In this chapter, we present profiles of these two categories of non-state actors that could, in our opinion, be considered serious participants in the power relationship in the state and at the supranational level. We leave out international organisations such as the European Union (EU), although their participation in the exercise of public power, both as to its regulation, its exercise and the settlement of disputes, is unquestionable and oftentimes crucial. This is a subject that has long been thoroughly analysed in the literature, including with regard to accountability,[1] yet it must be recognised that international organisations

1 For example: Thorsten Benner, Wolfgang H. Reinicke and Jan M. Witte, "Multisectoral Networks in Global Governance: Towards a Pluralistic System of Accountability", *Government and Opposition* 39, no. 2 (2004): 191–210; Erik O. Eriksen, "An Emerging European Public Sphere", *European Journal of Social Theory* 8, no. 3 (2005): 341–63; Ruth Grant and Robert O. Keohane, "Accountability and Abuses of Power in World Politics", *American Political Science Review* 99, no. 1 (2005): 29–43; Carol Harlow and Richard Rawlings, "Promoting Accountability in Multi-Level Governance: A Network Approach", *European Law Journal* 13, no. 4 (2007): 542–62; Deirdre M. Curtin, "Betwixt and Between: Democracy and Transpar-

DOI: 10.4324/9781003493419-6

hold the mandate given by states and are closely linked to the power structures in the state – both in their origins and composition and the competencies precisely prescribed by treaties and secondary legislation.

In this chapter, however, we deal with those who have nothing to do with the state – and that is actually the only thing they have in common. Non-state actors is a broad term, taken from international law[2] and stands, in the most straightforward sense, for all those who are not bound to the state by a structural bond. They are not elected by the citizens to exercise power and do not formally wield it. Nor do they fit into the organisation of the state and its authorities. Such entities do not constitute a system or regime; instead, they are a collection of actors completely different from each other, hardly recognised by the law in the context of the exercise of power as well as responsibility for it. Such entities have only recently been recognised under international law. Although the state of affairs established by the Westphalian system recognised only states as subjects of international law, using the triad that is classical according to Clausewitz: government-army-civilians, today certain international documents refer to the competence and position of non-state actors, such as non-governmental organisations (NGOs) and business-oriented entities.[3] Non-state actors are subject to certain obligations[4] in the area of humanitarian law and armed conflict[5]– this includes especially terrorist

---

ency in the Governance of the European Union", in *Reforming the Treaty on European Union: The Legal Debate*, ed. Jan A. Winter et al. (The Hague: Kluwer, 1996); Yannis Papadopoulos, "Problems of Democratic Accountability in Network and Multilevel Governance", *European Law Journal* 13, no. 4 (2007): 469–86; Christopher Lord, *A Democratic Audit of the European Union* (Basingstoke: Palgrave Macmillan, 2004), 195; Navdeep Mathur and Chris Skelcher, "Evaluating Democratic Performance: Methodologies for Assessing the Relationship between Network Governance and Citizen", *Public Administration Review* 67, no. 2 (2007): 228–37 at 235.

2 Markus Wagner, "Non-State Actors", in *Max Planck Encyclopaedia of Public International Law*, ed. A. Peters and R. Wolfrum (Oxford: Oxford University Press, 2009), available at: www.mpepil.com.

3 To name a few, after Wagner: the Ottawa Convention on the Prohibition of the Use, Stockpiling, Production and Transfer of Anti-Personnel Mines and on Their Destruction, as well as the rules of international organisations – e.g. the International Labour Organization (ILO). Two of the ILO's main bodies, the International Labour Conference and the Governing Body, consist of state but also of labour and industry representatives.

4 Andrew Clapham, "Human Rights Obligations for Non-State Actors: Where Are We Now?", in *Doing Peace the Rights Way: Essays in International Law and Relations in Honour of Louise Arbour*, ed. Fannie Lafontaine and François Larocque (Cambridge: Intersentia, 2019), 11–36, available at SSRN: https://ssrn.com/abstract=2641390

5 This is mentioned, for example, in the Security Council resolution: SC Res. 1368 of 12.09.2001 and UN SC Res. 1373 of 28.09.2001 passed as a result of the 11.09.2001 attack, addressing the need to defend against terrorist attacks. See: Anne Peters et al., "Self-Defence against Non-State Actors: Impulses from the Max Planck Trialogues on the Law of Peace and War: Editors' Introduction: Self-Defence in Times of Transition", *Max Planck Institute for Comparative Public Law & International Law (MPIL) Research Paper No. 2017-07*, available at SSRN: https://ssrn.com/abstract=2941640 or http://dx.doi.org/10.2139/ssrn.2941640

groups, but non-state armed forces too, as well as corporations and their obligations with regard to human rights.[6] Their impact on these relationships has already been recognised and is beginning to be regulated – both in terms of human rights[7] and obligations arising from other relationships, particularly in the digital environment,[8] but the scope and nature of these responsibilities and obligations remain unclear. As Wagner points out,

> the State as the sole actor for the purposes of international law no longer appears to be a viable characterization: it is (and has been) descriptively incorrect and normatively problematic. At the same time, it should be recognized that while non-State actors are crucial in today's international relations.[9]

However, this statement is also true for state-level politics. Contemporary public policy is no longer shaped only in relations between citizens and public authorities, but between the state and its agencies, organisations of business representatives, civic society organisations and intergovernmental organisations, within the framework of a highly complex and often concealed negotiated process. This is how matters are settled, be it healthcare, the environment, poverty, exclusion, justice, the economy or more broadly: the provision of all the public services that the state is responsible for.[10] Furthermore, as we will try to demonstrate, it is the various non-state actors who in various situations assume influence over decision-making and participate in the exercise of public power, significantly transcending the role defined by private law and their previous positioning in the legal system. Meanwhile, the constitutional order is still stuck in the identified liberal dichotomy between the individual and

6 Gro Nystuen et al., eds., *Human Rights, Corporate Complicity and Disinvestment* (Cambridge: Cambridge University Press, 2011); John Gerard Ruggie, *Just Business: Multinational Corporations and Human Rights* (New York: W.W. Norton, 2013); David J. Karp, *Responsibility for Human Rights: Transnational Corporations in Imperfect States* (Cambridge: Cambridge University Press, 2014); Surya Deva and David Bilchitz, eds., *Human Rights Obligations of Business: Beyond the Corporate Responsibility to Respect?* (Cambridge: Cambridge University Press, 2013); Juan Pablo Bohoslavsky and Jernej Letnar Èerniè, eds., *Making Sovereign Financing and Human Rights Work* (Oxford: Hart Publishing, 2014).

7 This includes, in particular, the protection of children's rights (i.a. General Comment 16 (2013) on state obligations regarding the impact of the business sector on children's rights, at para 8) and the prohibition of discrimination – e.g. the new General Recommendation 35 (2017) on gender-based violence against women adopted by the UN Committee on the Elimination of Discrimination against Women which tackles under the heading "non-state actors" the violence perpetrated by both corporations and armed groups.

8 Nicolò Bussolati, "The Rise of Non-State Actors in Cyberwarfare", in *Cyberwar: Law and Ethics for Virtual Conflicts*, ed. Jens David Ohlin, Kevin Govern and Claire Finkelstein (Oxford: Oxford University Press, 2015), 102–26.

9 Wagner, *Max Planck*, comm. 4.

10 Lisa Jordan, "Mechanisms for NGO Accountability", *GPPI Research Paper Series*, no. 3 (2005): 5, available at: https://www.gppi.net/media/Jordan_2005_Accountability.pdf.

the state. It guarantees human rights and freedoms, while on the other hand it regulates the position and powers of the subjects of power, making them strictly governed by the rules of law. Non-state actors (NSAs) are treated as entities that enable the realisation of individual rights, regarded almost as the essence of civil society, where every person has the right to unfettered expression of their views, economic activity, association, protection of their status and property. In this sphere, they are free from state interference, and therefore also the entities with the help of which they do this (associations, corporations, media) are traditionally endowed with a status that derives from the guarantee of individual rights. They let people associate to achieve common goals, organise them to provide shared activities and express shared views. Relations between NSAs and state power are constitutionally regulated rather sparingly. But this kind of treatment, based on classical liberal thought, sometimes fails to describe its function and significance.

Attempts to regulate the position of non-state actors are severely hampered by the fact that they are very different entities, formed for different purposes – from profit-making (commercial corporations, companies), through organisations working for the realisation of certain ideologies, to cultural organisations, associations bringing people together for a variety of reasons, communities aimed at spiritual development or worship (religious movements). The typology of non-state actors is complex – or even not possible – due to the diversity of their features, aims and modes of activities. Some of them are linked to the state and perform some of its functions; e.g. in the law-making process (public consultations, bills, petitions), performing the activities of the administration within public-private partnership framework, or tasks associated with public service (like running schools, hospitals, etc.). This allows them to establish their status and obligations towards the state. Such NSAs are structured and accountable for the tasks entrusted to them through fiscal auditing, managerial performing and public reporting within their activities run on the behalf of the state and often – within the scope of using public funds. However, this group of NSAs is not very broad and does not overlap in any way with those that actually affect the authority. Therefore, we will focus on two groups that sometimes elude attention in this context and hardly fit into the classical framework of public law in general. These are the mass social movements and the large Big Tech corporations.

The selection of these two seemingly completely unrelated groups of actors as parties to the power relationship in the state, coming from a different world than the state power, must be motivated at the outset.

First of all, they are powerful actors. Their power comes from the mobilisation and participation of huge numbers of people, interestingly enough – people usually uninvolved in existing politics, often contesting it openly (so in the case of mass social movements) or behaviourally, simply remaining (at times ostentatiously) outside of public power relations.

Secondly, the actors mentioned exert a difficult to ignore, huge influence on the community in a completely different way than the actors of public power. This influence means entering into a relationship with actors of state power (also at the international level), and sometimes even directly stepping into their position. Mass movements confer identities and attitudes on people – including political ones; digital corporations with vast amounts of information about their users, previously unknown to even the most dystopian totalitarian regimes. This knowledge and the ability gained through it to form strong ideological attitudes among members in a way provide a link between individuals and the state. According to a number of metaphors, such non-state actors can be "brokers", "norm entrepreneurs"[11] or the third apex of the triangle in the triad we should use to replace the hitherto classical state-individual dichotomy.[12] These metaphors, while illustrative, do not seem to fully capture all the complexity and depth that non-state actors are bringing to modern political life. Just as the churches of yesteryear shaped the religious and daily lives and worldviews of the vast majority of people (if not all), and just as the media shaped the image of the world and its assessment as recently as two decades ago – so do Big Tech and the mass movements erupting now and again heavily shape our attitudes, daily lives and the choices we make in our private and public lives.

Thirdly, power actors are becoming clients of these non-state actors, though of course in different ways when it comes to Mass Social Movements (MSM) and Big Tech. In both cases, however, politicians seem to believe that they are the ones using the non-state actors, treating them as an instrument to recognise and elevate certain ideological and political attitudes (MSM) or to recognise and shape opinions and gather information about the governed (Big Tech). However, it is becoming increasingly apparent that this relationship is mutual, and it even happens that non-state actors simply assume the functions of power, albeit without any spectacular revolutions and with rare recourse to clear caesuras or declarations. Furthermore, this power is backed by knowledge on a scale hitherto unknown, and (as far as Big Tech is concerned) by the unbelievable global scale of the involvement of people and resources.

And fourthly, non-state actors are completely transcendent to the rules of a democratic and constitutional state. They exist outside the world order recognised by the norms of constitutional law – as we have already mentioned, they formally take the form of spontaneous associations or permanently organised entities: businesses, unions and thus entities hitherto considered to be emanations of human freedoms (freedom of association, expression or economic freedom). Thus, according to the liberal order, they function in constitutional law and enjoy privileges only slightly curtailed (and often ineffectively) by competition law, at least when it comes to Big Tech. They are not subject to any regimes characteristic of political actors like political parties, nor do the

11 Cass R. Sunstein, "Social Roles and Social Norms", *Columbia Law Review* 96 (1996): 903–68.

12 Jack Balkin, "Free Speech Is a Triangle", *Columbia Law Review* 118 (2012): 2011–56.

constitutional or legal restrictions of the countries in which they operate apply to them.

Fifthly, the two categories of non-state actors distinguished here are exceptionally tightly coupled, which gives them an extraordinary capacity for exerting influence. They create (or co-create) the sphere of technopolitics, their own space in which they reign indivisibly, rendering the traditional media and its control irrelevant and without influence. Understanding the conjunction of these forces is essential for comprehending contemporary challenges of communication (like information overload, filter bubbles, career of fake news) strategies and networking of power.[13] These entities replace public debate, govern the agenda setting, create new cultural codes.[14] In doing so, they are doing what was previously sacred – abolishing the division between the private and public spheres, combining them. Civil society, in turn, transfers there not only its attention, but also its data, it draws knowledge from there and after migrating to the virtual world, makes choices accordingly.[15]

Finally, and most relevant to our argument, these actors are completely unaccountable. As actors operating outside the power structure of the state and international order, they are not constrained by the rules of democracy, and consequently – they do not submit to classification in the Agent-Principal relationship. They act in their own name, creating, as it were, their existence and position from scratch, outside the chains of entrustment; meanwhile they easily assume the voice of the Principal, set the tone and sometimes directly speak with its voice or take that voice away from it. On the other hand, they themselves are neither responsible for their actions and words nor ready to give an account of their performance. Moreover, there is no room even for someone who could exercise the function of receiving such an account of power from them in the order of a democratic state.

In the meantime, the problem of lack of accountability is not in their case (as it is, among others, for NGOs, and the interest groups centred around them)[16] accentuated in the reflection on this sociological and political phenomenon. The colonisation by Big Tech and mass movements of the collective identity and attitudes of individual users/sympathisers, or even just observers, often

13 Cristina Flesher Fominaya and Ramón A. Feenstra, "Introduction: Contemporary European Social Movements: Democracy, Crisis and Contestation", in *Routledge Handbook of Contemporary European Social Movements*, ed. Cristina Flesher Fominaya and Ramón A. Feenstra (London: Routledge, 2020), 10; Dirk Helbing et al., "Will Democracy Survive Big Data and Artificial Intelligence?", in *Towards Digital Enlightenment*, ed. Dirk Helbing (Cham: Springer, 2019), 73–98.

14 Alberto Melucci, "The Symbolic Challenge of Contemporary Movements", *Social Research* 52, no. 4, Social Movements (1985): 789–816.

15 David Betz and Tim Stevens, *Cyberspace and the State: Toward a Strategy for Cyber-power* (London: Routledge, 2011), 58.

16 Ondřej Císař, "Social Movement Diffusion in Eastern Europe", in *Routledge Handbook* (see note 13), 240, 243–4.

need not be a coincidence, but may instead be a conscious strategy calculated to achieve certain goals. Their demands, the promoted or stigmatised attitudes towards social and economic phenomena, the postulated changes in the law, the focusing of attention on certain phenomena and events – after all, these are extremely powerful instruments of influence, of mobilisation at the state and supranational level, and thereby political action par excellence. The non-state actors mentioned change two basic principles of democracy, namely, through their action there is a change in the rules and environment of participation and deliberation.[17] These are the key elements of the environment in which power is entrusted, its legitimacy is gained, and – as discussed in this work – the conditions of accountability are created, the account of the exercise of power is received.

Of course, the communication strategies of the two non-state actors that we have distinguished are different: while the MSM openly and loudly express their demands, conduct vigorous activities to articulate their attitudes and requests, Big Tech conducts activities far more discreetly and usually indirectly, by moderating the discourse, and influencing its course according to their own preferences. Such activity takes place outside the borders of states and even outside the space and known structure of the public sphere in general, outside the real world order, making it hardly graspable, transcendent in this context as well.

The dynamics of non-state actors' assumption of power over people's attitudes and ultimately their actions and choices, i.e. political power, coincides with a deep crisis of confidence in the economic and political order of modern states.[18] This deficit in the legitimacy of institutions considered up to now as necessary and permanent elements of the demoliberal order, the end of grand narratives, to use Jean-François Lyotard's term, also applies to the story of the state and power, to the hitherto dogma of the liberal order, democracy as the rule of the enlightened and the elected, a public sphere in which the enlightened debate and all participate and monitor those appointed to exercise power. Many European societies are therefore experiencing mobilisations demanding greater or "real democracy" like pro-democracy "movements of the squares".[19] The reaction to this crisis can be observed in particular in the anti-austerity and anti-globalist movements. The vociferous activity of MSM and Big Tech strategies, and most importantly: the conditions they create for the development of preferred attitudes find fertile ground.

These dynamics and features of both categories of non-state actors deserve our attention also from the perspective of accountability. Let us therefore trace

17 Donatella della Porta, "Democratic Models in Europe", in *Routledge Handbook* (see note 13), 75.

18 Peter Mair, *Ruling the Void: The Hollowing of Western Democracy* (London: Verso, 2013), passim.

19 Flesher Fominaya and Feenstra, 1, 9.

the characteristics and actions of both these categories in terms of their participation in public power, their relevance to modern states and the unsuccessful attempts to curb them by public authorities, operating in the classical paradigm.

Features of mass social movements as political and social agents

Mass social movements as a kind of mixture of organisation and campaign,[20] are usually described as spontaneous communities, emerging suddenly as a result of disappointment with the dysfunctions of the state, gaining quickly massive support from people. The sociology of mass movements is developed,[21] but mainly based on the phenomenon of 1960s experiences of mass mobilisation in civil rights movements. Their image is rooted in a rather optimistic view of their origins in righteous anger and their potential to change social attitudes – but it is a rather naive one, according to the words of Alain Touraine.[22] As Jenkins put it, sociology focuses on individualistic participation, or resource mobilisation theory. However, it was also noticed, they have their political strategies and alliances and participate in political and social processes.[23] Therefore movement mobilisation needs to be recognised as agencies of not only social but also cultural and political changes – and conflicts. Four main types of mass movements were distinguished in sociology: movements of revolutionary, reform, reactionary and religious nature, but this division does not pretend to be complete; many MSM can change their character, goals and mode of operation during their life cycles. From our perspective, however, it is worth highlighting "political social movements" among them, according to Amenta defined as actors and organisations seeking to alter power deficits and to effect social transformations through the state by mobilising regular citizens for sustained political action.[24] Many authors argue that mass social movements have a great impact on politics, by mobilisation framing, constructing

20 Lewis M. Killian, "Social Movements", in *Britannica*, https://www.britannica.com/topic/social-movement.

21 John D. McCarthy and Mayer N. Zald, "Resource Mobilization and Social Movements: A Partial Theory", *American Journal of Sociology* 82, no. 6 (1977): 1212–41; J. Craig Jenkins, "Resource Mobilization Theory and the Study of Social Movements", *Annual Review of Sociology* 9, no. 1 (2003): 527–53.

22 Alain Touraine, "An Introduction to the Study of Social Movements", *Social Research* 52, no. 4, Social Movements (1985): 749–87.

23 Edwin Amenta et al., "The Political Consequences of Social Movements", *The Annual Review of Sociology* 36 (2010): 287–307. For a study of movements' strategies in Latin America, see: Leonidas Oikonomakis, *Political Strategies and Social Movements in Latin America: The Zapatistas and Bolivian Cocaleros* (Cham: Springer, 2018).

24 Amenta et al., at 288. A full overview of social movements and their impact on politics in Charles Tilly, "Social Movements and National Politics", *CRSO Working Paper #197,* 1979; Charles Tilly, Ernesto Castañeda and Lesley J. Wood, *Social Movements, 1768–2018* (London: Routledge, 2019).

collective identity boundaries.[25] Interestingly, this impact is not necessarily synonymous with the success of the movement – moreover, measures of this success are also difficult to determine.[26] Success does not necessarily mean winning an election or realising demands. In terms of success, one can also see the mere concentration and mobilisation around certain expectations, and therefore engaging and forcing politicians to adopt certain attitudes towards them. This could involve the enactment of a new legal regulation, but also a change in the practice of its application or the implementation of some public policy, even to a limited extent. Therefore, their impact on the political and public life of movements definitely goes beyond their immediate goals and stated demands, it is much more complex and multifaceted. It frequently means simply a change in the political agenda, a change in the axis around which public debate takes place (Black Lives Matter [BLM] in the United States, LGBT in the United States and Europe). Often, it also results in the replacement of political elites, as in the case of Chile in 2020. Success can be greatly postponed and hard to see, and has many stages and many faces.[27] For this reason – despite the considerable amount of sociological literature on the subject, we will devote some attention to mass movements and their impact on politics.

From this point of view, in our opinion, two groups of mass movements in particular deserve attention, which have become the most visible in the space of modern democratic states in recent years: anti-austerity and anti-discriminatory movements. The first group includes all mass movements that emerged on the grounds of agitation in times of economic crisis and the actions of states (and institutions treated as allied with the liberal state, primarily banks and corporations). Such movements erupted in Europe and Latin America at the beginning of the second decade of the 21st century and easily crossed national borders. The second includes movements such as BLM or #MeToo, emerging amid growing mass frustration over a sense of discrimination, a social practice that permits unacceptable treatment of certain groups.

Sociological reflection usually focuses on the emergence of mass movements and their life cycle. However, there is no full consensus on why mass social movements occur; traditional explanations emphasised their increases

25 Frank R. Baumgartner and Christine Mahoney, "Social Movements, the Rise of New Issues, and the Public Agenda", in *Routing the Opposition: Social Movements, Public Policy, and Democracy*, ed. David S. Meyer, Valerie Jenness and Helen Ingrampp (Minneapolis: University of Minnesota Press, 2005), 65–86.

26 See further: William A. Gamson, *The Strategy of Social Protest*, 2nd ed. (Belmont, CA: Wadsworth, 1990); Lee Ann Banaszak, *Why Movements Succeed or Fail: Opportunity, Culture and the Struggle for Woman Suffrage* (Princeton, NJ: Princeton University Press, 1996); Amenta et al., 290.

27 See further: Daniela R. Piccio, "The Impact of Social Movements on Political Parties", in *The Consequences of Social Movements*, ed. Lorenzo Bosi, Marco Giugni and Katrin Uba (Cambridge: Cambridge University Press, 2016), 266.

in short-term grievances created by the "structural strains" of rapid social change.[28] Resource mobilisation theory[29] claimed that such grievances are important but also constant and that movements form because of long-term changes in group resources, organisation, and opportunities for collective action.[30] Deprivation, discontent, and frustration are frequently assumed to be sufficient causes for initiating or joining a social movement. The reasons for the beginning of MSM are not always very clear; but often are linked with one particular restraint or an occurrence. The Black Lives Matter movement in the United States as an ethnic civil right movement emerged in the circumstances of tragic incidents of police brutality, indicating racial inequalities, also in the resources of concentration of minority groups and their marginalisation. Large-scale "peasant" rebellions have typically emerged after the coercive capacity of the state has collapsed, leaving cohesive villages free to act on long-standing grievances.[31] As for the anti-austerity movements, the cause appears easy to diagnose; they usually appear in situations of recession, crisis and austerity measures taken. Well-known representatives of such movements are the Indignados, Podemos or Syriza, the Yellow Vests (*Gilets Jaunes*),[32] the Estallido Social movement in Chile which occurred in October 2019 and a somewhat forgotten case can be the movement formed in Iceland, initiating the so-called Saucepan Revolution, which led to the draft constitution in 2014 in a non-precedential procedure (the draft was lost in a referendum).[33]

But the genesis of MSM is not as simple as such. Some authors questioned this model and emphasise that there is little evidence that the most deprived segments of a population are the most likely to participate in social movements. Their genesis is often symbolic but hard to predict in the social environment. Probably a good clue is to see their rise in importance in the weakening position of political parties and existing ideologies. The ideologies that until recently organised people's political attitudes, previously recognised and functioning in the public consciousness as right-wing and left-wing visions of a good society, have become unpersuasive, and democratic institutions have largely become detached from the idea of representative government. As Torney points out:

28 Joseph Gusfield, "Tradition and Modernity: Conflict and Congruence", *Journal of Social Issues* 14 (1968): 1–8.

29 Charles Tilly, *From Mobilisation to Revolution* (Boston: Addison-Wesley, 1978), 70–9, 86–9.

30 Jenkins, 530.

31 Theda Skocpol, *States and Social Revolutions: A Comparative Analysis of France, Russia and China* (Cambridge: Cambridge University Press, 1979), 125–38.

32 Josep Lobera, "Anti-Austerity Movements in Europe", in *Routledge Handbook* (see note 13), 267.

33 Björg Thorarensen, *Why the Making of a Crowd-Sourced Constitution in Iceland Failed by 2014*, at: Constitutional Making and Constitutional Change, 2014 https://www.constitutional-change.com/why-the-making-of-a-crowd-sourced-constitution-in-iceland-failed/

> Not only have we lost our belief in the redemptive qualities of particular ideologies, we are losing our belief in representative politics as the best way to engage in politics broadly understood. This is both opportunity and threat for social movements whose self-understanding is often as a means of participating in the democratic process rather than a means of supplanting it, a kind of monitory conscience to complement the activities of political parties.[34]

It is an easily observable fact that in the last decade, starting back in 2010, movements against austerity, for democracy, numerous movements have conquered the world. They have freely crossed national boundaries both in terms of goals and demands and methods of action.[35] This ease of crossing borders, the extraordinary rate of dissemination of slogans, demands and demonstrations of attitudes observed in many movements, including the migration of the national Arab Spring movement and the unions of Spanish Indignados and Occupy Wall Street,[36] is, in an obvious and oft-described way, induced by social media.[37] As already mentioned, today's mass movements are operating faster and easier than ever before due to the operation of the digital public sphere.[38] Movements create a collective identity extremely effectively: by viral posts, videos, slogans and symbols, the concept spreads, and then the idea, and finally the identification with the movement. Thus, select online communication spaces (such as certain social media groups, platforms, communicators) act as para-institutions that mediate the flow of information and

34 Simon Tormey, "Visions of a Good Society: European Social Movements in the Age of Ideologies and Beyond", in *Routledge Handbook* (see note 13), 28. Also: Pierre Rosanvallon, *Counter-Democracy: Politics in an Age of Distrust* (Cambridge: Cambridge University Press, 2008); John Keane, *The Life and Death of Democracy* (London: Simon & Schuster, 2009).

35 Esther del Campo, Jorge Resina and Yanina Welp, "Crossing the Ocean: The Influence of Bolivia's MAS Movement on Spain's Podemos Party", in *Routledge Handbook* (see note 13), 250 et seq.

36 Eduardo Romanos, "Brokerage and the Diffusion of Social Movements in the Digital Era", in *Routledge Handbook* (see note 13), 223, thoroughly elaborated theories of diffusion of mass movements (ideological, behavioural), i.a.: Sean Chabot, "Dialogue Matters: Beyond the Transmission Model of Transnational Difussion between Social Movements", in *The Diffusion of Social Movements: Actors, Mechanisms, and Political Effects*, ed. Rebecca K. Givan, Kenneth M. Roberts and Sarah A. Soule (Cambridge: Cambridge University Press, 2010), 99–124. In the same vein, the links between the movements are demonstrated by del Campo, Resina and Welp, 250 et seq.

37 A good example is the evolution of the Indignados movement and the impact on the rise of the Occupy Wall Street by distributing documents created in Spain (most well known: "How to Cook Up a Non-Violent Revolution") on the sites of marches, and then – via web pages as: https://takethesquare.net/2011/07/15/how-to-cook-a-pacific-revolution/, in: Romanos, 231.

38 Josep Lobera and Victor Sampedro, "New Intermediations of the Electoral Information Flows: Changes in the Digital Public Sphere in Election Campaigns in Spain (2008–2015)", *Social Science Information* 57, no. 4 (2018): 553–72.

the organisation of protesters, strongly influencing the evolution of mobilisations.[39] This new structure of public sphere of debate makes it simple to cross local, as well as national and continental borders. It allows, in real time and for free, the dissemination of whatever the movement wants to communicate. Or at least, whatever the administrators of platforms and social media deem appropriate to communicate and in accordance with their internal regulations.

Mass movements are closely linked to the pursuit of social change. As early as the 1980s, a thesis was formulated that social movements bring about cultural change by building a new collective identity beyond the political realm.[40] As Melucci notes, the movements "translate their action into symbolic challenges that overturn the dominant cultural codes".[41] They create then their own culture encompassing norms, values and patterns of behaviour, which shape the new social order that the movement proposes to bring about.[42] This is a profound change that draws on new criteria and references,[43] a new construction of a sense of identity. These spontaneous communities, emerging suddenly as a result of disappointment with the dysfunctions of the state, shape individual and collective identities, define new created attitudes and build strong moral compelling demands. Such a change may even include a reinterpretation of history – e.g. BLM in some activities and demands caused removal of statues symbolising racism in past centuries. According to Touraine mass social movements create new cultural orientation: social control of the main cultural patterns through which our relationships with the environment are normatively organised – society becomes an enemy of the community.[44]

This is accompanied by strongly underlined polarisation, the Manichaean vision of the world. By using unequivocally expressed narratives and expressing claims they become a powerful force influencing societies and state powers. Instrumentation of movements includes such methods as: forming speeches of the leaders, regular marches or rallies, other forms of common rituals and even martyrs symbolising commitment and the burden of sacrifices for the aims of the movement.[45] These are factors that not only strengthen the sense of identity, but at the same time result in clear separation of (*we*) from the others (*they*).

39 Lobera, 271.

40 Alberto Melucci and John Keane, *Nomads of the Present: Social Movements and Individual Needs in Contemporary Society*, ed. Paul Mier (Philadelphia: Temple University Press, 1989), 34; Amy Bartholomew and Margit Mayer, "Nomads of the Present: Melucci's Contribution to New Social Movement Theory", *Theory, Culture and Society* 9, no. 4 (1992): 141–59.

41 Melucci and Keane, 75.

42 Alain Touraine also pointed out the need for such a broad, including cultural view of social movements in "An Introduction to the Study of Social Movements", *Social Research* 52, no. 4, Social Movements (1985): 749–87.

43 Melucci, passim.

44 Touraine, 755

45 https://www.britannica.com/topic/social-movement/The-consequences-of-social-movements

The main feature from our point of view is their ability to create a new meaning of public interest,[46] defining challenges and desired attitudes of society and political community. In this sense, they tend to replace the old meaning of public agenda with the new one, which is focused on a particular issue. As movements gain popularity and achieve victories in their influence on public life, their expectations grow to an increasingly holistic vision of society and the state. And this is a momentum when mass social movement may touch and tend to change a core of constitutional order. It was, among others, the case in two anti-austerity movements in the last decade: the Iceland movement in 2010, called "Saucepan" or "Pots and Pans Revolution", and a similar change took place in Chile in 2019–22.[47] Both attempts failed,[48] but it is noteworthy that they proposed not only a new political order, but also an economic and social order, and above all a completely new way of working and passing new constitutions. We used to refer to such changes (attempts) as revolutions, changes in the rules of succession of power. However, it should be remembered that under the slogan of revolution there is also concealed a certain subject, and it often has the face of a social movement that strives for change and is the driving force for organising it.

This subject has special characteristics – mass social movements are all essentially collective, perfectly visible, they present worthiness, unity, numbers and commitment (WUNC), as called by Tilly,[49] and derived from the spontaneous coming together of people without previous rules and procedures, only by sharing a common outlook on social problems or change. All of them have to attract a large number of participants to succeed. They are therefore inherently inclusive. Their strength lies precisely in their ability to quickly attract a significant number of supporters. The clearest symptom of this is the slogan of one of the movements: (#WeAreThe99%),[50] which referred to opposition to the rich, but so aptly conveyed the idea of universal unification against the power and will of a minority.

However, their subjectivity is difficult to grasp. They are born outside of mainstream institutions, and they are by nature non-institutionalised, usually loosely organised. For example, the organisers of the Yellow Vests movement rejected all links with formal organisations, such as political parties and trade unions; they relied solely on social media to spread their message and organise protests around the country. They rejected also the proposal to become a

46 Jenkins, 530–1.

47 This country witnessed a revolution that started with protests against the increased transport tariffs in Santiago. Protesters assembled in the movement called the Estallido Social; in two years it completely changed the establishment and political order in the country (more below).

48 In 2022, the draft constitution was lost in a referendum, and another one failed again in December 2023 (on a proposal for a new constitution, prepared by the Constitutional Council) – see more below.

49 More on the mechanisms for creating a collective identity: Tilly, Castañeda and Wood, 10.

50 Romanos, 226, 229, 231.

regular civic organisation or coalition of organisations. While the movement never became institutionalised, it cannot be treated as such, and can act operating in revolutionary, extraordinary circumstances, since it does not have one leader, one structure and sources that could be eliminated or marginalised. The case of BLM's movement is also instructive – mobilising structures by BLM was decentralised and led exclusively by social media, which facilitates the nationwide mobilisation of local actors from different sides, like feminists, African-American youth movements and leftists.

They are organised in amorphic and liquid manner, they do not offer any formal membership and leadership and clear decision-making procedures. Leaders are absent or of charismatic nature – in the sense of being not endowed with authority through some formal process, then they must constantly substantiate their claims to leadership by demonstrating the effectiveness of their influence on the followers. These features make mass social movements an actor who is difficult to combat or even with whom it is challenging to establish a dialogue.

All these features relating to the structure and functioning of movements make them a unique participant in public life, especially in comparison with the standards of functioning of state bodies, but also parties and even associations and trade unions – all these entities which have their own structures, (elected) authorities, rules and procedures of operation, and most importantly are included in public life on clear principles and within certain limits.

Mass social movements within constitutional framework

The social mass movements can change the political agenda and language of public debate, but there is more to it. The expression of specific expectations or anger sheds new light on facts, phenomena and attitudes and norms. Such change also applies to the law. Mass social movements refer to the law, quote the law (sometimes: arbitrarily interpreted) or formulate how the law should be changed. They sometimes make legal claims,[51] and often criticise the existing legal order. What does this mean for the constitutional framework, traditional political order?

The features of mass social movements: the informal nature, open and amorphous structure, diagonal relations with other actors, within the movement, as well as the ability to build a strong identity and polarising influence on society have turned mass social movements into a strong competitor for political parties. This competition is all the more dangerous because movements tend to engage people who have not previously been interested in

51 Tomiko Brown-Nagin, "Social Movements and Social Change in Twentieth-Century America", *Harvard Law School Lecture Series*, 2016, https://www.lej4learning.com.pk/single-lecture/59995 (accessed 12.08.2024) also: "The Civil Rights Canon: Above and Below", *The Yale Law Journal* 123 (2014): 2698–740.

politics and convert them into devoted followers. People who favour movements and identify with them often come from disadvantaged groups, mostly neglected or marginalised in the existing political discourse, not perceived as a serious social resource. The Yellow Vests movement is a good example – the movement has involved many hitherto unnoticed, essentially alienated groups in rural areas mainly, who had not previously been involved in political protests. This movement took over the main narrative in society, focusing public attention on these people's living conditions and a need to provide profound reforms of social and political conditions. So, the mobilisation and articulation of new demands in public debate is the first important feature, which can influence the political order. Social movements, either locally, nationally or internationally, are able to develop new attitudes towards the newly raised and newly defined issues. While building strong moral claims, they employ a clear and highly categorical narrative exerting an extremely powerful influence over political communities, even effecting a kind of resegregation in them centred around new issues. Mass movements operate in the logic of opposite interests, while the public sphere and politics demand activity and deliberation of a public character, which was mentioned as a problem of exceptionalism.[52] Mass movements practically nullify the possibility of broad-church arrangements, and a degree of shared responsibility for the public world. As Hoffer put it: "All mass movements (…) irrespective of the doctrine they preach and the program they project, breed fanaticism, enthusiasm, fervent hope, hatred, and intolerance".[53]

This, of course, provokes reactions from the authorities and political forces. They must redefine their position in the face of these newly reported attitudes, which can capture public discourse and determine people's individual choices. This is not an easy mission. The slogans and demands of social movements evolve rapidly, and in addition, they are not always clearly formulated. Addressing them in a responsible and accountable manner – and this is what we expect from political forces and authorities in the constitutional system – is a sometimes Sisyphean task

Movements usually arise as a protest against specific social policies (or their shortcomings): the Yellow Vests, Estallido Social, crime fighting policies (BLM) or against phenomena more broadly defined as a vision of the position of the state in the modern economic world (Occupy Wall Street). At the same time, the strong identity accompanying the movements makes it necessary for every member of society to take a stand in relation to it. This causes a reorganisation of political forces, a new division according to the criterion chosen by the movement. As Jenkins put it:

52 Adam Szetela, "Black Lives Matter at Five: Limits and Possibilities", *Ethnic and Racial Studies* 43, no. 8 (2020):1358–83.

53 Eric Hoffer, *The True Believer: Thoughts on the Nature of Mass Movements* (New York: Harper Perennial, 2010), 141.

> The basic goals of movements are defined by conflicts of interest built into institutionalised power relations. The grievances generated by these conflicts are sufficiently ubiquitous that the formation and mobilisation of movements depend on changes in resources, group organisation, and opportunities to social action.[54]

The escalating nature of the demands of social movements leads to a second consequence that is important from the point of view of the constitutional order. Social movements are closely linked to social conflicts or political struggles where the opponent is identified as the state. This exposes the weakness of the state and its agendas and, as a consequence, can lead to undermining the function of the state in its current form. Often, the debate on the role of the state initiated in this way seeks to call into question the existing institutions of the state, but also the existing political divisions and parties, or at least their corrosion in the face of new demands and challenges that they have not confronted until now. New demands based on a strong identification with the movement create a new social and political creed, shaping a new standard of political behaviour and even restructuring the social fabric around new phenomena and demands.

This new polarisation founded on strongly expressed interests and protest is not subject to the rules of constitutionalism, checks and balance or rule of law. It leads to growth of public irresponsibility, procedural impatience and general contempt of "traditional sources of authority" (according to Hannah Arendt's words) and simply: constitutional institutions. This change in society is flexible, easily adapted to the dynamic of the movement increasing, even to take over directly political power and even constituent power. Chilean Estallido Social (2019–20) can be a very illustrative example – this movement removed old political elites and made efforts to change completely the political and legal order. Then: mass social movements can quickly lead to serious institutional changes – legal reforms, taking over the logic and structure of political power. And the states seem to be defenceless against this process.

These processes make for very strong competition for political parties which operate in a strictly legal manner and are bound by internal conditions. Parties operate on a long-term basis, and are a permanent fixture in the democratic game, while movements form and make demands spontaneously, unfettered in the formulation of claims and accusations. They are not bound by the will of their voters (because no one elected them and no one will dismiss them), the conditions of coexistence with other partners or even their own programme, which is freely shaped. They act in the state, set the agenda and make demands, hold themselves accountable – and they themselves are not held accountable or bound by any rules. They operate within a revolutionary paradigm, marginalising or outright contesting the existing rules. Their amorphous structure

54 Jenkins, 528.

and the unclear status of their leaders do not legitimise them under democratic principles to influence public affairs. Nevertheless, it often happens in practice that political parties have to succumb to them, and public institutions have to initiate dialogue with them. In many cases, it is the mass movements that actually define not only what the public interest is, and therefore stipulate the public agenda, but also compel parties and state institutions to make specific declarations or take action. This applies to politicians in office, but also to incumbents. All candidates in general elections will sooner or later (and this only depends on the power of the mass movement) be asked about their attitude to their claims. And depending on the answer, they will be positioned by the movement and its supporters. This way, movements become a new tool in the constitutional toolbox – and a very versatile one at that.

Responding to the demands of mass movements on account of their amorphous and populist nature on the part of public authorities is then extremely difficult. The authorities are bound by the rules of law, the existing institutional structure and public policies, fiscal considerations, the commitments they have made both to citizens and in international relations. Moreover, public authorities are held accountable for their words, and even if it is not the case, they are mindful of the consequences of their words. An unfortunate and overstepping statement, let alone an action, is, first of all, irresponsible from the point of view of the authority entrusted to it, and can give rise to legal consequences, not to mention political or economic repercussions. Mass movements are much less constrained in their words and actions. Indeed, it is precisely their incalculability, their ability to bid for demands, that is the strength of mass movements. Thus, they change the rhetoric and language of the debate to their convenience, confrontational and unrestricted by any of the considerations indicated earlier.

Viewed from the perspective of constitutional law, it is precisely this feature – lack of accountability – that is perhaps most interesting. Mass movements can shape their statements and demands in any way they like, and even spread information without regard to its veracity. No one will hold them accountable for those words. There is no entity that can effectively and authoritatively deny or debunk them. Nor do they have to reckon with the practical consequences of their slogans, demands and claims. They simply act outside the system, in a revolutionary-like fashion and therefore to some extent in anarchic manner, without the bonds of law, hierarchy, legal or political accountability, guided by the goal they have formulated in a completely arbitrary manner. This is outside the logic of democracy and the rules of constitutionalism. Movements do not need democratic legitimacy and a chain of entrustment. They grant themselves this legitimacy. And the only measure of their effectiveness is the measure of popular support. They do not need to take responsibility, and in fact – they have no one to answer to.

MSM's finances and sponsored goals are usually far from disclosure and transparency, sometimes even for donors. Mass movements create networks of their organisations, agencies and affiliates. BuzzFeed News reported in 2020 that Apple, Google, Microsoft and other corporations nearly donated $4 million to an entity called the BLM Foundation before realising it had no connection to the group started by Patrice Cullors.[55] It should also be added that many of the movements of a pacifist, anti-globalisation, environmental, anti-discrimination or libertarian nature (Anonymous) are symptoms not only of certain attitudes, but also of forces operating on a global scale, shaping the worldwide debate, and often involved in purely domestic, local problems. By appropriately shaping public opinion and the perception of government actions, they influence core governmental decisions, decision-making processes, they increase political conflicts and polarisation in the social and political sphere. If they are held accountable – it is rather to their, often invisible, donors.[56]

Why is it dangerous for the state or for the societies? Since movements are often ephemeral in nature, and so many agree with their postulates?

The threat to the constitutional order is not too apparent in the short term. Social or political change – if any occurs as a result of movements – is often greeted with relief, as a necessary replacement of elites. But from a distance, it can be noted that mass movements change the logic of the political system and blow up the intricate system of checks and balances, as well as the paradigm on which democracy is based: the power game is played out in cyclical elections, succession follows stable rules and entities of those in power bear responsibility for this and have competences closely related to the sphere of accountability. Although these assumptions are sometimes illusory, they constitute a certain scenery in which democratic power is exercised. Mass social movements change it completely. This is a phenomenon completely external to the law system and constitutional order – moreover: it is designed as such. This is something that the constitutional system experiences – but the logic of the phenomenon of mass movements lies outside its rules and sources. And since the changes brought about by mass movements affect the law, policies and institutions of the state, they cannot be ignored by constitutional order.

Mass movements in the adult world – parties vs. movements

The previously described distance of mass movements from democratic and constitutional rules, this "adult world" is convenient, yet the expectations of supporters, the demands made, their evolution and escalation (especially in the field of anti-austerity movements) often lead to direct participation in political life. This is generally the case when their individual participants become socially recognisable through their activities in the movement, and at the same time the ambition to celebrate this popularity by holding public offices or functions grows in them. The temptation to convert real behind-the-scenes

55 https://nymag.com/intelligencer/2022/01/black-lives-matter-finances.html
56 Jordan, 7–8.

power into formal power becomes stronger. The movement faces a dilemma, as Cristina Flesher Fominaya notes:

> Do they maintain their distance from policy and governance, maybe at the cost of influence and the realisation of the outcomes they desire? Or do they participate in the creation of citizen platforms, new parties, and connective initiatives to help create the basis for new forms of democratic governance, and beyond that a new vision of democracy?[57]

The stories of such involvements in institutional political life, when simply discrediting institutions is no longer enough, are quite instructive. They did happen in many countries and affected numerous movements, yet it seems that some regularities can be found. We should start with the history of two attempts to introduce radical changes to the constitutional order triggered by the economic crisis. The first is the story of Iceland's Pots and Pans Revolution. A mass movement of resistance to the effects of the 2008 banking crisis, which was exceptionally severe in Iceland, attempted to hold previous elites accountable for their actions, using a special investigative commission examining the financial sector collapse, and a special tribunal, which ruled (among others) that former Prime Minister Geir H. Haarde was guilty of failing to inform his cabinet of the pending bank crisis in the months before the collapse. At the same time, parliament (the Althing) decided that a new constitution should be drafted as a "crowdsourced" constitution. In June 2010, it passed the law[58] which regulated the procedure for the appointment of the bodies involved in the constitution-making process: Constitutional Commission, Constitutional Assembly and National Assembly to work on the new constitution.[59] The Constitutional Commission, composed of seven members, five of whom had legal training, was tasked with preparing a special process: organising a National Assembly of about 1,000 participants, compiling the results of this National Assembly, and submitting ideas for amending the Constitution.

The National Assembly was a debate held on 6 November 2010. Its purpose was to gather the main views and wishes of Icelanders about their constitution. The event was attended by 950 people, drawn randomly from among the Icelandic citizens (taking into account the representativeness of the participants from all over the country and equal gender distribution). At the event, participants were divided into groups and sat at round tables with a facilitator who guided the group through the day-long discussion.[60] In November 2010,

57 Flesher Fominaya and Feenstra, 2, 3.
58 Act on a Constitutional Assembly, 90/2010.
59 The course of events as recounted in the report by Jón Ólafsson and Salvör Nordal, "The Icelandic Constitutional Process, 2010–2020", https://pihrb.org/wp-content/uploads/2021/06/PHIRB-RS_1_2021_IS-Proces-Konstytucyjny-final.pdf.
60 See more at http://www.thjodfundur2009.is/english/index.html.

Icelanders also elected the Constitutional Assembly, which was to consist of 25 delegates. However, the election was annulled by the Supreme Court due to minor procedural errors. Subsequently, Parliament appointed a Constitutional Council which would replace the Assembly. The delegates who received the highest number of votes in the Constitutional Assembly elections were given seats on it. The Constitutional Council worked from April to July 2010. The work of the Council proceeded in a very transparent manner, and was broadcast on major social media (Facebook [FB], YouTube and Flickr). The results of the work (working versions of the draft chapters) were made available via the website and could be commented on by everyone. The Constitutional Council received 395 formal suggestions from individuals, groups and NGOs, and some 3,600 comments on social media.

The Council presented its report to Parliament, but the result of its work was not effectively binding on Parliament. The Icelandic constitution stipulates that the constitution can only be amended by Parliament, and that amendments require approval by two successive parliamentary assemblies separated by parliamentary elections.[61] The role of the previously indicated civic bodies, established *ad hoc* in 2010, was not clearly defined in this regard. Faced with ambiguity over who actually has the right to amend the constitution, relations between the Council and Parliament were strained from the very beginning. The draft was debated between 2011 and 2013, primarily in the Parliament's Constitutional and Oversight Committee. Finally, in May 2012, Parliament decided to hold a consultative referendum. Voters were to decide whether Parliament should proceed with the development of a new constitution, based on the Constitutional Council's proposal, and in addition, they were to answer five questions on systemic solutions. In the 2012 referendum, two-thirds of voters declared that they wanted the new constitution to be based on the Constitutional Council's draft. However, the draft was met with strong resistance from the academic and political community.[62] They stressed the eclectic nature of the constitutional borrowings proposed in the draft, the difficult-to-predict impact of the introduction of certain institutions, as well as the possibilities for risky interpretation of the new provisions.

Eventually, the Constitutional and Oversight Committee presented a revised draft constitution, which, however, was very different from the one known to voters at the time of the referendum. In the end, parliamentary leaders reached an agreement to postpone the revision process until the next

61 Art. 79 sec. 1 of the Constitution of the Republic of Iceland: "Proposals to amend or supplement this Constitution may be introduced at regular as well as extraordinary sessions of Althingi. If the proposal is adopted, Althingi shall immediately be dissolved and a general election held. If Althingi then passes the resolution unchanged, it shall be confirmed by the President of the Republic and come into force as constitutional law".

62 Jón Ólafsson, "The Constituent Assembly: A Study in Failure", in *Iceland's Financial Crisis: The Politics of Blame, Protest, and Reconstruction*, ed. Valur Ingimundarson, Philippe Urfalino and Irma Erlingsdóttir (London: Routledge, 2016), 260, 264.

parliamentary term. In the April 2013 elections to the Icelandic Parliament, the ruling coalition, which had been in power since February 2009, lost its majority. The two parties that had ruled between 1995 and 2007 returned to power. The new government was opposed to the constitutional draft, and only established a committee to discuss possible constitutional amendments. Even another government crisis of 2016, however, did not effectively restart constitutional work. Subsequent elections showed that the political fuel of constitutional work had lost its potency.[63] The issue appeared not to have affected voting behaviour in the parliamentary elections. For this reason, the parties were clearly uninterested in reviving the constitutional project. The political and economic establishment was even less interested in changing the political and economic rules. The mass movement of protest against both the existing rules and the establishment, which had transformed itself into a force capable of holding the process of creating a new regime, ultimately bogged down and succumbed to the existing elites of the state and the constitutional order it was just about to change.

In several respects, similar events unfolded a few years later in Chile. This country witnessed a revolution that started with anti-austerity protests (against the increased transport tariffs in Santiago). Protesters initiated a series of riots called the Estallido Social, which in two years changed the establishment and political order in the country. On 15 November 2019 negotiations between the government and protesters produced the “"Agreement for Social Peace and the New Constitution”" and led to voting for the Constitutional Convention. The national plebiscite in October 2020 voted to draft a new constitution (78% agreed, and 79% chose the Constitutional Convention as a body legitimate to prepare a new act). On 16 May 2021, 155 citizens of Chile were elected to form the Convention which drafted the new constitution. The Convention was composed equally of men and women, as well as the representation of the indigenous peoples; many of the representatives in the Convention were independents. The Convention elaborated a draft of constitution and presented it in May 2022. In September 2022 voters in Chile overwhelmingly turned down the new constitution (in a referendum, almost 62% voted against the draft). The political commentary on the rejection was that the Chilean public feared that the new constitution would put their country on the Venezuelan path, that the draft was not representative of the many citizens with conservative attitudes. But from our point of view, all that matters is that the movement, which was able to mobilise the vast majority of the electorate to support the idea of a new constitution, failed in the process of drafting it.

President Gabriel Boric, the leader of the protests and negotiator of the constitutional agreement, who won the presidential election obtaining 55.9% of the votes (the highest number of votes in Chile's history) in 2021, decided

63 Thorarensen (see note 33).

not to resign and to continue works on a "new constitutional process". But this time political parties had more control over the new process: the 24-member expert committee was set up to prepare a draft. Members were appointed by political parties represented in Congress.[64] The next constitutional referendum held on 17 December 2023 rejected the proposed constitution with 56% against it.

These two examples from two places with completely different political and systemic traditions can serve as an example of a mass movement that mobilised "conscience constituency", turning it into a constituent power. There are some regularities to be found in them that concern not so much the content of the projects, but rather the course and defeat of the constitutional process.

In both cases the mass movement born during the social protest revealed new political forces, new leaders and changed the political scene. This opens not only the political, but also the legal-systemic framework to this new order. New bodies have been instituted, formed under the banner of full representativeness, implementing the idea of popular participation in the formation of the political system. These bodies are constituted by universal suffrage, the elected representatives to the Constituent Assembly often have little political experience, so to speak, as opposed to the existing political structure (native people). Yet the initial enthusiasm and mass support for the constitutional process (as expressed in the referendum) erodes rather quickly. First of all, the constitutional process proves to be quite sophisticated, and despite the earlier interest in the slogan of the new system, the public fairly quickly loses its interest in the constitution-making process. The enthusiasm and the fervour of constitutional awareness gets mired in the details. Secondly, the work is contested by the existing establishment, and this is both because of fears of experimenting on the living flesh of the nation, and also for procedural reasons. The course of the process in Iceland is striking in this regard, when the failure to accurately prioritise the new constitutional bodies in the face of the existing mode of constitutional amendment virtually paralysed the work. Finally, when the constitutional work proceeds to the painstaking stage of determining the details and actual choices of legal institutions, it turns out that the movement is unable to meet them to its satisfaction – not just the lawyers and the establishment anymore, but also the people, as the Chilean referendum in 2022 illustrated. The tension between the civic movement and the political forces and institutional arrangement turns out to be the beginning of a losing streak for the movement proclaiming change.

64 As Sergio Verdugo wrote: "Unlike the 2022 proposal, which was drafted in a Convention that sidelined major parties and voted against these parties' interests in many areas, the new proposal seems to do exactly the opposite". See: Sergio Verdugo, *Chile's New Constitutional Proposal: A Balance between Change and Continuity?*, ConstitutionNet, International IDEA, 30 June 2023, https://constitutionnet.org/news/chiles-new-constitutional-proposal-balance-between-change-and-continuity.

In fact, similar regularities can be found in the history of mass movements, which entered the world of institutional democracy through the creation or co-creation of political parties. Some European movements, fractions or divisions of them, joined or created political parties. This happened in Greece[65] – the Syriza party emerged from Aganaktismenoi as a protest movement against the rule of the incumbent political elite and the Troika (the European Commission, the European Central Bank [ECB] and the International Monetary Fund). It garnered considerable electoral support in 2012 (16.7%), while in subsequent elections it received 26.9% of the vote. In 2014, Syriza won the elections to the European Parliament, winning approximately 26.6% of the vote (6 seats).[66] It won early parliamentary elections in January 2015, receiving more than 36.3% of the vote and 149 seats in the 300-seat parliament. Alexis Tsipras, Syriza's leader, went on to become Prime Minister. However, six months later, Syriza backed the adoption of austerity reforms that were the condition negotiated with the Troika entities to provide further aid to Greece.[67] Nonetheless, Syriza won again in the next early elections (35.5% of the vote and 145 seats), but in 2019 it received only 31.5% of the vote (86 seats) and lost its majority, shifting to being the opposition. In May 2023 and June 2023 elections, the formation saw further decline in support, receiving 20.1% of the vote (71 seats) and 17.8% of the vote (48 seats), respectively. Syriza became the second largest party, with a noticeable downward trend in popularity, however. It became an element of the institutional order in 2017, succumbed to the political game, its demands were verified in practice and it lost the momentum of the mass movement.[68]

A similar fate befell Spain's Podemos, dubbed the "a hurricane in the Spanish Crisis of Trust",[69] which began with a wave of mass protests spreading from Spanish cities in 2011 and 2012.[70] Podemos was registered as a political party on 11 March 2014. The 2015 elections broke the two-party system in Spain that had existed since 1978; the Popular Party (Partido Popular, PP) and the Spanish Socialist Workers Party (Partido Socialista Obrero Español, PSOE) lost votes and two new parties appeared: Podemos and Ciudadanos (a centre-right party rooted in Catalonia). Podemos became the third largest

65 del Campo et al., 252; Marina Prentoulis and Lasse Thomassen, "Movement Parties: A New Hybrid Form of Politics?", in *Routledge Handbook* (see note 13), 252.

66 del Campo et al., 349.

67 "Greek Crisis: MPs Approve Bailout Measures, after Clashes in Athens – As It Happened", *Guardian*, 15 July 2015, https://www.theguardian.com/business/live/2015/jul/15/greek-crisis-mps-bailout-imf-debt-relief-alexis-tsipras-live.

68 More in: Cas Mudde, *SYRIZA: The Failure of the Populist Promise* (London: Palgrave Macmillan, 2017).

69 Jose Pavía, Anselm M., Bodoque and Joaquin Martín, "The Birth of a New Party: Podemos, a Hurricane in the Spanish Crisis of Trust", *Open Journal of Social Sciences* 4, no. 9 (2016): 67–86.

70 About Podemos, see: Ramón Feenstra et al., *Refiguring Democracy: The Spanish Political Laboratory* (London: Routledge, 2017).

national party, with 69 seats.[71] It has become a permanent fixture on the political landscape, but the number of seats has now dropped significantly: United We Can (UP Unidas Podemos) had only 35 out of 350 seats in the 2019–23 term. In the 2023 elections, the Sumar party, which is made up of Podemos activists, among others, won 31 seats, and in the Senate – 3.

These cases reveal that mass movements, insofar as they are subject to the same rules as political parties, quickly share their fate and even succumb to existing forces in a relatively short time. Their momentum and ability to create a collective identity fades away, yielding to the framework of institutional democracy – as if they could not permanently and successfully find their way within it. As noted by Esther del Campo, Jorge Resina and Yanina Welp: social movements moved from generating a feeling of initial euphoria and great expectations to an impasse and later the disappearance or dissolution of local democratisation processes.[72] If we compare them to revolutions, every revolution ends at some point after all – and not necessarily with a takeover of power.

How is it that mass movements lose their ability to act effectively right when they have already gained that opportunity?

First of all, the careers of mass movements in the world of institutional democracy when they adopt its rules demonstrate perfectly the tension between the civic and political worlds. As long as they want to stay true to their origins and followers, movements must be unambiguous and categorical. This means no skill in the political game and no compromise – not even the ability to reach one. The case of Syriza – which knew how to protest, but not how to negotiate – is instructive here. Similarly, as with the Icelandic mass protest and the Constitutional Council born out of it, the Constitutional Council members lacked the ability to debate with parliamentarians. They were not inherently political.

In contrast, the examples of Greece's Syriza and Spain's Podemos indicate that movements often become subservient, discredited by political players with more experience and institutional advantage. The position, structure and nature of the mass protest movement is not suited to the cyclical struggle for votes. As researchers studying the movement parties point out, the movement represents the direct, participatory and bottom-up model of democracy: as opposed to the top-down competition among elites for the votes of otherwise passive masses. In short, one that was more horizontal and less vertical.[73] The central values were horizontality, voice, inclusion through participation,' and autonomy from existing organisation (the state, but also parties and unions).[74]

71 del Campo et al., 254.

72 E.g. most of the cases of the "Arab Spring" revolts, see: del Campo et al., 253.

73 Simon Tormey, *The End of Representative Politics* (Cambridge: Polity, 2015), 136.

74 On Podemos: Prentoulis and Thomassen, 348, 351.

Movements can evolve into parties, or colonise them – but such a transformation changes both sides. From the phase of expressing claims, proclaiming demands and slogans, the movement must advance to the phase of decision-making, it must become more vertical in its structure, it is no longer possible to maintain an open civil society structure.[75] At the same time – not all expectations are to be met. Compromise is necessary, and this is not the face of the mass movement.

The example of the Yellow Vests (*Gilets Jaunes*) movement, a French mass anti-austerity movement that gained huge support in 2018, is also worth mentioning here. This movement wanted to lower "all taxes", to raise the minimum wage and pensions, and to reintroduce the wealth tax abolished in 2018. Many of their demands were in line with the promises made by President Emmanuel Macron during the 2017 campaign: lower taxes, more purchasing power and greater democracy. Soon, it was clear that this movement gained great social support – initially over 70% of the French population agreed with the protesters' demands. Then, President Macron found himself in a very difficult situation. In December 2018, he suspended the planned gas tax increase and announced four crucial changes in social policy: to subsidise the minimum wage by up to 100 Euros per month with public money; to bring forward the tax and duty exemption for overtime payments; to exempt all pension payments below 2,000 Euros from taxes. But it was not enough; when it became clear that these concessions failed to satisfy protesters, Macron has begun to bring the movement into the political game on his terms. He arranged a "grand débat national": in January 2019 citizens of the country were invited to express their opinions and ideas on the following topics online and in organised debates on numerous issues: ecological change, taxes, democracy, participation, representation and coexistence, and state structures and public services. This move allowed him to divide the Yellow Vests movement: they do not have a homogeneous attitude towards these issues. In that way, Macron set out an agenda and forced the Yellow Vests to express their views and demands in more detailed issues and in a way he proposed. It led to some splits in the movement and public support for it declined: while 71% of the population agreed with the demands of the Yellow Vests in November 2018, in March 2019 only 54% did so. Simultaneously, part of the movement joined the political life, making initial attempts to draw up a list for the European elections in May 2019. That way, Macron took over control of a crucial issue – citizens' participation and support for the public agenda submitted to him.[76] Macron also took advantage of politicising the movement – in that way, new politi-

75 Prentoulis and Thomassen, 350.

76 Ronja Kempin and Paweł Tokarski, "Macron, the Yellow Vests, and the National Debate: Playing for Time, Not Solving the Political Legitimacy Crisis", SWP Comment 2019–C 17, 26 March 2019, https://www.swp-berlin.org/en/publication/macron-the-yellow-vests-and-the-national-debate.

cal force emerged between his opponents (Le Pen's far-wing Rassemblement National and the left-wing populist La France Insoumise), taking over their support.[77]

Another strategy towards mass movements is to adopt mass movements' language and demands to make them parties' tools in political struggles. Thereby, the mass movement is to fulfil the role of initiating "diagnostic framing", which means how social, and consequently political, actors diagnose problems and define their grievances. That was partly the case with "Black Lives Matter" in the 2016 US election campaign, overshadowed by BLM from the beginning (August 2015), especially among Democratic presidential candidates. Nevertheless, while Clinton's references to implicit bias and systemic racism were clear, and Trump's reluctance towards the BLM movement rather evident,[78] their attitudes to BLM claims were at the forefront of the public agenda in the campaign. Hillary Clinton announced the need for criminal justice reform. But in October 2015, the speech by Hillary Clinton on such reform and race issues at Atlanta University Center was interrupted by BLM activists, who wanted her to apologise for her support for Bill Clinton's 1994 criminal reform law, which, according to the protesters, caused "mass incarceration". Thus, as can be observed, the declaration of full support for the movement to attract supporters to the candidate is also challenging at times – supporters demand devotion to a degree that is difficult to achieve in the reality of politics. Declared sympathies, even devotion to the attitudes and expectations of the mass movement, lead to growing appetites, and the movement – in order to maintain the needed distinctiveness and identity – demands more, proclaims that the candidate is not sincere or principled enough. Then, the sympathy can reverse easily.

77 It is worth adding that this idyllic image of public debate was not so perfect: all this happened in circumstances of a state of emergency that lasted nearly two years, which saw widespread use of violence by the police, including shooting at the "yellow vests" peaceful protest (Jane Kilpatrick, *When a Temporary State of Emergency Becomes Permanent: France as a Case Study* [Amsterdam: Transnational Institute, 2020], https://www.tni.org/files/publication-downloads/france_and_the_states_of_emergency_online.pdf). Similar events took place this year in the Netherlands directed against protesting farmers, and in Canada in 2021, where protesting truck drivers were deemed by the government to be a threat, which led to the introduction of a state of emergency. Fuel for trucks was confiscated. The government threatened that anyone bringing supplies for the drivers on strike, including food and cleaning products, could be arrested, and blocked a legal collection of money on the internet. Initially, the platform used to raise money, GoFundMe, which collected over 10 million Canadian dollars for the protest, declared that the money that had been blocked would be transferred to selected charitable organisations. It was only after protests, including by Tesla CEO Elon Musk, who called GoFundMe a "professional thief", that GoFundMe returned the money to the donors.

78 Meanwhile, the Republican campaign was influenced strongly by BLM. In March 2016, Black Lives Matter helped organise the 2016 Donald Trump Chicago rally protest that forced Trump to cancel the event.

This is when the power of the movement's influence is fully disclosed. Thus, as long as the movement remains on the sidelines, it exerts much more influence, much more impact on the world of politics, than when it begins to participate in it on an equal footing. So, it is not necessary to seize power to win, to take control of political discourse, while necessarily remaining on the sidelines of institutional politics.

There is one regularity: when mass social movement begins to engage in regular political life, it exposes itself to the requirements and risks of functioning in the systemic environment, the constitutionally designed system of checks and balances, requirements of transparency, funding restrictions and above all: the necessity to play according to the rules of democratic succession of power and accountability of public actors. Meanwhile, as long as the social movement does not work that way, liberal democracy is somewhat powerless against it. Mass social movement does not need to be representative in a democratic sense, deliberative and accountable.

Now let us examine this phenomenon from the point of view of accountability. Mass movements tend to act beyond the political system and the law. They do not have a duty to report on the exercise of public duties, political power and long-term responsibility. As long as movements act outside the system, there is no entrusting power, so nobody is entrusted with it and has a duty to give a report. Lack of organisation, acting out of the political regular order, as well as grassroots character, give them the unique opportunity to act without any constraints predicted for other organisations.

Within the framework of democratic accountability, mass social movements act as Principal (or: Proxy Principal), not as an Agent. They try to impose the conditions of the discourse, they play the role of the sovereign. They operate within revolutionary dialectic, rather than a democratic one.

In contrast, if a movement is integrated into the rules of democracy and politics on the same terms as other participants, its momentum wanes, it must be given structure and be subject to rules – including accountability for what it has accomplished and how. The inclusion of mass movements in the world of democratic institutions therefore deprives them of the basic attribute of being outside the world of politics, above the institutions. Submission to the rules of the parliamentary game, inclusion in the system of checks and balances or verification of the effect within the framework of a general election or referendum have shown that the momentum of the movement is not sufficient for long and the rhetoric it uses is not convincing enough. From the point of view of accountability, this is a very important moment, because it can be considered that mass movements start to be the Agent and stop being the Principal. This means that the movement's activists become accountable, subject to the ordinary rigours of political struggle and reaction from those entrusted with power. By becoming a regular actor on the democratic stage on the side of those entrusted with power, they must demonstrate the ability to conduct a victorious political conflict, to bring their goals and demands to fruition. The transformation of a movement into a party and participation in institutional politics exposes the movement to the risk of losing out to actors more suited to the game, and beyond that, most poignantly, exposes them to the judgment of who they have hitherto identified with. It is this transformation – i.e. the accountability relationship for the function entrusted to them – that is the most serious consequence of entering the world of democratic governance.

However, as long as they operate outside the system, mass social movements, like revolutions, seriously challenge constitutional order and political systems, acting beyond the chain of accountability. They take advantage of being irresponsible, intangible and ubiquitous in their demands and influence of collective imaginary of state affairs. And they boast a powerful ally that makes mobilising and managing collective consciousness easier than ever before.

Technopolitics – public sphere according to BIG TECH

Mobilisation of participants and acquisition of supporters has become unprecedentedly easy and inexpensive in times of digital communication. Social media mobilise, inform, give feedback, receive feedback from users[79] 24 hours, seven days a week – and it's free. As Castells writes, they create mass self-communication, where "the message is self-generated, the definition of the potential receiver(s) is self-directed, [and] the retrieval of specific messages (or content) is self-selected".[80] At the same time, the digital sphere greatly facilitates the networking across the structure and action of movements. It allows for the lack of clear leadership (BLM an example), while perfectly enabling a sense of collectiveness. A movement can gain followers without any effort on their part, often without physical contact, because it costs virtually nothing, requires no time, resources, actions on their part – other than "like" and "share" or other online activity. As Richard Hasen wrote: "Social media lowers the costs of collective action, for good and for ill".[81]

There is no need to describe this relationship between social movements and digital communicators more broadly – it is well known and has been analysed in recent years,[82] although we should share the observation that these studies are usually descriptive[83] and say little about the changing trajectories

79 Lobera, 272–3. On the change and the power of communication see: Andreu Casero-Ripollés, "Alternative Media and Social Movements in Europe's Digital Landscape", in *Routledge Handbook* (see note 13), 326 et seq.

80 Manuel Castells, *Communication Power* (Oxford: Oxford University Press, 2009), 55; Casero-Ripollés, 328.

81 Richard L. Hasen, Cheap Speech and What It Has Done (To American Democracy), First Amendment Law Review 16 (2007), ., 216. available at: https://scholarship.law.unc.edu/cgi/viewcontent.cgi?article=1248&context=falr (to

82 Igor Sádaba Rodríguez, "The Technopolitical Frameworks of Contemporary Social Movements. The European Case", in *Routledge Handbook* (see note 13), 313. Some authors claim that we are living in a process of *platformisation* – see: Casero-Ripollés, 337.

83 Rodríguez, 313.

of political power. For our deliberations on accountability in the democratic world, it is only worth pointing out a few nodal issues regarding this interplay, as well as features of digital communication in general.

First, the scale of digital communication is a unique phenomenon in the history of humanity. The services and products in this category are used by a number of recipients unmatched by any other in the history of human civilisation. Facebook has about 1.9 billion daily active users, about 2.9 billion monthly, which is more than a third of the world's population. Similarly, YouTube and Tik-Tok each have more than 2 billion monthly active users. Communication is universal, happens in real time and is generally either free or inexpensive.[84] This means that several companies around the world are arranging public space on a scale previously unimaginable.

New media have taken over the function of providing information, public discourse and running electoral campaigns. To give an example, in the period between 30 May 30 and 18 August 2023, campaign spending directly financed by Biden for President and Donald Trump online amounted to $83.5 million each, Mike Bloomberg spent $61.9 million, while Trump's Make America Great Again spent $47 million and the Biden Victory Fund spent $15 million.[85] The final tally of political campaign ad spending in the 2016 election cycle came at $9.8 billion.[86] Digital advertising in the 2016 US campaign grossed $1.4 billion,[87] almost eight times the campaign budget in 2012.[88] Most of that amount went to two service providers: Facebook and Google received up to 85% of that revenue, according to Hasen, although it's hard to pinpoint exact figures because both companies are reluctant to share them.[89]

However, it is not the numbers of users in the world or the sums spent by politicians that are central, but the fact that the people who use the services of these entities are at the same time the community that corresponds in scope to the public sphere; in short, the bourgeois-citizen milieu, described by J. Habermas as the sphere of private people who collectively form the public, which argues and debates with the public authority about the general

84 In autumn 2023, Meta announced a plan for paid access to Facebook and Instagram for EU residents, but these are still insignificant amounts of money (between €9.99 and €12.99 a month): https://www.politico.eu/article/facebook-and-instagram-to-offer-subscriptions-in-europe/. Similarly, X (formerly Twitter) users will pay $1 per month, as announced by the service's owner, Elon Musk: https://www.npr.org/2023/10/18/1206701241/some-users-of-x-formerly-twitter-will-have-to-pay-1-a-year-to-tweet-on-the-site

85 https://www.statista.com/statistics/910251/largest-political-advertisers-on-google/

86 Kate Kaye, *Data-Driven Targeting Creates Huge 2016 Political Ad Shift: Broadcast TV Down 20%, Cable and Digital Way Up* (3 January 2017, https://adage.com/article/media/2016-political-broadcast-tv-spend-20-cable-52/307346.

87 Kaye (see note 86).

88 Sean J. Miller, "Digital Ad Spending Tops Estimates", *Campaigns & Elections,* 4 January 2017, https://www.campaignsandelections.com/campaign-insider/digital-ad-spending-tops-estimates.

89 Hasen, 211.

rules of mutual relations under the so-called public discourse (*das öffentliche Räsonnement*).[90] Specific and historically unprecedented is the medium of this sphere, the decomposition of which under the influence of oligopolies and mass media, among others, was already prophesied by the author of this concept himself.[91]

Much attention has already been paid to how the operation of these entities affects the personal sphere and social life.[92] However, it is not difficult to see that global digital services have taken over the attention, imagination and memory of every user and therefore member of the public sphere, and have changed social behaviour by colonising the sphere of choices through shaping and predicting consumer needs and attitudes, but also the field of social and political behaviour. These are the special fields mass movements and Big Tech have in common – the capacity to instantly and with no cost bring together large masses of people and shape their collective and in fact: flock consciousness. Meanwhile, this new public sphere has its own peculiarities. First of all, what is special is the way the message is tailored to the recipient, often slogan-like, image-based, but also infused with emotion in a way that has been unusual so far. This is the new phenomenon of Twitter (now: X) messages – a politician addresses the audience almost non-stop, directly and in short angry statements, without filters, distance and seriousness.[93] In a world of messages directed at the recipient, recognising their preferences and programming their needs, there is little room anymore for deliberation, compromise and carefully considered individual decisions.[94]

It is the nature of the digital sphere that in addition to widespread and grassroots participation[95] it subordinates content to the ideology and identified attitudes of users. On the first sight, the users' recognised preferences, choices and responses shape what content reaches them. The process of disseminating information and opinions in the digital sphere therefore has nothing to do with the values and professional standards of mainstream journalism, mainly those that concern impartiality and neutrality. New media is an environment saturated with false information, fake news,[96] media bubbles

90 Jurgen Habermas, *The Structural Transformation of the Public Sphere: An Inquiry into a Category of Bourgeois Society*, translated by Thomas Burger and Frederick Lawrence, , Cambridge: Polity, 1989, 86 et seq.; K. Jaskułowski, "Jurgen Habermas's concept of the public sphere", *European Meetings* 3 (2010): 74–5.

91 Habermas, 52.

92 One example is the monumental work by Shoshana Zuboff, *The Age of Surveillance Capitalism: The Fight for a Human Future at the New Frontier of Power* (London: Profile Books, 2018).

93 Hasen, 212.

94 Zuboff, 589.

95 Casero-Ripollés, 327.

96 Defined as news articles that are intentionally and verifiably false, and could mislead readers. See: Hunt Allcott and Matthew Gentzkow, "Social Media and Fake News in the 2016 Election", *Journal of Economic Perspectives* 31, no. 2 (2017): 211–36, at 213.

and streams ideologically tailored to the user, creating "the translocal digital protest media imaginaries",[97] although to varying degrees. However, it is not simply a neutral environment that tailors messages according to user preferences. New media have their own agendas and goals, and pursue them in violation of their respective states' constitutions in a completely non-transparent and arbitrary manner: imposing bans, removing content – or failing to do so, while not being held accountable for these activities.

Mark Zuckerberg, speaking to podcast host Joe Rogan, admitted that Facebook censored the Hunter Biden laptop story during the 2020 US elections.[98] Next, on the Lex Fridman Podcast, he admitted that during the period of the Covid-19 pandemic, FB removed some information about it and distributed messages intensifying Covid panic. Zuckerberg said that only in 2021 his platform had removed 18 million posts containing alleged "misinformation" about Covid-19. Such censorship was also demanded of FB by government agencies.[99] This happened in the United States, where Facebook's headquarters is based, and in other countries where censorship is still formally prohibited, yet censorship has been widely implemented, and those implementing it have not been held legally accountable.

Facebook's political agenda is also clearly evidenced, for example (for there are many examples), by its activities during the riots in Sri Lanka in 2017. That year, statements inciting violence and disinformation against one ethnic group were distributed and propagated by Facebook with the help of algorithms. When Sri Lankan community activists asked Facebook's regional headquarters, which oversees four hundred million South Asian users, to intervene, Facebook refused, stating that the company would have to check for violations on its own. This was not easy, however, as the people tasked with such an inspection did not speak local languages. Government representatives, too, were told that they could report violations of the rules only by using a form available on the site. And yet, despite countless reports, statements calling for ethnic cleansing in Muslim neighbourhoods continued to spread. It should be added that social media in this country and at that time had long since

97 Emiliano Treré, Sandra Jeppesen and Alice Mattoni, "Comparing Digital Protest Media Imaginaries: Anti-austerity Movements in Greece, Italy & Spain", *tripleC: Communication, Capitalism & Critique, Open Access Journal for a Global Sustainable Information Society* 15, no. 2 (2017): 404–22; Rodríguez, 320.

98 "Mark Zuckerberg Admits Facebook Censored Hunter Biden Laptop Story during 2020 U.S. Elections", https://www.thehindu.com/news/international/mark-zuckerberg-admits-facebook-censored-hunter-biden-laptop-story-during-2020-u-s-elections/article65815040.ece (accessed 05.09.2023).

99 B. Bernstein, "Mark Zuckerberg Says Facebook Censored 'True' Covid Claims at Request of Health Establishment", https://www.nationalreview.com/news/mark-zuckerberg-says-facebook-censored-true-covid-claims-at-request-of-health-establishment/.

replaced local media. Thus, they were virtually the only source of information for residents.[100]

The power of social media, most notably Facebook, was used earlier (in 2016) by Philippine President Davao Duterte in cracking down on his opponents using online bloggers. They used their popularity from the world of entertainment and fuelled social conflicts, fake accounts were also used, practically displacing journalists and the press, and fully deserving of the term brigading, i.e. coordinated aggressive behaviour online.[101] This time again, the Facebook authorities remained inactive, despite repeated reports (the fake accounts were removed in 2018).

These stories bring to mind the role of Free Radio of the Thousand Hills from the civil war in Rwanda. The difference, however, is that in Rwanda the responsibility for inciting hatred could be attributed to some people.[102] In this case, algorithms effectively nullify the attribution of responsibility for hate speech to anyone because of little known local languages and vague procedures for reporting violations of rules and regulations.

The long investigation into Russian influence on the 2016 US election campaign revealed that Russian interference in the election was "sweeping and systemic"; major attack avenues in social media campaigns favoured candidate Trump including the hacking of Clinton campaign-related databases and the release of stolen materials through Russian-created entities and Wikileaks. Russia also targeted databases in many states related to administering elections, gaining access to information about millions of registered voters.[103] The investigation, however, did not lead to indictments or convictions of anyone other than a dozen Russian citizens. The few US officials who were indicted faced charges not directly related to these activities. Demonstrating the influence of foreign actors on a specific social media activity is extremely difficult, and new media activities are enigmatic, easily mystified and ephemeral.

New media completely change the conditions and functions of freedom of expression through their unaccountability. After all, they only serve as the environment for users (although it is noticeable that they nonetheless pursue their own agendas, such as promoting social change, criticism of traditional

100 See further: Max Fisher, *The Chaos Machine: The Inside Story of How Social Media Rewired Our Minds and Our World* (Little, Brown and Company, 2022).

101 See further: Maria A. Ressa, *How to Stand Up to a Dictator: The Fight for Our Future* (New York: Harper Collins Publishers 2022).

102 After the end of the civil war, several radio journalists, including Belgian Georges Ruggiu and Valérie Bemeriki, were convicted by the International Criminal Tribunal for Rwanda for incitement to hatred, "'Hate Radio' Journalist Confesses", http://news.bbc.co.uk/1/hi/world/africa/749079.stm.

103 Special Counsel Robert S. Mueller, III, U.S. Department of Justice, "Report on The Investigation into Russian Interference in the 2016 Election", 2019 Vol. I, 1–5, 36–51 and 1–4 14–35 (after:) American Constitution Society, Key Findings of the Mueller Report, https://www.acslaw.org/projects/the-presidential-investigation-education-project/other-resources/key-findings-of-the-mueller-report/.

institutions, not to mention the direction of social policies). Instead, they have inherited from traditional media the informative function,[104] and political accountability as a result. As Hasen points out, it also leaves plenty of room for manipulating the politicians, involving them in scandals and affairs. It makes democracy vulnerable to outside manipulation, practically making it harder (rather than easier) to hold them accountable.[105]

So it turns out that this combination of the realm of politics, new media and digital technologies called "technopolitics", "hybrids of technical systems and political practices that produce new forms of power and agency"[106] not only takes on the role of the media, politicians and the public sphere. It is also far less transparent and accountable than the world we have so far associated with the exercise of power and the struggle for it.

BIG TECH – a few facts about the new actor

Supranational digital companies, especially those that fall into Big Tech, the so-called Big Five,[107] are characterised by the global nature of their operations, an unprecedented number of customers using their services in economic relations and hyper-liquidity[108] that represents a unique economic advantage in the history of civilisation.[109] Historically, the highest capitalisation of any of the platforms, be it Google, Apple, Facebook, Amazon, Microsoft has exceeded $1 trillion. The value of the five Big Tech companies (about $10 trillion by mid-2021) is roughly equivalent to the combined GDP of France and

104 According to Statista daily news consumption in 2022, social media is the primary source of information for 47% in the 18–34 group, 45% in the 35–44 group and 33% in the 45–64 group. In the same time radio broadcasting was the source of information for : 12%, 21%, 21% i 14%, and local press for:: 6%, 7%, 13% i 19% . See: "Most Popular Platforms for Daily News Consumption in the United States as of August 2022, by Age Group", https://www.statista.com/statistics/717651/most-popular-news-platforms/

105 Hasen, 209.

106 Rodríguez, 315.

107 Initially, the term took the form of the Big Four, following the term coined by Eric Schmidt, chairman of Google's board of directors, first used in 2008 (Erick Schonfeld, "Eric Schmidt's Gang of Four: Google, Apple, Amazon, and Facebook", – TechCrunch, techcrunch.com).

108 The vast majority of modern states suffer from structurally unsustainable public finances, persistent budget deficits and chronic budget debt. For example, the public debt of individual European Union countries that are part of the euro area is higher than 100% of their gross domestic product (GDP) with an upward trend. The scale of the financial problems of the EU states (including those outside the euro area) is illustrated, for one, by the fact that in 2020 the EU has decided to take on further liabilities (over €700 billion) with repayment by 2058.

109 Tim Buthe and Walter Mattli, *The New Global Rulers: The Privatization of Regulation in the World Economy* (Princeton, NJ: Princeton University Press, 2011), https://doi.org/10.23943/princeton/9780691144795.001.0001.

Russia.[110] The financial advantage of Big Tech companies was reinforced particularly during the Covid-19 pandemic, especially with regard to the finances of states. When the effect of the pandemic in the vast majority of modern countries has been a rise in public debt, Big Tech companies have reported record profits; so, for example, in 2020, Facebook had a net income of more than $29 billion, and the results for 2021 were much better. Figures for 2021 indicated that revenues of Alphabet, Google's parent company, rose by 41% year-on-year, while those of Mark Zuckerberg's Meta company rose by 37%. Apple (up 33%) and Amazon (up 22%) saw slightly slower revenue growth. Microsoft reported a "mere" 17% increase.[111] All five companies are among the world's largest capitals.[112] These companies have been accumulating profits using technology and knowledge on a scale not experienced in the world since colonial times. However, it is impossible to identify their activities solely with these competencies and the use of IT tools. They are, in fact, institutionalising a new form of economic and social relations, building a "kingdom of knowledge" and using the means of surveillance and behavioural modification, and this is not an accompanying action – only an intentional one.[113]

Currently, more than 70% of the world's internet is owned by two corporations, Google and Facebook. We have already referred to the number of social media users, here we want to point out that the services of only the latest two versions of Microsoft software (Windows 10 and Windows 11) are being used by 1.4 billion users a month.[114] This means that a significant part of the world's population functions within a single environment of services and media. Accordingly, the experts indicate that this expansive nature of activity entails centralisation on a global scale covering the sphere of information in the broadest sense: Big Data, cloud computing, as well as media content and its distribution.[115] Moreover, it is becoming increasingly clear that we witness the conversion of economic and technological advantage into forms of influence and eventually into political power, and the classical categories of politics, authority and also law are becoming obsolete.

The dominance of global corporations is being extended into new areas of activity. There is a global accumulation of capital in the hands of a small group

110 Jacques Fontanel, *Big Tech, a Progress and a Danger for Civilization*, St. Petersburg State University of Economics (UNECON) 2019, 2, available: https://hal.univ-grenoble-alpes.fr/hal-02102188/document.

111 Carmen Ang, "How Do Big Tech Giants Make Their Billions?", 25 April 2022, https://www.visualcapitalist.com/how-big-tech-makes-their-billions-2022/.

112 The 100 largest companies in the world by market capitalization in 2023. https://www.statista.com/statistics/263264/top-companies-in-the-world-by-market-capitalization/

113 Zuboff, 34–5, 482, 492.

114 https://earthweb.com/windows-users/.

115 Juan-Carlos Miguel de Bustos and Jessica Izquierdo-Castillo, "Who Will Control the Media? The Impact of Big Tech on the MediaIindustries in the Digital Economy", *Revista Latina de Comunicación Social* 74 (2019): 803–21 at 808.

of owners. For example, as of 2020, the top 1% of the richest people have accumulated nearly two-thirds of all new wealth created worldwide. A billionaire has gained about $1.7 million for every dollar of new global wealth earned by a person in the bottom 90%.[116] It is telling that the process of creating global monopolies goes hand in hand with the process of global concentration. For example, Bill Gates is not only a global monopolist in computer software, but also a tycoon in Big Pharma or Big Agribusiness. Digital business owners are also key investors in vaccines or genetically modified seed promoted especially in African countries. As owners or shareholders of the agribusiness industry, they influence the so-called smartification of agriculture,[117] which contributes to the loss of states' ability to act independently and the formation of global monopolies. Big Tech owners are also among the largest landowners – both in the United States and worldwide.[118]

What is occurring here is bringing global Big Tech companies on par with states and even superpowers on the international stage, as well as the slow but relentless assumption of other important state powers – from legislation, administration and operation of public service spheres to the realm of judicial power.

Big Tech in international relations

The intensity of the influence of global Big Tech companies in the international arena and their primacy in relation to modern states gives us the right to conclude that they have joined the superpowers imposing their rules of conduct on other participants in political relations through *hard power* and *soft power*. Attention is drawn to their use of means similar to those employed in political relations,[119] such as pressure, lobbying activities, placing own supporters in the decision-making process (agents of influence) and eliminating

116 Sophie Kiderlin, "The Richest 1% of People Amassed Almost Two-thirds of New Wealth Created in the Last Two Years, Oxfam Says", Davos 2023, CNBC, https://www.cnbc.com/2023/01/16/richest-1percent-amassed-almost-two-thirds-of-new-wealth-created-since-2020-oxfam.html.

117 Felix Maschewski and Anna-Verena Nosthoff, *Big Tech and the Smartification of Agriculture: A Critical Perspecitve,*2022, IT for Change (eds) The State of Big Tech 2022, https://projects.itforchange.net/state-of-big-tech/big-tech-and-the-smartification-of-agriculture-a-critical-perspective/, available at SSRN: https://ssrn.com/abstract=4080210

118 In the United States alone, Jeff Bezos has around 170,000 hectares of land, mainly in Texas, while Bill Gates has 100,000 hectares (https://agtecher.com/unveiling-the-strategy-why-is-bill-gates-investing-massively-in-farmland/). John Malone, chairman of Liberty Media, owns as much as 890,700 hectares (2.2 million acres) of land worldwide (https://www.farmlandriches.com/largest-private-land-owners/)

119 С. Ю. Зайцев, *Модели взаимодействия транснациональных корпораций (ТНК) и современного государства, Диссертация на соискание ученой степени кандидата политических наук* (Санкт-Петербург, 2019), 58–9, https://www.dissercat.com/content/modeli-vzaimodeistviya-transnatsionalnykh-korporatsii-tnk-i-sovremennogo-gosudarstva (accessed: 12.08.2024).

those who could harm the interests of transnational corporations from the decision-making process.[120] In 2021, for example, this kind of pressure was observed on the part of FB owners. They were aimed at eliminating certain individuals from antitrust proceedings, shaping the antitrust policy of the US Department of Justice or US Federal Trade Commission (FTC) officials.[121] Big Tech companies must be viewed together with their instrumentation of a political nature, such as global corrupt practices,[122] lobbying or global foundations.[123] As their size increases, these companies tend to increase their spending to influence government decisions.[124] For instance, expenditures by Big Tech companies on direct lobbying of EU institutions is roughly €100 million per year, and this is the largest sectoral spending on Brussels lobbying. On top of that, though, there is the indirect influence, carried out through various associations or *think tanks* formally acting as advocates of good ideas or modern legal solutions, which has a direct impact on the activities carried out by EU bodies.[125] Especially in the high-tech biological and medical sectors, there is a deepening loss of the ability of states to act independently, and the networked activities of global companies are shaping global, networked monopolies that exert an overwhelming influence on social and economic relations without direct interference or declaration. It is also difficult not to see that the failure to shape uniform norms of copyright and related rights within the EU is linked to the actions of communities and organisations operating with the more-or-

120 Fontanel, 3.

121 "FTC Alleges Facebook Resorted to Illegal Buy-or-Bury Scheme to Crush Competition after String of Failed Attempts to Innovate", tc.gov/news-events/news/press-releases/2021/08/ftc-alleges-facebook-resorted-illegal-buy-or-bury-scheme-crush-competition-after-string-failed (accessed 22.01.2023); Cecilia Kang, "A Facebook Antitrust Suit Can Move Forward, a Judge Says, in a Win for the F.T.C.", *New York Times*, 11 January 2022, https://www.nytimes.com/2022/01/11/technology/facebook-antitrust-ftc.html (accessed 22.01.2023).

122 In particular, see SEC Enforcement Actions: FCPA Cases, https://www.sec.gov/enforce/sec-enforcement-actions-fcpa-cases.

123 The Gates Foundation's resources are over $50 billion, the Silicon Valley Community Foundation over $7 billion. The Gates Foundation's annual spending budget is at the same level as that of the World Health Organisation. These foundations operate globally, particularly in terms of creating economic awareness and attitudes (e.g. the Gates Foundation in African countries promotes genetically modified seed and food produced by global producers such as Monsanto, Syngenta and Bayer, thus eliminating farmers' ability to use their own seed). https://www.rp.pl/biznes/art146351-fundacja-gatesow-zarabia-dzieki-innemu-miliarderowi.

124 Song Kim and Helen V. Milner, "Multinational Corporations and Their Influence through Lobbying on Foreign Policy", in *Global Goliaths: Multinational Corporations in a Changing Global Economy*, ed. C. Fritz Foley, James Hines and David Wessel (Washington, DC: The Brookings Institution, 2019), 500, https://www.brookings.edu/wp-content/uploads/2019/12/Kim_Milner_manuscript.pdf.

125 Max Bank et al., *The Lobby Network: Big Tech's Web of Influence in the EU*, Corporate Europe Observatory and Lobby Control e.V., Brussels and Cologne 2021, 6, available at: https://corporateeurope.org/sites/default/files2021-08The%20lobby%20network%20%20 Big%20Tech%27s%20web%20of%20influence%20in%20the%20EU.pdf.

less discreet backing of such organisations. Even when a directive is issued at the EU level in a given area, its implementation is blocked in individual countries, as in the case of the Directive on copyright in the digital single market (Directive 2019/790/EU), which means that Big Tech companies may not pay authors their due royalties in years to come.

As for the scale of foundations established by major corporations, for example, the resources of the Gates Foundation are more than $50 billion, the Ford Foundation more than $12 billion, the Silicon Valley Community Foundation – over $7 billion. The Gates Foundation's annual spending is on par with that of the World Health Organisation. These foundations are globally active, especially in shaping political awareness and attitudes, indoctrinating children and young people, or, like the Gates Foundation in African countries, promoting genetically modified (GMO) seed and food produced by global seed producers such as Monsanto, Syngenta and Bayer, where the common denominator of the activities carried out is dependence on GMO seeds, which are unobtainable by farmers themselves.

Perhaps most striking is the way in which Big Tech companies form their relationships with individual countries. Unlike ordinary transnational companies, Big Tech companies do not operate under the laws of a particular country. They negotiate their legal status, tax obligations, with individual states and shape them in contractual form. In this regard, the 2020 case of Australia is distinctive. When the Australian government tried to enforce Facebook's compliance with that country's laws and payment of taxes owed, within a dozen days it was forced to capitulate, disguised under the guise of an agreement that changed Australian laws.[126]

In the case of Chinese Big Tech companies the relationship between a digital company and the government is taking shape in a different, yet also extremely interesting way, still corresponding to a close inter-state relationship. A prime example is the well-known dispute from a few years ago between Huawei, the Chinese telecommunications giant, and the United States (a dispute extended by the United States to other dependent countries) over the use of 5G technology – a dispute that, although it arose out of controversy and allegations against corporate executives and purely technical considerations, in fact turned into a struggle between the two superpowers, and more than that, a precedent-setting battle over the geopolitics of internet infrastructure.[127] And in 2020, President Trump's administration raised concerns about the use of TikTok, owned by the Chinese company ByteDance, and banned transactions

126 "Facebook to Reverse News Ban on Australian Sites, Government to Make Amendments to Media Bargaining Code", https://www.abc.net.au/news/2021-02-23/facebook-reverses-news-ban-on-australian-sites-media-code/13173984 (accessed 08.04.2022)

127 See further: Min Tang, "Huawei Versus the United States? The Geopolitics of Exterritorial Internet Infrastructure", *International Journal of Communication* vol. 14 (2020): 4556–77.

with the entity.[128] These cases involved concerns about the transfer of information on citizens to the government of a country considered authoritarian, and they were probably not unfounded, as Americans are well aware,[129] as – due to the transfer of personal data by US Big Tech companies – they are involved in a similar dispute with the EU.

These cases prompt us to consider digital companies no longer as mere beneficiaries of economic freedom, companies interested in conducting their business – but as actors engaged in international politics, equal (though not always working hand in hand) to states and even superpowers.

The confrontation between global digital companies and modern states takes the form, as it did in the case of China and the United States, of a new kind of *proxy war* – no longer in distant territory this time, but extraterritorially,[130] though still for influence over citizens and primacy over domestic power. Thus, these companies become a weapon in the international arena capable of applying power and influence on the territory of other countries,[131] guided by their own interests, often conflicting with those of the countries in which they are registered.

Big Tech companies vs. state power

By design, digital corporations are global, interacting with users extraterritorially in the vast majority of modern countries, without being based in the countries where they do business. They operate outside the legal order of individual countries where they operate, and even confront their activities with the laws of those countries. The rules of conduct they impose supersede state law. Citizen-state relations are being replaced by consumer-transnational

128 Executive Order on Addressing the Threat Posed by TikTok. The White House. https://www.whitehouse.gov/presidential-actions/executive-order-addressing-threat-posed-tiktok/ 2020. Similar restrictions were imposed on WeChat.

129 In 2007 the National Security Agency (NSA) and other law enforcement agencies have accessed data directly from major US internet firms, including Microsoft, Google, Yahoo, Facebook and Apple, without making a request to the firms and without individual court orders through programmes such as PRISM. According to the NSA, "over 2,000 Prism-based reports" are now issued every month. There were 24,005 in 2012, a 27% increase on the previous year. In total, by 2013, more than 77,000 intelligence reports have cited the PRISM programme (Glen Greenwald and Ewan MacAskill, 07.01.2013, https://www.theguardian.com/world/2013/jun/06/us-tech-giants-nsa-data).

130 Madison Cartwright, "Internationalising State Power through the Internet: Google, Huawei and Geopolitical Struggle", *Internet Policy Review* 9, no. 3 (2020), https://policyreview.info/articles/analysis/internationalising-state-power-through-internet-google-huawei-and-geopolitical.

131 Loriana Crasnic, Nikhil Kalyanpur and Abraham Newman "Networked Liabilities: Transnational Authority in a World of Transnational Business", *European Journal of International Relations* 23, no. 4 (2017): 906–29; Natasha Tusikov, "How US-Made Rules Shape Internet Governance in China", *Internet Policy Review* 8, no. 2 (2019): 1–22, also: Cartwright (see note 130).

corporation ones, and at the same time public law is being superseded by private law.

A good example of just such an operation is SWIFT – the Society for Worldwide Interbank Financial Telecommunication, which conducts about 80% of the world's banking traffic, with headquarters in Belgium – although data is processed and stored in the United States. The US Treasury Department has requested data from SWIFT since the 9/11 attacks as part of its Terrorist Finance Tracking Program.[132] Significant problems exist precisely in the area of data storage and control, key products in the operation of IT companies, including effective demands by US authorities for access to data collected by Microsoft's European branch.[133]

Also well known are the business tax avoidance strategies used by Google, among others, which, thanks to the transfer of revenues to tax havens from an Irish company (and previously a Dutch shell), paid no taxes in either the United States or the EU. Indeed, the Irish Google (Google Ireland Holding) was registered in Bermuda.[134] The European Commission's battle against Apple has ended in defeat. Although the Commission ordered the conglomerate in 2016 to reimburse Ireland for €13 billion in back taxes, the Court of Justice of the European Union recognised the legitimacy of the company's appeal. Meanwhile, there is still no instrument to effectively claim the tax due on the turnover of these companies within the EU.[135]

Another feature of Big Tech companies is that their revenue does not depend on the stability of the countries in which they do business, because they conduct their business virtually, they do not build industrial plants or chains of physical stores. For such entities, crises can actually become a source of additional profits. Their interests do not necessarily coincide with those of the countries in which they operate, and their practices vis-à-vis the governments

132 Marieke De Goede, "The SWIFT Affair and the Global Politics of European Security", *Journal of Common Market Studies* 50, no. 2 (2012): 214–30.

133 Microsoft initially refused to release the suspects' mail at the request of federal prosecutors, arguing that it was being stored on an external computer server in an "IT cloud" at Microsoft's Irish branch, and therefore outside the jurisdiction of US authorities, and releasing it would be a breach of European data protection laws. Initially, a federal appeals court in 2016 agreed with Microsoft's argument, but the US Department of Justice appealed the ruling. At the same time, the rules regarding the release of such data were changed; under the new law, a service provider is required to comply with obligations to store, back up or disclose the contents of communications and any records or other information relating to a customer or subscriber, regardless of where such communications, records or other information are located (CLOUD Act §103(a)(1)). Following this, the Government obtained a new warrant that covered the requested information. The Supreme Court 584 USA (2018).

134 https://www.reuters.com/article/us-google-taxes-netherlands/google-shifted-23-billion-to-tax-haven-bermuda-in-2017-filing-idUSKCN1OX1G9/?utm_source=reddit.com.

135 On efforts in this regard: Adel Abdel-Sadek, *Big Tech and Digital Taxation reforms in the EU and MENA*, European Institute of the Mediterranean 2021, https://www.euromesco.net/publication/big-tech-and-digital-taxation-reforms-in-the-eu-and-mena/.

of these countries go beyond business practices. As opposed to traditional global companies, they are active not only in promoting their economic interests, but also claim the right to take over the function inherent to the state, i.e. the regulatory function, and impose it on the citizens of modern states. The measures taken by the EU to protect against unfair competition practices or to protect personal data can solve this problem only partially.[136]

When we adopt a systemic perspective, the most interesting are the manifestations of influence on strictly state activities, previously reserved for public authority, exercised in accordance with the requirements of democratic principles, including the accountability of authorities for the functions entrusted to them. Three areas are especially noteworthy. The first is the issue of regulating freedom of expression. As a consequence, creating a unified global communications space also results in the existence of information and opinion control on a global scale. In lieu of states, Big Tech companies are independently defining the framework for freedom of expression. Significantly, the rules and limits are set in action and quite fluid. Big Tech companies are involved in restricting hate speech, which gives them the tool to suppress the standard of freedom of expression quite arbitrarily. This is partly due to the US government encouraging the construction of an "algorithm of radicalism".[137] Since 2017, Microsoft, Google and Twitter have been active in the Global Internet Forum to Counter Terrorism working together to solve the problem of content classification, to eliminate hate speech (counterspeech) and to develop a common database to identify terrorist accounts.[138] However, as we indicated in the section on the convergence of mass movements and new media, content classification policies occasionally produce unexpected results.

Companies report such activity to the authorities, and independently apply sanctions, mostly exclusion – a kind of digital banishment. Typically, this is done through anonymous actions. That is, FB or Twitter employees grant permission to participate in public debate or eliminate from it. This happens arbitrarily, i.e. without applying what is obvious under domestic legal orders, i.e. domestic administrative or judicial procedure, namely, without the right to open and objective consideration of the legality of the actions taken. Nor are they subject to public scrutiny or otherwise held accountable for their actions. This aspect distinguishes them from traditional participants in political relations, such as states or social organisations, whose acts of law-making and application are subject to legal scrutiny usually not exhausted by the right to

136 By way of example: by decision of 18 July 2018, 3 the European Commission fined Google for having abused its dominant position by imposing anticompetitive contractual restrictions on manufacturers of mobile devices and on mobile network operators, in some cases since 1 January 2011. The General Court in its judgment T-604/18 of 14.09.2022 (*Google and Alphabet v. Commission (Google Android)*) confirmed the Commission's decision and imposed a fine €4.125 billion.

137 Zuboff, 527.

138 Zuboff, 527.

a domestic remedy, but also with extensive international scrutiny of acts taken by national legal protection bodies.

It is already a truism to say that platforms belonging to Big Tech take an active part in electoral campaigns by positioning the attitudes and preferences of voters, and by promoting convenient politicians and eliminating from the public debate politicians not approved by them. Those who hold views different from those of Big Tech owners are being censored. The most famous example is that of President Donald Trump, whose account was simply blocked on Twitter, on Facebook and YouTube (his posts were followed by 88 million people). Accounts of other participants in the public debate not approved by the company's anonymous employees are being deleted in a similar manner.[139] This happens for a variety of sometimes obscure reasons. Removing from the public debate part of its participants, part of the arguments formulated in it, deprives democracy of its key component, i.e. the deliberative dimension. It contradicts the Enlightenment idea of the free exchange of ideas as a necessary condition for the knowledge of truth and the rational formation of political relations.

Control over the formulation and distribution of ideas and views is exercised by informal, external centres of influence. Unlike domestic participants in political relations, they are subject to neither political nor legal accountability. As some views are removed from public debate much like Nikolai Yezhov from his photo with Joseph Stalin, other views are promoted. The process of eliminating views not shared by Big Tech companies from the public debate goes hand in hand with the process of funding selected views or entire ideologies through the system of foundations or directly. Big Tech companies fund the activities of selected political formations, such as movements like Black Lives Matter in the United States or the US Senate-affiliated Business Coalition for the Equality Act, funded by more than 500 major global companies.[140]

The significant impact of GAFAM companies on states' political systems is related to the form of communication they carry out. The public space, the space of common action, which is essential for the formation of social relations, has been segmented: divided into small forums, with no relation to each other. Small social groups have been formed, and people who do not fit into them are removed from them using an algorithm. People with similar views are grouped, and information like that to which the participant has already reacted positively is offered. This reinforces the conviction of members of a given social group that the way they think is the way the majority thinks,

139 For example, in 2020 FB removed the account of the most popular Polish MP on FB, whose account was followed by around 800,000 people. In turn, in January this year FB removed the account of the largest account of a Polish parliamentary faction on FB. It was followed by more than 670,000 people, i.e. roughly as many people as are following the accounts of the ruling party and the largest opposition party on FB combined.

140 https://www.hrc.org/resources/business-coalition-for-equality.

except for some so-called "outliers" who should be re-educated. A society of platforms comes into being,[141] or the phenomenon figuratively named Babel Tower Substack.[142] By intruding into the political sphere, Big Tech companies are shattering collective identity. Instead of uniting, they are polarising and fragmenting the modern world. The induced atomisation of society generates an intensification of political polarisation. In turn, associated with it is the progressive dehumanisation of those who dare to think differently, stirring up mutual hatred between various, algorithmically demarcated social groups and fuelling resentment and a sense of alienation of one towards the other. Paradoxically, therefore, by acting to eliminate hate speech, they are a mass generator of loss of connection with other people. Losing its collective identity, an emotionally fractured, fragmented society loses its capacity for self-organisation. It forfeits self-awareness, self-control. It loses the ability to read its own self-interest. It is thus prone to serve in the name of other people's interests, which are presented as an expression of progress and what is scientific and, as such, necessary.

The number of users of Big Tech companies, and their business relationships, causes disputes between them to be increasingly resolved through internal procedures. This is the reality, and it must be admitted that the fear of an internal arbitration disciplines users much better than the risk of a real lawsuit. The penalty is exclusion from the service, or at least tarnished reputation – and in a world where information and trust are handled, such a threat is serious. It does limit the role of the classical judiciary as a monopolist (except in the form of the tenuous share of arbitration accepted in arbitration provisions) in resolving civil disputes. Besides, technology, especially communication platforms, is also encroaching more and more heavily on this traditional justice system. In some countries, hearings are held via the Microsoft platform. This is, of course, a low-cost and convenient solution, but it results in a significant dependence of the exercise of judicial power on the provision of services by an entity not anchored in a country's procedure or even its law. This raises questions about fairness, access to the court for the digitally excluded and especially the public nature of such a process – or more precisely, a hearing to which only explicitly invited participants have access.[143] In turn, this definitely affects the accountability of the judiciary for its exercise of power, realised, among other

141 José van Dicjk, Thomas Poell and Martijn de Waal, *La parola chiave per capire il mondo. Perché è importante comprendere tutti i significati di 'platform societ'*, https://open.luiss.it/2021/04/26/democrazia-futura-platform- society-ovvero-societa-delle-piattaforme/.

142 Jonathan Heidt, "Welcome to the After Babel Substack. How Do We Adapt to a World in Which It Is So Much Harder to Understand One Another?", https://jonathanhaidt.substack.com/p/welcome-to-the-after-babel-substack.

143 Marcin Szwed, "Sądownictwo w Polsce a nowe technologie – początek drogi czy przystanek na drodze do cyfryzacji?", in *Nowe technologie, nowa sprawiedliwość, nowe pytania. Wdrażanie nowych technologii w wymiarze sprawiedliwości*, ed. Piotr Kładoczny and Katarzyna Wiśniewska (Warsaw: Helsińska Fundacja Praw Człowieka, 2021), 154 et seq.

things, precisely through open access to the hearing, and also about the extent of this openness – open especially to the entity providing the remote access service.

The issue of storing and processing information (not only personal data) is also treated with some degree of embarrassment in the administration, the so-called cloud services, which are one of the main resources of Big Tech companies.[144] This means that about 60% of resources are owned by the three Big Five players. What impact this has on political life was demonstrated by President Donald Trump when – after his Twitter and FB accounts were blocked for his supporters – the Parler service was created in 2018. It had 10 million users, but in January 2021 Amazon (AWS) suspended the use of the service from its cloud, and so Trump's supporters lost this opportunity for social communication as well.

Full dependence on cloud services, dominated by US companies,[145] prompted the creation of an initiative on the Old Continent, supported by the European Commission (GAIA-X). However, its launch is hindered by major obstacles. The more so because Microsoft has a stake in the initiative. Countries are making efforts to create their own services of this kind – so, for example, in the emerging Polish National Cloud, Microsoft and Google Cloud act as strategic partners.[146] In this context, the words from the Polish side of the Government Security Center about the fact that cooperation with industry is aimed at developing "transparent rules and procedures" between the owners of facilities of critical infrastructure installations or equipment sound particularly clear, since "a significant part of it, of crucial importance to the state, is currently in private hands".[147]

These are the most visible manifestations to date of the state's dependence or limitation in performing its traditional functions and reliance on unaccountable entities. Here we leave aside the issue of the increasingly powerful market for online currencies, and it is worth adding that Big Tech companies are also working on creating their own currencies (Facebook) or launching payments in cryptocurrencies (Amazon), which is likely to revolutionise the current currency markets and the monopoly of central banks (the ECB in the case of euro zone countries). At the outset, Facebook's bank would find itself

144 According to 2023 Report there are: Amazon Web Services (AWS) with a market share of over 30%, Microsoft Azure (a market share of over 20%), Google Cloud Platform (10% of the market share) after: Jana Brnakova, "The Top 10 Public Cloud Providers in 2023", https://www.revolgy.com/insights/blog/the-top-10-public-cloud-providers-2023.

145 Practically the only competition is Chinese Alibaba Cloud, the leading cloud provider in China, with a 42.4% market share, and the Asia Pacific, with a 19.6% market share, around 6% of global market share. Brnakova (see note 144).

146 A. Marczyński, "Na Podsłuchu, wywiad z P. Koniecznym, Niebezpiecznik", 24 March 2021, https://niebezpiecznik.pl/post/na-podsluchu-odcinek-33-ten-o-chmurze-krajowej-i-jej-bezpieczenstwie/.

147 rcb.gov.pl (accessed 12.04.2022).

in the top group of the world's largest retail banks, and the electronic money it creates would become the world's main settlement currency.

Summary

Needless to say, all these activities of Big Tech companies belong to the sphere of their business activities, and therefore enjoy complete freedom, limited only rarely by defence against monopolistic practices. However, this is a cloak that has nothing to do with reflecting on the classical powers of states. In fact, Big Tech companies influence legislation, create their own laws – including limits on freedom of expression, their own rules and preferences for election campaigns. They promote, and often fund, movements with key political influence, and have created the infrastructure in which the state exercises its power and administration. Their influence on the state and on society is as powerful as it is invisible.[148]

Subject exclusively to the rules of the free market, they enjoy freedom of activity and property rights, but imperceptibly begin to constitute a second pillar of power, in the sense of rule-making and enforcement. This situation is beginning to resemble the well-known dual authority of church and state from European history, but for the time being the dispute over investiture is won by Big Tech, which is much better equipped and devoid of the constraints characteristic of authorities operating under constitutionalism, including accountability for functions performed – through term limits and the electoral process, like a system of mutual balancing and control.

What is more – it is not bound by any democratic principles, including transparency and accountability – including in the sphere of those activities that go beyond purely service. Big Tech is a political actor, it is a partner to international relations, and the specifics of its structure and activities make it completely transcendent to states, laws and borders. It is not subject to the obligation to pass relations, because no one has entrusted Big Tech with power either. It has a primordial, self-contained character. Before the advent of the digital environment and the large entities that manage it, it did not exist at all. However, it has emerged and seems to be assuming rather on its own the function of its own accountability, according to its own not-so-transparent set of rules. Big Tech is beginning to take on the role of not only replacing public authority (e.g. in the area of controlling the limits of freedom of expression, control over broadcasting, education, general elections), but also replacing the Principal. When Twitter removes the US president's account, Facebook

148 The world of Big Tech is not hiding this at all; FB authorities declare that their goal is to create a society, and the best evidence is in the words of Lawrence Page, CEO of Google (from 2015 to 2019 Alphabet): "in my very long-term vision of the world, our software deeply understands what you know and what you don't, and how to organise the world so it can solve important problems", in Zuboff, 548.

fails to act to police speech inciting violence in Sri Lanka and the Philippines. Google, Amazon and FB gather knowledge and databases from all parts of the world and know the preferences of each of its inhabitants who use them, skilfully using this knowledge in political elections (either on their own or by sharing it with Principals), eliminating views they do not share. It is hard not to assume that Big Tech is no longer just held accountable – it holds accountable, and with tools that no tyrant could even dream of. They are taking on the role of proxy or perhaps super Principal. At the same time, they are effectively shaping the consciousness of citizenry and policy framing, influencing the Principal in a remarkably powerful way in the traditional perception of power.

And unlike the social movements previously described as proxy Principal – they are not ephemeral. They are truly enduring as it were, and their power and knowledge is growing at a tremendous rate and branching out into other dimensions of human existence. Perhaps, then, this is where the efforts of analysing the phenomenon of accountability should focus – on new actors. For now, however, this category is totally inapplicable to these subjects, and its existing framework is completely inadequate.

Conclusions

Accountability – the story about the exercise of power

We have presented the protagonist of our book: accountability as a major player in constitutional law and the political order of democratic states. A significant one, although somewhat secondary, at times episodic in specific representations and renditions of the exercise of power.

It was our task, however, to present it in a slightly different light – not as a new, rebranded form of scrutiny, liability or political responsibility, but as a story about the exercise of power, about the communication between those who entrust power to others, and those who exercise it by this delegation, explaining their actions and motives behind them. In this sense, it is a key feature of constitutional systems, a keystone for demonstrating the meaning and reality of rule of law, checks and balances and democracy as a system of entrustment and control of power by the community.

Our observations demonstrate that although accountability, conceived as an obligation to give an account of what has been done within the framework of entrusted power, lies at the heart of the democratic system, and is an important if not the key element of the democratic system, its actual incarnation is either illusory or appears rarely, on the margins of other functions of political and systemic life. Although many voice the need for accountability, both in science and in practice, in reality, communication about entrusted power happens rarely, and even more sparsely under conditions that enable it to be meaningfully received and assessed. There is neither a sense of importance nor much interest in such accountability. And yet, at the same time, all this is accompanied by a heated discussion about the crisis of democracy and the need to further deepen it – not a crisis, but precisely democracy.

This is hardly surprising to the reader (and to us) since, along with the belief in Santa Claus, we have forfeited the belief that the democratic system works in such a way that a political community, if not of enlightened then at least of citizens driven by the common good, deliberates on the solutions applied by those who have been elected to carry out particular tasks and as a consequence grants them further mandate or removes them from power, electing those who are more suited to carry out these responsibilities. All this,

DOI: 10.4324/9781003493419-7

in turn, takes place under conditions of discourse about public affairs, with the development of a common agenda and a common hierarchy of values, and with representatives (the political elite and, in terms of the judiciary, also the legal elite) openly and honestly reporting on their every action. Such a world does not exist and probably never has. But despite this, it is astonishing how accountability, especially a narrative one, gets overlooked in the realities of the system and fades under the pressure of the need for blame managing, incomprehensible messages, or has no chance to exist at all.

The last 30 years of the history of democracy have been a transition from triumphalism, as exemplified by Francis Fukuyama, who proclaimed that progress had reached its glorious finale in the form of liberal democracy – to increasingly serious crises, a decline in trust in political and state institutions (in countries claiming to be democratic and under the rule of law), and the last two decades have also witnessed, especially in the social media environment, a polarisation of civic attitudes – social atomisation, which meant the destruction of the very idea of political community. At the same time, the period since 1990 has seen the emergence of a number of new democratic systems – these emerging democracies, especially in Eastern and Central European countries, have provided an interesting field of research, for they allowed new data to be collected, new observations to be made about how parliamentary systems work and how accountability might exist (or disappear) in democracies so enthusiastically emerging. It was under such conditions of accountability inherent in different forms of democracy, with different durations and different institutional settings, that we observed accountability, seeking to discover its paths, the reasons for its disappearance – or development.

This led us to several general conclusions.

Epistemic asymmetry versus accountability

Narrative accountability is stretched between authority and knowledge.

The subject of power does not only determine the behaviour of the ruled, but also enjoys a vast advantage of knowledge – and it is knowledge that it is not very willing to share. This body of knowledge is immensely rich, complex, full of tedious details and nuances and arguably often leading to ambiguous conclusions. Under such conditions, those in power: members of government, parliament and also judges, have to make choices and decisions: tangible acts of power. The slogans and principles of transparency that are promulgated and implemented: openness of public life, access to public information, public access to parliamentary sittings, open court hearings, constitute an environment that is necessary and conducive to reducing epistemic asymmetries, but they fail to provide per se what accountability is all about, because, as we have tried to prove, accountability is about what has happened within the framework of entrusted power in terms of recognition of the will of the entity that exercises it. The account given as part of the accountability process should communicate what the governing body did, what was within its discretionary power, why its will was formed this way, what factors influenced it and what consequences were taken into consideration when this decision was made.

Yet the confluence of power and knowledge brings to mind the ideas of Michel Foucault, according to whom power and knowledge functions and aims are inextricably related: to control is to know and in knowing there is a control.[1]

This control manifests itself also in discourse – an institutionalised way of speaking or writing about the entire reality. Whoever imposes the discourse has, in fact, the power, because he or she decides on the agenda and on the way of expressing thoughts and the thinking itself, the formulation of opinions on the topics that are covered by the discourse. Other topics, on the other hand, disappear from it. As constitutionalists, we do not follow in the footsteps of postmodern thought about authority as a network of connections – we refuse to accept without criticism. Yet the thought of knowledge and power has to accompany us – just like the question of who imposes the narrative, i.e. the threads and tone of the discourse in Foucault's words.

So, does accountability seen as an obligation to give an account of the exercise of power have the potential to reduce epistemic asymmetry – the disparity in the pool of knowledge between the governed sovereign and the ruling elites? Or does the mastery of discourse also give the subjects of power an advantage when it comes to power over what is reported, when and how it is done – or even what the ruled could ask, if they had the opportunity and knew what to enquire about? In other words: is the epistemic asymmetry insurmountable, since the authority imposes the discourse using its leverage, carefully hiding what it does not want, does not need or (sometimes) cannot say about its actions? Or maybe it is even worse; namely, perhaps the subjects of power are no longer concerned with governing but with reporting it, focusing on what will be said – and not done. They are preoccupied with

1 "With the notion of apparatus, I find myself in a difficulty which I haven't yet been properly able to get out of. I said that the apparatus is essentially of a strategic nature, which means assuming that it is a matter of a certain manipulation of relations of force, either developing them in a particular direction, blocking them, stabilising them, utilising them etc. The apparatus is thus always inscribed in a play of power, but it is also linked to certain coordinates of knowledge which issue from it but, to an equal degree, condition it. This is what the apparatus consists in: strategies of relations of forces supporting, and supported by, types of knowledge. (…) what I call an apparatus is a much more general case of the episteme; or rather, that the episteme is a specifically discursive apparatus". Michel Foucault, Interview "The Confession of the Flesh", a conversation with Alan Grosrichard, Gerard Wajeman, Jacques-Alain Miller, Guy Le Gaufey, Domonique Celas, Gerard Miller, Catherin Millot, Jocelyne Livi and Judith Miller, in *Michel Foucault, Power/Knowledge: Selected Interviews and Other Writings 1972–1977*, ed. Colin Gordon, trans. Colin Gordon et al. (New York: Pantheon, 1980), 196–7.

Also the sentence of Michel Foucault is worth to cite here: "There is no power relation without the correlative constitution of a field of knowledge, nor any knowledge that does not presuppose and constitute at the same time power relations". Michel Foucault, *Discipline and Punish: The Birth of the Prison* (New York: Vintage Books, 1977), 27.

designing narratives about their activities, with how to convey and perpetuate their image of power, the justification of its legitimacy and rightness, polarising attitudes towards opponents and supporters accordingly.

Does accountability, as the obligation to give an account at the request of the one who entrusted the power, have a chance to reduce this epistemic asymmetry, and does it really serve such a function?

The answer to this question required solving three problems:

Are there two sides to this accountability relationship, that is, is there a sense of entrusted authority, a reciprocal bond entitling the Principal and binding the Agent to the actual relationship?

Are there procedures in place that effectively implement the giving of accounts by those to whom power is entrusted, that is, does the Agent – the one who exercises power indeed give it, and is the Forum (the Principal) capable of receiving it?

Finally, is the Principal even capable of being the recipient or initiator of this type of account?

It is time to address these three issues.

Agents and the Forum – a troubled entrustment relationship

The analysis conducted in the book indicates that the multicentricity and networked nature of contemporary legal and political relationships result in changes in the vectors of accountability, and it is increasingly difficult to identify the entities involved in these relationships (Forum/Principal and Agent).

It is difficult to pinpoint the mutual relationship between them, and even more difficult: to operationalise for the purposes of assembling this relationship and the obligation to communicate it. In a democratic system, the Principal cannot be personified any other way than as the subject of primary and sovereign power, i.e. the political community – the totality of citizens subordinated within the state to the authority they shape and control. It is the sovereign, the people, irrespective of the chain of entrustment – it is in the sovereign that power rests and it alone entrusts it. This assumption is highly convenient and provides sound justification for democratic well-being, but when looked at more closely, it turns out to be rather unprepared.

As we demonstrated in the chapter on electoral accountability, this fine assumption is rather mythical. "The people" is a fictional figure, not just in legal terms, but also in political terms, which serves as a perfect justification for the legitimacy of power, but lacks creative or controlling capacity. We arrive at findings similar to Olsen's, that it is probably not fruitful to assume a sovereign Principal with normative and coercive authority, command and control.[2]

2 Johan P. Olsen, "Democratic Accountability and the Terms of Political Order", *European Political Science Review* 9, no. 4 (2017): 519–37 at 529.

Neither, therefore, does it have the capacity to receive an account of the actions taken by its representatives, and systemic practice has consistently confirmed this – there are no forms of giving or receiving an account of actual communication from representatives through the actions of the political community. Such a role – one might have believed – was or was supposed to be played by the media, but their role, in view of the growing bias and the decline in trust in them, has been steadily diminishing for years now.

The lack of a clear chain of entrustment, i.e. of a bond forming the basis for reporting on the entrusted power, is indirectly evidenced by the complete lack of accountability in respect of legislative activity – the procedures undertaken in this regard and described in Chapter 3 are still ineffective and despite declarations to that effect hardly ever take the form of general orders, while sporadic reports on the effects of undertaken legal regulations rarely meet the requirements of authoritative and complete reporting. Reporting on the effectiveness of regulations therefore barely meets the requirement of accountability for the exercise of legislative power – and there are no other paths of accountability to be found.

A different issue presents itself with regard to the accountability of the executive and, more specifically, of the government. The accountability of the government finds numerous procedures and ways by which it can be exercised, and they all remain in the relationship between the government and the parliament, i.e. the Principal that entrusts the exercise of executive power. Therefore, we see an intermediate link: the parliament entrusted with the power to scrutinise the executive receives the accounts from the government. This chain of entrustment is the only clear one in the accountability relationship, which stems from the traditional rather than conscious shaping of scrutiny of the government. In this case, however, much – if not all – depends on the established procedures and the guarantee of the rights of the minority – that is those who do not support the appointed government and have not influenced its composition. The Principal here is usually identified with the parliamentary majority, although there are exceptions. Nevertheless, the accounts are given and in certain situations (notably parliamentarians' enquiries with members of the government and committees of inquiry) it leads to the parliamentarians obtaining important information about the government's actions and motives, although the chain of accounts, which is the reverse of the entrustment of power, continues only between the representatives and their exponents, without even the formal participation of the actual Principal. Moreover – the dual role of the parliamentarians as Agents of their constituents and also acting as Principals to the members of the government is sometimes very much evident in the course of giving an account. Many of these demands are made not so much to get data or a report, but to give the impression that the questioners themselves are performing their role well. So again we are faced with the problem of not doing but only talking about making policy.

As for the judicial power – the problem of accountability between the Forum/Principal and the Agent is even more enigmatic. The courts are that branch of authority that hardly ever faces any elections. Who is, or can be, the recipient of the court's account of its exercise of power? The particular risk of internal accountability, which, as we see it, does not meet this criterion, but also does not work in practice.

According to internal accountability logic, the reasons behind most of the claimable judicial decisions are produced not for the sole purpose of presenting the motivation of the decisions made to the defendants and other interested parties, but also with the intention of defending the position before the appellate court. The instance-based nature of the proceedings, as a process of identifying and correcting errors in the adjudication of cases, results in the lower court presenting its position arguing that it is in conformity with the law and logic, moral judgment and life experience, but also with the existing line of case law. This may mean that the true motivations are hidden behind the message that the superior court wants to receive in order to deem the decision to be in accordance with the law. Thus, the risk arises that it is the appellate court that becomes the primary recipient in place of those who have entrusted the authority.

The political emancipation of the power entities has a strong impact on the power of the judiciary, which balances between being politically independent and being engaged in resolving political disputes.

In contemporary states, there is a growing discrepancy between the constitutional model of accountability and practice. The ongoing process is conditioned by the political activity of entities other than public authorities, such as international organisations or corporations, i.e. entities that were unknown when the canons of divided and balanced power were being forged.

The complexity and interconnectedness of legal and political interactions lead to a change in the vectors of accountability, which is evident in EU countries where public authorities are subject not only to national accountability, but also to EU bodies, using different criteria for accountability.

The accountability of political power has lost most of the features recognised by traditionally established canons of separation and balance of powers. It has also been scattered among new participants: entities which are not recognised in national or international law as being part of political systems.

Procedures of narrative accountability

According to our analyses, the constitutional system is designed for the government to give a report to parliament. Several institutions traditionally associated with scrutiny of the government are used for this purpose. Among these, we can distinguish ones that indeed consist of a demand to give an account, as well as an obligation to do so – under conditions that at least exemplarily guarantee the reliability (veracity) of the account and an objective assessment of it. This kind of accountability can materialise especially in activities such as questions and information provided by members of the government at parliamentary and committee meetings and, in particular, the operation of committees of inquiry, almost universally accepted in parliamentary systems as a specific source for obtaining information as part of the scrutiny of the government. However, if we take a close look at the function of giving and receiving an account in the various avenues of parliamentary scrutiny of government, particularly as part of the operation of committees of inquiry, we discover that while these bodies are designed to provide oversight of the government and perform investigations, they are also strongly linked to parliamentary structure and logic, subordinated to the will of the parliamentary majority and political parties. There is no such thing as objective truth-finding – every issue is a party-political matter;[3] and the outcomes of investigations cannot be universally satisfying in such an environment. The party bias condemns committees of inquiry to instrumental use, or at least marginalisation, when their investigations may prove to be inconvenient for the parliamentary majority. The only clear task remains the promotion of committee members as indomitable seekers of truth in the eyes of their voters. At the same time, they are definitely responsive in nature – as evidenced by their appointment after an event or scandal arouses great interest and public outrage. This in turn produces increasing affect-mobilised participation under conditions of decreasing and impoverished access to information.[4] They give an "illusion of involvement",[5] with a predominant function of blaming rather than learning,[6] working instead within the inherited legal framework, designed to make political bodies accountable for their exercise of entrusted power. Therefore, we are dealing here with a special kind of over-accountability, or double accountability and over-narrative practices rather than pure and only accountability of executive power.

As for the accountability of the judicial power, we assume that full accountability for the power exercised is reflected in its operation by giving reasons for the decision. Therefore, the judicial procedure here operates in a manner ideally suited to the conditions of accountability that we outlined in Chapter 1: it is both a public and comprehensive explanation of not only the action taken (the decision), but also an indication of its motives, evidence and arguments for and against its taking. Accordingly, it is a report on the exercise of an act of power. Insofar as it is addressed to the real Principal – that is the Forum, to the general public and, above all, to those who are directly and indirectly interested in these decisions. No avenue for seeking judicial

3 Klaus von Beyme, "Parliamentary Crisis and How to Strengthen Democracy", in *Constitutionalism and Democracy: Transitions in the Contemporary World*, ed. Douglas Greenberg et al. (Oxford: Oxford University Press, 1993), 275–86 at 278.

4 Giovanni Sartori, *Comparative Constitutional Engineering: An Inquiry into Structures, Incentives and Outcomes* (Basingstoke: Macmillan, 1997), 150.

5 Pierre Bourdieu, *Language and Symbolic Power* (Cambridge, MA: Harvard University Press, 1991), 180.

6 Raanan Sulitzeanu-Kenan, "Reflection in the Shadow of Blame: When Do Politicians Appoint Commissions of Inquiry?", *British Journal of Political Science* 40, no. 3 (2010): 613–34 at 633.

accountability elsewhere – that is, in the means of their appointment, disciplinary responsibility or appellate review – meets either of these requirements. There is no objective accountability for the act of power performed, or (in the case of appellate review) – there is no Principal, no entrustment relationship. We made an attempt to show what the false positioning of the accountability relation within the exercise of judicial power can lead to, using the vivid and illustrative example of the Polish developments of 2016–22. Their outcome included not only the nullification of the essence of judicial independence, but also the negation of the idea of their accountability for the power actually exercised and entrusted to them.

Yet, the emancipation of judicial power, which in a sense corresponds to holding the judiciary accountable by receiving an account in justification of a judicial decision, faces challenging practical and procedural obstacles within the accountability framework. The risk is related to the actions of the court, acting as the Agent in this accountability relationship. For it has plenty of means at its disposal to make its account of how the case was handled and how it was resolved compelling, without having to always report on its acts of authority. The court gives an account, but is in almost complete control of the communication. The institutional author of the account acts as a narrator who is not only omniscient but also omnipotent as to the management of information and arguments. The conditions of reporting are also very specific. It is a situation occurring in a particularly formalised environment that determines the form and content of the account. Indeed, in the accountability relationship, the application of the law becomes a communicative situation in which epistemic asymmetry takes on a particular shape, the predominance of the court as ruler and expert and interpreter of the authority of the law is huge. Consequently, the court's persuasive function and instrumentality can effectively mask the account of the essential elements of the court's act of authority.

Here, the "information asymmetry", namely the way in which justifications are drafted and the lack of substantive preparation of the audience in relation to this style, is particularly highlighted, as well as challenges such as the huge number of rulings delivered over time and the lack of a point of reference, of relevant comparative material. These barriers render accountability carried out in this way highly illusory.

However, what is rather astonishing is that no accountability procedures are provided for by the relationship of entrustment of the legislative power, in the sense that parliament is at no point obliged *in corpore* to give an account of its actions. This absence can be explained by constitutionalists in two ways. Firstly, the primary and fundamental relationship of entrustment of power by the sovereign to parliament takes place through free and universal suffrage. Thus, MPs are held accountable for their actions by the electorate in their renewal (or refusal) of their mandate. Secondly, constitutionalists might argue: admittedly, there is no obligation to report, but MPs are in constant contact with their constituents, and parliament's deliberations are open to the public, enacted laws with justifications are promulgated during the process. In view of this kind of interaction and openness, it is unnecessary to make additional provision for avenues for requesting and reporting, or even for cyclical provision of accounts.

Neither interpretation, however, clarifies the essence of the problem. Accountability via the electoral process is illusory, while openness and contact with the constituency do not provide an alternative to giving an account of the power exercised. Firstly, the power of the legislature is exercised *in corpore* and should be accounted for as such, which both arguments seem to disregard. Secondly, the realities of politics bring to mind the all-too-obvious observation that the fate of an MP depends not so much on his or her constituents, but on the will of the party (parliamentary club) with which he or she is politically affiliated, as well as the interest groups that are allied with it either temporarily or permanently. As Aziz Huq notes, any democratic constitution should address precisely and clearly whether and how misconduct of elected leaders can be sanctioned[7] – and almost all of them fail this test.

Thus, there are no paths to accountability for specific acts of power, i.e. especially decisions taken regarding the content of the law passed (or amended), and our analyses of an instrument that could create a foothold for such a path indicate that if this is not a dead end, it is at the very least an extremely narrow and winding alley. Should parliament, or only the enacting majority bear such responsibility – and if so, where does the relationship of entrustment of power and the distribution of responsibility between the government (which drafts the law) and parliament lie? Leaving aside even these considerations, however, impact assessment is unlikely to fulfil its accountability function. The technical reasons and the poor data collecting and analysis methods as noticed in the literature, as well as the lack of a coherent and efficient model for their execution, are a consequence rather than a root cause. Hence, it is not overly difficult to perform, but inconvenient for all actors to give an account of the operation of a law. If, however, one takes the promise of a democratic form of government seriously; public scrutiny of the actions of the authorities, under conditions of transparency in connection with the assumption that the Agents owe the Principal a proper account – then the absence of a report on the validity of the law prepared by its creators, responsible for its content, as well as its execution constitutes a breach of obligation. Giving an account cannot be substituted with media or court actions. And it is indeed quite intriguing that this does not happen, and even when it does – it does so to such a narrow extent.

In spheres where accountability can be identified within the constitutional framework, practice and regulation show that we are confronted with either its excess (parliamentary scrutiny), deficits (judicial power) or even absence (parliamentary accountability).

7 Aziz Z. Huq, "Democracy as Failure", in *Democratic Failure*, ed. Melissa Schwartzberg and Daniel Viehoff (New York: New York University Press, 2020), 42.

What is more, the public power branches identified here are only some of the actors that could find themselves in an accountability relationship. There are, in fact, other actors who assume influence over decisions taken, participate in the exercise of public power, considerably transcending the role defined by private law and their hitherto position in the legal system.

The Principal – new incarnations

There are many such actors – media, non-governmental organisations (NGOs), international organisations and institutions to name a few. We focused our attention on two categories of non-state actors: mass movements and Big Tech corporations. These are powerful players, able to mobilise and engage huge numbers of people, exerting an influence on the community that is difficult to overlook, in quite a different way from actors of public power. This influence means entering into a relationship with actors of state power (also at the international level) and sometimes even stepping directly into their position. Mass movements give people identities and attitudes – including political ones; digital corporations with volumes of information about their users, previously unknown to even the most dystopian totalitarian regimes. The resulting capacity to form strong ideological attitudes of members is the link between individuals and the state, heavily influencing attitudes, daily life and the choices made in private and public life.

Non-state actors are completely transcendent to the rules of the democratic and constitutional state. They come from the outside of the world order recognised by the norms of constitutional law and therefore function, according to the liberal order, with privileges only slightly restricted by law.

By creating the sphere of technopolitics, they replace the traditional media and the control exercised by it: they replace public debate, govern the agenda setting, create new cultural codes.[8] In doing so, they are removing the distinction between the private and public spheres, bringing them together. Civil society, in turn, transfers not only its attention but also its data there. It gains knowledge from there and migrates to the virtual world, then makes choices[9] in the very real world of political relations under its influence.

Finally, and most crucially from the point of view of our argument, these actors are completely non-accountable. As entities operating outside the power structure of the state and the international order, they are not constrained by the rules of democracy, nor, by extension, are they subject to classification in the Agent-Principal relationship. They act on their own behalf, establishing, as it were, their own existence and position from scratch, outside the chains of

8 Alberto Melucci, "The Symbolic Challenge of Contemporary Movements", *Social Research* 52, no. 4 (1985): 789–816.

9 David Betz and Tim Stevens, *Cyberspace and the State: Toward a Strategy for Cyber-power* (London: Routledge, 2011), 58.

entrustment, meanwhile they easily assume the voice of the Principal, set the tone and sometimes speak directly in its name or deprive it of that voice. They themselves, on the other hand, are neither responsible for their actions and words nor ready to be held accountable. In fact, there is no room for anyone to hold them accountable for the exercise of such power in the democratic state order.

Meanwhile, the problem of the absence of accountability is not accentuated in their case (as, for instance, in the case of NGOs, and the interest groups centred around them)[10] in the reflection on this sociological and political phenomenon. Whereas the identified non-state actors change two basic principles of democracy, in other words, through their action the rules and environment of participation and deliberation change.[11] These constitute the key elements of the environment in which the entrustment of power, its legitimacy and, as discussed herein, the creation of the conditions of accountability and the reception of an account of power exercised take place.

From the perspective of constitutional law, it is precisely this feature – the lack of accountability – that is perhaps the most interesting. Mass movements are free to shape their statements and demands as they please, and even to disseminate information without regard to its veracity. No one will hold them accountable for their words. There is no entity that can effectively and authoritatively deny or debunk such statements. Nor do they have to reckon with the practical consequences of their slogans, claims and assertions. They simply act outside the system, in a near-revolutionary order, to a certain extent anarchically, without the bonds of law, hierarchy, legal or political accountability, pursuing their formulated goal in a completely arbitrary manner. This means acting outside the logic of democracy and the rules of constitutionalism. Movements do not need democratic legitimacy and the chain of entrustment. They grant such legitimacy to themselves. And the only measure of their effectiveness is the measure of popular support. They have no need to take responsibility and, moreover, they have no one to answer to. They are designed to act as Principal, or they cast themselves in that role; they represent the direct, participatory and bottom-up model of democracy: as opposed to the top-down competition among elites for the votes of otherwise passive masses. The central values were (at least in the declarations) horizontality, voice, inclusion through participation and autonomy from existing organisation (the state, but also parties and unions).[12] Bringing these actors together – that is, mass movements and the social media sphere led by Big Tech – poses

10 Ondřej Císař, "Social Movement Diffusion in Eastern Europe", in, Routledge Handbook of Contemporary European Social Movements, Cristina Flesher Fominaya and Ramón A. Feenstra eds, (London: Routledge, 2020), 240, 243–4.

11 Donatella della Porta, "Democratic Models in Europe", in *Routledge Handbook* (see note 10), 75.

12 On Podemos: Marina Prentoulis and, Lasse Thomasssen, "Movement Parties:. A New Hybrid Form of Politics?", in: Routledge Handbook (see note 1) 348, 351.

a new challenge for accountability. Firstly, the scale of digital communication is an unprecedented phenomenon in the history of mankind. Its services and products are used by an audience unparalleled in the history of human civilisation, leading to the situation where a few companies in the world are organising public space on a scale hitherto unimaginable, with new media taking over the function of informing, engaging in public discourse and campaigning. And all this is happening when traditional accountability mechanisms for political power are failing.

Global digital services have taken control of the attention, imagination and memory of every user and therefore member of the public sphere and have changed social behaviour, colonising the sphere of choices through shaping and anticipating consumer needs and attitudes, but also the field of social and political life. These are the special fields mass movements and Big Tech have in common – the ability to bring large masses of people together instantly and at no cost as well as to shape their collective and even: flock consciousness. Meanwhile, this new public sphere has its own specific characteristics. First of all, what is unique is the way in which the communication is tailored to the audience, often buzzword-like, image-based, but also infused with emotion in a way that was previously uncommon. This is the new phenomenon of Twitter (now X) messages – a politician posts updates almost non-stop, in direct and short angry statements, without filters, distance or expected seriousness.[13] This makes the process of providing information meaningless and communication becomes a conduit for emotions in the setting of pseudo-debates, pseudo-information, temporary but heated disputes. Politics, and therefore the exercise of power, is an area which guarantees a constant stream of excitement, a sense of conflict around latest issues, tribal division and a sense of heroic (though never victorious) struggle against an opponent, usually imaginary. We have known since the early 1990s that the notion of truth under such conditions makes less and less sense, and so the account of governance falls victim to this transformation too. In the post-truth world, the truth means only things that ensure that the attention and sympathy of the audience is maintained, that desired attitudes and a sense of belonging to the right group are forged. Such communication bears no relation to the actual account of the exercise of power, much less to its reception. The truth about the exercise of power is sometimes complex, does not lead to definite conclusions, and does not allow for easy culpability or heroism. Just as mass movements fade away when entering the world of politics, so does the factual and complex account of data, indicators, criteria and alternatives in the exercise of power.

Accountability has no place in a communication that celebrates constant excitement and the sustaining of thrills through brief and *ad hoc* statements.

13 Richard L. Hasen, Cheap Speech and What It Has Done (To American Democracy), First Amendment Law Review 16 (2007), available at: https://scholarship.law.unc.edu/cgi/viewcontent.cgi?article=1248&context=falrHasen, 212.

In the world of audience-oriented communication, which recognises the preferences of the recipients and programmes their needs, there is no longer any room for deliberation, compromise and carefully considered individual decisions,[14] but above all there is neither space nor time to give an account of what really happened. The truth – and therefore accountability – is not only difficult – it is boring – and that is its biggest sin.

In conclusion, in both old and new democracies, accountability is becoming post-accountability that is closer to revenge or militant, theatrical outcries than to a factual account and its evaluation as to how power was exercised on behalf of and for the political community. The new communication, like new wine poured into old beakers, bursts the previous imaginarium of the political world, the systems of government, the law and the rules that used to govern it. Unless they never actually did.

14 Shoshana Zuboff, The Age of Surveillance Capitalism: The Fight for a Human Future at the New Frontier of Power (London: Profile Books, 2018), 589.

Index

access to court 160
access to information 117, 119, 127, 138, 231, 251
accountability: concepts vi–viii, x, 1–2, 9–10, 14, 16, 19–20; definition viii, 1, 2, 4, 6, 10–11, 14–16, 21; distinction viii, 7–9, 12–13, 15–20; electoral ix–x, 6–7, 9, 15, 23–24, 28, 30–31, 35, 47–52, 55–65; etymology 1–5, 9, 17; forensic 12, 133, 162; function 2–5, 14, 18, 21; governmental ix, 89, 92, 101, 123, 133–35, 143, 217; internal 22, 25–26, 93, 160, 170–71, 190–91, 194, 250; narrative ix, 12, 16, 18, 24, 194, 246–48, 250–51; objects 4, 10–14; subjects ix, 4, 8, 14–15, 18–19, 21, 23–25
administration 2, 4, 5, 7, 78, 87, 119, 133, 136–38, 140, 160, 162, 167, 171–72, 183–86, 188, 193, 197, 203, 234, 242–43
Amazon 232–33, 242, 244
Anglo-Saxon legal tradition 3, 29, 115, 166, 195
answerability vii, 9, 12, 161, 163, 169, 172, 190–93
anti-austerity movements 206, 208–10, 212, 217, 220, 224
Apple 217, 232–33, 238
arbitrary/arbitrary rule viii, 2, 40, 42–43, 168, 187, 216, 230, 255
Ástrádsson v. Iceland test 168, 182
audience 11, 27, 173, 192–93, 196, 198–99, 229, 252, 256–57
audit institutions 83, 87, 105, 115–16, 119; *see also* supreme audit institutions
Australia 77, 82, 84, 139, 143, 164–66, 236
Austria 117, 120, 121, 123, 127, 134–35, 144–45
Bangalore Principles of Judicial Conduct 151, 166
Belarus 155
Belgium 35, 87, 93, 120, 135, 140, 174, 238
bias and accountability 138, 150, 167, 180, 187, 189
Big Tech x, 137, 203–06, 227, 229, 232–44
blame managing 11, 138, 246
Brazil 59–60, 65, 115, 154–55, 157
Bulgaria 117, 120, 128, 131, 141–43, 154, 166, 174, 176
bureaucracy 87–88, 93, 95

Canada 40, 77, 105, 165–66, 225
checks and balances vi, 97–98, 137, 215, 217, 226, 245
Chile 115, 156, 208–09, 212, 215, 220–21
China 166, 237, 242
citizens participation viii, 7, 60–61, 66, 68–69, 72, 87–89, 96, 101, 109, 138, 209–10, 212, 217–18, 221, 223–24, 226–28, 234, 239–40, 249–51, 254–55
civil society organizations 154, 203, 205, 224
Colombia 115
committees: of inquiry (COI) 25, 28, 61, 86, 89, 93, 114, 120–35, 147, 249, 251; parliamentary 25, 28, 61, 83–85, 93, 101, 114, 118–22, 127–28, 132, 136–37, 147
common good 38, 46, 54, 245
confidence 8, 16, 17, 28, 38, 44, 71, 76, 86, 113–17, 141, 152, 154, 161, 181, 206
constitutional courts 40, 103, 120, 127, 129, 131, 154–55, 192

constitutionalism viii, 2, 17, 30–31, 38–39, 47, 200, 215–16, 243
constitutional liability 18, 128
control vii–ix, 7–8, 13–15, 17–20, 23–25, 30, 44, 47–52, 68–70, 84–88, 93–94, 97–98, 109–10, 116, 132, 135, 156, 159–60, 162, 171, 176, 180, 193, 200, 205, 211, 221, 224, 226, 238–41, 243, 245, 247–49, 252, 254, 256
correct legislation 103
corruption 56–57, 130, 132–36, 156–59, 190; judicial 150, 156
courts 22, 35, 40, 103, 111–12, 125–31, 133, 137, 146, 149–99, 241, 246, 250, 252, 254
Croatia 94, 120, 131, 154, 176
Czech Republic 94, 120, 131, 154, 176

delegation of powers 22, 34, 73, 97, 170, 173
democracy vi–ix, 2–3, 6–9, 22–24, 27–29, 32, 35–36, 39, 44–48, 50–51, 62, 68–73, 151, 156–57, 205–06, 210, 216–18, 222–24, 226, 232, 240, 245–46, 255–56; representative viii, 8, 32, 36, 44
democratic legitimacy vi, 56, 152, 216, 255
Denmark 49, 77–80, 90, 93, 96, 99, 105, 120, 135, 174
disciplinary responsibility of judges ix, 26, 160, 162, 164–68, 171–72, 175–76, 179, 181–85, 189
disinformation 66–69, 230

efficiency 1, 5, 8, 75–76, 78, 84, 92, 95–98, 100, 103, 106, 116, 147, 161, 172, 183, 185, 197
egalitarianism 66
election campaign 43, 48, 52–53, 69–70, 152, 225, 231
elections vii, ix, 8, 23–24, 30, 34–37, 40–44, 46–48, 56–57, 62–63, 65, 68–73, 87, 106, 130, 154, 216–17, 219–24, 243
electoral accountability ix, 15, 23–24, 28, 30, 47–58, 70, 73, 170, 248
enforcement 17, 25, 93, 103, 121, 127, 136–37, 147, 161–63, 168, 172, 189–90, 235, 237, 243
England and Wales *see* United Kingdom
equality, principle of 38, 47, 69, 163
Estonia 80, 89, 120, 121, 131, 142
European integration 55, 100
European Union 3, 30, 39, 53–56, 78–79, 90, 114, 155, 179, 189, 200, 238
ex ante evaluation 13, 25, 77, 80, 87, 89–96, 99, 103, 107, 110, 180
executive power vii, 7, 18, 24–25, 42, 85, 93, 98, 109, 113–14, 116, 118, 122–23, 128, 130–31, 136, 139, 146, 153, 164, 174, 178–79, 182, 200, 249, 251
ex post evaluation 25, 74–112, 137

Facebook (FB) 26, 67, 219, 228, 230–37, 240, 242–43
failsafe mechanisms 94
Finland 80, 90–91, 93, 129, 141, 174
forum viii–ix, 10, 16, 21–22, 78, 117, 123, 126, 139, 141, 159, 161, 169–73, 176–77, 192, 240, 248, 249, 251
France 2, 37, 71–72, 80, 85–86, 93, 97, 99, 115, 119–21, 124–25, 128, 130, 136, 139, 145, 174, 192, 225, 232
freedom of expression 27, 231, 239, 243

GAFAM/Big Five 232, 240
Germany 49, 72, 77, 80, 87–88, 93–94, 96, 113, 115, 118, 120, 122–24, 126–31, 135–37, 140, 144–45, 154, 156
Google 26, 217, 228, 232–33, 237–39, 242–44
government's accountability 29–32, 113, 148, 256
Greece 71–72, 80, 174, 222–23, 230

human rights 38, 149–50, 155–56, 177, 179
Hungary 80, 154, 166, 174, 177

India 164, 166, 173
individual accountability 3, 4, 11, 48, 56, 58–59, 118, 123, 140–42, 145, 169, 194
inquiry: outcomes 127–29, 131–37; process 25, 83, 89, 120–41
interpellation 24, 57, 117, 139–42, 144–46, 181
Ireland 39, 84, 139, 164, 174, 238
Italy 49, 54, 57, 70–72, 80, 88, 93, 96, 99, 120, 122, 124, 129–31, 133, 137, 145, 156, 165–66, 169, 174, 230

Japan 3, 80, 99, 115, 164–66
judge ix, 10, 22, 26, 124, 128, 149–95, 197
judicial accountability x, 22, 149–199
judicial activism 157–78
judicial appointments 168, 173, 175
judicial independence ix–x, 22, 128, 149–53, 156–57, 161, 164–90
judicial minimalism 195
judicial misconduct 165–66, 169
judicial offences 165–66, 183–85
judicial responsibility 189
judicial review 153
justification and accountability 18, 26, 62, 160, 171, 187–88, 191–98, 248

Kenya 49, 156

Latvia 80, 120, 123, 131, 145, 174
legal reasoning 192, 196, 199
legislative 8, 15, 25, 52, 61, 74–89, 92, 97–101, 103, 106, 109–11, 126, 133, 136–37, 140, 174, 179, 182, 187, 200, 249, 252
legitimacy ix–x, 8–9, 20–21, 32, 34, 37, 53, 66, 75, 94, 111, 128–29, 152, 181–83, 189, 192, 196, 199, 206, 216, 238, 248, 255
liability 3, 7, 11, 13, 17–18, 26, 74, 103, 119, 128, 135, 154, 159–60, 176, 189, 198, 245, 251
Lithuania 120, 140, 142, 154, 174

mandate vi, 2, 7, 11, 19, 21, 23, 30, 34, 41–42, 45–46, 59, 90, 97, 122–23, 152, 157, 163, 184–85, 198, 201, 245, 252
mass social movements x, 203–04, 207–08, 211–13, 215, 217, 226–27
meritocracy 65
Mexico 141
Microsoft 217, 232–33, 239, 241–42
ministerial accountability 17, 109, 146, 182
misinformation *see* disinformation
Muzzle Act 183

Netherlands 35, 77, 80, 91, 93–94, 96, 115, 120, 166, 169, 174, 225
New Public Management 5, 78
non-governmental organizations (NGOs) 171, 193, 201, 205, 219, 255
Norway 49, 80, 90

ochlocracy 65
openness vi, 2, 5, 8, 26, 63, 75, 130, 160, 171, 191, 242, 246, 253
opposition 2, 39, 54, 61, 74, 85, 104, 117, 123, 125, 134, 140, 143–44, 146, 148, 212, 222, 240
Organisation for Economic Co-operation and Development (OECD) 75, 78–82, 87–90, 94–100, 104–05, 107–10

parliament 4, 25, 33–35, 39–42, 45, 51, 53, 55, 61, 74, 78, 85–87, 89, 92, 97, 100, 106, 109–11, 113–18, 122–25, 128–32, 135, 137–38, 140–47, 164, 172, 218–19, 246, 249, 252–53
parliamentary debate 61–62, 117, 142, 145
parliamentary oversight x, 85, 119, 135
parliamentary scrutiny 31, 85, 111, 113–14, 118, 251, 253
Philippines 142, 231, 244
Poland 18, 22, 38, 40–43, 45, 53–54, 57, 62, 80, 88, 99, 115, 119–21, 124–31, 134, 136–38, 142, 144–46, 154, 156–58, 169, 177, 179–90, 197
political decision-making 13–14, 38–39, 41, 50–51, 53, 55–58, 62, 64, 71, 73, 75–76, 99, 106, 116, 120, 126, 136, 143, 155, 197, 202, 213, 217, 234–35
political parties 29, 60, 62, 69–71, 117, 130, 135–36, 138, 154, 204, 209–10, 212–16, 221, 223, 251
political representation 32–35, 37–38, 44, 46, 51, 55, 73
political responsibility 17–19, 114, 245
Portugal 80, 120, 123, 131, 145, 169, 174
post-implementation review (PIR) 81–85
post-legislative scrutiny (PLS) 81–85
Principal-Agent relationship 10, 14, 21–22, 24, 27, 111, 168, 189, 198
private sector 5, 29, 204–5, 254
procedural fairness 167
programmed review mechanisms *see* failsafe mechanisms
proportionality 75, 79, 98, 104, 124, 167
public administration accountability 4, 93, 136
public authorities x, 1, 4, 5, 28, 34, 37, 43, 54–55, 72, 90, 93, 110, 119, 121–22, 126, 128, 135, 146, 180, 200, 202, 207, 216, 250

public interest 43, 45, 57, 117–18, 124, 131–32, 157, 160, 212, 216
public opinion 5, 38, 68, 95, 132–33, 135–36, 217
public sphere 5, 6, 205–06, 210–11, 214, 227–29, 232, 254

regulatory impact assessment (RIA) 25, 74–112
reliable assessment 76, 106
representative democracy viii, 8, 32, 36, 44
republican form of government, principle of 38, 47, 163, 225
Republic of South Africa 42, 49, 156, 166
responsibility vii, xi, 3, 7, 9, 11–12, 14, 16–19, 25–26, 28, 59, 74, 114, 140, 159–60, 162–65, 167–68, 172, 175, 181, 183–85, 189–92, 197–98, 201–02, 214–17, 226, 231, 245, 252–53, 255; responsiveness vi vii, 1, 7, 9, 11, 13
retrospective electoral accountability 51–52, 57–59, 64, 69, 70, 134
right to fair trial 161, 168, 191
right to truth 155
Romania 119–20, 128, 154, 174
rule of law viii, 2, 8, 47, 55, 103, 128, 149–50, 153–54, 156–58, 177, 179, 182, 187, 195, 215, 245, 246
Russia 54, 135–36, 155, 209, 231, 233
Rwanda 231

Salvador 156
sanction-based accountability *see* forensic accountability
separation of powers, principle of viii–ix, 7–8, 21, 24, 29, 127, 188, 200
Sierra Leone 156
Slovak Republic 120, 141, 174
Slovenia 80, 120, 123, 166, 174
social atomisation 123, 241, 246
social movements vii, x, 203–5, 207–15, 217, 223, 226–27, 244
sovereign vi, 8, 21, 32, 34, 36–39, 49, 51, 64, 72–73, 96, 99, 102, 152, 163, 170, 226, 247–48, 252
Spain 29, 80, 120, 122, 131, 145, 154, 169, 174, 210, 222–23
Sri Lanka 230, 244
stocktake reviews 94, 97
subsidiarity 79, 122
sunset rules 94
supreme audit institutions (SAIs) 115–17
Sweden 49–50, 80, 89, 142
Switzerland 86

Tik-Tok 228, 236–37
transition 28–29, 32, 93, 155–56, 159, 186–87, 190, 201, 246
transparency vi, vii, 1, 8, 9, 11, 53, 60, 68, 75–76, 100–1, 104, 108–11, 126, 130, 137, 150, 160, 191, 216, 226, 243, 246, 253
trust x, 25–26, 71, 104, 113, 119, 130, 156, 168, 170, 182, 241, 246, 249
Turkey 115, 155

United Kingdom 26, 72, 77, 80, 82–84, 93–94, 115, 118, 120, 139, 143, 145–46, 174
United States of America 5, 26, 29, 46, 48–50, 53, 71, 77, 96, 99, 164–65, 175, 208–09, 230, 234, 236–38, 240
Uruguay 156

voters 33, 36, 41, 43–45, 47–48, 52, 56–60, 62–65, 68–71, 133, 138, 215, 219–20, 231, 240, 251
voting 39–41, 47, 60–63, 65, 69–71, 129, 154, 220; prospective 57, 70; retrospective 51–52, 57–59, 64, 69–70, 134

YouTube 219, 228, 240

For Product Safety Concerns and Information please contact our EU representative GPSR@taylorandfrancis.com
Taylor & Francis Verlag GmbH, Kaufingerstraße 24, 80331 München, Germany

www.ingramcontent.com/pod-product-compliance
Lightning Source LLC
LaVergne TN
LVHW021121300926
849160LV00010B/812